Phänomenologie der Natur
(Phenomenology of Nature)

Beiträge von

Kah Kyung Cho
Helmuth Vetter
Klaus Held
Hans Rainer Sepp
Aiko Ogoshi
Toru Tani
Nam-In Lee
Otto Pöggeler
Bernhard Waldenfels
Hwa Yol Jung
Kiyoko Shimizu
Seung-Chong Lee
Yoshihiro Nitta
Ernst Wolfgang Orth
Harry P. Reeder
Lester Embree
Jae-Chul Youm

Herausgegeben von

Kah Kyung Cho und Young-Ho Lee

Verlag Karl Alber Freiburg/München

Die „Phänomenologischen Forschungen" werden von Ernst Wolfgang Orth und Karl-Heinz Lembeck im Auftrag der Deutschen Gesellschaft für phänomenologische Forschung e. V., München, herausgegeben.

Im Abonnement ermäßigter Preis. Für Mitglieder der Deutschen Gesellschaft für phänomenologische Forschung Pflichtbezug zum Mitgliederpreis. Für Studenten gegen jährlichen Nachweis Studentenabonnement. Die Kündigung des Abonnements ist erst nach Abnahme von mindestens vier Heften möglich und dann nur zum Ende eines Jahres.

Die Deutsche Bibliothek – CIP-Einheitsaufnahme

Phänomenologische Forschungen = Phenomenological studies / im Auftr. der Deutschen Gesellschaft für phänomenologische Forschung hrsg. – Freiburg [Breisgau] ; München : Alber
ISSN 0342-8117
Sonderbd. Phänomenologie der Natur. – 1999

Phänomenologie der Natur = (Phenomenology of nature) /
Beitr. von Kah Kyung Cho ... Hrsg. von Kah Kyung Cho und Young-Ho Lee. – Freiburg [Breisgau] ; München :
Alber 1999 (Phänomenologische Forschungen ; Sonderbd.)
ISBN 3-495-45651-1

Texterfassung und Druckvorlage durch die Herausgeber

Gedruckt auf alterungsbeständigem Papier (säurefrei)
Printed on acid-free paper

Druck: WB-Druck, Rieden 1999
ISSN 0342-8117
ISBN 3-495-45651-1

Inhaltsverzeichnis

III. Epistemologie, Logik, und Wissenschaft

Anhang

Vorbemerkung

Die hier vorgelegten Beiträge erscheinen, bis auf einen einzigen* zum ersten Mal öffentlich. Eine unverkäufliche, limitierte und in manchen Punkten abwei-chende Ausgabe wurde im Oktober 1998 an die Konfernzteilnehmer in Seoul anlässlich der 20. Gründungsfeier der Koreanischen Gesellschaft für Phänomenologie verteilt.

Wir sprechen allen verehrten Kollegen, die uns mit ihren Beiträgen geehrt haben, unseren Dank aus. Besonders Herrn Professor Dr. E. W. Orth, Herausgeber der *Phänomenologischen Forschungen*, und dem Verlag Karl Alber sind wir uns zum Dank verpflichtet. Ferner bedanken wir bei der Alexander von Humboldt-Stiftung für eine Druckkostenbeihilfe.

Herausgeber

*Siehe Anmerkung auf S. 115.

Introduction: The Naturalness of Nature

Kah Kyung Cho

I

It would be more appropriate to indicate our intention to philosophically rethink the meaning of *nature* by resorting to the Greek term *physis*. *Phenomenology of Physis* was the initially proposed title for the collection of essays in this volume. Though for the simple reason of clarity we settled on the English word "nature," the choice of the word is a conditional one, as the real issue is more about the gap that exists between the two terms rather than about their seeming approximation.

Our modern world view is shaped by the overpowering presence of the physical science that has all but eclipsed the original meaning of *physis* which amounted to *Being* as such and as a whole. However, what was significant in this all-encompassing notion of nature was not so much the fact of man's being a part of nature as the reversal of the relation or the role between man and nature. Literally, nature looked more like the subject in the modern sense, comporting toward man as the object. An indication of this is the frequency of the middle voice in Greek grammar in which man is acted upon while performing what we consider today a simple "action," such as washing oneself. Even with the hybristic pride in their self importance and dominance over all the creatures, as Sophocles sang in *Antione*, the ancient Greeks were acutely aware of the limits of their power. Their uncanny skill to subdue nature was surpassed only by the sense of ultimate submission to fate.

Fortunately, we owe to some phenomenologists that even in our midst today the reversal of man's relationship to nature may not be perceived as totally strange. Husserl himself, in spite of his ever deeper exploration of the life-worldly structure which reached the level of nature not only as object, but as *corporeity* constitutive of subjectivity itself, never saw *physis* as something that transcended conscious experience. However, to those familiar with the more involuted turns of the phenomenological movement, such as the early leanings of Hedwig Conrad-Martius toward a "Real Ontology" in which even plants are creatures with souls, Eugen Fink's return to cosmological contemplation and, of course, Heidegger's thought on *physis*, it should be apparent that these approaches to the phenomenon of nature cannot be aligned with the Husserlian sense of constitutive phenomenology. For these thinkers, nature is no longer an *object*, least of all a mere physical object, no matter how a wide region it claims to encompass. It is not something to be tallied by means of a parsimoniously measured *act series*, as if water is let in through the controlled sluice gate, whereas in reality nature is more like the sea - full of waves and tides in which we float, and at whose mercy we are most of the time. Nature not only "weaves and strives", and "takes us by surprise", but as the totality of being, of which we are a part, it is *physis*, very much in the sense in which the pre-Socratics understood it. *Physis* is prior to the separation of man and nature, history and nature, and all other such "self-evident" bifurcations.

Physis is also the way a thing is in its essential structures and relations, its Being *by nature*. *Phenomenology of Nature* makes it clear at once that our purpose is to steer the course of phenomenology to go (literally, *metaphysically*) beyond nature as a mere correlate of consciousness, i.e. to free nature from the confining methodological grid which allows nature no other status than that which can be correlated to human *consciousness*. Only by reflectively surpassing the functional primacy of the meaning-bestowing consciousness can we face the *otherness* of nature, and experience nature's *other kind of nearness* which the phenomenology of Husserlian provenance has little appreciated. It is also in this sense of letting nature's own magnitude come to the fore, and not taking any ingrained conventional view of nature for granted, that Heidegger's talk about the "naturalness of nature" should be understood.

In the process of breaching the hardened shell of subjectivity preoccupied with itself, we found no advance in the recent history of Western philosophy more germane to this purpose than Heidegger's query of the "naturalness of nature". Starting out as an internal phenomenological development that took an existential-ontological turn, Heidegger's thought on the "issue itself", i.e. Being, increasingly took on the character of thinking about *physis*.[1] This led us to discern in the later thought of Heidegger a tendency which we may call "physicocentric". Also in this connection, it should be recalled that Max Scheler similarly employed the term "cosmomorphic" (*kosmomorph*) to point to the need for counterbalancing the extremely human-centered way of looking at nature.[2] Thus defining not merely the ex-*static*, but also the ex-*centric* position of man *within the physical universe* has been a clearly visible strand of thought among some prominent thinkers who for various reasons departed from the Husserlian phenomenology.

But in contradistinction from various other phenomenological attempts that explicitly address the question of nature, we shall integrate Eastern perspective[3] into the discussion of overcoming the consciousness-centered

---

[1] Heidegger, *Basic Concepts of Metaphysics* Chapter III, 8.

[2] See Kah Kyung Cho, Chapter IX, Verstehen in kosmischen und akosmischen Perspektiven, in: *Bewußtsein und Natursein* (quoted as BN below.)

[3] Karsten Harries struck the right cord when he reviewed the present author's book and found its subtitle, "*Phänomenologischer West-Ost-Diwan*", more revealing of the author's intention than the main title, for it did not echo the well known *West-östlicher Diwan* of Goethe fortuitously. If Goethe's collection

anthropomorphism in an attempt to go beyond the limit of Europe's already radically self-critical tradition. Here again Heidegger's thought of Being led the way. Specifically, the twofold directional sense of his "turn" (*Kehre*) implies the "turning toward" nature in order to re-appropriate the ancient Greek experience of *physis*, and concomitantly, the "turning away" from the anthropocentrism ("metaphysics of subjectivity") into which modern Western philosophy has lapsed.

In his critical re-appropriation of the early Greek experience of Being, Heidegger's thought was guided not so much by the question of how the way it had happened was possible, as by the question of whether what had happened could possibly have taken a different course. Like the *physis* of Heraclitus, the truth of Being has the innate tendency of showing itself and concealing itself at the same time. *Erring* is considered co-primary with the emergent truth. As such, thinking the *other possibility* of Being belongs essentially to the thought of Being. Already Heidegger's attempt to re-think the Greek beginning implied going beyond it. But when one lets go of the last foothold after climbing up the summit of antiquity, how could one tell whether it is a blind fall into an abyss or it is like straying into an unknown territory, only to find there someone else's footprints? What if a basically similar primordial experience beckons from an entirely opposite quarter?

We submit that it is against the backdrop of a global oblivion of Being, as manifested by the *planetary* ascendancy of technology, that Heidegger could momentarily ignore the gulf between East and West and feel himself addressed by the kindred spirit of Lao Tzu. For, essentially, Lao Tzu also thought against his age, an age of pervasive "humanism", which came to pass as soon as the great *Tao* was abandoned. We further submit that the characteristic of self-withdrawal attributed to *Tao*, along with its *modus operandi* that accomplishes things in an uncanny way and therefore deservedly called "non action" (*wu-wei*), may have so attracted Heidegger as to engage him in a "dialogue" with Lao Tzu.[4] Today, Heidegger's intriguing question about whether there was a *common origin* of the thought of both the Occident and Orient may be regarded as an aborted speculative adventure.

However, quite apart from the question of a common origin, the signifi-

---

of poems "intended to lead poetry beyond European parochialism and to give voice to the universally human", so too was the author's (Cho's) a work, even if not in poetry, but in phenomenology "that calls that (Europe's) tradition and its logocentric presuppositions into question," Karsten Harries, "Phenomenology Beyond the Spirit of Revenge", in *Research in Phenomenology*, Winter 1990, p. 275.

[4]See "Gedanken abseits der dichotomischen Weltansicht", Chapter III, BN., and Cho's three other articles cited in Footnote 2 of Vetter's contribution, *Die Frage nach dem "Natursein" bei Heidegger aus der Sicht von Kah Kyung Cho*, this volume, p. 15, below.

cance of Heidegger's entire involvement with Lao Tzu may be obscured or trivialized if the *philological* scruple that Heidegger had shown in this matter were allowed to stifle the genuine philosophical concern that was clearly there. For, growing more and more wary of the difficulties surrounding the Chinese language, Heidegger seemed, toward the end of his life, to have leaned in the direction of recanting[5] his purported "dialogue" with Lao Tzu. Even with the help of a native Chinese scholar, the risk of interpreting some key Chinese words to conform to his thought of Being must have appeared too great for him.

But this should not deter us from pursuing the question of what has been said, be it philologically correct or not. A half truth brought to daylight is better than a half truth swept under the carpet. And certainly we are here concerned with nothing less than the whole truth about Heidegger's attempted East-West dialogue, in spite of his own dissatisfaction with its outcome. Hence we are fortunate to obtain Otto Pöggeler's contribution, *Noch einmal: Heidegger und Laotse*, which pointedly addresses the extent to which Heidegger was engaged with the thought of Lao Tzu.

Previously, Pöggeler had dedicated to this subject an exhaustive, three part discussion which appeared in Japanese translation.[6] In view of some new misunderstanding that appears to be swirling around this problem, we cannot help attaching due significance to the fact that Pöggeler's steadfast position on Heidegger's involvement with Lao Tzu as a historical fact once and for all is the first public vindication of the present author's criticism dating back to 1967,[7] which pointed out the risk involved in Heidegger's tendentious[8] "translation" of Japanese and Chinese language into his own idiom.

---

[5] About translation notes on Lao Tzu being destroyed, see Pöggeler's article in this volume, pp.112-113, below.

[6] "Heidegger and Lao Tzu, The East-West Dialogue", in *Riso* (The Ideal), No. *634, 635, 636*. 1987.

[7] See Footnote 4 above.

[8] Intervening against Heidegger purely on linguistic grounds would be the last thing the present author had in mind. As Pöggeler stated clearly toward the end of his article in this volume, Cho "consistently interpreted the issue that was Heidegger's very own, in a new situation". This meant avoiding the popular topic of inquiring how much Heidegger was indebted to or influenced by Lao Tzu. Our primary concern was to flesh out Heidegger's thought of Being, to which his detour over Lao Tzu had added some significant stylistic enrichment, but no change in substance. As for the substance, there was undeniably a certain felt common element, as revealed by Heidegger's gesture of taking Tao to be an older "primary word" (*Urwort*) than some of the basic Greek concepts. If Heidegger felt that *Tao* can somehow speak more primordially for what Greek words like *logos*, *physis* and *moira* meant, then this only confirms that the direction he sought by re-thinking the Greek experience of Being did not end in the dark, but was echoed by a voice coming from beyond, - the East. But here the whole issue gets pushed over the bounds of the historical, into Heidegger's own speculative dimension.

According to Vetter, whose article is placed at the beginning of this volume for its insightful overview of the question of the "naturalness of nature", the answer to this question translates, in a hermeneutical sense, into how man should recover the lost "center and measure". Since Tao is ultimately an expression of such a measure (*Maß*) to which nature itself (heaven and earth) must conform, but from which man, priding himself on his self-made measure and knowledge, has turned away, the "naturalness" is no simple and primitive condition of man. Rather, Taoist metaphysics has all the elementary trappings of the classical myth surrounding the emergence of man who, equipped with his cunning reason, has to turn against nature for survival and yet, because of this *hybris*, has to suffer the consequences of disrupting the larger order of the universe. Naturalness, after the loss of the initial innocence, is something man has to *un*-learn to come near to, and stoop to re-appropriate.

II

The rivalry between the Taoist naturalism and the Confucian humanism in ancient China is a historical parallel which careful readers might find re-enacted in a modern setting in Heidegger's *Letter on Humanism.* The lesson is in each case the same: Before insisting on what to *do* to bolster the image and dignity of man, man had better empty his ego and humbly ask the question of what it is to *be* human. But can this question be answered within the confines of a human-centered world? Can the determination of humanness be derived from a human being who has already established himself as the "subject"? Wouldn't the privileged *ego*-centricity of subjectivity, as the origin of all possible and real meaning of being (*Seinssinn*) in the world, annul the distance for man to look at himself and at his being as an issue unto itself? If phenomenology were to make an essential contribution to this problem, could we, as phenomenologists, retain our own (human) perspective (*Eigenperspektive*) as the only valid yardstick for measuring other, non-human perspectives as well?

Husserl asserts that if animals have "their own perspectives" which are "different from ours", it is because our transcendentally constituting subjectivity is capable of "attributing" those *altered* perspectives to the animals.[9] On this intellectualistic premise of transcendental phenomenology, the difference in the order of *being* is reduced to the difference in the order of *knowing.* In this sense there is no hiatus separating the human world from the non-human world. The latter is only the logical extension of human perspectives.

Heidegger, on the other hand, filed a caveat against looking at insects and animals as objects correlated to the subjective consciousness of man. Ani-

[9]BN., pp. 297 f.

mals have their very own "basic way of being" (*Grundart von Sein*) which is quite different from their "present at hand-ness" as accessed through the "representation" by man. Animal life "lives an inner life of its own" and has its self-sufficient nexus of meaning which requires no extraneous bestowal of meaning from human subjectivity. The being of nature "rises above itself" and thus defies being commensurate to our consciousness, scientific or otherwise. Nearly a half century before the world community awoke to the clarion call of ecological crisis, Heidegger defended in 1929/30 this unique sense of the *naturalness of nature* in the following memorable words:

> ... nature, whether living or lifeless, is not the plank, not the lower layer, upon which human being is erected, in order that he can go on a rampage on it.
>
> (*Grundbegriffe der Metaphysik*, p. 403)

The discussions of Klaus Held and Nam-In Lee also cut deeply into the problem of nature. But they do so on the horizon of "life-world" and "world" respectively. While world as such is for Husserl the "total horizon" within which any meaningful talk about world in all its real and possible variations can take place, *life-world* opened up a depth dimension of our oxic life which in an important sense converges on the issue of the *natural* side of subjectivity. i.e. the human corporeity. Held delves into the elementary influence of the climate on human body and traces how nature as the one basic form of life-world starts to be differentiated into many cultural life-worlds. Though he quotes only one modern Japanese philosopher T. Watsuji, the author of *fudo* (Wind and Earth), it should be noted that the Neo-Confucian cosmology exhibits not only similar climatological observations that Held extrapolates here, but developed a vast system of organic correlations between man, heaven and earth.

This is why through the means of phenomenological analysis at the level of life-world, East and West could be brought together for a more meaningful conversation. New astronomical and physical discoveries have revolutionized many times our scientific world views. But the intuitive style of life of humans as *earthlings* retained its inner stability each time, assimilating the results of new inventions and discoveries into its familiar horizon. Thus when we say today that earth is not moving, this sense-based experience includes the reflective awareness of the limited validity of this statement, but this kind of doxic possessions is phenomenologically defensible on the grounds of life-worldly a priori. Husserl's research in this direction has given us a heightened awareness of the human life on the planet earth and a certain sense of sanctity for the ecosphere of which the earth is the invariant center.

One can forcefully argue the case of Husserl prioritizing the worldhood over nature, which was, incidentally, also Heidegger's position in *Being and Time*. But one has yet to come up with a defense against the charge that Husserl's is a humanized world in which subjectivity is so absolutely posited, that it precludes any meaningful reference to a consciousness-transcending reality, particularly the "naturalness of nature". Some Husserlian phenomenologists may disagree that a question of this magnitude can be left out unanswered. Although Husserl himself never went so far, these scholars might argue that, in principle, it is possible to trace the origin of the so-called indexSNaturalness of Nature"naturalness of nature", as our indexSDoxa, doxic"doxic possession", to its transcendental source, thereby demonstrating that it has its genesis in the anonymously functioning subjectivity.

If one is confined to the history of Western philosophy, it would not be easy to gauge how far apart Husserl's and Heidegger's views on nature are. Only when we call upon a third position, outside of the purview of the European tradition, which has a certain visible affinity with the one or the other view or both, such as Taoism, does Heidegger's criticism of the Husserlian anthropocentrism begin to sink in. The teaching of Chuang Tzu is fraught with lessons on what we called earlier "*ex*-centric vision", - lessons designed precisely to deflate man's aggrandized image of himself. Chuang Tzu did not pass by Heidegger unnoticed. But there is also in 17th century Europe the example of Newton and Leibniz. Few would have disagreed with Newton's physics at that time and felt the impulse to revise it. And yet this unquestioned Euro-centric science was perceived by his contemporary, the philosopher Leibniz, *as Euro-centric* because of his knowledge of China. His monadology was much closer to the organicistic cosmology of Neo-Confucian cosmology than to Newton's mechanistic world view.

It is significant that Leibniz called China by the name "anti-Europe".[10] It is a mirror standing opposite to Europe. By looking into it, Europe would gain a distance toward itself. Today, more than ever, knowledge of Eastern philosophy is becoming a bench mark for the *drift* that is Eurocentrism. Pöggeler's advice should be heeded when he stresses the importance of Asian languages for Western philosophers. The *exchange* of thought should not be a one-way street, if for no other purpose than for the Western thought to orient itself in a larger world than its own, and for the Eastern philosophy to become conscious of its own limits.

Hans Rainer Sepp, in his turn, presents here the two luminaries of Freiburg phenomenology: Eugen Fink and Oskar Becker. While Sepp situates these two on the side of Heidegger because of their kindred attempts to internally overcome (*verwinden*) the shortcomings of the philosophy of consciousness, he maintains that they stood nearer to Taoism than Heidegger himself did. This may sound surprising, since we know that Heidegger went quite a

---

[10]Daniel Cook & Henry Rosemont, Jr., "The Pre-established Harmony between Leibniz and Chinese Thought", in *Journal of the History of Ideas*, 1981, p. 265. Cook and Rosemont also cite "oriental Europe" as the term Leibniz used to describe China.

distance seeking some sort of dialogue with Lao Tzu, while Becker and Fink made no such efforts. The explanation for this lies in Heidegger's "hermeneutic" point of departure, which singles out human *Dasein* as the privileged "agent" in whom the truth of Being (*physis*) comes to *language*.[11] Sepp shows here a salutary lesson that even within the same family of phenomenologists in Freiburg, there were some more discerning members who resisted Heidegger's hermeneutic turn.

If the name of the game is the consistent avoidance of any logo-centric and therefore humanized reading of nature, then language indeed becomes a stumbling block for the "naturalness of nature". Since Lao Tzu was not given to any anthropomorphic prejudices, the possibility of nature (Tao) revealing itself in human language would be out of the question for him. But it is interesting to note that Sepp apparently agrees with Fink and Becker that this "a-logical" or hermeneutically inaccessible side of nature should be taken as the state of its "concealment" (*Entzug*), and for this reason brings them closer to the neighborhood of Taoism. In truth, though, the negative characteristics commonly attributed to Tao, such as "non-action", "emptiness" and "self-withdrawal" are conceived more in direct antithesis to the *artificiality* of the human will and action than to man's *linguisticality.*

Absence of language in nature was so *natural* to Taoism that to call it a "concealment" would have required a measure of logocentric consciousness equal to that of the European tradition. Both Fink and Becker were certainly legitimate heirs to that tradition. That meant that they also had to work out their philosophy so as to reconcile the tension between man who has language (and, with it, freedom and history) and nature which, in contrast to Heidegger's view of Being, does not have it. Suffice to say for the moment that Becker and Fink found in "art" and "play" (*Spiel*) respectively the form of such mediation between man and nature.

In his essay bearing the characteristic title "*Phenomenology and Metaphysics of Nature*", ToruTani places Cho at the end of the stages of development that runs from Husserl through Heidegger and Merleau-Ponty. Tani sees a gradual intensification in the way nature has become problematized by phenomenology, until it appears warranted to call the whole movement "metaphysical". Though Husserl's aversion to "a historically degenerate metaphysics" is well known, it is also in keeping with his phenomenological spirit to call "ultimate cognitions of being", such as the results of his own monadological investigation, metaphysical. But for the most part, Husserl, like Kant, reserved this title for the drive and motivation directed toward the "supreme and ultimate" questions,[12] rather than answers and systems

---

[11] In 1967, the present author critically commented on this as the "lingering shine" (*Abglanz*) of Europe's glorification of man in spite of Heidegger's ostensive disavowal of anthropocentrism. BN., p. 102.

[12] Husserl, *Cartesian Meditations*, translated by Dorion Cairns, The Hague 1973, p. 139, 156.

built around those answers.

The meta-physical significance of Merleau-Ponty's phenomenology of nature is that it has effectively dislodged the subjectivity from the innermost recesses of consciousness and brought it into the open where it is now present as *flesh*, coalesced with nature. We may also read it backward and say that nature has now revealed itself, in its noumenal reality, as flesh. Flesh is, as it were, the very quick of nature, the zero point at which the constitution of any object begins. If, however, both the noumenal man and noumenal nature are revealed in flesh, has not philosophy somehow reached its final end? Does not this spell fulfilment and death of philosophy at the same time? Fulfilment, because the search for the concrete reality that has been an imperative of phenomenology has now run its course. And death, because from this concretum of flesh back to the abstract thought poses the same difficulty Schelling once charged Hegel with, namely, that Hegel's absolute idealism had to introduce the *brute existence* through the back door. Only this time it is *mind (spirit)* that has to be smuggled in.

Can this drive for concretization of philosophical reason be extended even beyond Merleau-Ponty? Tani seems to think so when he observes that "Cho opened a new possibility of phenomenology in connection with the East Asian Taoism".[13] But most of the points he raises deal only with formal aspects of East-West dialogue. It would be interesting to show, for instance, how far the chiasmal ontology of flesh in Merleau-Ponty runs parallel to an apparently cognate structure of micro-macrocosmic correspondence in the Neo-Confucian cosmology.[14] But as Tani implies, heightening the awareness of the *difference* in the traditions of East and West would be also in itself a positive outcome of an intercultural dialogue. On a more specific note, since Tani appreciates the Taoist aspect of nature for its being remarkably free of anthropomorphic traits, the question might be directed to him as to whether Merleau-Ponty could really move away unscathed from the charge of anthropocentrism with his chiasmal ontology.

III

The phenomenological development culminating in Merleau-Ponty's philosophy of flesh is an extention of the Husserlian kinesthetic theory and shares with it the essentially same technique of constitutive analysis. Both located in human corporeity an *Archemedean* principle with which they attempted to explain the genesis of the meaning of all objects. The only important difference between the two is in the shades, as the active and

---

[13]See below, p. 77 f.

[14]See Hyung-Hyo Kim, "Yulgok Yi Yi und Maurice Merleau-Ponty: in K. Cho and J. Hahn (ed.) *Phänomenologie in Korea*, Freiburg 1999.

passive sides of the motor function of body are blended in markedly different ways. Husserl was still very much preoccupied with the active "I *can* move my body" side of intentionality, whereas Merleau-Ponty found in the more localized interface of touching and touched flesh the seismographic ripples that are eventually to cover and map the world.

Body and flesh are *concrete* in the typical sense that in them two things, subject and object, are inseparably grown together. In order to show, however, that we are not at the end of the road in our search for concreteness, let us turn to a similar, related problem. In recent years, it has become fashionable to talk about "human face". It is, more generally speaking, about the necessity to restore the lost or faded human face to where it properly belongs. If it makes sense to give human face back to a political system, to make it "kinder and gentler", it should also make sense to soften the contour of the rigid and canonized philosophical reason. If the appeal to "humanize" reason sounds untoward, let us remember Kant, for whom the arduous task of mapping the territory of speculative and practical reason was not just for the sake of science and morals, but ultimately in the service of knowing what we humans are. But here we can raise again the same question that we have directed to Husserl earlier: would we be able to know who we are, purely *out of reason*? Or must we not orient ourselves *in the world* through intuition and find the sense of bearing in relation to heaven and earth, to animals and plants, and receive the determination of man through these vitally interconnected and interdependent relationships?

Landgrebe once summed up the achievement of Husserl in having rehabilitated the much neglected rights of *intuition*, i.e. by bringing the "thinking reason" into a concrete relationship with "the immediate reality".[15] To the extent that such a relation to immediate reality was accessible only through sensibility, Husserl took a giant step forward in *humanizing* the function of subjectivity. The more humanized subjectivity became, the more minutely would the receptive side of its function, namely, sensibility (intuition) become differentiated.

Soon man's state of "being attuned" (*Gestimmtsein* or *mood*, Heidegger) was revealed as the still deeper lying layer of the initial contact between man and world. The next main stages were "felt and affected" state of our mind (*sympathy*, Scheler), "constituting and constituted" body (*Leib*, Husserl), and the "incarnate corporeity" as the topos of being in general (*flesh*, Merleau-Ponty). But there was finally to come an encounter with the face (*visage*, Levinas) of a third person, and with that occurred something the uni-directional thrust of the Husserlian intentionality was not quite prepared for: the *reversal* of intentionality. The spontaneous function of the Ego is itself subjected to interrogation. The questioner is turned around to become an accused. Suddenly, philosophical reason is no longer

[15] L. Landgrebe, *Der Weg der Phänomenologie*, Gütersloh 1963, p. 134.

the sovereign lawgiver it once was, standing over against a world of objects. Wearing human face, which is not a mask, but thing in itself, or *noumenon*, humanized reason is pushed back into a position of having to respond to, and to share responsibilities with, *others*. Shouldn't this otherness of others include the "animal perspectives" other than the ones constituted by human subjectivity? And wouldn't this necessarily entail that the human-centered world must be taken for what it is: an *enclave* within a larger universe, an enclave which we must be free to bracket and view from an opposite perspective, lest we should develop the proverbial cave dweller's syndrome?

The contributions by Waldenfels and Hwa Yol Jung may be considered in part as spirited sequels to the line of development that we have followed all the way to the reversal of intentionality. Dialectics of presence and absence, hermeneutics of question and answer, eco-ethical responsibility of giving and taking, - drawn from traditions of East and West, provide a multiple chiasmus of a global dimension. Jung is a virtuoso in English philosophical prose, but of Korean descent, Waldenfels an embodiment of Gallic esprit d'empiétement, but of German provenance, both of whose voices are heard in intercultural forums far away from home.

A genuine East West dialogue in philosophy is a rare occurrence in spite of so much surface traffic in today's world. The language barrier is a real problem. But if we measure the success of a dialogue by the response a certain theme touches off among people groomed in different cultures, then *Phenomenology of Nature* may have begun an important step in the right direction. The Korean Society for Phenomenology feels fortunate to open a conversation on a theme broad and timely, one about which traditions of East and West have had distinctly different views, and yet around which many people could come together because of their training and interest in phenomenology. The responses which scholars from various countries have shown to the appeal of phenomenology and criticism of it, as manifested in the process of planning this volume with its central theme, Phenomenology of Nature, were certainly spontaneous and unexpectedly intense.

The cooperation among phenomenologists in the East began in Japan where Yoshihiro Nitta, influential leader in the field, and others took an active interest in the views presented in the volume *Bewusstsein und Natursein*, and particularly the interpretation of Husserl and Heidegger attempted therein from a different angle than the one the Japanese are used to. To the Japanese, Zen Buddhism constituted usually a stable frame of reference in their effort to assimilate new Western philosophical theories. But *Bewusstsein und Natursein* employed the internal logic of European philosophy and accentuated it by means of some Taoist arguments, a possibility which was greatly enhanced by Heidegger's own involvement with Lao Tzu. Encouraged by these circumstances, time has become ripe for announcing a physico-centric program of phenomenology, as this volume may be looked upon by some. But this is just a humble beginning. If this message reached

Japan earlier than Korea by several years, it is largely due to Professor Nitta's commitment to phenomenology as a task in cooperative thinking across national boundaries. It is, therefore, not by chance that the first translation from the original German edition of ***Bewusstsein und Natursein*** appeared in Japan.

The reminiscing article by Kiyoko Shimizu gives a glimpse of the backstage preparation of the Japanese translation of the book. Though the volume has, prima facie, the format of an East-West dialogue, it helped open another real, much needed living dialogue between scholars of Asian countries, eventually to include Chinese, because Taoism often took the center stage of discussions. Aiko Ogoshi's critical analysis of the Japanese Buddhist approach to nature, its dual status, lays bare the ambivalent consciousness of man who has yet to come to grips with the seriousness of ecological crisis. The problem of dual standard, however, is not limited to just Japanese Buddhism. Asia, supposedly a tradition in which man had lived in harmony with nature, has also a most deplorable record of ecological calamities today. But this paradox only highlights the timeliness of scrutinizing the complex relationship between man and nature, going back all the way to the roots of ***physis*** expeience.

On the other side of the ledger, we have an in-depth look at the parallel development of modern physics and phenomenology. As if realizing that the phenomenon of nature ought not become a sellout to practicing metaphysicians, psychosomatic analysts and ecologists, Harry Reeder delivered a much needed, sober research on what relevance phenomenological philosophy is having to physical science, in fact or by implication. Here obviously the correlational schema of the observer/observed has a great positive significance. Furthermore, if ***life-world*** can be shown in its "founding" role for the world of science, and as a result the study of life-world achieves its own "scientific" dignity, such a work would have met with a much more positive approval of the founder of phenomenology, than certain other exercises of anthropological and psychoanalyzing variety.

Lester Embree's focus is on the traditional Chinese medicine, and he shows how its practice is rooted in the Neo-Confucian and Yin-Yang cosmology. Man's organism as small cosmos has corresponding regions and functions in the larger cosmos. Disturbance and harmony between the macrocosm and microcosm are the difference between ill and good health. A phenomenological observation in this regard may not expect to square with empirical facts, as the Chinese have carried the correspondence very far afield, into social and political realities as well. Their inability to rationally separate and categorize objects has often been blamed for the retarded state of Chinese science. If, however, the objective was to achieve multiple, correlational harmony between man and nature, to explain "ambient" causality rather than linear causation, then phenomenologically descriptive and hermeneutically understanding approaches have clearly their place here.

Ernst Wolfgang Orth opens up a wider coulisse on the stage of current philosophical historiography and reading of history of ideas. To him, some of the lesser known "academic" philosophers of 19th century do not really deserve the fate of obscurity that they met, as they have helped the so-called non-academic philosophers, Nietzsche, Kierkegaard and Marx, to name a few, become known, understood and celebrated. Orth draws from the work of Karl Löwith, who set the tone for our current century's attitude to look at the recent historical past, meaning that a tree is judged by its fruit, and one could tell the father by looking at his son. We could go against Löwith and say the tree had its own life much different from its fruits, and agree with Orth that Kierkegaard or Marx could not have risen to their fame on their own. But controversy aside, we should recall that Löwith was trained under Husserl, and the method of phenomenology left its trace in his "de-structuring", i.e. removal technique of all theological presuppositions from historiography, as demonstrated in *Meaning in History.*[16]

By way of concluding this Introduction, we may observe that the reversal of intentionality was inevitable because, after all, who would seriously expect that the "otherness" of the magnitude of a self-subsisting *physis* could be elicited from the filigree work of a tactile, visual or whatever other kinesthetic principle of "I can" or "I touch"? Even if we concede that Heaven and Earth are pre-given, it does not bring us far enough toward adopting an ex-centric world view, because such a datum presupposes a dator consciousness that always reserves the right to be a fulcrum which can move things around, but which refuses to be moved. Ex-centric and physico-centric vision has become "unnatural" to man because he has so securely established himself as the measure of all things. But the wisdom of East and West has known the necessity of effacing the Ego all along in deference to a higher order than man. There is today an even more compelling reason to adopt the physico-centric perspective, because man has proven beyond doubt that, with him as measure and center, he has brought the world around him only in disarray.

---

[16]Karl Löwith, *Meaning in History*, University of Chicago Press, 1949.

Die Frage nach dem „Natursein“ bei Heidegger aus der Sicht von Kah Kyung Cho

Helmuth Vetter

> „ Wer vermag Stille so in Spannung zu halten, daß sie Lebendiges austrägt? “
>
> „ [...] erst die griechische Hybris schuf mit der Hypothese, der Zusammenhang der Dinge sei dem Geiste nach Gesetzen begreiflich, eine dem Geiste begreifliche Welt. “ [1]

I.

Vor genau einem Jahrzehnt erschien in dem um die phänomenologische Forschung so verdienten Alber-Verlag in Freiburg im Breisgau eine Sammlung grundlegender Aufsätze von Kah Kyung Cho, *Bewußtsein und Natursein: Phänomenologischer West-Ost-Diwan.* [2]

„Diwan“ oder „Divan“ heißt im Alltagsdeutsch ein Ruhebett. Mit dem Wort „Diwan“ wird in seinem persischen Ursprungsland auch eine Gedichtsammlung bezeichnet. So wurden die Gedichte des großen persischen Lyrikers Hafis (1389 gestorben) posthum von seinen Schülern unter dem Titel *Divan* herausgegeben. In der Übersetzung des bedeutenden österreichischen Orientalisten Joseph von Hammer-Purgstall las Goethe erstmals im Juni

---

[1]Das erste Motto ist die Wiedergabe eines Verses aus dem Tao-te-king, der Versuch einer interpretierenden Übertragung durch Erhart Kästner: *Aufstand der Dinge*, Frankfurt 1976, 61. Vgl. dazu auch Heideggers Brief an Kästner, in: *Martin Heidegger/Erhart Kästner: Briefwechsel*, Frankfurt 1986,122. Das zweite Motto ist entnommen Heinrich Zimmer, *Spiel um den Elefanten: Ein Buch von indischer Natur*, Düsseldorf/Köln 1976, 167.

[2]Kah Kyung Cho, *Bewußtsein und Natursein: Phänomenologischer West-Ost-Diwan*, Freiburg/München 1987. Im folgenden im Text mit „BN“ und Seitenzahl zitiert. Vgl. meine Rezension: *Philosophischer Literaturanzeiger*, 40 (1987) 315-317. - Weitere Abkürzungen der Aufsätze von Cho: „HU“ = Heidegger und die Rückkehr in den Ursprung. Nachforschungen über seine Begegnungsmotive mit Laotse, in: Dietrich Papenfuss/Otto Pöggeler (Hg.), *Zur philosophischen Aktualität Heideggers*, Band 3. Frankfurt 1992, 299-324. „AH“ = Der Abstieg über den Humanismus. West-Östliche Wege im Denken Heideggers, in: Hans-Helmuth Gander (Hg.), *Europa und die Philosophie*, Martin-Heidegger-Gesellschaft - Schriftenreihe, Band 2. Frankfurt 1993, 143-174. „IB“ = Zur Idee der ‚Bewahrung‘ des Naturschönen, in: *Facetten der Wahrheit*, Festschrift für Meinolf Wewel. Freiburg/München 1995, 57-80.

1814 darin und war so entzückt, daß er noch im selben Monat seinen eigenen *West-Östlichen Divan* zu schreiben anfing.

Die allgemeine Bedeutung des Wortes „Diwan" ist „Sammlung". Doppelsinnig trifft dies auf *Bewußtsein und Natursein* zu: Als Sammlung von Aufsätzen im buchtechnischen Sinn sammeln sie sich inhaltlich auf ein Grundthema, das durch die Suche nach „Mitte und Maß" bestimmt wird (BN 29). Darüber hinaus verstehen sie sich als „phänomenologisch" - darin liegt gleichfalls ein Doppelsinn. Edmund Husserl und Martin Heidegger sind die bevorzugten Gesprächspartner; aber auch Maurice Merleau-Ponty und der aus Wien stammende Husserlschüler Ludwig Landgrebe (von dem auch das Geleitwort stammt) kommen zu Wort. Die einzelnen Beiträge innerhalb dieser Sammlung übernehmen aber keineswegs nur das von den genannten Autoren (im übrigen sehr unterschiedlich) entfaltete Vorverständnis von Phänomenologie.

Der Themenkomplex, den Cho entfaltet, ist um die Frage nach Mitte und Maß geordnet; es geht dabei (was sich nicht von selbst versteht) um die Natürlichkeit der Natur. Dies führt zu kritischen Anfragen vor allem an Husserl und Heidegger. Es wird geprüft, wieweit diese sogar dort noch in gewisser Weise „logozentrisch" denken, wo sie die abendländische Tradition in Frage stellen; das trifft im besonderen auf Heidegger als den radikalsten Kritiker dieser Überlieferung zu. Eine solche an europäisches Denken herangetragene Herausforderung hat nicht zuletzt deshalb Gewicht, weil hier westliches Denken östlichem begegnet, einem Denken also, das aus anderen Quellen herkommt.

Nun ist seit langem bekannt und mehrfach dokumentiert, daß Husserl und Heidegger einerseits, japanische Philosophen auf der anderen Seite schon in der Frühzeit der Phänomenologie in Kontakt kamen.[3] Dabei spielt infolge seiner eminenten Bedeutung für die östlichen Gesprächspartner der Zenbuddhismus eine herausragende Rolle; die Schule von Kyôto zeigt exemplarisch, wie die von Heidegger empfangenen Anstöße angeeignet wurden, ohne die eigene Herkunft zu verleugnen.[4]

Angesichts dieser Dominanz Japans wird leicht übersehen, daß Heideggers Gespräch mit dem Fernen Osten auch und nicht nur am Rande dem chinesischen Denken gegolten hat; verhaltener zwar und lange der Öffentlichkeit verborgen, doch nach Heideggers eigenem Zeugnis für ihn selbst von ganz besonderer Bedeutung. Es sei ihm, wie er einmal gesprächsweise bezeugt hat, gerade hier die Fremdartigkeit von Sprache und Denken Asiens aufgegangen. Er sagt weiter, er habe zwar von früh an „mit Japanern

---

[3]Vgl. etwa Ernst Wolfgang Orth: Interkulturalität und Inter-Intentionalität, Zu Husserls Ethos der Erneuerung in seinen japanischen Kaizo-Artikeln, in: *Zeitschrift für philosophische Forschung*, 47 (1993) 333-351. Ferner Hartmut Buchner (Hg.), *Japan und Heidegger*, Sigmaringen 1989.

[4]Ryôsuke Ohashi (Hg.), *Die Philosophie der Kyôto-Schule: Texte und Einführung*, Freiburg/ München 1990.

zusammengearbeitet"; jedoch: „Von Chinesen habe er indessen mehr gelernt."[5] Dabei bezieht er sich auf seinen Umgang mit Laotse. Gemeinsam mit dem chinesischen Philologen und Philosophen Paul Shih-Yi Hsiao ist der Versuch einer Übertragung des *Tao-te-king* zustandegekommen. Bis Ende des Sommers 1946 werden acht der einundachtzig Sprüche bearbeitet, darnach wird allerdings die Zusammenarbeit beendet.[6]

Das *Tao-te-king* ist Quelle auch für den koreanischen Philosophen Kah Kyung Cho. Durch Laotse und dessen Grundwort „Tao" erhält die Frage nach Maß und Mitte und der Natürlichkeit der Natur - dem „Natursein" - erst jene eigentümliche Zuspitzung, die mitten in das Gespräch mit abendländischem Denken führt. Hier findet die Begegnung mit Heidegger statt. So zurückhaltend dessen Annäherung an Laotse gewesen sein mag, sie gehört doch in das Ganze seiner Denkbewegung, zu jenem Weg, dessen erste Hauptstation *Sein und Zeit* gewesen ist (auch wenn wir heute sehen, wieviel eigenständige Schritte in den Vorlesungen vor dieser ersten großen Veröffentlichung getan wurden). Dort spielt allerdings die Frage nach der Natürlichkeit der Natur noch keine wirkliche Rolle; erst mit der Deutung der Natur als *Φύσις* unter Aneignung des frühen griechischen Denkens kommt es zu einer bedeutenden Vertiefung des Naturverständnisses. Gegen das Ende hin führt dieser Weg gleichsam zur Einkehr bei sich selbst: im Gedanken des Tao als des allumfassenden Weges.

Der Haupttitel der Sammlung kennzeichnet präzise das schon erwähnte Gespräch mit der Phänomenologie. Mit den Substantiven „Bewußtsein" und „Natursein" werden gleichsam zwei Pole des Spektrums phänomenologischer Themen benannt. Das erste Thema ist eng mit Husserl verbunden; das zweite knüpft bei Heidegger an, führt aber im Ausgang vom Tao zu einer Anfrage an Heideggers Auslegung des Menschen als Dasein. Die hin zu Laotse verlaufende Bewegung deutet Kah Kyung Cho als nichts Geringeres denn als ein Freiwerden der Seinsfrage zu sich selbst. Als Leitsatz für das Folgende sei dieser Gedanke wörtlich wiedergegeben: „Die durch Jahrzehnte hin fast auf der Stelle tretende Seinsfrage Heideggers entpuppte sich, so möchte es scheinen, am Ende als die Frage nach der Natürlichkeit der Natur, wiewohl diese Natur keineswegs als das, was die Heutigen zumeist darunter verstehen, sondern erst als das am ehesten Fragwürdige genommen werden soll." (BN 292).

---

[5]Wiedergegeben von Hans A. Fischer-Barnikol: Spiegelungen - Vermittlungen, in: Günther Neske (Hg.), *Erinnerung an Martin Heidegger*, Pfullingen 1977, 87-103; 102. - Das berühmte Gespräch mit Prof. Tezuka („Aus einem Gespräch von der Sprache", GA 13, 79-146) bleibt einseitig (vgl. HU 303; BN 95, Anm. 18). Der japanische Gesprächspartner hat später selbst bezeugt, daß „sich keine neuen Gedanken mehr im Verlauf des Gesprächs entfalten" (zit. HU 304).

[6]Paul Shih-Yi Hsiao: Wir trafen uns am Holzmarktplatz, in: Neske, (Anm. 4) 119-129, bes. 125 ff. Zur erhofften Veröffentlichung der dazu entstandenen Notizen Heideggers ist es nicht gekommen; sie wurden auch im Nachlaß nicht gefunden (vgl. HU 299, Anm. 1).

Drei „Baustellen" (GA 12, 105)[7] dieses Weges werden im folgenden näher in Augenschein genommen; auf ihnen zeigt sich das Verhältnis von Mensch und Natur in je verschiedener Weise: Auf dem durch *Sein und Zeit* gekennzeichneten Wegstück stehen Welt (das In-der-Welt-Sein des Daseins) und Natur einander gleichgültig gegenüber, was zumindest die ausdrückliche Darstellung betrifft; diese Nichtbeziehung läßt sich als Kluft charakterisieren. In der Vorlesung *Die Grundbegriffe der Metaphysik* vom Winter-semester 1929/30 tut sich ein neuer Anblick auf: Die nichtmenschlichen Lebewesen werden einer überaus genauen Analyse unterzogen, in präziser phänomenologischer Deskription in ihrem Eigenwesen bedacht und kategorial angemessen bestimmt. Doch ist die Untersuchung davon geleitet, durch den Aufweis der „Weltarmut" des Tieres die Welthabe des Menschen erst recht hervortreten zu lassen. So offen daher der phänomenologische Blick auch ist: er ist vorweg auf die Verschiedenheit gerichtet, die zuweilen auch als „abgründig" gedeutet wird. Demnach stellt sich auf dieser Ebene das Verhältnis von Welt und Natur in Gestalt eines Vergleichs dar, wobei die Ungleichheit überwiegt. Im Spätwerk - auf dieser dritten „Baustelle" findet sich z. B. *Unterwegs zur Sprache* - kommt es zur Annäherung an das Tao; es ist der Aufbruch zu einer universalen Sicht der Natur, wo alle Wesen ihren Platz haben. In einem Punkt kommt allerdings hier immer noch dem Menschen ein Vorrang zu: als demjenigen, dessen Auszeichnung es ist, die „Erde" - hier der Name für die wachstümliche Natur und ihre Wesen - zu „retten". Das auf dieser Stufe gedachte Verhältnis von Menschenwelt und umfassender Natur mag mit dem Namen „Nähe" angemessen benannt sein, so wie von einer „Nachbarschaft" zu Laotse gesprochen werden darf: Nachbarn haben einander etwas zu sagen, auch und gerade wenn sie nicht auf ein gemeinsames Vorverständnis zurückgehen können.

II.

Ein erster entscheidender Schritt in *Sein und Zeit* ist die Auslegung des Menschen als Dasein. Das besagt zum einen eine Gegenstellung zu der vom „Bewußtsein" bestimmten Position der Neuzeit, die grundlegend von Descartes bestimmt wurde, aber auch in Husserls Phänomenologie weiterlebt - so jedenfalls Heideggers Kritik, derzufolge die Phänomenologie ihres Begründers nur „vermeintlich phänomenologisch" ist (GA 20, 178). Husserl sei gegen seine eigene Maxime „Zu den Sachen selbst! " von einer hinsichtlich ihrer Voraussetzungen nicht weiter untersuchten Frage geleitet: „Wie kann überhaupt das Bewußtsein möglicher Gegenstand einer abso-

[7] Heideggers Schriften werden, wo nicht anders angegeben, im Text nach Band- und Seitenzahl der Gesamtausgabe („GA") zitiert. Weitere Abkürzungen: „VA" = Vorträge und Aufsätze. Pfullingen 1954. „ZS" = Zollikoner Seminare. Hg. v. Medard Boss. Frankfurt 1987.

luten Wissenschaft werden? " (Ebd. 147) Bewußtsein wie Idee einer absoluten Wissenschaft seien hier unphänomenologisch vorausgesetzt.

In dieser in der Vorlesung vom Sommersemester 1925 vorgetragenen Distanzierung des eigenen Lehrers Ververgen sich auch die Momente, von denen her der Ansatz beim Bewußtsein als unzureichend für die Bestimmung des Menschen relativiert wird. Zwei sind hervorzuheben: erstens die Frage nach der Seinsart des Bewußtseins, zweitens die Abweisung der Idee einer absoluten Wissenschaft; beide Momente gehören zusammen. Denn mit der Kritik am Bewußtsein verbindet Heidegger - und dies von seinen ersten Vorlesungen an - eine Kritik an einer einseitigen Auslegung des Menschen, so als wäre dieser primär „Theoretiker".

Damit wird der Rückgang auf etwas „Vortheoretisches" nötig.[8] Heidegger verzichtet dabei nicht auf den wissenschaftlichen Charakter seiner Arbeit, revidiert allerdings eine seiner Meinung nach auch noch von Husserl unkritisch vorausgesetzte Idee von Wissenschaftlichkeit. Indem dieser den Menschen vom Bewußtsein her versteht und dieses neuzeitlich mit Descartes mit dem Index der Evidenz versieht, begibt er sich der phänomenologischen Aufgabe, die „Sachen selbst" in ihrer jeweiligen Seinsart in die „Vorhabe" zu bringen.

Daß Bewußtsein überhaupt möglich ist, d. h. die Dinge in der von der Evidenz geforderten Klarheit erscheinen können, setzt voraus, daß sie sich dem Menschen zuvor schon gelichtet haben bzw. umgekehrt, daß dieser für solche Lichtung offen ist. Diese Offenständigkeit des Menschen für das Seiende nennt Heidegger das „Da", und weil in solcher Offenheit das Auszeichnende des Menschen liegt, erhält er den Namen „Dasein". Dieses vollzieht sich vor aller Theorie im praktischen Umgang mit Gebrauchsdingen, in Rede und Gegenrede, Tun und Lassen, Schweigen und Aufeinanderhören mit anderem Dasein, insgesamt in der Dimension eines „Vortheoretischen", in dem alle Theorie erst gründet. Konstituiert wird solches Dasein daher primär nicht durch das Erkennen, sondern durch Verstehen, Befindlichkeit und Rede - alle drei ausgesetzt dem Verfallen. Die entscheidende Eröffnung dieser Gedanken liegt im Einstieg über etwas, das vor aller Theorie und vor dem Bewußtsein liegt.

Damit fällt auch die für Husserl prinzipiell (wenn auch nicht faktisch) vorausgesetzte völlige Durchsichtigkeit des Subjekts.[9] Aus diesem Rückgang

---

[8]So heißt es schon in der ersten der frühen Freiburger Vorlesungen: „Das wissenschaftliche Denken, in dem sich das Theoretische leibhaft verdichtet, hat einen sicher zugänglichen, objektivierten Charakter. [...] Diese Vorherrschaft des Theoretischen muß gebrochen werden, zwar nicht in der Weise, daß man einen Primat des Praktischen proklamiert, und nicht deshalb, um nun mal etwas anderes zu bringen, was die Probleme von einer neuen Seite zeigt, sondern weil das Theoretische selbst und als solches in ein Vortheoretisches zurückweist." GA 56/57, 59; vgl. ebd. 93.

[9]Den Gedanken, daß Husserls (Descartes folgende) Tendenz nach jedem Zweifel standhaltender Gewißheit im Verfallen des Daseins gründet, entfaltet Hei-

ergibt sich eine grundlegende Bestimmung des Daseins, das In-der-Welt-Sein.

Mit ihr wird das Dasein einerseits über die Enge des Bewußtseins-Subjektes hinausgeführt, verliert damit aber auch dessen Selbstgewißheit. Mit diesem Ansatz wird zwar deutlich, daß Dasein zu Erfahrungen befähigt ist (ein Bewußtsein enthält, wie die Monade bei Leibniz, alle Möglichkeiten in sich, auch wenn viele nie zur Entfaltung kommen); aber indem es erfahren kann, *widerfährt* ihm auch etwas, wird es verletzbar. Als Ort solchen Ausgesetztseins inmitten des Seienden nennt Heidegger die Stimmungen, die Befindlichkeit.

Die Einführung dieses konstitutiven Moments markiert den entscheidenden Unterschied zwischen ihm und seinem Lehrer Husserl.[10] Die fundamentale Bestimmung des Menschen als Dasein scheint die Frage nach der „Natur" schon aus Gründen thematischer Beschränkung nicht aufkommen zu lassen. Zur Analyse der Umwelt gehört freilich auch ein Blick auf die „Natur", weil Schuhe aus Leder und Nägel aus Eisen hergestellt werden: Die „Natur" wird hier im Lichte der „Naturprodukte" entdeckt (GA 2, 94). Doch jenseits der durch die „Naturwissenschaften" zugänglich gewordenen „Natur" sowie der für die Herstellung der *techne onta* vorausgesetzten *physei onta* gibt es noch ein Drittes: „die Natur als das, was, webt und strebt, uns überfällt, als Landschaft gefangen nimmt."(ebd.) Diese Natur wird hier nicht weiter bedacht, was aufgrund der Fragestellung in *Sein und Zeit* auch völlig einsichtig ist.

Nun läßt sich aber noch ein vierter Naturbegriff denken, der hier gänzlich unbeachtet bleibt; es handelt sich um jene Natur, die zum Menschen selbst gehört und wesentlichen Anteil an dessen Verletzlichkeit trägt: die leibliche und geschlechtlich differenzierte Natur. Auch wenn Heidegger keine ausgearbeitete Anthropologie intendiert, mag hier das Versäumnis schwerer als im Fall der an dritter Stelle genannten Natur sein, handelt es sich doch um eine inhaltliche, nicht um eine durch die Ökonomie der Gesamtthematik bedingte Unterlassung, das *Fehlen einer Analytik der leiblichen Natur.*

Dazu zwei Hinweise aus Heideggers Spätzeit. Medard Boss hat ihn nach eigenem Zeugnis auf Sartres Vorwurf hingewiesen, daß in *Sein und Zeit* ganze sechs Zeilen dem Thema „Leib" gewidmet seien. Heidegger dazu: „Sartres Vorwurf kann ich nur mit der Feststellung begegnen, daß das

---

degger GA 17, § 50.

[10]Vgl. auch Ludwig Landgrebe, *Philosophie der Gegenwart*, Frankfurt 1958, 69: Für Husserl gelte, „daß der letzte Grund des konstituierenden Bildens von Welt in der freien Aktivität der Subjektivität selbst zu finden" sei. Heidegger dagegen frage „*über die bildende Aktivität des Subjektes hinaus* [...] nach der Betroffenheit und Bedrängnis, in der es sich schon immer befindet, und die es erst sein Gehäuse von ‚Welt' um sich bilden läßt. Das heißt, Welt kann nicht verstanden werden als Produkt intentionaler Leistungen, sondern als das, ‚worin' sich der Mensch in seinem Dasein schon immer befindet."

Leibliche das Schwierigste ist und daß ich damals eben noch nicht mehr zu sagen wußte." (ZS 292) Immerhin verrät dieser Satz, daß Heidegger nach eigener Auffassung später doch „mehr zu sagen wußte", als dies in *Sein und Zeit* möglich war. Weshalb aber „das Leibliche das Schwierigste" ist, wird damit nicht beantwortet.

Skeptischer noch stimmt eine Äußerung Heideggers, die Wolfgang Blankenburg wiedergibt: „Bei meinen Gesprächen, die ich mit Heidegger in den fünfziger und sechziger Jahren, zuletzt 1968, in Freiburg führte, verwies er mich diesbezüglich immer mit Nachdruck auf die französischen Phänomenologen, insbesondere auf Merleau-Ponty, und meinte - fast ein wenig wehmütig -, er selbst habe das Leibproblem nicht bewältigt, deshalb sei es in *Sein und Zeit* ausgespart geblieben."[11] Hier ist nicht die Rede von einem Noch-nicht-bewältigtsein dieses Themas, sondern von einer Nichtbewältigung überhaupt. Eine Begründung bleibt indes wiederum aus.

Insgesamt bestätigt ein Blick auf *Sein und Zeit* die These von Cho, mit der dortigen Ausarbeitung des Weltbegriffs sei der Naturbegriff durch eine fast unüberbrückbare Kluft getrennt (BN 35). Wenn dabei vor allem an jene Natur gedacht wird, die der Wissenschaft und noch ihrem technischen Gebrauch vorausgeht und mehr ist als bloß ein Korrelat zum Bewußtsein, so möchte ich darüber hinaus auch die spezifisch menschliche Natur einbeziehen, die Leiblichkeit, zu der das „viszerale Empfinden" (BN 254) nicht weniger gehört als Erotik, Verletzbarkeit und Bedrohung des Daseins durch Krankheit und äußere Gewalt und nicht zuletzt seine Hinfälligkeit durch Prozesse der Demenz - Phänomene, die nicht nur biologisch gedeutet werden sollten und in die Konkretion einer nicht dualistisch mißzuverstehenden Einheit des *auch* naturhaften Daseins gehören.

III.

Die Auswahl der Heideggertexte (vor allem mit *Sein und Zeit*, den *Grundbegriffen der Metaphysik* sowie *Unterwegs zur Sprache*) ist dadurch bestimmt, daß hier gewisse Schwerpunkte von Chos Interpretation markiert werden. Darüber hinaus sei auf eine Vorlesung aus der Zeit noch vor den *Grundbegriffen* hingewiesen, die letzte Marburger Vorlesung *Metaphysische Anfangsgründe der Logik im Ausgang von Leibniz* . Im § 10 behandelt Heidegger rückblickend und in äußerst konzentrierter Zusammenfassung „Das Problem von *Sein und Zeit*". Er tut dies in Gestalt von zwölf „Leitsätzen", wobei der für das Problem des Leibes bedeutsamste der Leitsatz 6 ist.

Heidegger setzt bei der „Neutralität" des Daseins an, die sowohl der „faktischen Konkretion" als auch der Differenz der Geschlechter vorausgeht. Dies sei keine Indifferenz, „sondern die ursprüngliche Positivität und

[11] Wolfgang Blankenburg: Phänomenologie der Leiblichkeit als Grundlage für ein Verständnis der Leiberfahrung psychisch Kranker, in, *Daseinsanalyse* 6 (1989) 161-193; 167.

Mächtigkeit des Wesens" (GA 26, 172). Im Leitsatz steht folgende Aussage: „Das Dasein ist als faktisches je unter anderem in einen Leib zersplittert und ineins damit unter anderem je in eine bestimmte Geschlechtlichkeit zwiespältig." (Ebd. 173)

Betrachtet man den ganzen Abschnitt, so wird zunächst ausgesagt, daß Dasein nicht neutral und dann auch faktisch existiert, sondern sich Existenz stets als faktische in Leiblichkeit und Geschlechtlichkeit vollzieht. Leiblich ist jeweiliges Dasein in seine Welt geworfen, die Leiblichkeit bestimmt mit über das In-der-Welt-Sein. So werden - um das auffälligere negative Beispiel zu bringen - leibliche Gebrechen oder Anfälligkeiten „kompensiert"; Karl Jaspers z.B. litt zeitlebens an einer Herzinsuffizienz und mußte lernen, sein In-der-Welt-Sein darnach einzurichten.

Heideggers Beschreibung der im faktischen Existieren gelegenen Leiblichkeit und Geschlechtlichkeit folgt einer bestimmten Rhetorik: „Zerstreuung", „zersplittert", „zwiespältig", „Mannigfaltigung" sind die von ihm gebrauchten Ausdrücke. Dabei sind die ersten drei vom vierten her zu verstehen, der den negativen Beiklang mildert: „Mannigfaltigung" ist die Wiedergabe des lateinischen „multiplicatio". (Der Wortteil „mannig" kommt wie „manch" vom lateinischen „nonnullus", Plural „nonnulli", „einige" ; das deutsche „-faltigung" ist wie „Falte" mit dem lateinischen „plica" verwandt). Faktisch existiert Dasein vielfältig, nämlich: zerstreut, zersplittert, zwiespältig. Aber hört sich „Zersplitterung" nicht trotz allem eher negativ an? Wenn Dasein faktisch existiert, weshalb dann überdies ein neutrales Dasein in der „Mächtigkeit des Ursprunges", wo doch die Mannigfaltigung zum Sein selbst gehört?

Hört man auf den äußeren Wortklang, legt sich der Gedanke an eine gewisse Nähe zur Gnosis nahe. Dazu ist zu bemerken, daß Hans Jonas 1928 (also genau im Jahr dieser Vorlesung) seine grundlegende Arbeit über diese bedeutende spätantike Bewegung der Religionsgeschichte bei Heidegger und Rudolf Bultmann eingereicht hat. Es wird dort ausgeführt, „daß das Leben in die Welt und in den Körper ‚geworfen' sei."[12]

Heidegger behandelt jedenfalls in dieser Vorlesung die Leiblichkeit - ohne ihm damit eine gnostische Leibfeindlichkeit zu unterstellen - vom Existieren her, also von der dem Menschen und nur diesem eigenen Weise zu sein.

---

[12] „Wie grundlegend der Begriff [der Geworfenheit] für die Gnostiker ist, geht daraus hervor, daß in der berühmten Programmformel der Gnosis, die dem von den Mandäern doch weitabliegenden Kreise der valentinianischen Gnosis entstammt, das so konkrete Bild des Geworfenseins unter sonst lauter formalen, abstrakten Kategorien begegnet; ‚Gnosis' soll dort sein ‚die Erkenntnis, wer wir waren, was wir wurden; wo wir waren und wohinein wir geworfen wurden (*pou eneblethemen*); wohin wir eilen, woraus wir erlöst werden; was Geburt und was Wiedergeburt'." Hans Jonas: Gnosis und spätantiker Geist. Erster Teil: Die mythologische Gnosis. Göttingen 1964, 106. Der Verfasser bezieht sich ausdrücklich auf *Sein und Zeit*, doch mit dem Zusatz: „dies alles erschöpft freilich noch nicht den Heideggerschen Begriff der ‚Geworfenheit' "(ebd. 108, Anm. 1).

Dessen Eigentümlichkeit wird auch mit Blick auf die Transzendenz bestimmt. Darunter versteht Heidegger den mit der Existenz gegebenen je schon vollzogenen „Überschritt" zum Sein, von wo aus jegliches Seiende erst offenbar wird. Dazu ist aufschlußreich, wie im § 11 der Vorlesung, wo von der Transzendenz des Daseins die Rede ist, dessen Leiblichkeit kurz erwähnt wird, u. zw. im Zusammenhang mit der „Natur" - und in Distanz zu dieser.

Als faktisches, geworfenes Dasein ist es „ganz inmitten der Natur". Transzendierend geht es aber „über die Natur hinaus, obzwar es als faktisches von ihr umschlungen bleibt". Dabei ist Dasein gerade in dem, was ihm eigentümlich ist, also in seinem Transzendieren, „der Natur etwas Fremdes" (ebd. 212). Dasein ist „über die Natur hinaus" - obzwar „von ihr umschlungen": Die Natur, die menschliches und nichtmenschliches Sein gleichermaßen umfaßt, wird hier als etwas den Menschen Umschlingendes beschrieben. In diesem Wort „umschlingen" klingt wohl etwas Hemmendes mit. Wenn in *Sein und Zeit* die Natur beispielsweise „als Landschaft gefangen nimmt", ist das ein anderer Sprachgebrauch, weil hier die Schönheit der Landschaft, die bezaubert und berückt, angesprochen wird. Dagegen läßt „umschlingen" an etwas Bedrohliches und Hemmendes denken. „Schlingen" und „Schlange" gehören sprachlich zusammen, die Vorsilbe „um" in „umschlingen" bedeutet wie das verwandte griechische *amphi* „auf beiden Seiten, ringsum": Wer aber so von der Natur (wie von einer Schlange oder auch einer Schlingpflanze) „umschlungen" ist, der muß sich seiner Freiheit gegen diese erwehren: „Freiheit" und „Natur" bilden einen Gegensatz.[13]

Die Vorlesung *Metaphysische Anfangsgründe der Logik* wurde im Sommersemester 1928 gehalten. Im übernächsten Wintersemester hielt Heidegger jene Vorlesung *Die Grundbegriffe der Metaphysik*, die wohl nicht nur wegen ihres Umfangs ein „heimliches Hauptwerk" genannt werden konnte.[14] Was sie unter anderem auszeichnet, ist die umfassendste, ja in Heideggers Schrifttum singuläre Analyse der Seinsart des Tieres.

---

[13] Daß der Ausdruck „umschlungen" die Fremdheit der Natur anzeigt, wäre etwa mit Hinweis auf Heideggers Cassirer-Rezension und die Davoser Disputation genauer zu belegen. Dort spricht Heidegger von der „Bezogenheit eines Menschen, der gewissermaßen in einem Leib gefesselt ist"; wenn Dasein aus solcher Situation heraus „als freies einen Einbruch in das Seiende vollzieht" (GA 3, 290), stehen auch hier Leibgebundenheit und Freiheit im Widerstreit. Vgl. auch Jean Greisch: Das Seinsverständnis und der Leib des Anderen, in: Albert Raffelt (Hg.), *Martin Heidegger weiterdenken*, Freiburg, München/ Zürich 1990, 105-124; 122: „In Heideggers Darstellung handelt es sich um eine Bewegung, deren terminus a quo die Natur und deren terminus a quem die ‚Welt' bildet." Während es Greisch aber vor allem um die „Leibvergessenheit" (ebd. 109) geht, die in Richtung auf den Bezug zum Anderen bedacht wird (dabei nimmt Emmanuel Lévinas eine Schlüsselrolle ein), kommt es im vorliegenden Beitrag auf das „Natursein" des Leibes an.

[14] Rüdiger Safranski: Ein Meister aus Deutschland. Heidegger und seine Zeit. München/Wien 1994, 226.

Im oben erwähnten Leitsatz 6 der *Anfangsgründe* steht die etwas kryptische Aussage, die Leiblichkeit stelle für die Mannigfaltigung des Daseins einen „Organisationsfaktor" dar (GA 26, 173). In gewisser Weise nehmen die *Grundbegriffe* diesen Gedanken auf, allerdings jetzt auf den Organismus des Tieres bezogen. Es heißt dort: „Organisiertsein heißt *Befähigtsein.*" (GA 29/30, 342) Nun ist mit „Fähigkeit" die Seinsart des Organs bezeichnet, wobei zu beachten ist, daß sich das Fähigsein Organe verschafft, und nicht umgekehrt. Nicht das Organ „hat" eine Fähigkeit, sondern diese als bestimmte Art des tierischen Seinkönnens („zum Sehen, Riechen, Greifen, Fressen, Verdauen und den dazu gehörigen Organen", ebd.) im Unterschied z. B. zur „Fertigkeit des Zeugs" (ebd. 322) [15] bringt die entsprechenden Organe hervor.

Die Beschreibung der Eigentümlichkeit des Organismus und der von ihm in Gebrauch genommenen Organe (die Heidegger auch mit Beispielen aus der Biologie erläutert) läßt sich aber trotz der sprachlichen Nähe nicht mit dem Organisationsfaktor des Daseins zusammenbringen. Denn die Intention der Grundbegriffe ist es gerade, das Tier in seinem Unterschied zum Menschen herauszustellen. Das Gemeinsame, die „Habe" eines Organismus, wird ausschließlich aus der Differenz zu den anderen Wesen bedacht, gemäß jenen drei Ausgangsthesen, welche die Erörterung des dem Tier eigentümlichen Seins erst einleiten: „1. der Stein (das Materielle) ist weltlos; 2. das Tier ist weltarm; 3. der Mensch ist weltbildend." (Ebd. 263, vgl. auch GA 25, 19 f.) Wo der Anschein der Nähe zwischen menschlichem und tierischem Wesen besteht, beharrt Heidegger darauf, „daß diese nächste Nähe beider Wesensverfassungen nur täuschend ist, daß zwischen ihnen ein Abgrund liegt, der durch keine Vermittlung in irgendeinem Sinne überbrückt werden kann" (GA 29/30, 409; vgl. ebd. 384). Daß der Anschein von Affinität durch die leibliche Organisation hervorgerufen wird, bestätigt später der Humanismusbrief, wo Heidegger „die kaum auszudenkende abgründige leibliche Verwandtschaft mit dem Tier" mit der „Wesensferne" des Göttlichen in Zusammenhang bringt: Diese sei uns trotz ihrer Ferne „vertrauter" (GA 9, 326).

IV.

Der „Brief über den Humanismus" stammt vom Herbst 1946. Etwa zur gleichen Zeit wurde dem Bericht Paul Hsiaos zufolge die gemeinsame Arbeit am *Tao-te-king* unterbrochen, ohne später fortgesetzt zu werden. In einem Brief an Karl Jaspers nennt Heidegger als Grund für das Ende dieses Versuchs seine Skepsis gegenüber einer ihm fremden Sprache, wenngleich er die

[15] Zur Kategorie der „Fertigkeit" vgl. GA 2, 326 („Bestimmung eines Vorhandenen oder Zuhandenen"), GA 24, 160 („das herstellende Verhalten"), GA 29/30, 330 („kann in seinem spezifischen Sein [Zeugsein] als solchem nicht weiter").

„Anklänge an das östliche Denken", die Paul Hsiao in seinen Vorlesungen über Heraklit und Parmenides herausgefunden hat, nicht in Abrede stellt.[16]

Diese Anklänge reichen weit zurück. Heideggers Biograph Heinrich Wiegand Petzet berichtet von Heideggers Lesung von Tschuang-Tses „Die Freude der Fische", 1930 anäßlich eines Aufenthaltes in Bremen.[17] Otto Pöggeler interpretiert diesen frühen Beleg mit Hinweis auf die vorausspringende Fürsorge in *Sein und Zeit*, fügt aber hinzu, diese taoistische Legende habe doch auch „den weitergehenden Sinn, an die universale Sympathie zu erinnern, die alles Lebendige - z. B. Fische und Menschen - miteinander verbindet."[18] Cho bezieht einen Gesichtspunkt ein, der den von Pöggeler genannten einer universalen Natur ergänzt: den des *logos*: „Als Beispiel eines nicht-sprachlichen Kommerzes steht diese Lehre Tschuang-Tses eigentlich im direkten Gegensatz zu Heideggers ontologischer Voraussetzung, welche das Tierreich abgründig vom menschlichen Dasein trennt." (HU 302) Diese Abgründigkeit wird bald, wie oben ausgeführt, zum Kennzeichen der Trennung zwischen dem Menschen und den übrigen Lebewesen. Als Wesen, das nie etwas als etwas vernehmen kann und damit des *logos* entbehrt, ist das Tier in seinem „Benehmen" (im Gegensatz zum „Vernehmen") von dem, worauf es bezogen ist, „hingenommen" (GA 29/30, 450); auch hier meldet sich - wie beim Wort „umschlungen" - ein Moment der Unfreiheit oder besser: ein Zustand jenseits von Freiheit und Unfreiheit, sofern unfrei nur Wesen sein können, denen Freiheit grundsätzlich offensteht.

Das Jahr 1946 weist in verschiedener Hinsicht auf Heideggers Annäherung an taoistische Gedanken hin. Zur gleichen Zeit, als er mit dem chinesischen Philosophen am *Tao-te-king* arbeitet, schreibt er die Abhandlung *Der Spruch des Anaximander*, auch wenn es dort „keinen direkten Hinweis auf ein bevorstehendes Gespräch mit dem Osten" gibt (AH 158), gleichwohl der Sache nach ein Vergleich möglich ist (AH 157 ff). Es ist auch das Jahr, in dem der *Brief über den „Humanismus"* abgefaßt wird, dessen „Bezüge zum Osten" Cho gleichfalls eingehend gewürdigt hat (AH 152 ff). Darüber hinaus darf an den gleichfalls auf 1946 datierten Vortrag *Wozu Dichter?* erinnert werden, in dem Heidegger Rainer Maria Rilkes Gedicht mit der Anfangszeile „Wie die Natur die Wesen überläßt" Wort für Wort einer tiefschürfenden Interpretation unterzieht.

Nähe und Ferne Heideggers zum Taoismus: daß eine gemeinsame Wurzel von altchinesischem und frühgriechischem Denken gesucht wird, deutet der Jaspersbrief an, und nicht nur er. Wenn hier ein rechtes Gespräch in Gang kommen soll, bleibt die unterschiedliche Herkunft der Gesprächspartner im

---

[16] *Martin Heidegger/Karl Jaspers: Briefwechsel 1920-1963*, Frankfurt, München/Zürich 1990, 181.

[17] Heinrich Wiegand Petzet, *Auf einen Stern zugehen: Begegnungen und Gespräche mit Martin Heidegger 1929-1976*, Frankfurt 1983, 24.

[18] Otto Pöggeler, *Neue Wege mit Heidegger*, Freiburg/München 1992, 395.

Spiel. Es ist der Unterschied zweier Welten. Die „augenfälligste Differenz“ zwischen dem späten Heidegger und dem Denken des alten Ostens erkennt Cho in der „Unterscheidung des Menschen von dem übrigen Seienden der Natur“ (BN 103). Dieses Trennende ist zu achten und nicht vorzeitig zu versöhnen. Aber läßt sich, bei bleibender gegenseitiger Achtung des je Anderen, nicht doch auch weiterfragen?

In der gebotenen Kürze sei dies mit wenigen Bemerkungen unternommen. Bei Heidegger ist auch im Rückgang hinter die neuzeitliche Engführung bis hin zu den Wurzeln abendländischen Denkens der Mensch das ausgezeichnete Seiende, offen dem Seienden im Ganzen. Dagegen erschiene es, so Chos Einwand, taoistischem Denken „wie eine letzte Verstiegenheit, wollte man behaupten, daß sich Tao nur dem Menschen lichtet und daß Tao ihn für die eigene Botschaft braucht“ (BN 102[19]). Im Lichte des Taoismus erscheint hier wiederum bei Heidegger jene Einschränkung der Lebewesen auf das eine, ausgezeichnete Wesen „Mensch“, wie er dies früher schon in dessen „abgründiger“ Unterscheidung vom Tier zum Ausdruck gebracht hat. „Dasein“ und „Natursein“ sind offenbar doch durch eine unüberbrückbare Kluft geschieden.

Vermutlich kann aber diese Trennung unter zwei unterschiedlichen Aspekten betrachtet werden. Der erste kommt zum Zug, wenn man jene Aufzeichnung aus dem Konvolut „Überwindung der Metaphysik“ betrachtet, dem die folgenden Sätze entnommen seien: „Das unscheinbare Gesetz der Erde wahrt diese in der Genügsamkeit des Aufgehens und Vergehens aller Dinge im zugemessenen Kreis des Möglichen, dem jedes folgt und den doch keines kennt. Die Birke überschreitet nie ihr Mögliches. Das Bienenvolk wohnt in seinem Möglichen. Erst der Wille, der sich allwendig in der Technik einrichtet, zerrt die Erde in die Abmüdung und Vernutzung und Veränderung des Künstlichen.“(VA 98)

Das Gesetz der Erde wahrt „diese“, nämlich die „Hirten“, die nicht darauf aus sind, die Erde bloß zu nutzen, berechnend sicherzustellen, daß sie sich für menschlichen Gebrauch eignet. Die Hirten sind jene, die sich dem „unscheinbaren Gesetz der Erde“ anvertrauen. Während Pflanzen- und Tierreich in ihrem Möglichen bleiben, zwingt der Wille die Erde über das Mögliche hinaus in das Unmögliche. Die allseitige, „planetarische“ Einrichtung dieses Willens entfaltet sich in der Technik.

Dieser Prozeß geht Heideggers Erkenntnis zufolge auf die Anfänge abendländischen Denkens zurück, ist also älter als der neuzeitliche Anspruch, die Natur zu beherrschen. Das heißt in der frühen griechischen Philosophie, die selbst noch nicht dem Geschick der Technik verfallen ist, bereitet sich

[19] In dieser Wendung „für die eigene Botschaft braucht“ klingt offenbar das „Gespräch von der Sprache“ an, wo es am Ende von der „Botschaft“ heißt, daß sie „uns als Botengänger braucht“ (GA 12, 146). Über die Bedeutung des „Brauchens“ AH 165 ff.

dieses schon vor. Der europäische Herrschaftswille hat hier seine Wurzeln.

Nun ist Heidegger von dem Gedanken geleitet, diese Heraufkunft der europäischen Technik sei nur im Rückgang auf die Wurzeln Europas recht zu bedenken. In einem Brief an den japanischen Professor Takehiko Kojima hat er diese Aufgabe, aber auch die Grenze, die damit dem abendländischen Denken gezogen ist, mit dem Satz umrissen: „Solches Nachdenken ist nicht mehr durch die bisherige abendländisch-europäische Philosophie zu vollziehen, allein auch nicht ohne sie, d. h. ohne daß ihre erneut angeeignete Überlieferung auf einen geeigneten Weg gebracht wird."[20]

Diese Aufgabe, die eigene Überlieferung auf einen geeigneten Weg zu bringen, schließt zwar das Gespräch mit außereuropäischem Denken nicht aus. Aber offensichtlich gehört es dem Eigensten zu, jener Vermutung nachzugehen, von der er im späten Hölderlin-Vortrag „Hölderlins Erde und Himmel" sagt, daß in der Gewalt der Herausforderung der Technik eine Herausforderung waltet, die (ich kürze ab) dem Menschen ein neues Wohnen auf der Erde ermöglicht: „Es ist die Hochzeit von Erde und Himmel, da die Menschen und ‚irgend ein Geist', d. h. ein Gott, gemeinschaftlicher die Schönheit auf der Erde wohnen lassen." (GA 4, 179)

Die ausgezeichnete Stellung des Menschen bestünde hier, grob gesagt, darin, einem neuen Verhältnis zur Erde vorauszudenken. Wäre - und dies führt auf den zweiten Aspekt - die „Unterscheidung des Menschen von dem übrigen Seienden der Natur" in einem solchen *hieros gamos* aufgehoben und er damit in ein neues Verhältnis zur Natur gebracht? Was könnte dies aber meinen, will man nicht hinter die seit der Frühzeit der Phänomenologie vorgebrachte Kritik an naturalistischen oder biologischen Mißdeutungen zurückfallen?

Unter dem Gesichtspunkt des Vorrangs des *logos* sind solche Mißdeutungen unvermeidlich. Natur ist hier *entweder* bloße Natur, blind und dem Gesetz des struggle for life unterworfen; oder sie wird, wie Heidegger dies tut, als *physis* gedeutet, als Lichtung, die aber ihrerseits des *logos* bedarf, der sie entbirgt (vgl. VA 247). Sosehr hier freilich *physis* mit Bezug auf das Dasein gedacht wird, so darf anderseits nicht vergessen werden, daß Heidegger mit Hölderlin die „allebendige" Natur bedenkt (GA 4, 65; vgl. IN 70 f). Aber heißt dies, daß die Trennung zwischen dem Dasein und den übrigen Wesen der Natur aufgehoben ist?

Nochmals: Der eine Aspekt dieser Trennung zeigt sich daran, daß das Seiende „Mensch" insofern ausgezeichnet unter allen Wesen der Natur ist, als es diese durch den Einbruch der Technik gewaltsam in den Griff zu bringen vermag und damit ihr, der Natur, Mögliches überschreitet. Zu dieser fragwürdigen Auszeichnung gehört aber auch jene andere, daß im denkenden Vernehmen ein neues Verhältnis zur Natur gestiftet werden kann, was keines der übrigen Wesen von sich aus vermag. Aber - und

[20] Zitiert nach Buchner (Anm. 2) 226.

dies führt zum zweiten Aspekt dieser Überlegung - sind das denkende Vernehmen, das *noein*, die Offenständigkeit im *logos*, das *aletheuein* nicht trotz aller berechtigten Kritik am abendländischen Intellektualismus und seiner Umdeutung des „Denkens" zur berechnenden ratio immer noch „einseitig"? Wäre nicht das Gemeinsame mit der „Natur" auch noch in jenem anderen zu sehen, das den Menschen mit den anderen Wesen verbindet, ohne diese Verbindung bereits naturalistisch mißdeuten zu müssen, nämlich daß Dasein zwar leiblich *existiert*, aber auch *leiblich* existiert? Dem stehen freilich Heideggers entschiedene Absagen entgegen, wenn er etwa schreibt, der Leib des Menschen sei „etwas wesentlich anderes als ein tierischer Organismus" (GA 9, 324), und: „Das Leibliche am Menschen ist nicht etwas Animalisches." (GA 15, 237)

Wird in solchen Aussagen, die sich auf die Auszeichnung des Menschen durch den *logos* gründen, nicht deshalb etwas zur Leiblichkeit wesenhaft Gehöriges ausgeklammert, weil von vornherein das Trennende von Dasein und Leben (das heißt nichtdaseinsmäßigem Seienden vor allem von der Seinsart des Tieres) in den Blick genommen wird? Ein Hinweis auf taoistisches Denken mag diese Überlegungen konkretisieren.

Wir lesen bei Cho: „Die osmotische Beziehung zwischen Natur und Mensch ist eine Art Telepathie, die ebensogut zwischen Mensch und Mensch wie zwischen Menschen und beliebig [!] anderen Lebewesen stattfinden kann." (BN 101) Durch den *logos* sind die Menschen und die anderen Lebewesen getrennt. Was macht dann ihre Einheit aus? In dem eben zitierten Satz ist von Telepathie die Rede. Dieses Fremdwort bezeichnet im Deutschen ein Gefühl für Fernes ohne leibliche Vermittlung. Es sei hier demgegenüber die umgekehrte Variante ins Spiel gebracht.

Das griechische *tele* (epische Form von *tely*) heißt „fern". Das Wort *pathos* meint solches, das widerfährt; daher auch Leidenschaft, Affekt oder äußere Einwirkung. Die oben gemeinte Telepathie wäre dann gerade nicht ein leibloses Ferngefühl, sondern ein auch das Ferne umfassendes Betroffenwerdenkönnen. Widerfahrnis oder Betroffenheit ist aber nur Wesen möglich, denen ein Leib eigen ist. Die Erfahrung der Verletzlichkeit anderer (nicht nur menschlicher) Wesen ist möglich, weil Verletzlichkeit am eigenen Leib erfahrbar wird. Selbst die Bedrohung durch den Tod, die immer eine gewisse Vorwegnahme bedeutet, setzt voraus, das endgültige Erlöschen des eigenen individuellen Leibes zumindest zu ahnen. Sollte man diese Ahnung der Sterblichkeit den Tieren völlig vorenthalten können?

Heidegger hat - worauf Landgrebe so klar hingewiesen hat[21] - in den Prozeß der Weltbildung über Husserls reines Bewußtsein hinaus die „Betroffenheit und Bedrängnis" hineingenommen. Sie bleiben jedoch auf die Befindlichkeit fokussiert, die wiederum als Offenheit für das Seiende im Ganzen ausgelegt ist. Aber wie sind Betroffenheit und Bedrängnis ohne

[21] S. o. Anm. 10.

Leib erfahrbar? Wie könnten Bedrängnis und Bedrohung zu Wirklichkeiten werden, gäbe es nicht auch einen Leib, hinfällig für Krankheiten und ausgesetzt einem irreversiblen Prozeß des Alterns? Und wie könnten die Menschen die werden, die sie sind, die Sterblichen, müßten sie nicht auch dazu herbeilassen, mit der „großen Vernunft des Leibes" (Nietzsche[22]) ihren Frieden zu schließen?

Vom Ansatz her ist Heideggers Denken solchen Überlegungen gegenüber nicht grundsätzlich verschlossen. Doch bleibt das „Naturhafte" des Leibes ausgespart. So wird zwar dem großen Zusammenhang alles Lebendigen Achtung erwiesen, die Reiche des Daseins und der Lebe-Wesen bleiben aber durch einen Abgrund getrennt. Daß das Leibhafte der ganzen Natur zu einer Sache des Denkens wird, ist nicht das Geringste, das von diesem Ost-West-Diwan zu lernen ist.

Ein Gleichnis des Tschuang-Tse lautet: „Wie Vögel ihren Schnabel unbewußt beim Zwitschern schließen und, ohne ihn zu schließen, nicht zwitschern können - also an Himmel und Erde geschlossen werden, ohne dessen bewußt zu sein, das ist göttliche Tugend, das ist der große Einklang."[23]

---

[22] *Also sprach Zarathustra I.* „Von den Verächtern des Leibes".

[23] *Reden und Gleichnisse des Tschuang-Tse: Deutsche Auswahl von Martin Buber*, Zürich 1951, 99 (Erstdruck 1910).

Lebenswelt und Natur: Grundlagen einer Phänomenologie der Interkulturalität

Klaus Held

Daß uns alles, womit wir in unserem Verhalten zu tun haben, in unthematisch vertrauten Horizonten begegnet, darf als die Grunderkenntnis der Phänomenologie, so wie sie Husserl auf den Weg gebracht hat, bezeichnet werden. Die Horizonte sind die „Welten", in denen wir Menschen leben, die Welt der Politik oder des Sports, die Welt des Angestellten, die Welt des Computers usw., und schließlich die umfassendsten Welten: die verschiedenen Kulturen. Wir müssen uns in unserem Denken und Handeln in Horizonten orientieren, weil sie uns als Verweisungszusammenhänge die Regeln dafür vorgeben, in welchen Bahnen unsere Aufmerksamkeit verläuft: Alles, womit wir zu tun haben, verweist uns auf andere Vorkommnisse, mit denen wir uns ebenfalls beschäftigen könnten. Es gibt kein Verhalten, das unabhängig von solchen Verweisungszusammenhängen stattfinden könnte.

Die Horizonte erregen normalerweise nicht unsere Aufmerksamkeit; sie bleiben für uns im Hintergrund und liegen gleichsam im Schatten dessen, was jeweils zu einem Pol wird, worauf wir mit einer bestimmten Verhaltensweise ausdrücklich abzielen, und was wir so - wie Husserl formuliert - zu unserem „Thema" machen. Alles, worauf sich unsere Aufmerksamkeit richten kann, ist in einem buchstäblichen Sinne ein „Vorkommnis", nämlich etwas, was für uns aus dem dunklen Hintergrund einer unthematisch vertrauten Welt „hervorkommt" und in diesem Sinne „erscheint"; es gibt keine horizontfreien Vorkommnisse in unserem Leben.

Alle überhaupt denkbaren Horizonte des Menschen gehören durch wechselseitige Sinnverweisungen in einem durch seine Offenheit allumfassenden Verweisungszusammenhang zusammen, „der" Welt als *singulare tantum*, die Husserl als „Universalhorizont" bezeichnet. Die Welt, in der wir Menschen vor und neben aller Wissenschaft unser konkretes Leben führen und uns zu Hause fühlen, ist diese eine horizonthafte Welt, die Husserl in seinem letzten Werk terminologisch als die „Lebenswelt" bestimmt hat.[1] Gelegentlich kann uns schon im Alltag einer der normalerweise unthematisch vertrauten Horizonte der Lebenswelt bewußt werden, etwa wenn uns

[1] Eine relativ neue Bestandsaufnahme der Literatur zum Husserlschen Begriff der „Lebenswelt" findet sich im gleichnamigen Artikel des V.s in: „Theologische Realenzyklopädie", Berlin/New York, Bd.XX, 1991. Vgl. v. Vf. außerdem „Husserls neue Einführung in die Philosophie: der Begriff der Lebenswelt", in: C.F. Gethmann (Hrsg.): Lebenswelt und Wissenschaft, Bonn 1991.

auffällt, daß ein Horizont sich durch Umorientierungen in unserem Verhalten geändert hat. So haben wir auf unsere Horizonte einen gewissen Einfluß, aber er geht nicht so weit, daß wir uns von allen vorgegebenen Horizonten befreien könnten; in jeglichem Verhalten bleiben wir von der Vorgegebenheit der Lebenswelt abhängig.

Das Ziel der modernen Wissenschaft, sofern sie sich in ihren methodischen Normen nach der Naturwissenschaft richtet, ist die unbedingte „Objektivität", worunter eine Erkenntnis der Welt zu verstehen ist, die von allen subjektiven, d. h. durch die jeweiligen Horizonte eines Menschen bedingten Gesichtspunkten unbeeinflußt wäre. Mit ihrem von Husserl als „Objektivismus" bezeichneten Streben, sich von allen solchen Gesichtspunkten unabhängig zu machen, versucht die moderne Wissenschaft eine Welt zu erkennen, die vollständig von ihrem Horizontcharakter befreit wäre. Doch eine solche Welt gibt es nicht, weil auch für alle Verfahren, Instrumente und Ergebnisse wissenschaftlicher Forschung gilt, daß sie dem Menschen nur in irgendwelche Horizonte eingebettet begegnen können. Gleichwohl kann die moderne Wissenschaft den unaufhebbaren Horizontcharakter der Welt aus ihrem Bewußtsein verdrängen, weil die Horizonte in unserem Leben normalerweise unthematisch bleiben. In diesem Sinne kann Husserl sagen, daß die moderne Wissenschaft auf einer tiefgreifenden Vergessenheit der Lebenswelt beruht.

Keine Situation in unserem Leben - mag sie noch so aussichtslos erscheinen - kann damit enden, daß wir auf nichts mehr verwiesen würden. Der universale Verweisungszusammenhang der Lebenswelt erneuert sich in jeder Situation; d. h. das - im phänomenologischen Sinne verstandene - „Erscheinen", das Auftauchen von Vorkommnissen in Horizonten, bricht niemals ab. Dieses Nicht-Abbrechen des Erscheinens, das nicht aufhörende Geschehen, das darin besteht, daß das Verweisen sich immer weiter fortsetzt, ist nichts anderes als die Welt, sofern wir darunter die konkrete Lebenswelt als Universalhorizont verstehen; das Sein der Welt hat den Charakter des Geschehens. Die gewöhnliche Vorstellung, die Welt sei so etwas wie ein statisch existierender gigantischer Behälter für alles, was es gibt, oder sie sei die Gesamtmenge dessen, „was der Fall ist", wie Wittgenstein formuliert hat, ist ein unzureichender Begriff von „Welt", den die Phänomenologie durch die Klärung der Horizonthaftigkeit allen menschlichen Verhaltens überwunden hat.

Daß sich für uns immer wieder neue Verweisungszusammenhänge auftun, ist ein Geschehen, das sich „von selbst" abspielt, d. h. ohne daß wir Menschen eigens dafür sorgen müßten. Im Gegenteil: bei allem, was wir aus eigener Kraft bewerkstelligen können, sind wir darauf angewiesen, daß die Selbsterneuerung des Erscheinens, das Geschehen der horizonthaften Welt, schon immer ohne unser Zutun stattgefunden hat und weiter stattfindet. Die Art von Sein, die „von selbst" stattfindet, bezeichnet die Philosophie seit alters als Natur. Die Natur, die *physis*, erregte als erstes die Aufmerksamkeit, als bei den Griechen Philosophie und Wissenschaft entstanden.

Mit der *physis* der frühgriechischen „Naturphilosophen" war nichts anderes als die Welt gemeint, wenn wir unter „Welt" das Geschehen des Erscheinens verstehen, das allem menschlichen Eingreifen vorgegeben ist, weil es sich jederzeit „von selbst" erneuert.

Das Geschehen des Erscheinens ist die Lebendigkeit der „Lebens"-welt, nämlich ihr Fortbestand durch die Selbsterneuerung der Horizonte. Das zeigt, daß es keiner nachträglichen intellektuellen Verknüpfung bedarf, um die Lebenswelt in einen Zusammenhang mit der Natur zu bringen: Die Lebenswelt hat vielmehr von vornherein als „von selbst" geschehendes Erscheinen den Charakter der „Natur". Andererseits leben wir Menschen in vielen verschiedenen Horizonten, und die umfassendsten Horizonte sind die der unterschiedlichen Kulturen auf dieser Erde. Die Kulturen aber sind ein Werk des Menschen; sie können dies sein, weil wir Menschen, wie oben gesagt, auf unsere Horizonte doch einen gewissen Einfluß haben. Demnach muß zwischen den *vielen* kulturellen Welten, die dem menschlichen Einfluß nicht ganz entzogen sind, und der *einen* allen Menschen gemeinsamen Lebenswelt als Natur, die allem menschlichen Verhalten vorgegeben ist, ein Unterschied gemacht werden.

Im Zeitalter des globalen Zusammenwachsens aller Menschheitskulturen stellt sich die Frage, welches Verhältnis zwischen der einen Lebensweltnatur der Menschheit und den vielen Welten der verschiedenen Kulturen besteht. Wie läßt sich der Unterschied zwischen der einen Natur der Menschheitslebenswelt und den vielen kulturellen Lebenswelten genauer bestimmen?[2] Zunächst ist man geneigt, das Von-selbst-Geschehen der Natur von dem Geschehen der Horizontbildung, das einem gewissen menschlichen Einfluß unterliegt, abzutrennen und dieses zweite Geschehen auf das erste folgen zu lassen. Deshalb hat Husserl in Übereinstimmung mit der philosophischen Tradition auf die besagte Frage die Antwort gegeben, die eine Natur bilde in unserer Weltvorstellung gleichsam die unterste Schicht, die von den unterschiedlichen Weltschichten der verschiedenen Kulturen überlagert werde.

Dieses Schichtenmodell bestimmt auch das Bild von der Welt, das die moderne Naturwissenschaft hat: Die *eine* und keinem menschlichen Einfluß ausgesetzte Welt ist die eine allgemeine Natur, wie sie von den Naturwissenschaften erforscht wird, und die vielen Kulturen sind gleichsam Interpretationen dieser einen Welt. Die Naturwissenschaftler erheben den Anspruch, die interpretationsfreie Basis für die vielen verschiedenen kulturellen Überformungen zu erforschen. Für die interkulturelle Verständigung bedeutet das, daß die Wissenschaftler wegen der Bezogenheit ihrer Forschung auf die eine allgemeine Natur eine gemeinsame Sprache sprechen

[2] Zum Verhältnis zwischen der Einheit der einen Menschheitslebenswelt und der Vielheit der vielen kulturellen Welten nach Husserl vgl. v. Vf.: „Heimwelt, Fremdwelt, die eine Welt", in: E.W. Orth (Hrsg.): Phänomenologische Forschungen, Band 24, Freiburg/München 1991.

können, während es zwischen den Menschen in ihrem Leben außerhalb der Wissenschaft latenten oder offenen Streit gibt, weil ihrer Verständigung durch die Verschiedenheit der vielen kulturellen Welten Grenzen gesetzt werden.

Aber die Vorstellung von zwei Schichten der Welt wird dem oben erläuterten Verhältnis zwischen Natur und Kultur in der Lebenswelt nicht gerecht: Die Lebenswelt ist nichts anderes als der universale Zusammenhang der Horizonte. Weil die Horizonte sich durch den Einfluß des Menschen ändern können, also ein Werk der Kultur sind, ist die Lebenswelt von grundauf Kultur, und es kann keine untere „Schicht" von reiner Natur geben, die jeder menschlichen Interpretation entzogen wäre. Aber auch das Umgekehrte gilt: Weil sich das Verweisungsgeschehen bei jedem Horizont, den wir Menschen haben können, von selbst erneuert, kann man von der Horizonthaftigkeit im ganzen sagen, daß sie den Charakter der Natur hat. Die Welt als Lebenswelt ist durch und durch Natur *und* Kultur, sie ist Natur als Kultur und umgekehrt.

Ein besonders instruktives Beispiel für die lebensweltliche Einheit von Natur und Kultur ist das Klima der verschiedenen Weltregionen. Einen antiken Gedanken aufgreifend hat J. G. Herder die Behauptung aufgestellt, die Verschiedenheit der Kulturen sei primär auf die Unterschiede des Klimas zurückzuführen. Diesen Gedanken hat in den dreißiger Jahren Tetsuro Watsuji in seinem Buch über das Klima konkret mit einem Vergleich zwischen Europa und Japan fortgeführt.[3] Für die Naturwissenschaft bedeutet „Klima" einen bestimmten Zusammenhang von Gesetzmäßigkeiten der Natur, die man statistisch bestimmen und erforschen kann. Wenn man dieses Verständnis von „Klima" voraussetzt, muß man annehmen, Herder und Watsuji wollten behaupten, alle typischen kulturellen Unterschiede - etwa zwischen Europa und Japan - seien aus naturwissenschaftlich erforschbaren Gegebenheiten ableitbar. Da die Gesetzmäßigkeiten, um die es der modernen Naturwissenschaft geht, nicht dem Einfluß der menschlichen Freiheit unterliegen, würde das auf die naturalistische These hinauslaufen, alle kulturellen Errungenschaften des Menschen seien durch Naturgesetze determiniert.

Der Naturalismus ist blind dafür, daß der Mensch die Freiheit hat, auf seine Horizonte Einfluß zu nehmen; er verleugnet genauso wie der Objektivismus den Horizontcharakter der Welt. Man würde Herder und Watsuji aber mißverstehen, wenn man ihnen einen Naturalismus unterstellte. Worauf sie mit ihrer These von der Herkunft der Kulturen aus dem jeweiligen Klima abzielten, auch wenn sie selbst das noch nicht mit den Mitteln einer Phänomenologie der Lebenswelt verdeutlichen konnten, war nicht das

[3] Übersetzt ins Deutsch: Tetsuro Watsuji, Fudo - Wind und Erde. Der Zusammenhang zwischen Klima und Kultur, Vorw. u. Übers. v. D. Fischer-Barnicol u. R. Okochi, Darmstadt 1992.

„Klima“ im Sinne eines naturwissenschaftlichen Objektivismus, sondern das Klima als lebensweltliche Einheit von Natur und Kultur. Die Gegebenheiten des so verstandenen Klimas sind zwar Geschehnisse, die sich einem gezielten Einfluß des Menschen entziehen, aber als „reine Tatsachen“, d. h. als von jeder Interpretation freie Gegebenheiten würden sie im Menschenleben keine Rolle spielen; Bedeutung für uns können sie immer nur dadurch gewinnen, daß wir sie durch unsere Interpretation zu Erscheinungen innerhalb bestimmter kultureller Horizonte machen.

Trotz der Einheit von Natur und Kultur in der Lebenswelt muß man die Frage stellen, wie sich die *eine* Welt, welche die Naturwissenschaftler als interpretationsfreie Natur zum Gegenstand ihrer Forschung machen wollen, von den vielen kulturellen Welten unterscheiden läßt. Gibt es die Möglichkeit, Bestimmungen der *einen* Lebenswelt der ganzen Menschheit zu entwickeln, ohne dadurch ins Fahrwasser eines Objektivismus oder Naturalismus zu geraten? Dies ist eine der zentralen Fragen, welche die Phänomenologie der Lebenswelt zu beantworten sucht. Dabei kann sie zunächst nicht anders als von den Grundbestimmungen der einen Welt auszugehen, welche die undiskutierte Voraussetzung für die Forschungen der modernen Naturwissenschaft bilden, ohne diese Bestimmungen zu übernehmen. Die wichtigste dieser Grundbestimmungen ist die Annahme, daß überall in der Natur das Kausalgesetz herrscht.

Dieses Gesetz bedeutet für die Naturwissenschaft, daß es im Prinzip möglich sein muß, aufgrund der in der Natur herrschenden Gesetzmäßigkeiten sichere und exakte Prognosen für den künftigen Ablauf bestimmter Naturprozesse abzugeben. Die Naturwissenschaft stellt sich die Aufgabe, diejenigen Gesetzmäßigkeiten ans Licht zu bringen, die solche absolut zuverlässigen Prognosen erlauben. Nun hätte aber die moderne Naturwissenschaft von vornherein nicht auf die Idee kommen können, sich diese Aufgabe zu stellen, wenn es nicht schon innerhalb des Lebens in der vorwissenschaftlichen Lebenswelt ein allgemeines Bedürfnis der Menschen gäbe, künftige Entwicklungen vorherzusagen, und auch schon Praktiken, welche diesem Bedürfnis gerecht zu werden versuchen.

Das lehrreichste Beispiel hierfür bietet der schon angesprochene Bereich des Klimas: das Wetter. Seit alters kennen die Menschen in allen Kulturen irgendwelche Wetterregeln, d. h. Verfahren, aus gewissen Anzeichen am Himmel oder auf der Erde auf die nächste oder fernere Entwicklung des Wetters Schlusse zu ziehen. Wesentlich ist nun die Feststellung, daß solche Wetterregeln in der Lebenswelt - gleichgültig worauf sie sich stützen - niemals von solcher Beschaffenheit sind, daß sie vollkommen zuverlässige und genaue Vorhersagen erlauben. Die Regeln können durchaus einigermaßen brauchbar sein, weil sie sich auf gewisse Kausalzusammenhänge stützen. Aber bei diesen Zusammenhängen handelt es sich immer um eine Kausalität der „Umstände“, und zu ihr gehört grundsätzlich eine gewisse Unbestimmtheit; die Prognose kann immer nur lauten: „unter bestimmten Umständen werden wahrscheinlich ungefähr die und die Ereignisse eintreten".

Natürlich haben alle Menschen ein Interesse daran, im voraus mehr über irgendwelche zu erwartenden Naturprozesse wie etwa die Wetterentwicklung zu wissen. Aber erst die moderne Naturwissenschaft macht mit methodischer Entschiedenheit den Versuch, die Zuverlässigkeit von Prognosen nicht nur graduell zu steigern, sondern solche Vorhersagen auf eine prinzipiell andere Grundlage zu stellen, als es bis dahin in der Lebenswelt aller traditionellen Menschheitskulturen selbstverständlich war. Diese andere Grundlage soll - und kann auch nur - dadurch gewonnen werden, daß die Prognosen sich nicht mehr auf die unbestimmte lebensweltliche „Kausalität der Umstände" stützen, sondern auf eine exakte Kausalität. Die lebensweltliche Kausalität und Prognostik kann deshalb niemals exakt sein, weil die „Umstände" immer den Charakter der „Situation" haben. Eine Situation ist ein zusammenhängendes Ganzes von Bedingungen für das Handeln, das dem Menschen zwar einerseits vorgegeben ist, aber andererseits auch Angebote für seine Freiheit enthält, weil die Bedingungen keine interpretationsfreien Fakten sind, sondern in Horizonte eingebettete Gegebenheiten. Der Versuch, zu exakten Prognosen zu gelangen, unterscheidet sich deshalb von allen Formen traditioneller lebensweltlicher Prognostik, weil er darin besteht, sich von der Bindung an die Situativität und damit an die Horizonthaftigkeit des menschlichen Verhaltens zu befreien.

Mit den letzten Überlegungen ist ein erster allgemeiner Zug der *einen* Lebenswelt der Menschheit ans Licht getreten: die von Husserls in seinem letzten Werk erstmals als solche beschriebene Umstandskausalität.[4] Sie ist zwar die Voraussetzung der naturwissenschaftlichen Idee einer exakten Kausalität, aber sie selbst ist keine Bestimmung der Lebenswelt, mit der die Welt oder das Menschenleben einseitig objektivistisch oder naturalistisch aufgefaßt würde. Ein zweiter Grundzug der einen Lebenswelt zeigt sich nun, wenn man darauf achtet, daß die traditionelle lebensweltliche Prognostik sich entsprechend der besonderen Bedeutung von Wetter und Klima in beinahe allen Kulturen vor allem auf den Himmel bezog, - ein Blickwinkel, dem Husserl noch nicht genügend Beachtung geschenkt hat.

Versteht man den Begriff „Himmel" als eine Bezeichnung, die am Bereich des lebensweltlich Erfahrbaren abgelesen ist, meint er den ganzen offenen Raum „über der Erde".[5] Die Erde ihrerseits, so wie sie uns in der Lebenswelt konkret erscheint, bildet den Untergrund des Bodens unter unseren Füßen. Dieser Untergrund enthält das Material, woraus die ma-

---

[4]Vgl. E. Husserl: Die Krisis der europäischen Wissenschaften und die transzendentale Phänomenologie, hrsg. v. W. Biemel, Den Haag 1954 (Husserliana Bd. 6), S. 357 ff.

[5]Die folgenden Ausführungen stützen sich auf den Aufsatz des Vf.s: „Sky and Earth as Invariants of the Natural Life-world", in: E.W. Orth u. Chan-Fai Cheung (Hrsg.): Phänomenologische Forschungen, Sonderband 1998 „Phenomenology of Interculturality and Life-world", Freiburg/München 1998.

teriellen Dinge bestehen; die Erde, welche die Dinge trägt, setzt sich in die Dinge hinein fort, und in diesem Sinne können wir sagen, daß die Dinge „aus Erde" bestehen. In die Erde als Untergrund und Material können wir Menschen durch irgendwelche praktischen oder theoretischen Aktivitäten „eindringen" und so in ihre innere Dunkelheit Licht bringen. Aber das setzt voraus, daß die Erde von sich aus dunkel und verschlossen ist.[6]

Daß die Erde für die materiellen Dinge den tragenden Grund und das Material bildet, zeigt sich uns in der lebensweltlichen Erfahrung nur dadurch, daß die Dinge in einem Raum erscheinen, der im Gegensatz zur Verschlossenheit und Dunkelheit der Erde eine Dimension der Offenheit und Helligkeit ist. Dieser offene und lichthafte Raum ist der Himmel. In ihm können die materiellen Dinge ans Licht treten, weil sie darin einen Platz finden. Ein Raum, der für etwas Platz gibt, ist leer. Bemerkenswerterweise ist das chinesische Schriftzeichen für „Leere" mit einem der Zeichen identisch, die den Himmel bezeichnen.[7] Das zeigt, daß der Himmel mehr ist als nur eine Teilregion der Welt; er ist in gewissem Sinne die Welt selbst, sofern er für alles Platz gibt, was unseren Sinnen erscheint. Charakteristischerweise bevorzugten die ersten Klassiker der Philosophie, Platon und Aristoteles, als Bezeichnung für das Ganze der Welt den Begriff „Himmel", *uranos*.

Aus dem Himmel als der für alles Materielle platzgebenden und in diesem Sinne „leeren" Offenheitsdimension ist in der neuzeitlichen Naturwissenschaft der „leere Raum" geworden, die zweite Grundbestimmung der objektivistisch erforschten einen Natur neben der exakten Kausalität. Der naturwissenschaftlich verstandene Raum ist das *eine* in drei Dimensionen erstreckte unendliche Stellenkontinuum, dessen einzelne Stellen man rechnerisch durch Angaben von drei Koordinaten bestimmen kann. In der Leere dieses Stellenkontinuums breitet sich die Materie aus, und in ihm wirken die im subatomaren Bereich beginnenden Kräfte, deren kausale Gesetzmaßigkeit die moderne Physik erforscht. Ohne die allgemeine menschheitliche Erfahrung des Himmels als *uranos* der Lebenswelt hätte die moderne Naturwissenschaft zwar niemals zu ihrer Raumvorstellung gelangen können, aber der lebensweltliche Raum des Himmels ist etwas ganz anderes als ein unendliches Stellenkontinuum.

Für die moderne Naturwissenschaft ist der „Himmel" das, was wir Menschen von der Erde aus vom sogenannten „Weltraum" sehen. Der Weltraum, das „Universum", ist eine „objektiv", d. h. unabhängig von unserer

---

[6] Der Sinn dieser Dunkelheit ist zum ersten Mal von M. Heidegger in seiner Abhandlung „Der Ursprung des Kunstwerkes" phänomenologisch erläutert worden. Vgl. M. Heidegger: Holzwege (Gesamtausgabe Bd. 5), Frankfurt a. M. 1977, S. 31 ff.

[7] Vgl. hierzu v. Vf.: „Welt, Leere, Natur. Eine phänomenologische Annäherung an die religiöse Tradition Japans", in: G. Stenger u. M. Röhrig (Hrsg.): Philosophie der Struktur - „Fahrzeug" der Zukunft? Für Heinrich Rombach, Freiburg/München 1995, S. 117.

subjektiven Erfahrung existierende unendliche Menge von Leerstellen, d. h. von Plätzen, die von beliebigen Dingen eingenommen werden können. Nach objektivistischer Auffassung kommt unsere menschliche Erfahrung erst nachträglich ins Spiel, indem wir einem gewissen Teilbereich dieser Leerstellen den Namen „Himmel" geben, weil der damit bezeichnete Komplex von Raumstellen uns aus unserer subjektiven Perspektive als der Bereich oberhalb von uns erscheint. Objektiv aber sind nach dieser Auffassung die Raumstellen, die dieser Bereich umfaßt, Plätze in der Unendlichkeit des Weltalls, die unabhängig davon, wie sie uns subjektiv erscheinen, vorhanden sind.

Aber wenn alles, was uns begegnet, uns aus Horizonten entgegentritt und nur von daher für uns eine Bedeutung bekommt, muß das auch für den Himmelsraum und für das, was es darin an Platz gibt, gelten. Bei unserem alltäglichen Leben in der vorwissenschaftlichen Lebenswelt sind wir auf bestimmte Dinge angewiesen, von denen wir wissen, daß sie da oder dort auffindbar oder erreichbar sind. Das Allermeiste von dem, womit wir uns beschäftigen, hat in diesem Sinne einen bestimmten „Platz", an den es hingehört. Zum alltäglichen Verweisungszusammenhang gehört, wie Heidegger in „Sein und Zeit" phänomenologisch gezeigt hat, die Vertrautheit mit solchen Plätzen und mit der Art und Weise, wie sie uns zugänglich sind.[8] Vom Raum wissen wir lebensweltlich zunächst und normalerweise nicht in der Form, daß uns eine unendliche subjekt-unabhängige Menge von leeren Stellen im Weltraum bewußt ist, an denen sich beliebig Gegenstände befinden können.

Nur solange wir im Objektivismus befangen sind, können wir annehmen, die Menschen hätten zunächst das Bewußtsein von einem Kontinuum leerer Stellen und füllten diesen Raum dann wie ein leeres Gefäß mit den Dingen auf, die sie an bestimmten Stellen in das Kontinuum einordnen. Phänomenologisch betrachtet verhält es sich umgekehrt: Wir wissen vom Raum, weil die meisten Dinge für uns an bestimmten Orten gleichsam zu Hause sind. Nur durch einen langen geschichtlichen Abstraktionsprozeß ist man im Europa der Neuzeit zu der Vorstellung vom Raum als einem unendlichen objektiven Stellenkontinuum gelangt. Entsprechend ist der „Himmel" keine subjektive Bezeichnung für einen objektiv vorhandenen Sektor dieser Unendlichkeit, sondern ein Ort, der uns deshalb vertraut ist, weil gewisse Vorkommnisse dort natürlicherweise ihren Platz haben. Der Himmel ist also ein Platz für viele Plätze. Ein solches Ganzes von Plätzen nennen wir „Gegend".[9]

Zu einer Gegend gehören gewisse für das menschliche Leben bedeutsame Geschehnisse, die sich dort regelmaßig ereignen oder einmal ereignet haben. Das für das alltägliche Leben wichtigste Geschehen, das sich in der

---

[8] Vgl. Heidegger, Sein und Zeit, §22, S. 102.

[9] Vgl. a.a.O., S. 103.

Gegend namens „Himmel" abspielt, ist das Wetter. Im Lateinischen heißt das Wetter *status caeli*, „Zustand des Himmels". Bei diesem Geschehen gibt es die Veränderungen, die wir von Tag zu Tag beobachten können, aber in den Kulturen außerhalb der Tropenregion vor allem auch die großen Veränderungen, die den Wechsel der Jahreszeiten kennzeichnen. Die Jahreszeiten verändern auch das, was unter dem Himmel ist: die Erde. Aber über den Himmel ziehen die Veränderungen des Wetters herauf, in denen sich die Jahreszeiten dramatisch ankündigen. Im Wetter spüren wir das Klima der Gegend der Welt, die wir bewohnen. So gehört zu jeder von Menschen bewohnbaren Gegend der Welt ein bestimmter Himmel, nämlich als die Gegend für das Wetter, das für ein entsprechendes Klima charakteristisch ist.

Über die Bedeutung des Wetters im Zusammenhang mit dem Himmel hat man in der Philosophie noch wenig nachgedacht. Eine phänomenologische Analyse der Lebenswelt, die den Naturalismus vermeiden und die unfruchtbare Opposition von Natur und Kultur hinter sich lassen möchte, kann davon ausgehen, daß es die menschliche Freiheit konkret nur gibt, indem sie verleiblicht ist, gleichsam inkarniert, und primär durch die Leiblichkeit eingebunden in Horizonte. Die inkarnierte Freiheit ist nicht einer rein biologisch zu verstehenden körperlichen Ausstattung und Verhaltensweise des Menschen aufgestockt - dies ist die Denkweise des Naturalismus -, sondern sie hat ihre Wurzeln schon in der Art und Weise, wie wir in unserem Leib leben und uns verhalten. Mit der Polarität von Himmel und Erde sind wir vertraut, weil wir mit unserem Körper zwischen beidem angesiedelt sind. Die Erde trägt uns, wir fühlen körperlich die Schwere, die uns nach unten zur Erde zieht, und wir gehen als Menschen aufgerichtet zum Himmel über uns.

Den Himmel haben wir aber nicht nur im räumlichen Sinne „über" uns, sondern auch in dem Sinne, daß uns die klimatischen Geschehnisse, die sich dort abspielen, beherrschen. Diese Herrschaft ist eine solche über unser leibliches Leben: Wir sind vom Himmelsgeschehen betroffen, indem wir uns bei dem einen Wetter wohlfühlen und bei dem anderen nicht. Die Veränderungen des Wetters am Himmel, denen wir in unserer leiblichen Befindlichkeit am meisten ausgesetzt sind, vollziehen sich aber zwischen zwei Polaritäten des Klimas, die uns bei jedem einschneidenden Wetterwechsel auffällig werden: Hitze streitet mit Kälte und Nässe mit Trockenheit.[10]

Wir kennen diese vier Qualitäten als Eigenschaften der materiellen Dinge, wie sie unserem Tastsinn erscheinen; wir können etwas Materielles intentional als kühl oder warm, als feucht oder trocken empfinden. Wichtiger

[10]Hierzu und zum folgenden vgl. die detaillierteren Analysen des Vf.s im Heraklit-Teil der Untersuchung: „Heraklit, Parmenides und der Anfang von Philosophie und Wissenschaft. Eine phänomenologische Besinnung", Berlin 1980, S. 355 ff.

aber ist, welche Rolle diese Tastempfindungen für unser leibliches Befinden spielen: Daß wir lebendige Wesen sind, können wir nur vor dem Hintergrund der Bedrohung durch den Tod erfahren. Diese Bedrohung spüren wir leiblich in der Labilität unseres Befindens. Wir fühlen uns wohl, wenn die Tastqualitäten, die grundlegend das Empfinden von unserem eigenen Leib bestimmen, dadurch für uns unauffällig bleiben, daß sie ein normales Maß einhalten. Wenn dieses Maß durch Extreme gestört und uns dadurch unser eigenes leibliches Befinden auffällig wird, meldet sich auf diese Weise die Gefährdung unseres leiblichen Lebens durch den Tod. Die Grundlage unseres ganzen leiblichen Befindens sind eine Empfindung von Wärme und von Flüssigkeit oder Feuchtigkeit, mit denen einerseits zwischen extremer Hitze und Kälte und andererseits zwischen extremer Trockenheit und Nässe das Gleichgewicht gehalten wird.

Das Warme und das Flüssig-Feuchte sind nicht zufällig die Empfindungsqualitäten, die das vorgeburtliche Leben des Menschen im Fruchtwasser der Mutter ermöglichen und die auch die erste Nahrung nach der Geburt kennzeichnen. Beide Qualitäten hängen eng damit zusammen, daß wir die materiellen Dinge nur wahrnehmen können, indem wir unseren Körper oder Teile davon bewegen. Beweglichkeit setzt Geschmeidigkeit voraus, und diese begegnet uns als Empfindungsqualität des Tastsinns in einem mittleren und unauffälligen Maß von Feuchtigkeit und Flüssigkeit, das wir als angenehm empfinden. Die dazu gehörigen lebensgefährdenden Extreme sind eine Nässe, in der das Lebendige ertrinkt und in der das Fleisch unseres Leibes verfault, verwest usw., und eine Leib und Leben ausdörrende Trockenheit. Daß das leibliche Leben gerade durch diese beiden Extreme gefährdet ist, wird kulturgeschichtlich durch die Tatsache bestätigt, daß der Tod als Zustand des Leichnams in manchen Kulturen - je nach dem Klima - als ein Vertrocknen, in anderen als Verfaulen oder Verwesung beschrieben wird.

Beweglichkeit setzt neben der Geschmeidigkeit Kraft voraus. Das Wohlbefinden durch ein Kraftgefühl empfinden wir in der Tastqualität maßvoller Wärme. Extreme Kälte und Hitze begegnen uns leiblich als lebenzerstörende Kräfte, weil sie unserer eigenen Kraft entgegengesetzt sind und sie zum Erliegen bringen, - die Kälte, indem sie unsere Beweglichkeit erstarren läßt, die Hitze, indem die Beweglichkeit in ihr erlahmt. Auch diese Extremerfahrungen werden kulturgeschichtlich durch den Umgang mit dem leiblichen Tod bestätigt: In den Kulturen herrschen traditionell zwei Formen vor, wie der menschliche Leichnam behandelt wird: Er wird einem der beiden das Leben zerstörenden Extremzustände anheimgegeben, entweder der Hitze des Feuers, worin man ihn verbrennt, oder der Kälte der Erde, worin man ihn bestattet.

Alle Wettererscheinungen, die über den Himmel heraufziehen, spielen sich zwischen den beiden Polaritäten von Hitze und Kälte und von Nässe und Trockenheit ab. Das Verhältnis zwischen den beiden Polen dieser Polaritäten ist ein Streit, und zwar in einem nicht metaphorischen Sinn des

Wortes: Das Sein der Hitze beim Wetter besteht in nichts anderem als darin, daß sie das Gegenteil von Kälte ist, und umgekehrt. Der Zustand solcher Hitze besteht deshalb darin, sich eine Zeitlang gegen das Gegenteil, die ihm widerstreitende Kälte, zu behaupten.[11] Dieser Kampf der polaren Elementarzustände um ihre zeitweilige Vorherrschaft wäre nicht möglich, wenn sie keine Kraft besäßen. Die konkrete Erfahrung dieser Kraft machen wir in der Kraft, die, wie oben erwähnt, der Erfahrung der Beweglichkeit unseres eigenen Leibes zugrundeliegt. Die Kraft der Elementarzustände, die wir lebensweltlich zugleich an unserem eigenen Leibe und am Wechsel des Wetters am Himmel erfahren, bildet die Grundlage für eine weitere Grundbestimmung der Natur in der modernen Naturwissenschaft: die Kraft.

Dadurch, daß jede Vorherrschaft eines Zustandes nur für eine gewisse Zeitdauer anhalten kann, hat die Abfolge der Wettererscheinungen einen periodischen Charakter. Auch die Erfahrung dieser Periodizität liegt einer naturwissenschaftlichen Grundbestimmung der Natur zugrunde; hier wird uns lebensweltlich die „Zeit" zugänglich. Die Naturwissenschaft versteht unter „Zeit" die Form des Nacheinander, die abzählbare und meßbare Abfolge der „Jetztpunkte". Aber dieses Verständnis von „Zeit" ist ebenso wie die Vorstellung vom Raum als einem Stellenkontinuum etwas Abgeleitetes. Es ist charakteristisch, daß in den romanischen Sprachen die Zeit und das Wetter mit dem gleichen Wort bezeichnet werden, das auf das lateinische „tempus" zurückgeht. Das zeigt, daß der Wechsel vom aktuellen Jetzt zum nächsten Jetzt ursprünglich, d. h. in der natürlichen Lebenswelt, nicht als bloße Form des Nacheinander der Jetzte erfahren wird, sondern als ein Wechsel unserer leiblichen Befindlichkeit, der von dem Wechsel der Zustände, die der „Himmel" durchläuft, nicht zu trennen ist.

Erst damit wird deutlich, was die Besonderheit des Himmels als Gegend ausmacht. Der Himmel ist nicht nur deshalb eine Gegend, weil er ein Ganzes von Plätzen für die dort anzutreffenden Dinge ist, sondern in erster Linie deshalb, weil dort im Wechsel der Tageszeiten, im Wechsel zwischen Tag und Nacht und im Gang der vier Jahreszeiten das Geschehen stattfindet, das für das leibliche Befinden des Menschen elementare Bedeutung hat und die ursprüngliche Erfahrung von Kraft und Zeit ermöglicht: der Kampf der polar entgegengesetzten Zustände Hitze und Kälte, Feuchtigkeit und Trockenheit um ihre Selbstbehauptung, der Streit zwischen ihnen um ihre zeitweilige Anwesenheit.

Die vier Tastqualitäten Hitze und Kälte, Feuchtigkeit und Trockenheit bestimmen nicht nur das Wetter und damit den Himmel, sondern ebenso auch die lebensweltlich erfahrene Erde. Daß Dinge „aus Erde" sind, also materiell, wird uns zugänglich durch den Tastsinn; denn alle anderen Sinne

---

[11] Auch diese Verhältnisse sind vom Vf. genauer analysiert in: „Heraklit, Parmenides und der Anfang von Philosophie und Wissenschaft", S. 342 ff.

können uns hinsichtlich der wirklichen Existenz von etwas Materiellem täuschen. Schon Aristoteles, der Phänomenologe vor der Phänomenologie, hat darauf hingewiesen, daß wir die Körper nur dann *als* Körper erfahren, wenn wir sie mit dem „Fleisch“ unseres Körpers unmittelbar, ohne ein „dazwischen“, berühren.[12] Die elementaren Empfindungen bei dieser Berührung aber sind Hitze und Kälte, Nässe und Trockenheit, weil sie, wie oben skizziert, für unsere leibliche Befindlichkeit die maßgebende Rolle spielen. Deshalb erscheinen uns in diesen vier Qualitäten, wie ebenfalls Aristoteles schon beobachtet hat, die wahrnehmbaren Körper *als* Körper. Damit sind wir auf die lebensweltliche Grundlage für eine weitere Grundbestimmung der Natur in der modernen Naturwissenschaft gestoßen: ihre Materialität.

Für die ganze europäische Kosmologie und Naturwissenschaft in Antike und Mittelalter bestand die materielle Welt aus den vier Elementen Feuer, Wasser, Erde und Luft. Als naturwissenschaftliche Theorie ist diese Elementenkosmologie heute überholt. Aber die Begründung, die Aristoteles dafür gegeben hat, daß es genau vier Elemente und gerade diese Elemente gibt, hat dadurch keineswegs ihre Bedeutung für uns verloren. Für Aristoteles gibt es deshalb diese vier Elemente, weil sich die vier Elementarqualitäten des Tastsinns nur in vier Paaren miteinander kombinieren lassen: Hitze mit Trockenheit oder Flüssigkeit, d. h. Feuer und Luft, und Kälte mit Trockenheit oder Flüssigkeit, d. h. Erde und Wasser.

Den Streit der vier Elementarqualitäten in der Lebenswelt erfahren wir nicht nur im Wetter des Himmels als den Kampf von Hitze und Kälte, Feuchtigkeit und Trockenheit um ihre Selbstbehauptung. Wir erfahren diesen Streit zugleich auf der Erde an unserem eigenen materiellen Leibe dadurch, daß uns die Luft, das Element des Himmels, warm oder kalt, feucht oder trocken umweht und als Wind von wechselnder Richtung und Stärke unser leibliches Befinden bestimmt. Bezeichnenderweise enthält das japanische Wort fur „Klima“ - „fudo“, das ist auch der Titel des erwähnten Buches von Watsuji - das Wort „fu“, „Wind“. Der andere Wortbestandteil - „do“ - bedeutet „Erde“. So bringt das Wort „fudo“ auf konkrete Weise zum Ausdruck, daß die vier polaren Qualitäten Himmel und Erde verklammern und deshalb die naturhaften Grundbestimmungen der Lebenswelt bilden. Deswegen hat Watsuji seine Erklärung der Verschiedenheit der kulturellen Lebenswelten aus dem Klima auf den beiden Tastpolaritäten Hitze und Kälte, Nässe und Trockenheit aufgebaut.

Es ist charakteristisch, daß Aristoteles die elementaren Empfindungsqualitäten von Hitze und Kälte, Nässe und Trockenheit nicht etwa in seiner Kosmologie eingeführt hat, d. h. in seiner Schrift über den Himmel, *De caelo*, sondern in seiner Schrift über das Lebendige, *De anima*.[13] Das zeigt den engen Zusammenhang zwischen der Erfahrung der elementaren Tast-

---

[12] De anima 422 b 17 ff.

[13] 423 b 27 ff.

qualitäten und dem Leben in der Lebenswelt. Die Elemente sind das, worin und woraus die Lebewesen „zu Wasser, zu Lande und in der Luft" leben können. Dieses Verständnis vom Element wird heute wieder lebendig, wenn man im Zeichen der ökologischen Krise von der lebensgefährdenden Verschmutzung der Elemente Erde, Wasser und Luft spricht. Die Bemühung um eine philosophische Begründung der Ökologie im Zeitalter der Umweltkrise wird philosophisch solange auf schwachen Füßen stehen, als man es unterlaßt, die lebensweltliche Erfahrung der elementaren Tastpolaritäten, die Himmel und Erde verbindet, phänomenologisch zu analysieren.

Eine solche Analyse bezieht sich auf die eine Lebensweltnatur der ganzen Menschheit. Aber im Unterschied zu der Natur, die in der objektivistischen Wissenschaft erforscht wird, eröffnet sie zugleich einen Zugang zur Verschiedenheit der Kulturen: Die grundlegende Erfahrung der Lebenswelt als Natur in den Urpolaritäten des Tastsinns und des davon nicht zu trennenden leiblichen Befindens hat das Leben in einem bestimmten Klima zur Grundlage; denn die Möglichkeiten des Wetters in einer bestimmten Klimaregion werden durch eine für die betreffende Region spezifische Konstellation der Elementarqualitaten Hitze und Kälte, Nässe und Trockenheit bestimmt.

Diese beiden Elementarpolaritäten sind das, was den lebensweltlichen *Raum*, den Himmel, mit der lebensweltlichen *Materie*, der Erde, verbindet. Der Streit der Elementarqualitäten ist das erste Erscheinen von *Kraft* in der Lebenswelt als Natur, und er ist ihre erste Gesetzmäßigkeit. Diese Gesetzmäßigkeit ist die elementare Grundlage für die in der Lebenswelt herrschende Kausalität der Umstände, und sie wiederum eröffnet das Feld für die elementarsten Prognosen. Die Periodizität, die durch den Streit der Polaritäten entsteht, bildet die elementare lebensweltliche Erfahrung der *Zeit*. So bestimmt das Klima die Grundzüge der Lebenswelt als Natur: Kraft, Kausalität, Raum, Zeit, Materie, also die fünf Züge, die dann von der neuzeitlichen Naturwissenschaft zu objektiven Bestimmungen der Natur gemacht wurden.

Die phänomenologische Analyse fördert eine Reihe von fünf miteinander zusammenhängenden Grundzügen der Lebenswelt als Natur zutage, die für jede Kultur gelten. Aber dabei ist zu beachten, daß sich diese Grundzüge nur bestimmen lassen, indem zugleich berücksichtigt wird, daß der Streit der polaren Elementarqualitäten, der in allen Kulturen Himmel und Erde verbindet, konkret immer nur ausgehend von einem bestimmten Klima und der ihm korrespondierenden Kultur analysiert werden kann. Die vorliegenden, von einem Angehörigen der Kultur Europas verfaßten Überlegungen sind vom gemäßigten Klima dieses Erdteils ausgegangen und stehen deshalb nicht zufällig in einer Beziehung zur alteuropäischen Kosmologie, die das Elementare, der Klimakonstellation in dieser Weltregion entsprechend, in einer Theorie der vier Elemente Feuer, Wasser, Erde, Luft systematisierte.

Aber was in den verschiedenen traditionellen Kulturen als elementar gegolten hat, war variabel. Die Vorstellung vom Elementaren war nicht auf die Zahl von vier Elementen festgelegt, und es mußte sich auch nicht um gerade die Elemente handeln, die in der alteuropäischen Kosmologie kanonisch wurden. Für das Monsunklima der Kulturen Ostasiens beispielsweise hat die Polarität der Elementarqualitäten, wie Watsuji gezeigt hat, eine ganz andere Bedeutung als fur das gemäßigte Klima Europas, und wieder ganz anders steht es mit den Kulturen der Tropen, in denen der jahreszeitliche Streit der Elementarzustände fast ganz fehlt. Hier ist noch ein weites Feld für die phänomenologische Erforschung des Klimas, der Einheit von Natur und Kultur in der einen Lebenswelt und den verschiedenen kulturellen Lebenswelten. Aber mit der Einsicht, daß es zwei voneinander unabtrennbare Polaritäten gibt, die Polarität von Himmel und Erde und die beiden Polaritäten der Elementarqualitäten, die in allen Klimazonen und Kulturen in jeweils anderer Konstellation wiederkehren, ist ein erster Schritt getan.

Natur-Entzug im Da? Oskar Becker und Eugen Fink auf dem Ost-West-Diwan

Hans Rainer Sepp

Kah Kyung Cho hat ein Hauptaugenmerk seiner philosophischen Arbeit immer wieder darauf gerichtet, wie in der westlichen Philosophie des 20. Jahrhunderts in einer Auseinandersetzung mit den eigenen europäischen Wurzeln eine Annäherung an dasjenige erfolgte, was die großen philosophischen Strömungen des Ostens von alters her zu denken suchten.[1] Hierbei brachte Cho vor allem das Seinsdenken des späten Heidegger, aber auch die Voraussetzungen, die hierfür der Autor von *Sein und Zeit* sowie die Phänomenologie Husserls schufen, in ein philosophisches Gespräch mit dem Taoismus. Cho ging und geht es dabei in erster Linie nicht um einen interkulturellen Vergleich, der Gemeinsamkeiten und Unterschiede lediglich verrechnet; sondern die ‚Sache des Denkens' selbst ist es, in deren Mitdenken Cho Heidegger und Laotse einander begegnen läßt. Mit dem Absehen auf ein solches Gespräch zur Sache und von der Sache her konnte Cho aufzeigen, daß das zeitgenössische westliche Denken zu etwas unterwegs ist, das offensichtlich auch schon für die überlieferten Philosophien des Ostens bestimmend war, aber auch worin die Geister nach wie vor sich scheiden. Seine Rechtfertigung fand dieses Vorgehen darin, daß auf westlicher Seite vor allem die Phänomenologie mit der Absicht auftritt, die europäisch-neuzeitliche Bewußtseinsphilosophie zu überwinden - eine Absicht, der Heideggers Versuch der „Verwindung der Metaphysik" auf bisher radikalste Weise nachkam. Cho legte dar, wie Heideggers Denken eine neue Haltung dem „Natursein" gegenüber einnahm, die dieses Denken in eine Nachbarschaft zum Taoismus stellt.

Doch nicht nur in Heideggers Denken begegnet jene Nähe zum Taoismus; Annäherungen in der Sache sind auch bei anderen Vertretern der Freiburger Phänomenologie zu konstatieren. Freilich wurden die philosophischen Positionen nahezu aller Vertreter der Freiburger Phänomenologie in der Generation nach Husserl nachhaltig von Heidegger beeinflußt. Nichtsdestotrotz bemühten sich nicht wenige von ihnen, wie etwa Oskar Becker und Eugen Fink, sich in entscheidenden Hinsichten von Heidegger abzusetzen. Nimmt man überdies die von Cho herausgearbeiteten Unterschiede ins Visier, bei denen die Wege von Heidegger und Laotse auseinanderlaufen, so kommen die genannten Philosophen ein erhebliches Srück *näher* an Positionen des

[1] Vgl. vor allem die hierfür grundlegenden Studien von Cho, vereint zu dem Band *Bewußtsein und Natursein. Phänomenologischer West-Ost-Diwan*, Freiburg/München 1987 (im folgenden zitiert mit der Sigle BN).

Taoismus heran. Im folgenden suchen wir diese These zu begründen. Für dieses Vorhaben wählen wir zwei für Becker wie für Fink zentrale Problembereiche, die nicht nur der Sache nach der Weltsicht des Taoismus näher stehen, als dies bei Heidegger der Fall ist, sondern in denen sich Becker wie Fink ausdrücklich gegen Heideggers Position aussprechen: einmal mit der Auffassung, daß sich Natur bzw. Welt einem hermeneutischen Zugriff *entziehen*, und zum anderen, daß ungeachtet dessen Natur einen eigentümlichen Charakter der Präsenz, des *Da*, besitzt.[2] Es ist fast überflüssig zu bemerken, daß damit auch wesentliche Gemeinsamkeiten im Denken von Becker und Fink zutage treten, die zum einen symptomatisch für Versuche von Vertretern der Freiburger Phänomenologie sind, sich von Heideggers Position abzusetzen, diese im wahren Sinn des Wortes zu entgrenzen; der Aufweis solcher Gemeinsamkeiten liefert zudem auch Bausteine für eine Beantwortung der Frage, inwieweit *der* Freiburger Phänomenologie eine Identität zuzusprechen ist. Was also vermögen Becker und Fink einem Ost-West-Diwan hinzuzufügen? Wir bitten die beiden, konkret gesprochen, auf dem Sitzmöbel Platz zu nehmen.

I. ‚Da' anders als Transzendenz

Es mag zunächst paradox erscheinen, wenn behauptet wird, Natur entziehe sich dem hermeneutischen Umkreis, ja sei vielleicht das sich Entziehende schlechthin, und ihr zugleich ein fundamentaler Anwesenheitsmodus zugesprochen wird. Auf ein ganz ähnliches Verhältnis macht Cho bezüglich des Taoismus aufmerksam, wenn er darauf hinweist, daß Tao „eine durchgängig *immanente Wirklichkeit*" darstelle (BN 324), deren Immanenz jedoch nicht mit dem Verstehen seitens des menschlichen Daseins korreliere (vgl. BN 47).

---

[2]Was das Projekt einer *Phänomenologie der Natur* betrifft, so hat sich Gernot Böhme jüngst zu der Behauptung verstiegen, „daß Phänomene der Natur als solche von der Phänomenologie bisher nicht bearbeitet wurden." (Gernot Böhme und Gregor Schiemann [Hg.], *Phänomenologie der Natur*, Frankfurt am Main 1997, S. 11.) Böhme reduziert die bisherige Phänomenologie der Natur auf Husserl (den „berühmten Pflaumenbaum" und die „Forderung nach regionalen Ontologien" [ebd.]) und Hermann Schmitz (a.a.O., S. 12). Die Geschichte der Phänomenologie lehrt anderes: So hatte sich Hedwig Conrad-Martius zeitlebens dem Projekt einer „Realontologie" gewidmet (vgl. Eberhard Avé Lallemant: „Hedwig Conrad-Martius. Bibliographie, in: *Zeitschrift für philosophische Forschung* 30 [1977] S. 301-309); so hatte Max Scheler eine „Metaphsik der Natur" konzipiert (vgl. *Schriften aus dem Nachlaß* , Bd. II: *Erkenntnislehre und Metaphysik*, hg. von Manfred S. Frings (*Gesammelte Werke* Bd. 11], Bern/München 1979) und beispielsweise von einer „Meta-Biologie" gehandelt (a.a.O., S. 156 ff.), ganz zu schweigen von den Ansätzen einer Naturphilosophie in der Freiburger Phänomenologie und deren Weiterwirken bis hin zu Kah Kyung Cho. Zu Husserl vgl. den Beitrag von Bernhard Rang, „Der systematische Ansatz von Husserls Phänomenologie der Natur," in: Böhme und Schiemann, a.a.O., S. 85-119.

Für den Taoismus gebe es ein transzendentes Jenseits ebensowenig wie ein verstehendes, entwerfendes Dasein, für das Transzendenz allererst einen Sinn besitzt. Die taoistisch gedachte Natur wäre demzufolge ein ,Anwesen' ins Da, ohne daß jedoch dieses ,Da' als das Da eines transzendierenden Daseins gedacht wäre. Heidegger selbst habe zwar, wie Cho des weiteren bemerkt, schon in *Sein und Zeit* „am Rande durchblicken" lassen, daß Natur „als das, was ,webt und strebt' "[3] - nicht also die Natur als Gegenstand der Wissenschaft und nicht die im praktischen Umgang mitverstandene Natur -, uns verborgen bleibe (BN 35), doch habe erst die ,Kehre' in Heideggers Denken „eine gewandelte Naturansicht" vorbereitet (ebd.). Heideggers Spätphilosophie sei dadurch gekennzeichnet, daß das Sein zunehmend „der Natur angeglichen" werde, so daß das Denken des Seins ein „*physikozentrisches* Gepräge" erhalte (BN 62). Beherrschend bleibe jedoch Heideggers Orientierung an der Sprache, die seinem Denken einen „*logozentrischen*" Grundzug verleihe und es gerade darin vom Taoismus abhebe (BN 45 f.).

Obgleich Heidegger die Zentralstellung des geworfen-entwerfenden Daseins in seiner ek-sistierenden Transzendenz im Spätwerk zugunsten einer Auffassung überwand, die schließlich den Entwurf als ein „Entsprechen" dachte, das auf den „Zuwurf" des Seins antwortet, blieb sein Denken als ein grundlegend *hermeneutisch* bestimmtes [4] im Bannkreis dessen, den Sprache und *logos* abstecken. Es ist schwer vorstellbar, wie in dieser Konzeption *Natur* gedacht werden kann als solche, die sich dem hermeneutischen Zugriff verweigert und doch volle Präsenz besitzt; dies wäre nur einem Denken möglich, das dem Hermeneutischen gegenüber eine zumindest *zwiespältige* Einstellung einnimmt. Bezüglich einer ausschließlichen Fixierung auf die eksistierende Transzendenz des Daseins hatte Oskar Becker, und zwar bereits zwei Jahre nach Erscheinen von *Sein und Zeit*, einen Korrekturvorschlag gemacht, der sich als eine bemerkenswerte *Ergänzung* der Heideggerschen Daseinsanalyse erwies.

Becker[5] hatte in seinem in der Husserl-Festschrift von 1929 erschienenen Beitrag „Von der Hinfälligkeit des Schönen und der Abenteuerlichkeit des Künstlers"[6] den Heideggerschen Existenzialien ein *Para-Existenzial* gegenübergestellt. Das Para-Existenzial versteht Becker als ein „Analogon" zu den Existenzialien der Geworfenheit und des Entwurfs, das jedoch nicht

---

[3] M. Heidegger: *Sein und Zeit*, Tübingen, 1972, S. 70.

[4] Vgl. Friedrich-Wilhelm Herrmann, *Weg und Methode. Zur hermeneuti-schen Phänomenologie des seinsgeschichtlichen Denkens*, Frankfurt am Main 1990.

[5] Zu Becker vgl. den Artikel von Otto Pöggeler: „Hermeneutische und mantische Phänomenologie," in: *Philosophische Rundschau*, 13 (1965) S. 1-39, wiederabgedruckt in: ders. (Hg.): *Heidegger. Perspektiven zur Deutung seines Werkes, Weinheim*[3] 1994, S. 321-357.

[6] Wiederabgedruckt in O. Becker: *Dasein und Dawesen: Gesammelte philosophische Aufsätze*, Pfullingen 1963, S. 11-40. Im folgenden wird nach dieser Ausgabe unter Verwendung der Sigle DD zitiert.

mehr im Rahmen der Daseinsanalyse, dessen Umfeld durch die genannten Existenzialen ‚abgesteckt' ist, lokalisiert werden kann. Vielmehr führen Geworfenheit wie Entwurf „an eine Grenze, die durch das Eingreifen des *naturhaften* Schicksals gesetzt wurde" (DD 34). Das heißt, Geworfenheit und Entwurf lassen in bestimmten Daseinsverhaltungen etwas aufscheinen, das nicht mehr mit ihnen selbst aufzufassen, nicht mehr *geschichtliche* Phänomenalität, sondern das zu Geschichtlichkeit und Freiheit Andere ist: *Natur.*[7] Diejenige Verhaltung des Daseins, die dies Andere erfährt, weil es in dieses hineingehalten ist, stellt für Becker die Kunst dar (vgl. die Ausführungen DD 25-33). Kunst besitzt ihm zufolge ihren Ort im Zwischen von Geschichte und Natur, indem sie, stets vom geschichtlichen Dasein ausgehend und in ihm sich realisierend, doch zugleich dem Para-Existenzial der „Getragenheit" (DD 34) unterworfen, von der „Gunst der Natur" abhängig ist (DD 32).

Becker verhehlt nicht, daß er in seiner Auffassung vor allem durch die deutsche Romantik, von Solger und Schelling, beeinflußt ist. Er bezieht sich insbesondere auf Schellings Unterscheidung zwischen dem „Bewußten" und dem „Bewußtlosen" (DD 23 f.): Der Kunst komme es zu, die antagonistischen Seinsprinzipien von Natur und Geschichte zu umspannen, wobei diese Umspannung, als in gleicher Weise abhängig von der ‚Gunst der Natur' wie dem ergriffenen „Augenblick" (DD 31), „fragil wie der Regenbogen" (DD 24) sei. Die Bestimmung des ‚Bewußtlosen'[8] ist für Becker offenkundig Anlaß, den mit der Sorge des Daseins bezeichneten, mit den Existenzialien von Geworfenheit und Entwurf umgrenzten hermeneutischen Zierkel zu durchbrechen, zur Geschichtlichkeit des Daseins eine Art von Pendant zu denken, das nicht in diese Geschichtlichkeit hineinsteht und doch, wenngleich auf ganz andere Weise, im Da, in einem anderen Da, dem Menschen ‚erschlossen' ist, indem dieser sich - in besonderen Weisen der Erfahrung wie dem künstlerischen Erleben - als von dem in diesem Da sich Bekundenden ‚getragen' erfährt.

Seine Grundansichten wiederholte und vertiefte Becker in dem späteren Artikel „Para-Existenz. Menschliches Dasein und Dawesen" (DD 67-102). Die antagonistischen Seinsprinzipien erhalten jetzt Namen, die auf ihr gleichursprüngliches Erschlossensein verweisen: Sie sind beide zugänglich im Da menschlichen Seins, doch auf je andere Weise. Während *Dasein* durch Geschichtlichkeit, Seinkönnen, Verstehen ausgezeichnet ist, entzieht sich

---

[7]Becker stellt der Natur als dem „Untergeschichtlichen" das „Übergeschichtliche" ideellen Seins an die Seite; beides zusammen bilde als das „Außergeschichtliche" den Gegenpol zum geschichtlichen Dasein des Menschen (vgl. Beckers Aufsatz „Para-Existenz. Menschliches Dasein und Dawesen" von 1943, ebenfalls wiederabgedruckt in *Dasein und Dawesen*, a.a.O., S. 67-102, bes. S. 72-74).

[8]Vgl. Chos Bemerkung, „daß nach Laotse eine bewußte Handlung niemals an die unbewußte Wirkungsweise der Natur heranreicht" (BN 317).

das *Dawesen* all dem: Es werde nicht durch ekstatische Transzendenz charakterisiert, sondern durch die „Unentstiegenheit des Wesens aus dem Wesenden," nicht durch die ontologische Differenz „Sein > Seiendes," sondern durch die parontologische Indifferenz „Wesen = Wesendes" (ebd.), was seiner Bestimmung als eines Wesenden *im Da* jedoch keinen Abbruch tut: „Denn in der ‚Anwesung' des Wesens selbst liegt eine Weise des ‚Da'."[9] Das paradoxe Verhältnis des Menschen zur Natur besteht demzufolge darin, daß er, weil er nur außergeschichtlich auf Natur *als solche* trifft, d. h. außerhalb aller Fernen und Nähen, vor aller Bedingung der Möglichkeit von Ferne und Nähe, ihr ‚näher,' ja am ‚nächsten' ist und zugleich ihr am ‚fernsten' steht.

Das Subhistorische des Naturseins besitzt seinen Präsenzcharakter mithin gerade darin, daß es diesseits von Transzendenz, diesseits des Systems der Nähen und Fernen und damit auch diesseits der Zeitlichkeit des Daseins seinen Ort hat. Mehr noch: Daß es im Diesseits außerhalb der Transzendenz der Ek-sistenz steht, verleiht ihm den Charakter seines Entzogenseins (nämlich vom geschichtlichen Umkreis) wie auch den seiner Präsenz (es verweist auf keine wie immer zu denkende ‚Hinterwelt'). Ja beides, Entzug und Präsenz, bedingen hier einander. Ohne den spezifischen Entzugscharakter fiele Natur in den Umkreis geschichtlichen Verstehens, ohne ihre Präsenz stünde man nicht ‚mitten' in ihr. Das Eigentümliche der im Anwesen, allein indem sie anwest, in eins sich entziehenden Natur besteht gerade darin, daß sie ihre eigene Zeitlichkeit hat, die nicht nur nicht mit der Zeitlichkeit des Daseins kongruiert, sondern offenbar von den Strukturmechanismen dieser gar nicht gefaßt zu werden vermag. Becker hatte versucht, diese andere Zeitlichkeit des Außerhistorischen mit der Kategorie der „ewigen Gegenwart" (DD 36) zu denken. Doch vielleicht ist dies noch zu sehr von der Zeitauffassung geschichtlichen Daseins her begriffen. Vielleicht könnte man, zumindest mit Bezug auf das Subhistorische, eher von einem perennierenden Anwesen sprechen, womit auch dem Faktum Rechnung getragen wäre, daß Natur nicht still steht, sondern daß ihre Bewegung zugleich die Weise ihres Da ausmacht (vgl. ebd.). In diesem Zusammenhang ist bemerkenswert, daß Becker den Begriff von Welt ausdrücklich auf das geschichtliche Dasein bezieht (vgl. „Para-Existenz," DD 85); der Ort von Natur als solcher läge demnach weder in der Welt noch in der ontologischen Ebene der Bestimmung von Welt noch würde sich Natur darauf reduzieren lassen, wie sie weltlich begegnet und in der Weise ihres Anwesens von einem Seinsdenken ontologisch gefaßt werden könnte. Um das Faktum zu verdeutlichen, daß Natur als solche aus all dem, was zur Welt als dem Umkreis des Geschichtlichen im weitesten Sinn gehört, her-

---

[9] O. Becker: „Von der Abenteuerlichkeit des Künstlers und der vorsichtigen Verwegenheit des Philosophen" (Artikel von 1958), wiederabgedruckt in Becker: *Dasein und Dawesen*, a.a.O., S. 103-126; hier zitiert S. 123.

ausfällt, wählt Becker zum Zweck der abhebenden Kennzeichnung für den Umkreis des Außergeschichtlichen den Begriff des „Kosmos" (ebd.). Das Kosmische ist zyklisch, nicht aber im Sinn des hermeneutischen Zirkels, der dem sinnverstehenden Dasein zugehörig ist. Das Zyklische des Kosmos ist an bestimmten Erscheinungen des rhythmischen Wechsels zu spüren (Jahres‚zeiten,' Lebens ‚zeiten,' ‚Zeiten' der Generationen), ohne daß es *als solches* verstanden werden könnte. Es kann nicht als solches aufgefaßt werden, da die Bewegungen dieses Zyklischen ihren Ort nicht im verstehenden Dasein haben;[10] dieses hat freilich, was etwas anderes ist, im Umkreis seines eigenen Verstehens diese Bewegungen immer schon ausgelegt. Mit dem Faktum, daß das Zyklische der Natur ursprünglich dem verstehenden Dasein nicht offen ist, korreliert der Befund, daß das ‚Subjekt' dieser Bewegungen nicht das jemeinige Dasein oder schlicht das Individuum ist, sondern die ‚anonyme' Generationenfolge (vgl. DD 78).[11]

Der Stachel, der in der Bestimmung der im Anwesen sich entziehenden Natur steckt, zielt nicht lediglich auf den bloßen Befund dieser Paradoxie ab, sondern vielmehr darauf, wie dieser Befund angemessen zu fassen ist. Wie können der Entzug von Natur und ihr spezifisches Anwesen im Da noch verstanden werden, wenn alles Verstehen sich schon im Umkreis des geschichtlich sich auslegenden Daseins hält? Oder kommt es vielmehr darauf an, im phänomenologischen Aufweis dem Nicht-mehr-aufgewiesen-werden-Können noch eine Nische einzuräumen?

II. Sprachentzogen

Daß das Sub- wie Suprahistorische dem Umkreis des Geschichtlichen entzogen sind, deutet Becker als ein Außerhalb von aller „seinsauslegenden

[10]Wir lassen hier offen, inwiefern z. B. die Naturphilosophie von Hedwig Conrad-Martius einem solchem Verstehen ‚auf halbem Wege' entgegenkommt, indem sie, verkürzt formuliert, danach fragt, wie dasjenige, das - wie Natursein - alles Bewußtsein transzendiert, noch für dieses gegeben sein kann. Meines Erachtens bildet der Beckersche Ansatz eine geeignete Grundlage, die Positionen von Vertretern der sog. ‚Münchener-Göttinger Phänomenologie' mit der ‚Freiburger Phänomenologie' ins Gespräch zu bringen.

[11]Cho spricht bezüglich der Naturauffassung Laotses von der „ ‚Unmenschlichkeit' des Naturmaßes" (BN 314), was besagt, daß Natur als solche nicht mit dem Bereich des Menschlichen korreliert. - Die Gegenüberstellung von Natur-Kosmos und Geschichts-Welt erinnert an Schopenhauers Kontrastierung der Welt als Wille und der Welt als Vorstellung, welch letztere selbst nur wieder Welt als Wille, jedoch unter Maßgabe der Subjekt-Objekt-Dichotomie sowie des principium individuationis: des Satzes vom Grund, ist. Nur auf dieser höchsten Stufe der „Objektität des Willens" treten Individuen hervor und korrelativ eine geschichtliche Welt, die sich nicht nur vom bloß Generativen, das die niederen Stufen der Willensobjektivierungen ausbilden, abheben, sondern ebenso von dem, was sie an sich selbst sind, nämlich unterschiedsloser Wille: Ihr Naturgrund liegt vor aller Individualität (vgl. *Welt als Wille und Vorstellung*, Band I, Paragraphen 26, 54).

(hermeneutisch-phänomenologischen) Betrachtung" (DD 92). Diese gegen Heidegger[12] gerichtete Auffassung weist in der Tat eine enge Parallele zu dem auf, worin Cho die offensichtlich wesentlichste Differenz zwischen Heidegger und Laotse erblickt: in puncto Sprache.[13] Der zentrale Ort, den in Heideggers Spätphilosophie die Sprache einnimmt, korrespondiert für Cho mit der „bevorzugten Stellung," die Heidegger dem Menschen als dem „Hüter des Geheimnisses des Seins," „Hirten des Seins" etc. „im Ganzen des Seins" zuweist. Und Cho merkt an: nur im Menschen „soll die Wahrheit des Seins zur Sprache kommen. Die sprachlose Welt des Seienden ist noch vom sprechenden Menschen verschieden" (BN 102).

Demgegenüber begrenzt Becker den Einflußbereich der Sprache, indem er sie mit dem Geschichtlichen kongruieren läßt und diesem das Außergeschichtliche zur Seite stellt. Zugleich wird jedoch auch bei ihm dem Menschen, als Künstler oder Philosophierenden, eine herausragende Rolle übertragen: nämlich die, zwischen den beiden Bereichen von Geschichtlichem und Außergeschichtlichem zu *vermitteln*.[14] ‚Vermitteln' in diesem Sinn heißt aber, das Zusammenbestehen des Divergenten, des ‚Bewußten' und ‚Bewußtlosen', und damit das Bewußtlose selbst in die Sichtbarkeit zu bringen - mit sprachlichen oder quasisprachlichen Mitteln. Becker ist sich der daraus resultierenden Schwierigkeit bewußt, wie dasjenige, das sich prinzipiell allem Sagbaren entzieht, doch bezeichnet, philosophisch-ontologisches Thema werden kann, ohne daß es in seinem Eigensein verkürzt wird. Daher gesteht Becker, daß das Dawesen „in der Tat in unmittelbarem geradem Zugriff nicht erfaßt werden" könne, es bedürfe des „ ‚schrägen Blicks' " (DD 126). Der schräge Blick verweist für Becker auf einen Standpunkt, der sich *über* Ontologie und Parontologie gleichermaßen erhebt, ein *„hyperontologischer"* ist (DD 107). Von ihm aus kann nicht mehr in direkter Weise gesprochen werden, sondern man muß sich einer „Metasprache" bedienen (DD 119 f.), was heißen soll, daß hier Aussagen in dem Bewußtsein gemacht werden, daß sie dem, von dem sie sprechen, von vornherein nicht angemessen sind. Der Preis ist hier allemal die Aufgabe der „Nähe zum Ursprünglichen" (DD 120).

---

[12]Becker bemerkt in „Para-Existenz," daß das „Begriffspaar ‚Welt-Erde' " im späteren Werk Heideggers „eine gewisse Ähnlichkeit mit unserer Zweiheit ‚Welt-Kosmos' " habe, jedoch „in wesentlichen Punkten, wie es scheint, in eine andere Richtung" weise, was von Becker nicht mehr näher expliziert wird (DD 92, Anm. 2; vgl. auch DD 86 f.). Einer dieser „wesentlichen Punkte" scheint mir darin zu liegen, daß Beckers Begriff des Kosmos auf ein Transhermeneutisches, Außersprachliches zielt.

[13]Bereits im Hinblick auf die Bewußtseinsphilosophie der Neuzeit bis hin zu Husserl heißt es bei Cho: „Zu einem andersartigen, sprachlosen Seienden, das gleichwohl lebendig ist, zu den Regionen der organischen und animalischen Natur, führt vom Bewußtsein aus kein Weg [...]." (BN 27)

[14]Schon im Aufsatz von 1929 heißt es: Der Künstler „ist das Zwischenwesen *κατ' ἐξοχήν* - und, da der Mensch als solcher Zwischenwesen ist - : er ist Mensch *κατ' ἐξοχήν* " (DD 37; vgl. 35; vgl. auch DD 115 und 117).

Obgleich Becker dem hermeneutischen Ansatz Heideggers mit Mißtrauen begegnet und auf einen Bereich hinweist, der durch Präsenz ausgezeichnet ist, ohne daß er mit den Kategorien des geschichtlichen Daseins zu fassen wäre, stehen hier beide Bereiche, der Bereich des außergeschichtlichen Kosmos, insbesondere der Natur, und der Bereich der geschichtlichen Welt unvermittelt nebeneinander und werden nur in den fragilen Augenblicken künstlerischen Erlebens oder vom Hochsitz philosophischer Reflexion aus ohne Beständigkeit verknüpft. Nach Beckers Auffassung steht der Mensch in der Natur und ist zugleich aus ihr herausgetreten. Beides, das In-der Natur-Sein und das aus ihr Herausgetretensein, wird als Faktum gesehen. Aus der ‚logischen' Unvereinbarkeit beider Fakten (indem hier Logos und A-Logos aufeinandertreffen) erwächst das philosophische Problem, wie über das A-Logische gesprochen werden kann. Demgegenüber würde es bei Laotse heißen, daß der Mensch gar nicht aus der Natur heraustreten könne; alles Herausgetretensein wäre nur ‚Schein.'

An diesem Punkt ging nun Eugen Fink einen entscheidenden Schritt weiter. Er faßt das Eingefügtsein des Menschen in die Polarität von Natur und Freiheit sehr ähnlich wie Becker auf, doch mit einem wesentlichen Unterschied: Er stellt nicht mehr Natur und Freiheit als zwei letzte Bereiche einander gegenüber, sondern denkt beides, ohne die Radikalität der Unterscheidung einzubüßen, in das *Weltverhältnis* des Menschen zurück. Ermöglicht hat diese Sicht eine intensivere Aufnahme von Grundeinsichten Heideggers; ungeachtet dieser Anlehnung an Heidegger schlägt Fink einen ganz anderen Weg als dieser ein und gelangt eher in die Nähe von Beckers Position. So heißt es bei Fink in Anknüpfung an die Hegelsche Terminologie, daß das menschliche Dasein nicht in den Kampf „zwischen Sitte und Natur" verstrickt sei, da es „im ganzen sittlich, d. h. weltbezogen" ist, aber es sei „verstrickt in einen Kampf gleichsam zweier Sittlichkeiten": „dem Weltprinzip des Geistes und dem Weltprinzip der Erde."[15] Der „Riß, der durch die Welt geht" (NFW 195), spaltet auch für Fink das Leben des Menschen, insofern er der ‚Natur in uns' wie dem ‚Göttlichen in uns' (vgl. NFW 194, 187, 189) eröffnet ist. Wie Becker (DD 25) spricht auch Fink diesbezüglich vom Menschen als dem Wesen der „äußersten *Spannung*" (NFW 195). Doch anders als Becker bestimmt Fink das Faktum, den „Weltprinzipien" auf zweifache Weise zu begegnen, einheitlich als ein Verhalten, das sich selbst aus der *Welt versteht.* Dieses Verhalten wird bei Fink dort am deutlichsten, wo er dessen Verlaufscharakter zu bestimmen sucht. Er wählte hierfür den Begriff des *Spiels.*

Die Figur des Spiels ist offensichtlich der *Zierkel*, sie konstituiert einen Kreis wechselseitigen Mitwirkens der am Spiel Beteiligten. Das im Spiel sich Hervorbildende wird so in seinem Hervorbilden weder in einem linearen

[15] Eugen Fink: *Natur, Freiheit, Welt. Philosophie der Erziehung*, hg. von Franz-A. Schwarz, Würzburg 1992, S. 82 (im folgenden zitiert mit der Sigle NFW).

Hinausstehen aus einem Subjekt noch in einem ebenso linearen Hereinstehen aus einem objektiven Grund gedacht. Finks Aussage, daß der Mensch „*Mit-Spieler im Spiel der Welt*" (NFW 193) ist, deutet an, daß beides, Entwerfen und Vorfinden von Sinnbeständen, in einem wechselseitigen einheitlichen Prozeß des Erscheinenlassens von Welt in und für das menschliche Sichverhalten verschmelzen. Doch die Feststellung, daß der Mensch Mit-Spieler im Spiel der Welt sei, besagt auch, daß er, obgleich er das Spiel mitgestaltet, doch in dieses eingetreten ist, daß es in einem bestimmten Sinn das Spiel der Welt selbst ist. Es wird hier also eine Differenz merklich zwischen dem Spiel der Welt und der Mitwirkung des Menschen an diesem Spiel. Der Mensch als Mit-Spieler im Spiel der Welt schreibt sich gleichsam in einen Kreis ein, der unter der sichtbaren Schrift seines Umgangs ein der Sichtbarkeit entzogenes Kreisen ahnen läßt. In diesen zweifachen Umgängen des einen Spiels deutet sich an, was Fink in der Differenz von in der Welt Sichzeigendem und Sichzeigen von Welt selbst (das „Sichzeigen aber zeigt sich nicht" [NFW 71]) zu denken versucht.

Das aber heißt, daß für Fink der Riß, der ‚durch die Welt geht' und Natur und Freiheit spaltet, eine weitere Verwerfung als Pendant erhält, nämlich die Differenz zwischen dem Spiel im Himmelt des Menschen, dem Spiel im Bereich des Erscheinenden, und der ‚Tiefendimension' ebendieses Spiels als dem Spiel der Welt, dem Erscheinenlassen, selbst. Obwohl hier das eine mit dem anderen zusammenfällt, ist es dennoch nicht eins: Das Spiel der Welt ist die der Phänomenalität abgekehrte Seite, das Nichtsichtbare. Das Problem der Phänomenologie liegt daher für Fink nicht wie für Becker im Verhältnis von Natur und Freiheit, darin, wie das ‚sprachlose' Außerhistorische zu Wort kommen und Begriff werden kann, sondern im Verhältnis des binnenweltlich Offenen, Phänomenalen, zu der Bewegung, die dieses Phänomenale erst Phänomen sein läßt und daher selbst nie Phänomen werden kann: zur Welt - liegt für Fink mithin im Weltverhältnis des Menschen selbst. Nun drängt sich freilich die Frage auf, in welchem Bezug in Finks Konzeption die eine Verwerfung von Natur und Freiheit zu der anderen von Welt und Binnenweltlichem steht. Eine mögliche Antwort kann hier nur angedeutet werden: Insofern Weltverhältnis stets ein Verhalten zur Natur - wie zur Geistseite besagt und sich jedes Verhalten dem Erscheinenlassen von Welt verdankt, besitzt alles Weltverhalten, Natur *wie* Geschichte, seine sichtbare und seine unsichtbare Seite. Jetzt wird deutlicher, wie für Fink der Hiatus zwischen Sichtbarem und Unsichtbarem, ‚Bewußtem' und ‚Bewußtlosem,' nicht zwischen Seinsbereichen verläuft (Natur-Geist), sondern quer durch diese nach Maßgabe des Erscheinenden und sich im Erscheinen Entziehenden selbst. Insofern denkt Fink im wahrsten Sinn phänomenologischer als Becker - insofern das Phänomensein selbst Maßstab für die Verwerfung abgibt -, doch zugleich mit dem Resultat, daß, ähnlich wie bei Becker, die Phänomenologie an eine für sie absolute Grenze geführt wird: Über das Spiel der Welt vermag, Fink zufolge, nur noch das spekulative Denken etwas auszusagen.[16] Der Entzug von Welt - und hier wendet sich Fink in gleicher Weise gegen Heidegger wie Becker bezüglich des Entzugs der Natur - ist nicht im Rahmen einer Problemstellung der Sprache zu behandeln.[17]

Die Sichtbarkeit ist somit auch für Fink durch geschichtliches Verstehen gekennzeichnet; doch zu ihr gehört auch ein Verhältnis zur Natur, sofern Natur immer schon Eingang ins geschichtliche Verstehen gefunden hat und sei es als das gänzlich Unverständliche *im Himmelt des Verstehbaren.* Doch beides, Natur und Geist, haben ihre Seiten, die nie erscheinen. Von diesem Unsichtbaren künden jedoch sichtbare Bruchstücke, die das Ganze erahnen lassen. Fink nimmt ausdrücklich Bezug auf das antike Symbolon: Symbola sind „abgerissene ‚Hälften,' denen eine andere, verborgene Dimension entspricht."[18] ‚Symbol' meint hier nicht zwei Bedeutungsebenen, derart, daß mit der einen auf die andere Bezug genommen wäre. Das Verweisen erfolgt nicht von einem zum anderen, sondern verläuft zwischen *Hälften*, die als solche vom Sinn eines *Ganzen* getragen sind. Die ‚bedeutsamen' Dinge sind mithin Symbole dergestalt, daß mit der Verweisung der einen Hälfte auf die andere gerade die ursprüngliche Ganzheit aufscheint, von der Binnenweltliches abgetrennt bleibt, gebannt in seine endliche, sichtbare Hälfte. Indem Dinge bedeutsam werden, geschieht eine Einung im Symballein, wirft sich paradoxerweise das, was sich aller Erscheinung entzieht: die Welt, im enthüllenden-verhüllenden Geschehen des Symbols in die Erscheinung.

Die Symbole lassen präsent werden, was sich aller phänomenalen Präsenz entzieht. Dies erinnert an die von Cho diskutierte „Idee der Unvollkommenheit in der taoistischen Ästhetik": „Nur einen Teil, ein Bruchstück der Natur, kann der Mensch im Glücksfall in seinem künstlerischen Schattenriß bergen." (BN 343) Diese „Symbole der Vollkommenheit" (BN 192) lassen nicht nur das als solche nie sich zeigende Ganze der Natur oder der Welt anwesen, sondern belegen, daß der die Symbole Schaffende und ihren ‚Sinn' Vernehmende, der Mensch selbst, *in* diesem Ganzen steht. In diesem Sinn ist auch Finks Satz zu verstehen: „Der Mensch ist ein ‚Verhältnis.' " (NFW 171) Das heißt, der Mensch *ist* der Bezug zu- , das Weltverhältnis selbst. *In ihm* öffnet sich der Riß zwischen Natur und Freiheit; *für ihn* besteht die Differenz von Binnenweltlichem und Welt selbst.

Freilich wird damit dem Menschen eine ähnlich zentrale, ihn von allem übrigen Seienden abgrenzende Rolle zugewiesen wie im Spätwerk Heideggers. Vielleicht kann man Finks Auffassung so interpretieren, daß diese

---

[16]Vgl. hierzu Fink: „Die intentionale Analyse und das Problem des spekulativen Denkens," in: ders.: *Nähe und Distanz. Phänomenologische Vorträge und Aufsätze*, hg. von Franz-Anton Schwarz, Freiburg/München 1976, S. 139-157.

[17]Vgl. z. B. Fink: *Philosophie des Geistes*, hg. von Franz-A. Schwarz, Würzburg 1994, S. 197 f.

[18]E. Fink: *Existenz und Coexistenz. Grundprobleme der menschlichen Gemeinschaft*, hg. von Franz-A. Schwarz, Würzburg 1987, S. 101.

Rolle zumindest abgeschwächt wird. An einer bedeutsamen Stelle in *Natur, Freiheit, Welt* spricht Fink von der „Verhaltenheit“ (NFW 175). Verhaltenheit ist Zurücknahme („Zurückstauung des Lebensvollzugs,“ „Unterbrechen der hinströmenden Lebenswoge“ [ebd.]) und doch zugleich dasjenige, das, so Fink, den Menschen vor allem anderen auszeichnet: Die Verhaltung ermöglicht „Selbstand“ und ist damit apollinischer Natur (ebd.). Als solche ist Selbstheit nicht nur „Maß-Halten“ im Sinn der „Besonnenheit,“ sondern zugleich „Maßgeben“ im Sinn von „messend im Bezug zu allem, was ist, zu existieren“ (NFW 176), d. h. Ausdruck menschlicher Freiheit als des „Verstehens des Seins alles Seienden“ (ebd.). Hier darf jedoch nicht übersehen werden, daß es sich dabei eben nur um die apollinische Seite menschlicher Existenz handelt. Mehr noch: Selbstand korreliert mit der *sichtbaren* Seite des Weltbezugs, auf der die Stücke der Symbola das Ganze nur „ahnen“ lassen (ebd.). Es mag dann eine besondere Weise der Verhaltung eine Voraussetzung dafür sein, denkend die Offenheit von Welt selbst so zu bestimmen, daß deren Bewegung als solche dem menschlichen Verhaltenkönnen ebensosehr sich entzieht, wie sie dieses zugleich ‚trägt.‘ Auf diese Weise wäre zwar der Mißdeutung menschlicher Freiheit als einer „abgelösten Selbstheit“ (ebd.) ein letzter Riegel vorgeschoben, doch auch diese Verhaltung bliebe noch Ausdruck menschlicher Freiheit. Damit steht auch Finks Konzeption (er selbst würde es am wenigsten bestreiten) in der europäischen Tradition, sofern auch er mit antagonistischen Prinzipien (Natur - Freiheit) operiert. Finks Denken kommt aber dem östlichen Denken insofern auf besondere Weise nahe, als er, anders als Becker, bei diesem Antagonismus nicht stehenbleibt, sondern ein kosmisches Geschehen denkt, dessen Vollzug selbst ein Kreislauf ist: *Spiel* - wobei ‚Spiel‘ freilich auch ‚nur‘ ein *Symbolon* verkörpert („Spiel als Weltsymbol“).[19] Es handelt sich jedoch um einen Kreislauf, der gleichsam von zwei verschiedenen 'Kraftfeldern' in Anspruch genommen wird und so mit sich selbst immer wieder zur Deckung kommen muß, der sich in zwei unterschiedlichen Verlaufsarten vollzieht: die eine orientiert am Weltverhältnis des Menschen (hermeneutisch), die andere an der Welt selbst (sprachentzogen).

Der europäisch-dichotomischen Weltsicht entgeht *tao* dadurch, daß es - wie Cho in seiner Studie „Das Absolute in der taoistischen Philosophie“ eindrücklich demonstriert -, *zweimal* auftritt: das eine Mal als Weltprinzip, das sowohl Einheit erzeugt (übergang vom Nichts zum Sein) wie die Spaltung dieser Einheit in die Polarität von *yin* und *yang* ermöglicht; das andere Mal als die jene Polarität in ihren Auswirkungen „vermittelnde Potenz“ (BN 185). Daher ist hier das, was im Unsichtbaren verbleibt und was doch immer erneut sichtbar wird, *dasselbe*. Es gibt nicht eine Differenz zwischen Sichzeigen und Sichzeigendem. Genau dies ist auch der Grund, warum man der taoistischen Weltsicht, obwohl sie sich an *einem* Prinzip orientiert, nicht

[19] Vgl. Finks gleichnamiges Buch, Stuttgart 1960.

einen Monismus unterstellen kann. Denn nur im europäischen Kontext, in dem die Möglichkeit nichtmonistischer Weltbilder erschlossen wurde, ist sinnvoll und mit Recht von ‚Monismus' zu sprechen. Dies ist nicht so zu verstehen, daß das chinesische Denken eine solche Unterscheidung lediglich nicht kannte. Vielmehr steht die Bewegungsfigur des zweimal auftretenden Tao ganz außerhalb des Schemas von Monismus vs. Pluralismus, weil in jener Figur das eine *als* anderes gedacht ist, ohne Identifizierung des einen mit dem anderen, und nicht wie im Fall von Monismus und Pluralismus entweder eine Identität oder eine Differenz zwischen dem einen und anderen angenommen wird.

Das „Mittlersein" des Menschen, sein Verhältnissein, mag bei Fink - im Kontext der europäischen Philosophie - denjenigen Ort beanspruchen, den das Tao als, wie Cho formuliert, „vermittelnder Funktionsbegriff" (BN 182) einnimmt. Dem Tao in erster Hinsicht entspricht aber nicht - wie bei Fink gedacht - ein von der vermittelnden Funktion verschiedenes, ein *anderes* Verhältnissein, das sich als *dasselbe* (bezüglich des Ganzen) entpuppen würde, ohne dasselbe (bezüglich der ‚Seite', des Symbolon) zu sein, sondern die Bewegung der Welt, von der allenfalls gesagt werden kann, daß sie das Verhältnissein ermöglicht, in dem Sinn, daß sie es ‚trägt.'[20] Und doch gibt es eine Entsprechung in den Bewegungsfiguren als solchen: Wenn bei Fink Weltspiel und Menschenspiel zur Deckung kommen und doch nicht dasselbe sind, oder dasselbe sind, aber nie zur Deckung kommen, dann liegt darin die gleiche Figur wie in den Bewegungen der beiden unterschiedlichen Hinsichten von Tao. Das in beiden Aufassungen nicht Zusammenstimmende mag jedoch auf solches hinweisen, was in den unterschiedlichen Kulturen jeweils ursprünglich erschlossen wurde, und es wäre gewiß verfehlt, wollte man eines dem anderen anzugleichen suchen. Hier liegt vielmehr die Chance, das, was verschiedene Augenpaare sehen, unverkürzt in einen neuen, breiteren Zusammenhang zu rücken. Es ist das besondere Verdienst von Kah Kyung Cho, im Bereitstellen eines *phänomenologisch* gepolsterten Ost-West-Diwans erste konkrete Schritte in diese Richtung unternommen zu haben.

---

[20] In diesem Sinn heißt es bei Cho, daß östliche Philosopheme „den tragenden Grund der *Seins*ordnung nicht in eine wie auch immer verstandene Subjektivität" verlegen, „sondern im Sein der *Natur* selber bergen" (BN 127).

A Critical Consideration on the View of Nature in Japanese Buddhism

Aiko Ogoshi

I. Introduction

Today almost everyone in the world recognizes that we must share global problems and make efforts to solve them. There are wars and genocides breaking out continuously along racial lines, sexual violence and rape of women and children, poverty and starvation of the third world and environmental crises. We have considered these problems to be political and economical and tried to escape the idea that our own culture is responsible for them.

Ecological and women's movements have asked what responsibility culture bears in relation to the problems faced today. Feminist studies have been able to elucidate that sexual violence and rape against women are based on patriarchal systems and culture. However, ecological studies, in trying to find what has brought about the environmental crisis on the earth, have not been as successful. As a result, these studies have started to examine the views of nature in various cultures, views which are internalized by the individuals living within those cultures.

Now many ecologists recognize that human history was nothing but the history of the exploitation and destruction of nature, and that the philosophies and religions which were esteemed as the crowning product of culture were guilty of the environmental crisis. They began to criticize these kinds of thought and tried to find alternative ones.

Ecological feminism which arose in 70's opens a new perspective on the relationship between nature and women. Eco-feminist Andree Collard says as follows:

> Nothing links the human animal and nature so profoundly as women's reproductive system which enables her to share the experience of bringing forth and nourishing life with the rest of the world.[1]

I agree with her assertion about women's affinity with nature, and her emphasis on the reproductive power of women, but I also think such affinity with nature and reproductive power are not essential only to women. In modernized society, men were forced to become conquerors of nature, and lost their sense of affinity with nature. In more nature-oriented culture, both women and men would be in tune with the Earth.

---

[1] Andree Collard, *Rape of the Wild*, London, 1988, p.102.

As for reproductive power, it does not belong only to women. All lives come into being by the cooperation of reproductive powers of both women and men. However in most cultures men were excluded from reproduction and they have been forced to engage in production. In patriarchal society, the value of reproduction was degraded, and women's rank was lowered. Women were identified with nature and became objects of men's exploitation.

Therefore it is very important to elucidate the problems found in each culture, especially those related to its view of nature. As religions are usually at the core of each culture, we must examine them. By considering how each religion views nature and what influence it has on secular society, a great contribution to the solution of Ecological issues will be made. In this paper, I want to make clear the issues on hand in Japan as seen from my perspective as a Japanese critical ecological feminist.

II. Ecological problems in Japan

The idea that highly developed countries are responsible for the ecological destruction of the earth is popular among people of the West. They attribute the major part of the blame for this phenomenon to the dualistic way of thinking within Western culture. This duality between nature and culture, or body and mind is believed to have originated in Greek thought, particularly Platonism, and in its Cartesian development, which became the essence of the West's rationalistic, scientific and industrial culture.

On the other hand, even though Japan is also a highly developed country, only a few Japanese people think they are to be blamed for the exploitation and destruction of nature and that they must do something to solve ecological problems, because most Japanese believe that they love nature and coexist with it. They know the environmental situation is at a critical point, but they also attribute the blame to westernization and modernization. They think the Japanese view of nature which regards human beings as part of nature is better than that of the West, which masters and exploits nature for the benefit of human beings.

One of the reasons why the Japanese are confident with their view of nature is that it is based on the view held by Buddhism, which has been highly esteemed as the ecological religion. However, I would like to make a distinction here between the greater tradition of Buddhism and Japanese Buddhism, the latter being the focus of discussion here.

Of course, Japanese Buddhism originated in the Buddhism founded by Sākyamũni in India, but its way of thinking is different from that of other types of Buddhism in many ways. The most important point is that Japanese Buddhism is so life-affirming and this-worldly that it tends to justify the desires of human beings, which were originally negated by Buddha and his disciples.

The main reason for the justification of desire in Japanese Buddhism is, not because it regards human beings as possessing special rights, but because it thinks them as part of nature. I will explain this way of thinking later.

Though many Japanese people think they coexist with nature and they are not guilty of destroying nature, Japan, as a highly industrialized country, is now responsible for exploitation and destruction of nature throughout the world. How can we explain this gap between the innocence of Japanese people and the real situation? I attribute this gap to the misunderstanding of the Japanese view of nature. In my mind, the view coming from Japanese Buddhism is no less guilty of the destruction of nature than that of the Western views of nature, but it is a deceptive way of thinking which keeps people from the awareness of their mistakes.

Today Japanese capitalism is skillfully making use of this view of nature and maneuvering to be exempt from the blame for the destruction of nature which it has caused. As a critical ecological feminist in Japan, it is my duty to elucidate this double-dealing in the Japanese way of thinking and make Japanese people aware of the problematic points in their notion of nature.

Why has the Japanese concept of nature been regarded as more harmonious than that of the West? Why does Japanese capitalism invade the developing countries and exploit and destroy the environment without feeling guilt? To answer these questions is the best way for me to contribute to our world's ecological issues.

III. The double standard within the Japanese view of nature

Recently not a few religious leaders and thinkers have been utilized as propagandists of the Japanese view of nature. Many of them do not realize their roles and think they are doing nothing but giving lectures on philosophy and religious thought for international goodwill. They often criticize Western rationalism which devalues nature and esteem their own view of nature based on Japanese Buddhism. I wonder if Western people who listen to their lectures might have questions as to why they can attribute the blame for the destruction of nature to the Western way of thinking so easily and not reflect on the problems within their own concept of nature.

The famous Japanese philosopher Kitaro Nishida and his disciples, who were called "the Kyoto School", had emphasized that the Japanese way of thinking is deeply connected with the Japanese view of nature attaching importance to harmony with nature and that it is one reason why Japanese philosophy can overcome modern Western civilization and its system of thought. Such a unreasonable view is still alive even now as the resource of Japano-centrism.

It is true that Japanese people love nature and regard themselves as part of nature, but they do not try to stop the destruction of nature and make no effort to protect nature. Those who love nature and grow flowers and plants in their garden, thoughtlessly throw gabarge away in mountains and rivers. Even those who are engaged earnestly in the protection of nature in Japan are indifferent to the destruction and devastation of nature in the third world.

Considering these contradictions, I can't help noticing a double standard working within the view of nature. They want to protect the nature which is directly related to them, but they are throughly indifferent to that part of nature which is out of sight. This view can be said to be far from environmental ethics in the true sense. It seems to be extremely dangerous for the environment of the world because it pretends to protect but in fact destroys nature. It is my belief, the double standard in this view of nature came from Japanese Buddhism. Therefore I would like at this time to elucidate this point.

IV. The view of nature in Japanese Buddhism

Recently I have often been confronted with the idea that Buddhism is an ecological religion, and that Buddhist teaching gives us the solutions to the global crisis. I will not discuss here whether this view is right or not, but I want to say that it is meaningless to assert that the original teachings were good or ecological. However good an idea might be, it can be easily transformed into a dangerous one when it becomes distorted through interpretation and practice.

For example, original Christianity was not a destructive religion as it became in modern times. As the one-sided understanding of Christianity led people to its distorted image, so one-sided appreciation of Buddhism will also lead us to misunderstanding the real situation. Buddhism had continuously changed through transmission into Asian countries, and created various kinds of teachings in each area. Therefore we must clearly elucidate the problems of the view of nature in Japanese Buddhism.

When Buddhism was introduced into Japan seventeen hundred years ago, it was understood as a highly civilized religion. At that time, Shinto, the animistic folk religion was prevalent in Japanese society. Its gods and godess personified natural phenomenon and some of them became the ancestors of Japanese noble families. For example, the supreme goddess Amaterasu was the sun-deity and became the ancestor of the imperial family after the establishment of the imperial system.

As the members of the imperial families esteemed Buddhism because of its spiritual and cultural characters, it soon became the state religion of the Asuka era (6-7th century). Since then, the mixing of Buddhism and Shinto, which was unique to Japan on many points, continued to form Japanese Buddhism. One feature of Japanese Buddhism is, as I described above, its this-worldly and life-affirming character. Hajime Nakamura calls this way of thinking 'absolute phenomenalism' and asserts that it emerged as the result of a unique interpretation of Buddhism by the Japanese, who promoted the syncretism of Buddhism and Shinto. He wrote as follows;

> The Japanese Tendai scholars were not very faithful to the original text of the Chinese T'ien-T'ai, but sometimes interpreted the original texts in a rather unnatural way, their interpretation being based upon the standpoint of Absolute Phenomenalism.[2]

'Absolute Phenomenalism' means, in this case, the way of thinking that recognizes absolute significance in the phenomenal world. According to Nakamura, this absolute phenomenalism deprived Buddhism of ideas of transcendence and transformed it into a this-worldly Buddhism pursuing this-worldly benefits rather than spirituality. As a result, Japanese people asked Buddha to give them tangible rewards instead of spiritual salvation. Concerning nature, they did not regard it as intimate in a spiritulal meaning, but in a materialistic meaning. They loved nature because it gave them everything they wished for. They wanted to depend on nature and be protected by it.

This life-affirming nature made Japanese Buddhism vulnerable to secularization. It didn't criticize the unfairness and unequality of secular society. It affirmed the hierarchical way of thinking and taught people passivity and endurance. I dare to say it became an authoritarian religion.

Another feature of Japanese Buddhism is that it has been penetrated by the dualism of 'pure' and 'impure'. This kind of dualism had existed in India before Buddhism emerged. Sākyamũni taught people to transcend this dualism; he was against the caste system which classified people as pure or impure.

Concerning women, however, his egalitarian attitude changed. He taught young priests that women were impure and to renounce their sexual desires for women. As a result, Buddhism contained the dualism of the pure and the impure, which has been used for discrimination not only against women, but against people excluded from society.

In contrast, in Shinto the concept of 'clean' and 'polluted' existed, but pollution was cleansed through ritual. The decisive dualism was established by Buddhism in the Heian era (8-12th century), when esoteric Buddhism was introduced into Japan and sutras containing discriminative teachings, like the *Lotus Sutra*, became popular. Women were regarded as impure beings and prohibited from entering sacred places.

According to the *Lotus Sutra*, there is no woman in Gokuraku, or Buddhist paradise. It teaches that women might enter Gokuraku after changing their sex, but that they must descend into various hells as long as they have female bodies. This teaching led people logically to the idea that the place where men existed was pure, and on the other hand the place where women

---

[2]Hajime Nakamura, *Ways of Thinking of Eastern Peoples*, Honolulu/Hawaii, 1964,p.351.

existed was impure. The dualism of the pure and the impure is not only ideological, but is also a topographical one. It was incorporated into the institution of Kekkai,the sacred citadels, into which women were not allowed to enter. Honen, the founder of Japanese Pure Land Buddhism, commented on the unlucky destiny of women as follows;

> Although women have two legs, there are peaks of the Law they cannot scale, there are gardens of the Buddha they are forbidden to enter. And how shameful it is, that although women have two eyes, there is hallowed ground which they cannot see, there are sacred images they cannot worship. A sacred place may be a mountain of rubbish and brambles, its crude sacred images may be made of wood and mud, and yet it will still refuse entry or worship to women. Far be it that a woman should be able to be reborn in the Pure land, built with every precious jewel, or to meet a Buddha endowed with every virture.[3]

Honen criticized the institution of Kekkai and sympathized with women, but he didn't negate it and preached to them to accept their destiny. This unreasonable institution has continued in one form or another until now.

V. The dualism of the pure and the impure in Japanese Buddhism

One of the reasons why women were degraded as impure was the notion of pollution connected with the discharge of blood during menstruation and childbirth. The 420-character Ketsubon-kyo (*Blood Bowl Sutra*), composed by a fourteenth-century priest of the Soto-Zen sect, was a sutra preaching the sins of women and their destiny, which is to fall into the Blood Pond Hell. The first half reads as follows.

> All women fall into this hell because of their *karma* ... The red blood flows seven days every month, this is eighty-four days in twelve months. This is why it is called 'moon water'. This 'moon water' is extremely evil and unclean. However, this evil blood spills upon the ground sullying the head of the Earth Gods, thus invoking the wrath of those 98072 Gods. If poured into water, it pollutes the Water Gods; if disposed of in the mountain forests, it defiles the Mountain Gods. When women wash their soiled clothing in the rivers, the good folk living downstream, ignorant of their act, draw this water and with it prepare tea and rice to offer to the Gods and Buddhas. Then the

[3]Honen, *Muryojukyo-shaku*, Trans. by Junko Oguri. In Young East., Osaka, 1984, p.351.

> deities cannot accept their offerings. Since women, by nature, soil the Gods and Buddhas, they will fall into the Blood Pond Hell after they die.[4]

This description defined the female body itself as unclean and defiled. By the early modern period, this sexist sutra was being used by many Buddhist sects and it had also become widely popular among women. Concerning this sutra,Junko Minamoto commented as follows;

> The *Blood Bowl Sutra* stands solidly in the tradition of Buddhist ideas on purity and pollution. It teaches that even in the world to come (after death), the pure (men) will be separated from the polluted (women), with women falling into the hells (a polluted place). Furthermore, their damnation was seen to be karmic retribution for sins committed in the past life; not only was it the result of bad *karma*, but it produced bad *karma* as well. Women herself is bad *karma*. – Under the spell of the Blood Bowl Sutra, women came to hold a negative view of their own sexuality. This was equivalent to negating their very existence.[5]

As Minamoto points out, this sutra, coming from the Buddhist tradition, degraded women because of their procreative sex and reproductive power. Considering that a human being can not come into being without this kind of discharge of blood, this teaching is nothing but absurd. But Buddhism taught that life is painful, since birth leads to old age, death, and further rebirth in an endless chain of causality, and as the life-negating religion degraded women as the sex responsible for this causality.

Japanese Buddhism, even though it was transformed into a life-affirming religion, approved only of men's sexuality, and continued to take a hostile attitude towards women's sexuality. It did not regard the chain of endless rebirth as symbolic of living nature, but as the source of troubles.

In androcentric society, Japanese women had led a life of constant self-affacement until the end of the war (1945). On the surface this traditinal view of women seems to have disappeared, but the absurd situation in which women are discriminated against because of procreative sex continues. Women can't participate in some religious rituals and even now are not permitted to enter into the Dohyo on which Sumo tournaments are held.

This dualism of the pure and the impure was not only applied to gender relationships but also used for discriminating against people who engaged in work regarded as impure at that time. Originally there were five precepts

---

[4]"Ketsubon-kyo: chi no ike jigoku", in "Nyonin Jobutsu Ketsubon-kyo", trans. Hirano Sojo, in "Dai Nikon zokuzokyo", Bd.87, Tokyo, 1912.

[5]Junko Minamoto, "Buddhism and the Historical Construction of sexuality in Japan", in "U.S.-Japan Women's Journal" 5, California, 1993.

in Buddhism: no killing, no stealing, no adultery, no lying, no drinking of alcoholic beverages. Therefore people who engaged in killing fish, birds and domestic animals were degraded as sinful and impure. Those people were not allowed to live with ordinary people. They were driven away into special areas like the riversides or outskirts of cities which were designated as impure places.

During the medieval period, this dualism became the basic ideology on which the Japanese feudal system was founded. At the top existed the Emperor who personified the concept of purity. In secularized society, there were four classes, which in descending order were the warrior-bureaucrats, the peasants or primary producers, the artisans or secondary producers and the merchants.

At the bottom existed the Japanese outcasts called Burakumin who were forced to perform occupations considered ritually polluting, including animal slaughter and disposal of the dead. Since outcasts who practiced jobs involving death and blood were thought to have been born to such a fate as a result of *karma* from a previous life; and seen subhuman by nature, their status was inherited through birth and they were forced to live within the reserved areas.

According to historian Hideo Kuroda, the division of the land by the rule of the dualism of the pure and the impure began in the medieval period.[6] The royal palace where the imperial family lived was regarded as the most sacred and pure place. The further from the royal palace, the more impure the land. One of the important responsibilities of the emperor is to purify the land through the performance of special ceremonies.

But the places where the outcasts lived were never visited and purified by the emperor, because the strong pollution of the people engaged in animal slaughter and the disposal of the dead was thought to menace the emperor. They were alienated even from the mercy of the emperor which was believed to be given to every place and people. The places called Hisabetsu Buraku or 'discriminated villages' were regarded as impure and defiled.

VI. The teachings of Shinran

Japanese Buddhism has to this day never resisted the Tennosei, or Japanese imperial system. It assimilated into this discriminative system and produced original teachings which preached the salvation of those discriminated people at the bottom. Shinran(1173-1262), who is one of the most popular figures in Japanese Buddhism and the founder of Shin Buddhism (Jōdo Shinshū), was famous for the paradoxical teaching that the most sinful people could be saved by their faith in the unfathomable compassion of Amida, the Buddha of Infinite Life. He also taught that their salvation

---

[6] Hideo Kuroda, *Kyokai no Chusei and Schocho no Chusei*, Tokyo, 1986, p.50

was actualized not by practicing austerities or performing religious rituals but by reciting the name of Amida (Nembutsu). Ruben Habito commented as follows:

> 'Even those who do good can be saved. How much more so those who do evil !' This is dictum attributed to Shinran, which subverts all our common sense notion of good and evil and salvation. Our ordinary moral sense would be more easily able to understand the reverse of the statement, namely, 'even those who do evil can be saved, how much more so those who do good! – implying that it is taken for granted that those who do good are saved on that account, i.e. for doing good. But Shinran's faith-experience which led him to the realization of the totally gratuitous nature of Amida's compassion is what lies at the basis of this emphasis, that "evildoers' are actually closer to that salvation given in the compassion of Amida: in recognizing oneself as an evildoer and powerless to save oneself by one's own merits, one is more easily able to submit oneself to that saving compassion than one who is under the impression that one's good acts merit one's salvation.[7]

I don't intend to negate this theological interpretation of Shinran's teaching, but I want to emphasize what kind of influence this teaching had on the real situation in Japanese history. It might be willingly accepted among the discriminated people who were degraded as evildoers, and thought to promise them salvation, but at the same time, it forced those people to accept the sinfulness and defilement placed on them, because their salvation could not be given without their self-negation.

However, I want to ask what could make them sinful and impure. Was it Buddhism? The Buddhist teaching of no killing forced the people dealing with the slaughter of animals and disposal of the dead to become sinful and impure. But nature itself contains birth and death, production and dissolution. Without the latter, the former can't be. This is the cyclical system of nature. It is Buddhism which applied the axiological dualism of the pure and the impure to the cyclical system of nature. It defined the production and ripening aspect of nature as pure and good, and on the other hand, the corrupting and dissoluting nature as impure and ominous.

The famous philosophy that teaches "the grass, the trees and all insentient objects; they are enlightened, every one" is often explained as proving that Japanese Buddhism is ecological, but I think that the nature which was regarded as enlightened was nothing but the "pure nature" which existed under the patronage of people. The "impure" nature which was too

[7]Ruben L. F. Habito, "Towards a Global Spirituality", in Zen Buddhism Today 8, *The Kyoto Seminar for Religious Philosophy*, Kyoto, 1990, p.116.

energetic to be tamed by human beings was excluded from enlightenment. Though Japanese Buddhism introduced this dualism into its concept of nature, it pretended to appreciate nature as a whole. It looks to me as a self-deception.

Shinran's teaching proves the dualistic view of Japanese Buddhism clearly. He preached that people whose occupations belonged to the dark side of nature were evildoers and they had to realize their sins and their defilement. They were powerless to do anything for themselves, to get rid of their sins except through dependence upon the compassion and grace of Amida (Tariki). Therefore they had to endure the discrimination against them. If they continued to endure their destiny without any resistance, they could go to the Pure Land, symbolizing pure nature after death.

Shinran was a great religious leader who made efforts to extend salvation to discriminated people, but in spite of his good intention, his teachings deepened the dualism of the pure and the impure. His school became very popular among the people at the lower classes in the middle ages. Farmers and peasants belonging to the "pure nature" which produced crops were also forced to lead poor lives of hard labour, but they could dissolve their frustration by discriminating against the people belonging to the "impure" nature.

Shin Buddhism justified the discriminative system and introduced the hierarchism into its religious order. The religious organization of the temple system stabilized in a pyramid-like pattern with Shinran's decendants dominant at the top of the pyramid. The main temples were respected as the pure ones, while the branch temples were degraded. Temples supported by the Burakmin were discriminated against and sometimes called impure ones.

VII. Discriminated people and their view of nature

Society was rigidly stratified under the Tokugawa Shogunate, beginning in 600. The degraded outcast status of those practicing "defiled" jobs was formally established. The Burakumin were forced to live in reserved areas which were in most cases barrens and situated at the verge of farming villages. The farmers discriminated against the Burakumin and also degraded the Buraku areas and the nature where they lived as impure. They threw away dead animals into the Buraku areas in order to avoid the pollution of death.

Even after the collapse of the feudal system, discrimination against the Burakumin has continued until now. At the beginning of the Meiji period (1868-1960), the government announced the liberation of the Burakumin, but the discriminating attitude toward the Burakumin never changed. Finally, the Burakumin established the radical organization struggling for their liberation, which was named Suiheisha in 1882. They tried to go beyond the traditional dualism of the pure and the impure, in order to justify their situation. The following declaration clearly shows their resolve.

> Burakumin throughout the country, unite! ... Brothers and sisters! Our ancestors sought after and practiced liberty and equality. But they became the victims of a base contemptible system developed by the ruling class. They became the martyrs of industry. As a reward for skinning animals, they were flayed alive. As a recompense for tearing out the hearts of animals, their own warm human hearts were ripped out. They were spat upon with the words of ridicule. Yet all through these cursed nightmares, their blood, still proud to be human, did not dry up. Yes! Now we have come to the age when men and women, pulsing with this blood, are trying to become divine. The time has come when the martyrs' Crown of Thorns will be blessed. The time has come when we can be proud of being Eta... Let there be warmth in the hearts of people, and let there be light upon all humankind. From this, the Suiheisha is born.[8]

In this declaration they justified their occupation and announced themselves divine for the first time in Japanese history. They tried to dissolve the traditional dualism and revive themselves as human beings and nature as a whole. They criticized the hierarchical views of human beings and nature which had divided them into the pure and the impure. And also they attempted to create a view of nature based on their own daily experience.

Shoichi Kawamoto, elucidating the history of the Burakumin, points out that the Japanese view of nature has lacked the concept of recycling. According to him, nature contains the cycle of germinating, growing, blowing, fruition, withering, decaying and reproducing itself, but the Japanese notion of nature has esteemed the first half of the cycle from germinating to fruition as pure nature and degraded the latter half part of that from withering to reproducing as impure.[9] From his suggestion it occurs to me that in Japanese folktales we can find old ugly women called Yamauba who symbolize the boundless energy and variety of untamed nature. They are said to live in mountains beyond any human habitation and kill or eat travellers whom they meet. They are feared and excluded from villagers, even though they want to be in their company. These folktales of Yamauba suggest that most Japanese people are afraid of raw and essential nature, and degrade it.

Kawamoto also points out that while the Japanese view of nature held by ordinary people was very one-sided, the concept of nature held by the

---

[8]Buraku Mondai Kenkyusho, *Suihei Undoshi no Kenkyu*, Bd.2, Kyoto, 1971, p.143.

[9]Shoichi Kawamoto, *Hisabetsu buraku no Seikatsu to Bunkashi*, Tokyo , 1991, pp.27-33.

Burakumin, on the other hand, esteems the total cycle. The Burakumin were excluded from farming and forced to engage in heavy labour such as cleaning communal places, slaughtering domestic animals, disposing of the dead, patroling, and executing criminals. They had the special technique of dissolving the dead cows and horses and reproducing them into daily necessaries. They made hide into leathers and drums, bones into handles of umbrellas, nails into combs, tails into writing brushes, suet into candles, blood into medicines and the remainder into fertilizers. Every part of a dead animal was reclaimed and never thrown away.

The dead animals gave many things to the Burakumin. They were proud of their technique of producing things and handed it down from generation to generation, even though this technique was the source of their discrimination. They knew from their experience that new things are made from the old, and circulation is the natural order. They regarded nature as a recycling system, and found themselves a part of nature in that sense. According to Kawamoto, such a view of nature was shared by all the people in pre-Buddhist days.

Fishermen at the seaside and hunters in the mountains also led their lives by killing fish, birds and animals, but they never killed more than they needed. They believed that they could lead their lives under the mercy of nature. They knew the circulation of nature and multifarious figures of it, but they were generally discriminated against because of the Buddhist precept against killing. In "Ukai", a famous Noh play of the middle ages, a fisherman killing fish was depicted as a sinner who had to fall into hell. In the play, we can find an interesting dialogue between a pilgrim-priest who looked for lodging and a fisherman as follows;

> Priest: We are pilgrim-priests. We asked for lodging in the village. But they told us that it was not lawful for them to receive us, so we lay down in the shelter of this shrine.
>
> Fisher: Truly, truly; I know of none in the village that could give you lodging.
>
> Priest: Pray tell me, sir, what brings you here?
>
> Fisher: Gladly. I am a cormonant-fisher. While the moon is shining I rest at this shrine; But when the moon sinks, I go to ply my trade.
>
> Priest: Then you will not mind our lodging here. But, sir, this work of slaughter ill becomes you; for I see that the years lie heavy on you. Pray leave this trade and find yourslf another means of sustenance.
>
> Fisher: You say well. But this trade has kept me since I was a

> child. I cannot leave it now.[10]

In this scene, it is clear that both the pilgrim-priest and the fisherman are excluded from villagers. The fisherman is kind enough to bring the priest back to his house and lodge him with uncommon care. However, he is criticized about his job, and after that, he is killed ruthlessly by villigers. It is true that his job can be reckoned a sin against life, but he never kills fish uselessly. In my mind, the villagers are crueler than the fisherman, but Buddhism always supports the discriminating people.

Kanichi Nomoto points out that human beings must live a life based on the killing of other animals.[11] According to him, co-existence contains not only intimate relationships, but also conflicting ones. The discriminated people, confronting the real situation, created their original belief that the dead animals would transform into spiritual beings, and they worshiped them as gods.

It seems that the view of nature of these discriminated people penetrates into the reality of nature more truly than that of the discriminating people. The people who know the circulation of nature have deeper insight than the people who see nothing but the pure side of nature. I think their view of nature is, in fact, much more ecological than that of the discriminating people, such as farmers, peasants, Buddhists and rulers. But it has been suppressed, ignored and degraded.

VIII. The self-deception of Japanese Buddhism

A famous Zen philosopher,Daisetsu Suzuki spoke of the Japanese concept of nature as follows;

> The love of nature the Japanese people originally had was no doubt their innate aesthetic sense for things beautiful; but the appreciation of the beautiful is at the bottom religious, for without being religious one cannot detect and enjoy what is genuinely beautiful. And there is no denying that Zen gave an immense impetus to the naive feeling for nature, not only by sharpening it to the highest degree of sensitiveness but also by giving it a metaphysical and religious background.
>
> In the beginning, probably, the Japanese were naively attracted to the beautiful which they saw about them. It is possible that they regarded all things in nature as uniformly animated with life, after the manner of primitive people who look upon even nonsentient things from their animistic point of view. But

---

[10]Ukai in *The No Plays of Japan* ed. by Arthur Waley, Tokyo, 1976, p.129.
[11]Kanichi Nomoto, *Kyosei no Folklore*, Tokyo, 1994, p.108.

> as they cultivated themselves in the Zen teaching, their aesthetic and religious sensitiveness was further nourished. And this nourishment came in the form of an exalted moral discipline and a highly spiritual intuition.[12]

We can find the self-deception of Japanese Buddhism in these words. As Suzuki states, Japanese Buddhism changed the original animistic view of nature into a different one, but a worse and not a better one. Pre-Buddhist people sympathized with all things in nature, both living and decaying.

It is Japanese Buddhism that introduced value judgement into the naive view of nature. Its dualism of the pure and the impure divided nature as a whole into a hierarchy. It ignored the circulating system of nature, and fabricated a one-sided model.

You can find how artificial the love of nature of Japanese Zen Buddhism is when you see the gardens of Zen temples. Zen priests don't like nature as it is and they always trim up their gardens. They like the white sand which gives the impression of purity. They surround the gardens with tall walls allowing only priests and apprentices to enjoy their beauty. A Korean scholar, O-Young Lee speaks of nature featured in Zen temple gardens as follows;

> Nature that has been pulled into the gardens as a dry landscape is no longer the nature of the outside world. It has been pared down, simplified to the extreme, and brought up to the veranda. It is a special kind of nature that exists on its own terms apart from what we usually call nature.[13]

He also points out that any dirt and useless elements are excluded from the Zen garden which most Japanese people esteem. According to him, the Japanese view of nature is very different from that of Koreans who take nature as it is, and it is rather like the Westerners who subjugate nature and make it their own, even though the aims and methods may differ.

We can find this unique Japanese view of nature in Bonsai or tray gardens. Those who like Bonsai try to transform nature in order to bring it closer to themselves, by dwarfing trees and cutting branches away. Considering their taste, we must conclude that most Japanese people love the closed-in nature found within the walls and under the patronage of human beings, regarding such nature as pure.

Though Japanese Buddhism has a one-sided view of nature, many Japanese Buddhists like Suzuki ignore this and assert that Buddhism is an ecological religion, while Christianity is a human-centered religion exploiting and destroying nature. I think this way of thinking leads to many mistakes. Indeed Japanese Buddhism can be ecological as far as pure nature

---

[12] Daisetsu Suzuki, *Zen and Japanese culture*, Vermont and Tokyo, 1988, p.363.
[13] O-Young-Lee, *The Compact culture*, Tokyo, 1982, p.48.

is concerned, but it discriminates against impure nature and leaves it to exploitation and destruction without any guilt.

Though famous Buddhists never admit it, Japanese Buddhism contained discriminating teachings against both women and the people whose jobs were regarded as impure. As I described in section V, many Buddhist schools taught women sexist sutras such as Ketsubon-kyo and degraded them as impure. They also taught the discriminating texts to the Burakumin and gave them demeaning Buddhist names after death.

Japanese Buddhism, as the central religion of Japan, has made many mistakes. However, I think, the greatest problem for Japanese Buddhism is that it has never become aware of its self-deception. Though it protects only walled-in nature, it pretends to be the protector of nature as a whole. Though it controls nature in its own way, it pretends to be an ecological religion.

IX. What is our responsibility?

Since the Meiji Restoration the "pure-impure" dualism seems to have disappeared and the discrimination based on the dualism is said to have dissolved. I think the true condition is not to be known by external appearance. Of course clear discrimination based on the impurity was forbidden, but it transformed into another kind of discrimination. During Meiji, when the new regime was established, the dualism of the internal and the external emerged.

As I describe in section VIII, Japanese Buddhism esteemed the surrounded and enclosed nature as pure and ignored the nature beyond the control of human beings and degraded it as impure. Under the influence of this view of nature, the notion that internal nature is pure and to be protected, and external nature is impure and beyond protection came to prevail among the Japanese. They loved internal nature and took great care of it, but external nature became the abstract world of expansion.

Since the end of Meiji, imperial Japan began to invade neighboring countries to protect the homeland. It aimed to plunder natural resources in Asian countries. The fanatic philosophy that Japan was the most sacred country in the world and other Asian countries should obey Japan was accepted among Japanese people. Imperial Japan colonized Taiwan and Korea and other Asian regions. Most Japanese discriminated against non-Japanese in Asia, and degraded them as inferior to themselves.

According to Junko Minamoto, as the theory of justification of the Japanese invasion into Asian countries, the dualism of the pure and the impure was availed. The Japanese army opened agressive wars, conquered and destroyed the lives and environment in surrounding countries. For these crimes, the Japanese government has not yet taken its responsibility.

After the atomic bombs were dropped on Japan, the war ended (1945). As the environment of Japan was also destroyed, the Japanese government and most of people concentrated on the reconstruction of Japan, and had no interest in the external world, even though a few people continued to warn against forgetting their crimes in Asian countries. Soon economic success enabled Japan once again to turn to the outside world.

The Japanese government did not take responsibility and express guilt for the war, but promoted enterprises to make an economic invasion into other countries in order to develop its industries. Japanese companies began to exploit and destroy the environment of those countries. Forests were exhaustively cut down, and big projects that changed the ecological condition were executed.

As for Japanese philosophers who had created Japano-centric dogmas like those called the Kyoto School, Hajime Tanabe wrote "Philosophy as Metanoethics"[14] and expressed his reflection of the failure to face up to the political and cultural realities that had landed the country in the war. But I must say that his reflection tuned only to the internal world and never to the external world. Though not only Tanabe but also other Japanese philosophers insisted in their writings to overcome the dualism of the modernity, their way of doing it was nothing but to ignore the dualism of the real world. In spite of their failures, their philosophies are reviving now as those of overcoming the Western dualistic ways of thinking and suggesting the Eastern nature-oriented view of the world.

Though Japanese people love nature and have a strong interest in protecting their own nature, they have no interest in the nature of other countries because they think it is nothing but their own natural resource. They want to live in the houses made of wood, enjoy healthy raw food imported from the other countries and they believe they coexist with nature. An Asian activist says that the Japanese is a kind of environmental racist.

It seems to me that these two attitudes of Japanese people toward nature reflect the dualism of "internal" and "external" lurking in their unconsciousness, more radically the dualism of "pure" and "impure". But many Japanese are not aware of this dualism. On vacation, some of them often enjoy the outdoor life, and think that they are part of nature. Some of them go to temples and shrines in the mountains in order to enjoy the religious feelings with which they can rest and make peace with themselves and nature. But when they start working, they forget their affinity with nature, they engage in business to exploit the environment of other countries.

Japanese must become aware of their ethnocentrism, which is that we love nature more than other people in the world. We do nothing but love and want to protect our "internal" nature, but are guilty of exploitation and destruction of the "external" nature. At first we must be free from the misunderstanding that the Japanese view of nature is more ecological

---

[14] Hajime Tanabe, *Philosophy as Metanoethics*, trans. Yoshinori Takeuchi, California, 1986.

than that of the West. We must also renounce the dualistic way of thinking dividing nature and people into a hierarchy.

Secondly we must revive the view of nature which grasps nature as a whole and recognizes the cyclical characters of nature. R.M. Ruether, who identifies herself as an ecofeminist theologian, recently says as follows;

> This cycle of production, consumption, and decomposition in nature prevents waste from accumulating. Nonhuman nature has developed a system of recycling that prevents the accumulation of waste as pollution. The crisis of pollution that afflicts modern civilization results, in large part, from its failure to imitate nature in this system of recycling. By failing to develop co-industries that break down and recycle technological wastes of production and consumption, as well as the natural wastes of food and excrement, these wastes are allowed to accumulate in concentrated forms that poison the soils, air and waters.[15]

This cyclic view of nature has been held by the discriminated people in Japan, like the Burakumin and the Ainu people living in Hokkaido, whom I have not touched upon in this paper. I think their views of nature can help to solve the ecological problems in the world, but unfortunately, many do not realize the worth of their views of nature, and continue to degrade them, while they esteem modern technology. For them, modern technology seems "pure" in contrast to traditional techniques. They eagerly attempt to invent new technology to protect internal nature in Japan. Of course such technology is also important and must be availed to protect the external nature.

As Val Plumwood, a critical ecological feminist in Australia, points out, the oppression of nature has been strongly connected with that of gender, race, and class. Therefore, ecological movements must be united with the movements against any discriminations based on gender, race and class. I also want to add that discrimination exists based on geographical areas. In the case of Minamata, where poor people in the fishing villages have suffered from pollution diseases, the modernized elite businessmen coming from Tokyo ignored the lives of the native people and destroyed their environment. The struggle against the big company which caused the pollution in Minamata is, at the same time, that of degraded people at the local areas against the central power. A journalist, who visited Minamata and saw the polluted sea, described it as follows;

> The enemy is before our eyes ... This brazen enemy, having confirmed through secret experiments that it was indeed poisoning the sea, concealed the results and continued its actions, even

[15]Rosemary Radford Ruether, *Gaia and God*, San Fransisco, 1992, p.53

> issuing threatening public statements suggesting that the local people had better not jeopardize themselves by incurring its wrath. Its attitude represents the worst kind of tyrannical capitalist oppression and exploitaion of the masses: the dumping of poison into local waters has exploited lives.[16]

Michiko Ishimura, a poetess living in Minamata, wrote many essays about the Minamata disease and made a great impression on the public. She described in her essays not only the miserable situations of victims, but also the people of Minamata, who led a peaceful life based on the cyclic view of nature. They loved nature and ate fish with the belief that the fish eaten by them changed into spirits living in their bodies. In fact, however, the modern technology changed the fish into poison in their bodies.

According to Ishimura, officials regarded such views as superstitious and forced the villagers to internalize the modern view of nature, but victims in Minamata refused this and kept their own cyclic view of nature. For example, a mother who has a daughter suffering from the disease venerates her daughter as a sacred being who saved her by absorbing the mercury poison in her womb. Such views give a great shock to the people who harbor suspicion about the modern view, but many people regard it as the product of ignorant people in marginal areas.

We Japanese have learned many things from the case of Minamata disease, but we have not yet changed our view of nature which has caused the destruction and exploitation of the environment. If we hope to be part of cyclic nature in the true sense, we must overcome not only our hierarchical view of nature but also that of human beings.

We must consider the reason why we can find the alternative environmental ethos not in the discriminating people in developed cultures but in the discriminated people like the Burakumin, the Ainu people, the Aboriginal people and native Americans, whose cultures and religions have been regarded as primitive and low. It is true that highly developed religions, like Christianity and Buddhism degraded these primitive cultures and religions, but at the same time they absorbed their essences and incorporated them into their teachings.

Therefore we can find the possibility of reviving their environmental ethos and putting them to practical use even within Christianity and Buddhism. As there are not a few Christians who try to establish a new environmental ethos, there are also some Buddhists who try to give new life to the Buddhist view of nature. We can find the following sentences in *Vimalakirtinirdesa-sutra*:

> And just like a soft breeze and a few blossoms on a branch that tell the coming of spring, so when a man attains Enlighten-

[16] Akiko Mishima, *Bitter Sea*, trans. by Richard L.Gage, Tokyo, 1992, p.39.

ment, grass, trees, mountains, rivers and all other things begin to throb with new life.

To attain enlightment here means to conquer worldly passions and to make efforts in order to build a Buddha land where all living beings revive their lives. In this world full of desires, it is very difficult for human beings to attain enlightenment, not only in an ideal sense but also in a practical sense. At first we must overcome the dualistic way of thinking which divides nature and humans into two realms.

We must overcome our egocentric ideas and take courage in the fight against all the discriminatory systems in the world. Because, I believe, if there is a Buddha land, it must not have discriminatory systems, like those of this world. I think it is the responsibility of critical ecological Buddhists to continue considering how we can establish such a Buddha land on our Earth.

Phänomenologie und Metaphysik der Natur

Toru Tani

Seit dem 17. Jahrhundert entwickelten sich die mathematischen Naturwissenschaften, die die Natur gegenständlich thematisieren. Im 19. Jahrhundert drohte jedoch die Gefahr einer „Bodenlosigkeit des Theoretisierens“[1], einer „Grundlagenkrisis“[2] der Wissenschaften. Diese Situation motivierte die Entstehung der Phänomenologie Edmund Husserls. Husserl fand Boden und Grundlage in den „Sachen selbst“, die in unmittelbarer Erfahrung gegeben sind. Diese Erfahrung weist in sich Schichten auf, die von der Intentionalität des Bewußtseins konstituiert werden, und die Aktivität des Bewußtseins fungiert auf dem Untergrund der Passivität. Die letzte Grundlage der Wissenschaften beruht also auf der letzten Schicht unmittelbarer Erfahrung. In dieser Schicht fungiert die Intentionalität noch nicht oder höchstens minimal. Diese Schicht ist die der letzten Passivität, ist „Urpassivität“. Gerade hier finden wir eine neue „Natur“, die weder Gegenstand noch eine Region der Naturwissenschaften, sondern die letzte Sache selbst ist.

In der Entwicklung der Phänomenologie, zu der nicht nur Edmund Husserl, sondern auch Martin Heidegger, Merleau-Ponty und Kah Kyung Cho beitrugen, kann man eine Tendenz zur Vertiefung der Erfassung dieser Natur finden. Husserl eröffnete den Zugang zur Natur. Heidegger fand sie im griechischen Begriff der „*physis*“. Merleau-Ponty, der nicht nur von Husserl und Heidegger sondern auch von Schelling inspiriert wurde, entwarf eine Naturphilosophie im Zusammenhang mit dem fleischlichen Sein. Cho eröffnete eine neue Möglichkeit der Phänomenologie des Naturseins im Zusammenhang mit dem ostasiatischen Taoismus.

In diesem Aufsatz verdeutlichen wir zuerst die Entwicklungslinie des Denkens der Natur in den Phänomenologien von Husserl, Heidegger und Merleau-Ponty. Die Phänomenologie in dieser Richtung böte eine neue Variante einer „Metaphysik der Natur“[3], obwohl diese nicht „spekulativ“, sondern „sachlich“ vollzogen wird. Als zweites charakterisieren wir das Problem der phänomenologischen Naturauffassung, die sich im westlichen „Vorgriff“ der Natur bewegt. Schließlich wird die Notwendigkeit eines interkulturellen Dialogs für die Aufklärung der Natur, dessen Möglichkeit erst Cho phänomenologisch eröffnete, dargelegt.

I. Husserls Zugang zur Natur

[1] Edmund Husserl: *Husserliana* (Hua), den Haag: Martinus Nijhoff Bd. IX S. 302.

[2] Martin Heidegger: *Gesamtausgabe* (HGA), Frankfurt a.M.: Vittorio Klostermann, Bd. 20 S. 4; *Sein und Zeit* (SZ), Tübingen: Max Niemeyer 1977, S. 9.

[3] Immanuel Kant: *Kritik der reinen Vernunft* (KrV), A S. XXI.

In Husserls Terminologie bedeutet „Natur“ zumeist die Region des Gegenstandes der Naturwissenschaft, wie in den *Ideen* II. Husserl bahnte jedoch noch einen Zugang zu einer ursprünglichen Natur in der Sphäre der Urpassivität. Er übernahm zuerst von Brentano den Begriff der Intentionalität als Bewußtseinsaktivität. Der Akt des Bewußtseins konstituiert aktiv „das Erscheinende“ (den Gegenstand). Die Intentionalität des Bewußtseins läßt „die Erscheinungen“ in den intentionalen Erlebnissen auf ein Erscheinendes hin, das die Erlebnisse transzendiert, konvergieren.

Die Konstitution bei Husserl besitzt, grob gesagt, zwei Seiten: einerseits die Bestimmung des „Sinnes“ des Erscheinenden und andererseits die Bestimmung des „Seins“ desselben. Im Urteil „S ist p“ zeigt „p“ die Bestimmung des Sinnes und „ist“ die des Seins. Husserl sucht nach der Grundlage dieser Bestimmungen und findet sie in der unmittelbaren Erfahrung, die dem im Urteil verwirklichten Theoretisieren vorangeht.

Diese doppelseitige Konstitution wird im und vom intentionalen Erlebnis (oder Bewußtsein), vor allem vom Zeitbewußtsein, ermöglicht. Dieses läßt alle Erscheinungen dauern und konvergieren. Ohne fungierendes Zeitbewußtsein würden alle Erscheinungen alsbald verströmen: „panta rhei“. Es gäbe dann keine Möglichkeit, Erscheinungen in einem Erscheinenden zusammenzufassen, und wir würden keine Zeitstrecke kennen. Das fungierende Zeitbewußtsein behält retentional im Griff, was ansonsten verströmen würde.

Das Zeitbewußtsein ist nach Retention-Urimpression-Protention strukturiert. Diese Struktur ist kein Produkt der aktiven Leistung des Bewußtseins, sondern das Zeitbewußtsein besitzt schon „passiv“ diese Struktur. Entsprechend weist das Zeitbewußtsein nicht nur urimpressionale, sondern auch retentionale und protentionale Erscheinungen auf. Es faßt alle Erscheinungen zusammen und ermöglicht die Bestimmung des einheitlichen Sinns des Erscheinenden. Es konstituiert z.B. durch die retentionale Erscheinung des Vierecks und die urimpressionale Erscheinung des Trapezes (und auch die protentionale Erscheinung des Vierecks) hindurch ein Erscheinendes, das den Sinn von „Quadrat“ besitzt.

Das Erscheinende wird andererseits auch als ein die Erlebnisse Transzendierendes konstituiert. Diese Transzendenz wird das Sein des Erscheinenden genannt. Der Akt der Konstitution des Seins ist das „Setzen“. Phänomenologisch gesehen, wird das Bestimmen der Transendenz oder des Seins (also das Setzen) zuerst dadurch ermöglicht, daß das Bewußtsein das Erscheinende der objektiven „Zeit“ (oder genauer „Zeitform“) zugehören läßt. Die objektive Zeit wird als eine linienförmige konstituiert, die Vergangenheit, Gegenwart und Zukunft umfaßt. Aber die Struktur von Retention-Urimpression-Protention gehört zur Gegenwart, obwohl sie eine Breite besitzt. Die Retention ist noch nicht die Vergangenheit und die Protention noch nicht die Zukunft. Das Zeitbewußtsein weiß zunächst noch nicht um Vergangenheit und Zukunft; es lebt in der Gegenwart. Was passiert, wenn die Erscheinung über die Grenze der Retention, also der Gegenwart, hinausgeht? Wird sie zu „nichts“ ? Das Bewußtsein kann aufgrund der Leistung der „Erinnerung“ die Abfolge der Retentionen wieder-holen. Diese erinnerte Abfolge heißt „Vergangenheit“. Das Bewußtsein „verlängert“ die Vergangenheit derart, daß es die voraufgehenden Abfolgen weiter wiederholt. Das Bewußtsein operiert so auch in Hinsicht auf die Protention: Dann wird „Zukunft“ konstituiert. Erst auf diese Weise wird die linienförmige „objektive Zeit“ ausgebildet, die nicht nur die Gegenwart, sondern auch die Vergangenheit und die Zukunft umfaßt. Das Bewußtsein läßt das Erscheinende in diese objektive Zeit gehören. Diese Leistung gibt dem Erscheinenden die Bestimmung als das in der objektiven Zeit von einer Zeitstelle zu folgenden Dauernde. Das Dauern in derselben Zeit bezeichnet den Charakter des Seins des Erscheinenden (oder des Gegenstandes) als „Realität“. „Für jeden Gegenstand der Wahrnehmung als solchen, d. h. als vermeinten, als vermeintlich wirklich seienden Gegenstand“ ist es entscheidend, in der objektiven Welt „seine feste Zeitstelle, Stelle in der objektiven Zeit“, zu haben.[4] In diesem Sinn ist die „objektive Zeit“ „die Form der mundanen Objektivität als seiender“.[5] Die Form hier bedeutet nicht so etwas wie die Bezeichnung des mathematischen Gegenstandes als eines nicht sachhaltigen, sondern die Bedingung der Möglichkeit der Bestimmung des Seins des Gegenstandes.

Das Bewußtsein kann statt der objektiven Zeit auch eine „Quasi-Zeit“ konstituieren. Diese ist die Zeitstrecke, die nicht der objektiven Zeit eingefügt wird. Das Dauern in der Quasi-Zeit bezeichnet den Charakter des Seins des Erscheinenden als „Neutralität“. Wenn ein Erscheinendes in den beiden Zeiten nicht dauert, sondern allzeitig erscheint, charakterisiert dies das Sein des Erscheinenden als „Idealität“. Die Zeit ist also die „Form“, die die Bestimmung des dreifachen Seins als Realität, Neutralität und Idealität ermöglicht. Alle seienden Gegenstände gehören in die Zeit als „Form“. Der Ursprung der Konstitution der seienden Gegenstände ist die Zeit und das Zeitbewußtsein.

Nun stellt Husserl fest, daß die Konstitution des Gegenstandes überhaupt von der intentionalen Struktur des Zeitbewußtseins, die die Konstitution der Zeit ermöglicht, abhängt. Was passiert aber, wenn die Intentionalität noch schwächer wird? Verschwinden dann alle Erscheinungen augenblicklich im Minimum der Intentionalität, also in der Urpassivität, weil das Prinzip von „panta rhei“ herrscht? Husserl unternimmt hier die letztmögliche Rückfrage nach der Urpassivität.

Hier deckt Husserl als einen erstaunlichen Befund auf, daß schon in der Urpassivität eine urtümliche „Form“ (oder „Urstruktur“) besteht. „Nun bedenke ich aber, daß in der Rückfrage sich schließlich die Urstruktur ergibt

---

[4] Edmund Husserl: *Erfahrung und Urteil* (EU), Hamburg: Felix Meiner 1985, S. 189.

[5] Hua VIII S. 86.

in ihrem Wandel der Urhyle etc. mit den Urkinästhesen, Urgefühlen, Urinstinkten. Danach liegt es im Faktum, daß das Urmaterial gerade so verläuft in einer Einheitsform, die Wesensform ist vor der Weltlichkeit." [6]

Diese „Urstruktur" oder „Einheitsform" ist diejenige, die eben in der Urpassivität das augenblickliche Verschwinden der Erscheinungen verhindert und die minimale Breite der Gegenwart ermöglicht. Die Erscheinungen strömen nicht nur, sondern sie stehen auch trotz des „panta rhei". Dieses strömende Stehen gibt eine urtümliche Form.

Husserl dachte die Form hauptsächlich in Hinsicht auf die Zeit. Wie steht es aber mit dem Raum? Der Raum spielt für Husserl bei der Bestimmung des Seins eine sekundäre Rolle. Doch fungiert er auch als Form. Deshalb soll beides, Zeit und Raum, integriert werden. Husserl führt später den Begriff „Weltform" als Integration von Zeit und Raum ein. Die objektive Weltform ermöglicht die Bestimmung des Seins des Gegenstandes. In dieser neuen Auffassung verändert sich der Seinscharakter der Welt. Früher faßte Husserl die Welt als „Gesamtinbegriff von Gegenständen".[7] Das Sein des Gegenstandes wird durch den Akt des Setzens (genauer des Zugehörenlassens in die objektive Zeit) konstituiert. Aber das Sein der Welt ist jetzt verschieden vom Sein der Gegenstände. „Weltbewußtsein ist [...] nicht durch einen im Lebenszusammenhang eigens auftretenden Akt der Seinssetzung [...] erworben."[8] Die Welt oder Weltform ist weder Realität noch Neutralität noch Idealität: Sie ist in Hinsicht auf das Sein vollkommen verschieden von dem, was in ihr zugehört, aber sie ist trotzdem nicht nichts. Sie besitzt schon von Anfang an und vor dem Setzen ein eigentümliches Sein, das das Sein der Gegenstände erst ermöglicht. Wie soll man dieses eigentümliche Sein benennen? Während die Gegenstände dem Sein im obengenannten Sinne (also dem Zugehören in die objektive Weltform) entsprechen, entspricht die Weltform, vor allem die urtümliche Weltform, dem „Vorsein," das dem Sein der Gegenstände voraufgeht.

Nun können wir fragen: Woher entspringt diese „Urstruktur" oder urtümliche „Form"? Sie stammt nicht aus der Struktur der Intentionalität (Retention-Urimpression-Protention) des Bewußtseins, weil das Bewußtsein hier urpassiv ist. Trotz des Minimums der Intentionalität ist die „Urstruktur" oder „Form", die das Bewußtsein später zur vollendeten objektiven Form konstituieren kann, schon vor der Beteiligung des Bewußtseins „gegeben".

Diese Gabe der Urstruktur oder Form besitzt keine Notwendigkeit, weil sie nicht von der Wesensstruktur der intentionalen Struktur des Bewußtseins abhängt. Sie ist ein „Faktum" oder besser ein „Urfaktum", weil sie der Intentionalität und also der Konstitution des normalen Faktums voraufgeht.

---

[6] Hua XV S. 385.
[7] Hua III/1 S. 11.
[8] EU S. 25.

Hier erblickt Husserl eine „Teleologie“. „Also im Faktum liegt es, daß im voraus eine Teleologie statthat.“[9] Wenn die Intentionalität des Bewußtseins fungiert, tendiert sie teleologisch die Erfüllung der Protention. Diese Tendenz gehört zur Wesensstruktur des Bewußtseins. Deshalb ist die Teleologie der Intentionalität nicht erstaunlich. In der Urpassivität fungiert die Intentionalität jedoch noch nicht. Gerade deshalb war diese in der Urpassivität sich vorab bildende Teleologie für Husserl erstaunlich. Er deutet hier „Gott“ an. Dann wäre die Urstruktur oder die Form eine Gabe von Gott.

Aber wir könnten dies auch anders denken: Diese Struktur findet „von selbst“ statt oder sie entsteht durch „Natur“. Hier müssen wir vorsichtig sein. Wie Husserls Denken von Gott typisch zeigt, weist das westliche Denken eine stärkere Tendenz zur Substantialisierung des Grundes oder der Ursache auf. Jenes sucht in der „Substanz“ nach dem „Grund“. Aber hier denken wir mit dem Begriff „Natur“ etwas Verbales: ein Entstehen von sich selbst aus.

So können wir Natur „sachlich“ denken. Dieser sachlichen Deutung nach eröffnete Husserl einen Zugang zur Natur: zum Entstehen von sich selbst aus. Wir können diese letztere Möglichkeit, die Husserl nicht selbst durchdachte, phänomenologisch weiterdenken. Dann treffen wir zuerst auf die Heideggers Auffassung von „*physis*“.

II. Heidegger und die Gabe der physis

Heidegger deckte im griechischen Begriff der „*physis*“ die Gabe der Natur auf. „*physis* ist arche kineseos - ausgängliche Verfügung über das Umschlagen dergestalt, daß jegliches Umschlagende diese Verfügung in ihm selbst hat.“ [10] Die *physis* waltet als arche von Anfang an in Bewegung und Veränderung. Bei Bewegung oder Veränderung entbirgt sich, was bisher sich verbarg. Die *physis* ist Sichentbergenlassen.

Heidegger unternimmt sozusagen eine Strukturanalyse der *physis*. Der Begriff *physis* verbindet sich mit den Begriffen *morphe*, *eidos*, *idea* und *logos*. Diese stehen im Verhältnis einer Familienähnlichkeit. Die Deutung, die Heidegger ihnen gibt, ist einzigartig.

Heidegger sagt: „Eidos meint das Aussehen eines Dinges und eines Seienden überhaupt.“ [11] Und „[...] idea ist jenes, was dem Sehen ein Sichtbares bietet, das Sichbietende, Sichtsame.“ [12] Kurz gesagt, die idea ist eine Art Kraft, die eidos als Aussehen austrägt.

Morphe, die in einer Verbindung zu idea und eidos steht, ist „die Gestel-

---

[9]Hua XV S. 385.

[10]Martin Heidegger: *Wegmarken* (WM), Frankfurt a.M.: Vittorio Klostermann 1967, S. 320.

[11]WM S. 345.

[12]WM S. 345.

lung in das Aussehen." [13] Sie ist keine unbewegliche Form, sondern eine Art Bewegtheit. Morphe ist Sehen- und Seinlassen.

In Heideggers Interpretation von Aristoteles „erhält [...] auch die morphe die Würde einer Wesenbstimmung der *physis*." [14] Die *physis*, die in der Verbindung mit der morphe steht, ist dann Sehen- und Seinlassen des Seienden. [15] In diesem Sinne ist die *physis* das Sein selbst als das Ermöglichende des Seienden. „Die *physis* ist das Sein selbst, kraft dessen das Seiende erst beobachtbar wird und bleibt." [16] Heidegger deutet die *physis* in Hinsicht auf eine Kraft oder Bewegung, die das Seiende sein läßt.

Auf diese Weise legt Heidegger Aristoteles aus. Aber die *physis* bei Aristoteles ist nach Heidegger „ein Abkömmling der anfänglichen *physis*".[17] Was ist dann die anfängliche *physis*? Sie erscheint im Spruch von Heraklit: „*physis* kryptesthai philei" Das Sein liebt es, sich zu verbergen.[18] Dies interpretiert Heidegger folgendermaßen: „Sein ist das sich verbergende Entbergen - *physis* im anfänglichen Sinne".[19] Heidegger faßt das Wort „philein" nicht als „Vermenschlichung" der Natur, sondern sozusagen als Wesenszug der Natur. Dann lautet der Spruch: „Das Aufgehen [der Natur] dem Sichverbergen schenkt's die Gunst."[20] Die *physis* (*φύσις*) erscheint, aber gleichzeitig verbirgt sie sich. Diese beiden Seiten sind die Gabe der Natur selbst.

Die *physis* ist bei Heraklit synonym mit dem *logos*, weil beide das, was bisher sich verbarg, erscheinen lassen. Das Sein bedeutet bei Heraklit vor allem *logos*. Heraklit benutzt das Wort *logos*, um das Sein als *physis* zu bezeichnen. [21]

Was ist aber der *logos*? Heidegger sagt: „[...] *logos* gehört zu legein, und dies besagt und ist dasselbe Wort wie unser *lesen* [...] *Lesen*, sammeln meint: mehreres Zerstreutes zusammenbringen auf Eines und dieses Eine zugleich beibringen und zustellen (para) - Wohin? In das Unverborgene der Anwesung [(parousia = ousia(apousia)]. Legein [...] meint soviel wie: vordem Verborgenes offenbar machen, es in seiner Anwesung sich zeigen lassen."[22] Weiter sagt Heidegger, daß *logos* und legein das in-seiner-Anwesung-Vorliegenlassen des Anwesenden sind.[23]

---

[13]WM S. 346.
[14]WM S. 345.
[15]Vgl. WM S. 83.
[16]HGA 40 S. 17.
[17]WM S. 370.
[18]WM S. 370.
[19]WM S. 371.
[20]HGA 55 S. 131.
[21]Vgl. Martin Heidegger: *Der Satz vom Grunde* (SG), Pfullingen: Günther Neske 1957, S. 179ff.
[22]WM S. 349.
[23]SG S. 179.

Aber sind *physis* und *logos* wirklich dasselbe? Die *physis* ist das Seinlassen, der *logos* das Vorliegenlassen. Gibt es keine Differenz oder Verschiebung zwischen beiden, wenn auch beides zum Teil sich deckt? Läßt der *logos* das, was die *physis* sein läßt, lediglich „zustellen"?

Überdies identifiziert Heidegger *logos* mit *polemos*: „*Polemos* und *logos* sind dasselbe." Heideggers Interpretation lautet: „Der hier gemeinte Kampf [=polemos] ist ursprünglicher Kampf; denn er läßt die Kämpfenden allererst als solche entspringen; er ist nicht ein bloßes Benennen von Vorhandenem. Der Kampf entwirft und entwickelt erst das Un-erhörte, bislang Un-gesagte und Un-gedachte. Dieser Kampf wird dann von den Schaffenden, den Dichtern, Denkern, Staatsmännern getragen. Sie werfen dem überwältigenden Walten [der *physis*] den Block des Werkes entgegen und bannen in dieses die damit eröffnete Welt. Mit diesen Werken kommt erst das Walten, die *physis*, im Anwesenden zum Stand. Das Seiende wird jetzt erst als solches seiend. Dieses Weltwerden ist die eigentliche Geschichte."[24]

Kann der Kampf [= polemos] aber die *physis* betrügen, wenn er „von den Schaffenden, den Dichtern, Denkern, Staatsmännern getragen" wird? Wird die *physis* mit ihren Werken mehr und anders zugestellt als früher? Kann „die eigentliche Geschichte," die erst hier entsteht, aufgrund dieser Differenz die Geschichte der „Verfehlung" werden? Findet nie eine Differenz oder Verschiebung zwischen Natur und Geschichte statt?

Aber Heidegger minimalisiert die Möglichkeit der Differenz. Mit dem Begriff „homologein" werden alle Differenzen in die „harmonia" überführt: In der ursprünglichen Natur waltet harmonia. Hier stoßen wir auf eine Teleologie in Heideggers Denken.

III. Merleau-Ponty und Naturphilosophie

Husserl fragte nach dem Ermöglichenden der Bestimmung des Seins des Seienden. Er fand es in der Weltform. Heidegger fragte nach der *physis* als Sein, das das Seiende ermöglicht. Sie war die Kraft oder Bewegung, die ohne Beteiligung des Bewußtseins das Seiende hervorbringt. Der späte Merleau-Ponty fragte nach dem Ermöglichenden der Bestimmung des Seins des Seienden, aber für ihn war das Sein nicht die Weltform, sondern sozusagen Weltmaterial, das den „Sinn" des Seienden ermöglicht. Es ist auch eine Kraft, die ohne Beteiligung des Bewußtseins das Was-Seiende und den Unterschied des Sinnes von Subjekt und Objekt stiftet. In dieser Auffassung entwickelte er im Zusammenhang mit Schelling eine phänomenologische Naturphilosophie.

Denken wir einen Fall, wo ein Seiendes, das den Sinn von „Weiß" besitzt, erscheint. Erst wenn es als „Weiß"-Seiendes thematisch wird, wird sein Hintergrund z.B. als „Grün" thematisiert. Wie steht es aber mit dem Hin-

---

[24]HGA 40 S. 66f.

tergrund vor dieser Thematisierung? Davor war er noch nicht ein „Grün"-Seiendes. Der Sinn des Hintergrundes war noch nicht als Sinn gegenständlich thematisiert. Er war trotzdem weder nichts noch un-sinnig. Er war sozusagen vor-sinnig, obwohl er noch nicht thematisch erkannt wurde. In der Terminologie Merleau-Pontys war er das „vorgegenständliche Sein," [25] das „Vor-Sein," [26] der „Prototyp des Seins," [27] das „wilde Sein," das „rohe Sein." Wir nennen dieses Sein, das den Vor-Sinn besitzt, *Weltmaterial*. Es ist keine Materie im naturwissenschaftlichen Sinn, sondern eine Vorstufe des „Sinnes."

Das Weltmaterial geht dem Was-Seienden vorauf. Zwischen beidem liegt ein dimensionaler Unterschied. Wir können das Was-Seiende erkennen. Wie steht es aber mit dem Weltmaterial? Merleau-Ponty erblickt im Chiasmus einen Zugang zum Weltmaterial. „Chiasmus" ist ursprünglich ein Begriff der antiken Rhetorik, der dem griechischen „x" entstammt. Merleau-Ponty eignet sich ihn als einen ontologischen Begriff an.

Wie äußert sich jemand, der nur zweidimensionale Begriffe kennt, beim Anblick einer dreidimensionalen Säule? Er sieht diese von oben (vertikal) und von ihren Seiten her (Himmeltal) und sagt vielleicht: „Dieser Kreis ist viereckig, dieses Viereck ist kreisförmig." Hier kreuzen sich die beiden Sätze: ein typischer Chiasmus. Aber „kreisförmig" und „viereckig" sind in ihren Sinngehalten verschieden. Deshalb ist der obengenannte Satz für jemanden, der nur zweidimensionale Begriffe kennt, „widersinnig." Für ihn sind „kreisförmig" und „viereckig" miteinander unverträglich. Für Andere jedoch übersteigt der Chiasmus den dimensionalen Unterschied und bahnt einen Weg zur dreidimensionalen, identischen Säule. In diesem Denkmodell liegt der Unterschied zwischen dem Zweidimensionalen und dem Dreidimensionalen. Aber wir können dies zum Unterschied zwischen dem Thematischen und dem Vorthematischen erweitern. Einige Sätze des Chiasmus bei Merleau-Ponty heraushebend können wir dieses Denkmodell anwenden: „Das Chiasma[28] ist [...] Austausch [...] zwischen dem Wahrnehmenden und dem Wahrgenommenen:

---

[25] Maurice Merleau-Ponty: *Résumé de cours* (RC), Paris: Gallimard 1968, S. 154; *La nature* (Nature), Paris: Seuil 1995, S. 164.

[26] Maurice Merleau-Ponty: *Le visible et l'invisible* (VeI), Paris: Gallimard 1964, S. 266. Vgl. auch die deutsche Übersetzung: *Das Sichtbare und das Unsichtbare*, übersetzt von Regula Giuliani und Bernhard Waldenfels, München: Wilhelm Fink 1986.

[27] VeI S. 164.

[28] Dieses Wort „Chiasma," das von Valéry stammt, besitzt die gleiche Bedeutung wie Chiasmus.

Was als Ding beginnt, endet als Bewußtsein des Dinges,
was als *Bewußtseinszustand* beginnt, endet als Ding."[29]

„Es gibt einen Leib des Geistes
und einen Geist des Leibes
und einen Chiasmus zwischen beiden." [30]

Mit dem Chiasmus drückt Merleau-Ponty das identische Vor-Sein(Fleisch) zwischen und unter beidem aus. Aus dem identischen Vor-Sein differenzieren sich das Bewußtsein und das Ding, das Subjekt und das Objekt. Nur jeweils dieses beide wird thematisch. Das Vor-Sein selbst bleibt unthematisch, obwohl es schon vor der Differenzierung gefühlt wird.

Wie differenziert sich aber beides? Merleau-Ponty sieht im Berühren (also im Selbstberühren des Fleisches) einen Anlaß zur Differenzierung. Das geschieht, „wenn meine rechte Hand meine linke berührt, während sie die Dinge abtastet, wodurch das *berührende Subjekt* zum berührten wird und sich unter die Dinge begibt, sodaß das Berühren sich inmitten der Welt und wie zwischen den Dingen abspielt." [31] Das Fleisch, das zuerst noch kein Ding und kein Subjekt war, differenziert sich und findet sich selbst erst beim Selbstberühren als Berührtes und Berührendes. Merleau-Ponty nennt dieses Geschehen „Aufklaffen oder Spaltung." [32] Das ist ein (verbales) Geschehen in der Dimension, wo die Intentionalität des Bewußtseins noch nicht fungiert. Ein solches verbales und vor-intentionales Geschehen gehört zur „Natur."

Bei diesem „natürlichen" Geschehen entstehen das Subjekt und das Ding. Doch zugleich bricht eine Kluft nicht nur zwischen dem Subjekt und dem Ding auf, sondern auch zwischen dem Subjekt und der ursprünglichen Natur. Wegen dieser Kluft kann das Subjekt die ursprüngliche Natur nicht mehr wieder-holen. Der Phänomenologie bei Merleau-Ponty begegnet eine Schwierigkeit. „Die Phänomenologie des vor-reflexiven Seins" [33] oder der ursprünglichen Natur muß eine neue Methodologie des Wieder-holens gewinnen. Merleau-Ponty spricht diesbezüglich von der „Dialektik von Anschauung-Reflexion."

„Die Dialektik von Auschauung-Reflexion ist keine Verfehlung in Hinsicht auf unsere Erkentnis vom Absoluten. Die Zirkelhaftigkeit des Wissens legt uns nicht vor das Gesicht, sondern ins Milieu des Absoluten." [34]

Anschauung bedeutet hier intellektuelle Anschauung: „[...] die ‚intellektuelle Anschauung,' die keine okkulte Fähigkeit, sondern die Wahrnehmung

[29]VeI S. 268.
[30]VeI S. 313.
[31]VeI S. 176.
[32]VeI S. 192.
[33]Nature S. 66.
[34]Nature S. 73.

selbst ist, bevor sie in die Idee reduziert wird, die in sich selbst schlafende Wahrnehmung, wo alle Dinge das Ich sind, weil ich noch nicht das Reflexionssubjekt bin.“ [35] Kurz gesagt, die Anschauung als intellektuelle Anschauung ist die Erschlossenheit des Fleisches, die schon vor der reflexiven Erkentnis entsteht. Diese Erschlossenheit ist passiver als die des „Bewußtseins“ bei Husserl und noch passiver als die des „Daseins“ bei Heidegger. Sie gehört zur urpassiven Schicht, und ist die Erschlossenheit des „Natur-seins.“ Sie wird von Merleau-Ponty auch als „*Erkennen durch Gefühl*“ [36] bezeichnet.

Die Reflexion wird nun mit dieser Anschauung verbunden. Die normale Reflexion kann wegen der Kluft zwischen dem Subjekt und der ursprünglichen Natur diese nicht wieder-holen. Die Reflexion verfehlt also die Natur. Merleau-Ponty versetzt daher Reflexion und Anschauung in eine zirkelhaftige Beziehung: Die Anschauung motiviert eine neue Reflexion, um die Verschiebung, die mit der ersten Reflexion stattfand, zu korrigieren. Hier kommt es zu einem Zierkel des Wissens.

Wenn dieser Zierkel aber ein einfacher Wiedervollzug wäre, würde er zu einer Sisyphosarbeit. Aber für Merleau-Ponty entwickelt das Fleisch (also das Erkennen durch Gefühl) sich selbst allmählich in dieser Kreisbewegung. Die Dialektik von Anschauung und Reflexion ist deshalb die Entwicklung des Selbsterkennens des Fleisches. Merleau-Ponty spricht in dieser Hinsicht auch von einer „Überreflexion.“[37] In der Selbstentwicklung und im Selbsterkennen des Fleisches entsteht Philosophie. Diese ist Naturphilosophie. Sie transzendiert nicht die Natur, sondern sie verkörpert ein kreisbewegendes Selbstwissen der Natur innerhalb der Natur selbst. Sie ist sozusagen eine Innen-Naturphilosphie. Deshalb sagt Merleau-Ponty: „[...] die Naturphilosophie, die nie eine Theorie, sondern ein Leben innerhalb der Natur ist.“[38] Die Naturphilosophie vollendet allmählich die Natur. Diese Auffassung ist von Schelling stark beeinflußt. Schelling sagt: „Ueber die Natur philosophieren heißt die Natur schaffen.“[39] Diese neuzeitliche Endgestalt einer Metaphysik der Natur übernimmt Merleau-Ponty.

Hier zeichnet sich eine starke Teleologie ab. Merleau-Ponty diagnostiziert die gleiche Teleologie in der Beziehung von Natur und Mensch. Die Natur läßt den Menschen als Bewußtseinssubjekt entstehen. In diesem Sinn verkörpert sie Elternschaft. Aber sie ist kein Geist, der den Sinn konstituiert. In der Natur gibt es noch keinen vollendeten „Sinn,“ sondern nur den „Anfang des Sinnes.“ „Was in der Natur wohnt, ist nicht der Geist, sondern

---

[35] RC S. 107.
[36] VeI S. 302.
[37] VeI S. 61.
[38] Nature S. 73.
[39] Friedrich Wilhelm Joseph Schelling: *Schellings Werke*, München: Beck'sche Verlagsbuchhandlung 1977, Bd. II S. 13.

der Anfang des Sinnes [...]." [40] Oder sie ist nur „eine Arrangierung des Materials, die den Sinn vorbereitet, den der Mensch ihr gibt." [41] Die Menschen (oder die Bewußtseinssubjekte) vollenden den von der Natur vorbereiteten Vor-Sinn hin zum „Sinn." In dieser Hinsicht sind die Menschen die Eltern der Natur. Merleau-Ponty sagt: „Wir sind die Eltern einer Natur, deren Kinder wir sind." [42]

IV. Harmonie und Begegnung

Husserl stellte eine Teleologie im Urfaktum der Gabe der Weltform fest, und Heidegger fand eine „harmonia" zwischen *physis* und *logos* (homologein). Jetzt sehen wir bei Merleau-Ponty eine noch stärkere Teleologie. Nicht nur der Chiasmus, sondern auch die Natur ist bei Merleau-Ponty „Wahrheit der prästabilierten Harmonie." [43]

Die Antike faßte das Verhältnis von Natur und Mensch harmonisch auf. Die europäische Neuzeit und bezeichnenderweise die Naturwissenschaften interpretierten die Natur als eine Summe von Gegenständen und eben als „Bestände" und entsprechend die Menschen als Subjekte. Zwischen der Natur und den Menschen brach eine große Differenz auf und wurde so ein Streitverhältnis begründet. Die Auffassung der Antike lebte nur in einigen Vertretern des Romantik (z.B. bei Schelling) fort. Die Phänomenologie, die den Ursprung der Wissenschaften auslegen will, entdeckt auf eine noch strengere Weise Teleologie und Harmonie von Natur und Mensch neu. Die Freilegungen der Gabe des Vorseins der Weltform bei Husserl, der Kraft oder Bewegung des Seinlassens (Sichentbergenlassens und auch Sichverbergenlassens) bei Heidegger sowie der Genesis des Sinns und des Unterschieds von Subjekt und Objekt bei Merleau-Ponty waren wichtige Beiträge. Cho eröffnet jedoch noch eine andere Möglichkeit der Phänomenologie: den Dialog zwischen dem westlichen und dem östlichen Denken. Dieser Dialog gibt uns eine Chance.

Einerseits gibt er die Chance zur Vertiefung gemeinsamer Probleme. Cho zitiert und erklärt einen Aphorismus von Laotse: „Unfaßbar und unerkennbar ist es (das Tao), aber es birgt Formen in seinem Inneren. Unerkennbar und unfaßbar ist es, aber es umschließt Kraft."[44] Wir können diesen Aphorismus auf die phänomenologische Analyse der „Form" und der „Kraft" beziehen;[45] und wir können im östlichen Denken eine wichtige phänomeno-

---

[40] Nature S. 68.
[41] Nature S. 67.
[42] Nature S. 68.
[43] VeI S. 315.
[44] Kah Kyung Cho: *Bewußtsein und Natursein*, Freiburg/München: Karl Alber 1987, S. 181.
[45] Vgl. meinen Aufsatz "The *physis* of Consciousness and Metaphysics" [erscheint in den Akten der Tagung "The Phenomenological Conference on Self-Awareness, Temporality and Alterity," Kopenhagen].

logische Analyse der Natur finden.

Andererseits gibt ein weiterer Aphorismus von Laotse (Sektion 5) die andere Auffassung der Natur wieder: „Der Himmel und die Erde sind nicht gnädig." Dieser Spruch verneint die gnädige Gabe der Natur und also auch die Harmonie von Natur und Mensch, die die obengenannten drei Phänomenologen erblickten. Noch negativer spricht Emanuel Levinas von der radikalen Äußerlichkeit der Natur, die gegenüber den Menschen indifferent oder feindlich sei.[46] Die so aufgefaßte Natur oder das „Il y a" bei Levinas gibt nichts. Die Naturauffassung Levinas ist von der jüdischen Tradition stark beeinflußt.

Mein Absehen gilt aber weder dem interkulturellen Vergleich von Denktraditionen noch der Verleugnung der Gabe der Natur. Mittels einer Kontrastierung möchte ich vielmehr den Grundzug (und auch die Möglichkeit der Verfehlung) der obengenannten Naturauffassungen der drei Phänomenologen noch deutlicher machen: Husserl, Heidegger und Merleau-Ponty suchten von der Seite einer gnädigen Gabe her nach einer Harmonie zwischen Natur und Mensch. Doch der Aphorismus Laotses und die These Levinas belegen die Auffassung, daß die Gabe der Natur nicht immer gnädig ist. Die Gabe der Natur kann schließlich gar ein giftiges Gift (ein Gift) sein. [47] Stets ist die Möglichkeit zu einer Disharmonie im Verhältnis von Natur und Mensch gegeben. Selbst die „guten" Menschen können eine Aufnahme der Gabe der Natur verfehlen, sollte diese denn gnädig sein, und können die Harmonie zerbrechen. Um eine phänomenologische Metaphysik der Natur zu entwickeln, muß auch die Möglichkeit einer Disharmonie gedacht werden. Die Begegnung zwischen verschiedenen Denktraditionen ist selbst die Gabe einer Chance zu solchem Durch- und Umdenken.

Es gibt jedoch unendliche Möglichkeiten der Begegnung: nicht nur zwischen dem Westlichen und Östlichen, sondern z.B. auch dem Griechischen und Jüdischen usw. Jede Begegnung kann unser bisheriges Denken als eine Verfehlung erweisen. Ich erwarte deshalb von einer phänomenologischen Metaphysik der Natur nicht „die Willfähigkeit und den Beistand eines Mithelfers"[48] als eines homologischen Denkers, sondern einfach die Begegnung mit den Anders-Denkenden. Erst an der Kreuzung zwischen der eigenen Naturauffassung und derjenigen anderer Kulturen wird die phänomenologische Metaphysik der Natur des weiteren auch den Zugang zur phänome-

[46] Überdies sagt Levinas, daß eine solche Äußerlichkeit der Natur zur westlichen Denkweise gehört. Aber diese Denkweise entstammt nicht schlechthin der westlichen Tradition, sondern vielleicht genuin der jüdischen.

[47] Fink sagt etwas Ähnliches: „Das Gebende ist in eins auch das Nehmende. [...] Das von der Natur, von der *physis* ins Sein Gelassene ist also gleich von ihr verlassen, sofern es überlassen wird an das Wagnis der Lust, dazusein." (Eugen Fink: *Welt und Endlichkeit*, Würzburg: Könighausen u. Neumann 1990, S. 208.)

[48] KrV A S. XXI.

nologischen Metaphysik der Sitten eröffnen. [49]

[49] Ich sehe einen fruchtbaren Ansatz zu einer phänomenologischen Metaphysik der Sitten in Husserls Begriff „Strahlensystem" der Welt (vgl. Edmund Husserl: *Briefwechsel*, Dordrecht/Boston/London: Kluwer Academic Publishers 1994, Bd. III S. 498). Dieser Ansatz könnte das „Seinlassen des Anderen" als ein zentrales Problem der phänomenologischen Metaphysik der Sitten ermöglichen (vgl. Jacques Derrida: *L'écriture et la différence*, Paris: Éditions de Seuil 1967, S. 202). Dies jedoch verweist auf eine andere Problematik.

* Dr. Hans Rainer Sepp hat sich des sprachlichen Gewandes dieses Aufsatzes angenommen. Dafür danke ich ihm herzlich.

Das An-sich-Sein und die verschiedenen Gesichter der Welt

Nam-In Lee

„Die Grundfrage der Phänomenologie läßt sich formulieren als die Frage nach dem Ursprung der Welt“[1], so schrieb einmal E. Fink. Diese Finksche These der Frage nach dem Ursprung der Welt als die Grundfrage der Phänomenologie wird vor allem dadurch bestätigt, daß fast alle phänomenologischen Analysen, die Husserl in seiner späteren Schaffensperiode durchgeführt hat, sich irgendwie zur Weltproblematik zusammenschließen. In diesem Zusammenhang ist es kein Zufall, daß man in den Schriften aus der späteren Schaffensperiode Husserls auf bunte Mannigfaltigkeiten des Weltbegriffs stößt wie Ideenwelt, mathematische Welt, physikalische Welt, geistige Welt, moralische Welt, soziale Welt, personalistische Welt, ästhetische Welt, Umwelt und Lebenswelt. Transzendental-phänomenologisch betrachtet, stellen diese Welten, wie unten gezeigt wird, mannigfaltige Formen der konstituierten Welt, oder was dasselbe heißt, der mundanen Welt dar. Freilich kann dieser Katalog der mundanen Welt durch die Einbeziehung der weiteren mundanen Weltbegriffe erweitert werden. Außer diesen mundanen Weltbegriffen findet man aber in der Spätphänomenologie Husserls einen ganz anderen Begriff der Welt. Es handelt sich dabei um das An-sich-Sein der Welt, also um die Welt, die aus dem All der transzendentalen Subjektivitäten besteht. In diesem Zusammenhang ist schon an einer Stelle der *Ideen II* von der „ ‚Welt‘ des reinen, phänomenologisch reduzierten Bewußtseins“(Hua IV, 211)[2] die Rede, also von der Welt, die Husserl später „die transzendentale Überwelt“(Hua XV, 591) oder „das transzendentale Monadenall“ nennt.

Der jeweiligen Welt, sei es der mundanen, sei es der transzendentalen Welt, entspricht die jeweilige Einstellung als eine habituelle Apperzeptionsweise des Subjekts. Das besagt nun, daß die mannigfaltigen Unterschiede, die zwischen den verschiedenen Welten feststellbar sind, „mit kardinalen Unterschieden der ‚Einstellung‘, mit grundverschiedenen Auffassungs- bzw. Erfahrungsarten“(Hua IV, 211) zusammenhängen. Die Einstellung als die habituelle Apperzeptionsweise des Subjekts birgt in sich ein Bewußtsein, das sich auf die Welt bezieht. Dieses Bewußtsein will ich mit Husserl im Unterschied zu dem Bewußtsein, das auf das jeweilige Seiende gerichtet ist, als

---

[1] E. Fink, „Die phänomenologische Philosophie Edmund Husserls in der gegenwärtigen Kritik“, in: *Studien zur Phänomenologie 1930-1939*, Den Haag 1966, 101.

[2] Die Husserliana-Bände sind zitiert mit der Angabe der Abkürzung „Hua“, der Nummer des Bandes und der Seitenzahl in Klammern.

das „Weltbewußtsein“ [3] bezeichnen. Wegen des untrennbaren Zusammenhangs zwischen der Welt und der dementsprechenden Einstellung bzw. dem Weltbewußtsein ist es zur Bestimmung der Struktur der Welt unumgänglich, auf die Struktur der Einstellung bzw. des Weltbewußtseins einzugehen.

Ich stelle mir nun die Aufgabe, die Finksche These etwas konkreter zu bestimmen. Zur Erfüllung dieser Aufgabe will ich zuerst im Hinblick auf die Wesenskorrelation zwischen Welt und Einstellung bzw. Weltbewußtsein die Grundstruktur der natürlichen Welt(1), der physikalischen Welt(2) und der transzendentalen Überwelt(3) enthüllen. Daran anschließend will ich versuchen, das Verhältnis von verschiedenen Welten zu bestimmen(4), wobei es einerseits um das Verhältnis zwischen mundanen Welten untereinander und andererseits um das Verhältnis zwischen den mundanen Welten und der transzendentalen Überwelt geht. Durch diese Analyse wird sich zeigen, was die Finksche These konkreter bedeutet.

I. Natürliche Einstellung und natürliche Welt

Die natürliche Welt[4], also die alltägliche Lebenswelt, ist immerfort für mich da, „solange ich natürlich dahinlebe.“(Hua III/1, 59) Sie ist diejenige Umwelt, die mir erscheint, solange ich natürlich eingestellt bin. Die natürliche Welt ist also das noematische Korrelat der natürlichen Einstellung und, um deren Grundstruktur zu enthüllen, ist es nötig, die natürliche Einstellung und das Weltbewußtsein, das in dieser enthalten ist, in Betracht zu ziehen.

In der natürlichen Einstellung führe ich mein Leben als eine Person, die verschiedenen Personenverbänden angehört. In der natürlichen Einstellung erscheinen für mich die anderen Menschen nicht als bloße Sachen, sondern ebenfalls als Personen wie ich, die mit mir verschiedene Personenverbände bilden können. Die natürliche Einstellung bedeutet also diejenige Einstellung, in der die Personen miteinander ihr Leben führen. Bei der natürlichen Einstellung handelt es sich um „die personalistische Einstellung, in der wir allzeit sind, wenn wir miteinander leben, zueinander sprechen, einander im Gruße die Hände reichen, in Liebe und Abneigung, in Gesinnung und Tat, in Rede und Gegenrede aufeinander bezogen sind.“(Hua IV, 183)

---

[3]Das Problem des Weltbewußtseins bildet ein wichtiges Thema der Spätphänomenologie Husserls. Das Problem des Weltbewußtseins behandelt Hussserl in Hua I, 97; Hua VI, 105, 111, 146; Hua XXIX, 191ff. 247ff. Ich habe die Struktur des Weltbewußtseins, das sich auf die natürliche Umwelt oder die vorwissenschaftliche Lebenswelt bezieht, ausführlich in Betracht gezogen in: N.-I. Lee, *Edmund Husserls Phänomenologie der Instinkte*, Dordrecht/Boston/London 1993, 144-150.

[4]Die natürliche Welt ist nichts anderes als die alltägliche Lebenswelt. Wegen der Vieldeutigkeit des Begriffs der Lebenswelt benutze ich in diesem Aufsatz den Begriff der Lebenswelt nicht.

Die natürliche Einstellung als „eine durchaus natürliche Einstellung“ unterscheidet sich also strikt von der „künstlichen Einstellung, die erst durch besondere Hilfsmittel gewonnen und gewahrt werden mußte.“(Hua IV, 183)

In der natürlichen Einstellung, in der ich anderen Subjekten als Personen begegne, erscheint die materielle Natur nicht als objektive Natur, also als der Gegenstand der physikalischen Naturwissenschaft, sondern eben als die Umgebung, in der wir unser Leben führen. Diese Umgebung enthält nicht die physikalischen Gegenstände, die für unser alltägliches Leben belanglos sind, sondern, wie Husserl sagt, „Gebrauchsobjekte (Kleider, Hausgeräte, Waffen, Werkzeuge), Kunstwerke, literarische Produkte, Mittel religiöser, rechtlicher Handlungen (Siegel, Amtsketten, Krönungsinsignien, kirchliche Symbole usw.)“ (Hua IV,182), die für unser alltägliches Leben ihren eigenen Sinn haben.

Bestimmte Gruppen von Dingen in der natürlichen Einstellung, beispielsweise der Nagel, der Hammer, der Ziegel usw., sind nicht zusammenhanglos, sondern sie alle sind als Zeuge zum Hausbau da und insofern bilden sie durch die Sinnesverweisung einen Verweisungszusammenhang, der mit Husserl als der Himmelt dieser Dinge bezeichnet werden kann. Jedes Ding hat für unser alltägliches Leben einen ihm eigenen Sinn, was darauf beruht, daß es in einem bestimmten Himmelt erscheint. Kein Ding ist also ohne den Himmelt vorstellbar, in dem es erscheinen kann. Ebenfalls bilden andere Gruppen von Dingen, beispielsweise der Schreibtisch, der Stuhl, der Kugelschreiber usw., durch die ihnen eigene Sinnesverweisung einen anderen Himmelt. Eine andere Gruppe von Dingen wie beispielsweise der Löffel, die Gabel, der Topf usw., bilden durch die ihnen eigene Sinnesverweisung einen weiteren Himmelt.

Es ist also möglich, in der natürlichen Einstellung mannigfaltige Horizonte der Dinge festzustellen. In diesem Zusammenhang ist es aber von großer Bedeutung, darauf aufmerksam zu machen, daß die mannigfaltigen Himmelte der Dinge in der natürlichen Einstellung nicht zusammenhanglos sind, sondern daß sie insofern aufeinander verweisen, als sie alle gerade die Himmelte für das alltägliche Leben des Menschen darstellen. Es ist also klar, daß alle Himmelte der Dinge in der natürlichen Einstellung in einen Verweisungszusammenhang des Sinnes als den Himmelt aller möglichen Himmelte der Dinge eingebettet sind, in dem sie alle ihren eigenen Sinn haben können. Dieser Himmelt aller Himmelte oder der universale Hori-zont der Dinge ist nichts anderes als die natürliche Welt als das noematische Korrelat der natürlichen Einstellung. Nur in diesem universalen Himmelt, also im Lichte der natürlichen Welt, kann für uns das jeweilige Ding mit seinem eigenen Sinn erscheinen, wie Husserl an einer Stelle der *Krisis*-Abhandlung schreibt: „Dinge, Objekte (immer rein lebensweltlich verstanden) sind ‚gegeben‘, als für uns jeweils ... geltende, aber prinzipiell nur so, daß sie bewußt sind als Dinge, als Objekte im Welt Himmelt. Jedes ist etwas, ‚etwas aus‘ der Welt, der uns ständig als Himmelt bewußten.“(Hua VI, 146)

Da das jeweilige Ding in der natürlichen Einstellung für mich nur im Lichte des Welt Himmeltes erscheinen kann, bin ich mir in jedem Moment, wenn mir ein Ding explizit erscheint, implizit dessen bewußt, daß vor dem Erscheinen der Dinge die natürliche Welt als der UniversalHimmelt der Dinge schon für mich da ist. Dem Bewußtsein der Dinge geht also notwendig das implizite Bewußtsein von der natürlichen Welt voran, das ich als das natürliche Weltbewußtsein bezeichnen möchte. Dieses Bewußtsein ist nichts anderes als das implizit vollzogene unmittelbare Bewußtsein davon, daß die natürliche Welt für mich existiert. Das natürliche Weltbewußtsein enthält in sich also das Moment der unmittelbaren Gewißheit der Existenz der Welt, die Husserl deshalb „die Generalthesis der natürlichen Einstellung" (Hua III/1, 60) nennt, weil es dabei nicht um eine Thesis der einzelnen Objekte geht, sondern ausschließlich um diejenige Thesis, die die Welt als den universalen Himmelt aller Dinge als existierend setzt und als solche den universellen oder generellen Modus zeigt.

Zur Bestimmung der Struktur der natürlichen Welt ist es unbedingt nötig, die Struktur des natürlichen Weltbewußtseins zu enthüllen. In diesem Zusammenhang ist folgendes zu bemerken.

1. Soeben wurde erwähnt, daß das natürliche Weltbewußtsein in sich das Moment der unmittelbaren Gewißheit der Existenz der Welt enthält. Dies besagt, daß das Subjekt in jedem Puls der natürlichen Einstellung eine implizite Vorstellung von der natürlichen Welt hat. Im Hinblick auf diese implizite Vorstellung läßt sich die natürliche Welt als eine Vorstellungswelt bestimmen. Das natürliche Weltbewußtsein besteht aber nicht nur aus der impliziten Vorstellung, sondern auch aus anderen Komponenten, nämlich der universalen Stimmung und dem universalen Willen, die mit der impliziten Vorstellung verbunden auf die Welt gerichtet sind. Wegen dieser beiden Komponenten läßt sich die natürliche Welt als die Güterwelt und zugleich als die praktische Umwelt bestimmen. Die Vorstellungswelt, die Güterwelt und die praktische Umwelt stellen also drei Aspekte der natürlichen Welt dar.[5]

2. Das natürliche Weltbewußtsein bedeutet das Bewußtsein von der natürlichen Welt als einer räumlichen Realität. Die natürliche Welt ist also eine räumliche Welt. Dabei gilt es unbedingt zu beachten, daß es sich bei der Räumlichkeit der natürlichen Welt nicht um die objektive Räumlichkeit der physikalischen Wissenschaft handelt. Bei dem Raum der natülichen Welt handelt es sich um einen Lebensraum, in dem sich das Leben der Subjekte abspielt. Deshalb hat jeder Teilbereich dieses Lebensraums seinen eigenen Sinn, der mit keinem anderen austauschbar ist, beispielsweise das Universitätsgelände, die Kirche, der Tempel, der Berg, die Ackerfläche usw. Insofern unterscheidet sich der Lebensraum strikt von dem objektiven Raum

[5]Diesen Problemzusammenhang habe ich ausführlich behandelt in *Edmund Husserls Phänomenologie der Instinkte*, 144ff.

der physikalischen Wissenschaft, der homogen und mathematisch bestimmbar ist.

3. Darüber hinaus bedeutet das natürliche Weltbewußtsein immer ein Bewußtsein von der natürlichen Welt als einer zeitlichen Realität. Bei der Zeitlichkeit der natürlichen Welt handelt es sich ebenfalls nicht um eine objektive Zeitlichkeit der physikalischen Wissenschaft, sondern um eine alltägliche Zeitlichkeit der Subjekte, wofür zwar die lebensweltliche Meßbarkeit von großer Bedeutung ist, aber die mathematische und objektive Meßbarkeit überhaupt keinen Sinn hat. Die alltägliche Zeitlichkeit in diesem Sinn umfaßt auch die Dimension der Geschichtlichkeit. Dadurch zeigt sich die natürliche Welt als eine zeitliche und geschichtliche Welt.

4. Das natürliche Weltbewußtsein ist wie alle Sonderbewußtseinspulse kein solipsistisches Bewußtsein, das ohne den Einfluß von und auf die anderen Subjekte bestehen könnte, sondern von Anfang an ein intersubjektives Bewußtsein, das sich im beständigen Kontakt mit anderen Subjekten befindet. Dementsprechend kann man mit Husserl von der „Intersubjektivität des Weltbewußtseins" (Hua XXIX, 197) sprechen. Die Intersubjektivität des natürlichen Weltbewußtseins besagt, daß die natürliche Welt ihrem Wesen nach eine intersubjektive Umwelt ist.

II. Naturalistische Einstellung und physikalische Welt

Die natürliche Einstellung kann sich unter Umständen in die naturalistische Einstellung umwandeln und dementsprechend kann aus der natürlichen Welt die naturalistische Welt, die nichts anderes als die physikalische Welt ist, entstehen. Um diesen Wandel der Einstellung bzw. der Welt zu verstehen, werfen wir einen kurzen Blick auf den Bewußtseinsstrom.

Im Bewußtseinsstrom der natürlichen Einstellung lassen sich mannigfaltige Intentionen, passive und aktive, objektivierende und nicht-objektivierende usw. beobachten. Die verschiedenen Intentionen sind im Bewußtseinsstrom nicht zusammenhanglos, sondern dort kann man mannigfaltige Zusammenspiele zwischen den Intentionen beobachten. Ziehen wir nun unter den verschiedenen Zusammenspielen der Intentionen dasjenige zwischen den objektivierenden und den nicht-objektivierenden Intentionen in Betracht. In der natürlichen Einstellung kann auf Grund einer objektivierenden Intention eine nicht-objektivierende Intention entstehen. Ein typisches Beispiel dafür wäre die Entstehung einer auf die Schönheit einer Blume gerichteten Intention aus einer auf das Sein derselben Blume gerichteten Intention. Freilich ist auch der umgekehrte Fall möglich, daß auf Grund einer nicht-objektivierenden Intention eine objektivierende Intention entsteht.

Bezeichnen wir nun im Hinblick auf dieses Zusammenspiel zwischen der objektivierenden und der nicht-objektivierenden Intention diejenige Intention, die die Grundlage der Entstehung einer anderen Intention bildet, als die fundierende Intention, dagegen die auf Grund der fundierenden Intention neu entstandene Intention als die fundierte Intention. Die fundierende

Intention übernimmt dabei die dienende Funktion für die fundierte Intention. Deshalb kann sie die dienende Intention genannt werden. Die fundierte Intention dagegen übernimmt der fundierenden Intention gegenüber die herrschende Funktion und kann deshalb herrschende Intention genannt werden. Im Bewußtseinsstrom der natürlichen Einstellung kann mal die objektivierende, mal die nicht-objektivierende Intention die herrschende Funktion übernehmen. Das Charakteritistische der natürlichen Einstellung ist dabei, daß weder die objektivierende Intention noch die nicht-objektivierende Intention beständig die herrschende Funktion übernehmen kann. Der ständige Wechsel der Herrschaft zwischen der objektivierenden und der nicht-objektivierenden Intention ist also das Wesen der natürlichen Einstellung.

Es ist aber doch wohl möglich, daß im Bewußtseinsstrom die objektivierende Intention nicht ab und zu, sondern habituell der nicht-objektivierenden Intention gegenüber eine Herrschaft errichtet. Mit der habituellen Errichtung der Herrschaft der objektivierenden Intention gegenüber der nicht-objektivierenden Intention im Bewußtseinstrom aber entsteht für das betreffende Subjekt aus der natürlichen Einstellung eine neue Einstellung, nämlich die theoretische Einstellung, wodurch alles in der Welt „objektiviert" erscheint. Die auf diese Weise entstandene theoretische Einstellung kann verschiedene Modi zeigen. Eine Möglichkeit davon ist, daß sie sich in diejenige Einstellung entwickelt, in der das Subjekt habituell alles als Natur im Sinne der physikalischen Wissenschaft betrachtet. Bei dieser theoretischen Einstellung handelt es sich um die naturalistische Einstellung, oder was dasselbe heißt, um die physikalische Einstellung, die zur Zeit der Renaissance entstanden ist und seitdem das wissenschaftliche Weltbild prägt.

Mit der Entstehung der naturalistischen Einstellung aus der natürlichen erfährt das natürliche Weltbewußtsein eine Modifikation. Dadurch entsteht eine neue Form des Weltbewußtseins, die die Grundlage der naturwissenschaftlichen Erfahrung bildet. Diese neue Form des Weltbewußtseins möchte ich im Unterschied zum natürlichen Weltbewußtsein als das naturalistische Weltbewußtsein bezeichnen. Indem sich das natürliche Weltbewußtsein ins naturalistische Weltbewußtsein modifiziert, entsteht aus der natürlichen Welt eine neue, nämlich die physikalische Welt, die nichts anderes als die Gesamtnatur im Sinne der Naturwissenschaft bedeutet. Zwischen dem naturalistischen Weltbewußtsein und der physikalischen Welt besteht also eine Wesenskorrelation. Im Hinblick auf diese Wesenskorrelation heißt es an einer Stelle der *Ideen II*: „Vielmehr eine wesentliche Idee von Natur liegt, wenn auch undefiniert zu Grunde. Korrelativ: das als naturwissenschaftliche Erfahrung und somit auch als naturwissenschaftliches Erfahrungsdenken fungierende Bewußtsein hat seine wesentliche phänomenologische Einheit, und dieses Bewußtsein hat in der Natur sein wesentliches Korrelat: eine herrschende ‚Apperzeption' bestimmt es im voraus, was naturwissenschaftliches Objekt ist und was nicht, also was im naturwissenschaftlichen Sinn Natur ist und was nicht." (Hua IV, 2)

Um die Grundstruktur der physikalischen Welt zu enthüllen, muß man die Struktur des naturalistischen Weltbewußtseins in Betracht ziehen. In diesem Zusammenhang ist folgendes zu bemerken.

1. Das naturalistische Weltbewußtsein besteht ebenfalls wie das natürliche Weltbewußtsein aus drei Komponenten: der objektivierenden Intention und den damit verbundenen anderen Komponenten, nämlich der Stimmung der Neugier und dem Willen zum objektiven Wissen. Dies besagt, daß die physikalische Welt, die sich als eine Vorstellungswelt zeigt, für die betreffenden Subjekte zugleich eine Güterwelt und eine praktische Welt ist. Die physikalische Welt als eine Vorstellungswelt ist insofern eine Güterwelt und zugleich eine praktische Welt, als sie das universale Feld darstellt, auf dem sich die theoretisch orientierten Subjekte bemühen, eine bestimmte Form des Wertes, nämlich des „Wertes des Wissens", [6] zu realisieren.

2. Das naturalistische Weltbewußtsein abstrahiert in bezug auf die Welt von allen Qualitäten, die mathematisch nicht bestimmbar wären. Im naturalistischen Weltbewußtsein verwandelt sich alles ins mathematisch Bestimmbare und insofern läßt sich darin ein Prozeß der Homogenisierung der Welt beobachten. Mit der Homogenisierung der Welt verwandelt sich der Lebensraum der natürlichen Welt in den physikalischen Raum und dadurch verliert jeder Platz der natürlichen Welt seinen eigenen Sinn, den er für das Leben der Person hat und der mit keinem anderen austauschbar ist. Jeder Platz im Lebensraum wird, wie Heidegger sagt, „gleichgültig" [7] und verwandelt sich in eine Raumstelle im homogenen Kosmos, die mathematisch bestimmbar ist. Für das naturalistische Weltbewußtsein besteht also nicht mehr „das Gebäude", „die Kirche", „der Tempel", „die Straße", „der Berg", „die Ackerfläche" usw. All das verwandelt sich im naturalistischen Weltbewußtsein in eine mathematisch bestimmbare Größe.

3. Durch die Homogenisierung der Welt modifiziert sich nicht nur die Räumlichkeit, sondern auch die Zeitlichkeit. Mit der Entstehung des naturalistischen Bewußtseins aus dem natürlichen Bewußtsein verwandelt sich die alltägliche Zeitlichkeit der natürlichen Welt in eine physikalische Zeitlichkeit. Das naturalistische Weltbewußtsein kennt nur die physikalische Zeit, die objektiv und mathematisch bestimmbar ist. Für dieses Bewußtsein besteht kein Gestern, kein Heute, kein Morgen, ja überhaupt keine Geschichte. Das alles ist mit der Entstehung des naturalistischen Bewußtseins verschwunden.

4. Die Homogenisierung der Welt, die sich mit der Entstehung des naturalistischen Bewußtseins vollzieht, beschränkt sich nicht auf die materielle

[6] In diesem Zusammenhang schreibt Husserl: „Richtiges Urteilen ist also ein Wert, unrichtiges ein Unwert, nämlich zunächst im Sinne eines Gefallenswerten bzw. Gefallensunwerten." (Hua XXVIII, 240)

[7] M. Heidegger, *Sein und Zeit*, Tübingen 1976, 361.

Natur, sondern sie kann sich auch auf die seelische und geistige Sphäre erstrecken. Dadurch verliert diese jeden Sinn, den sie für die Menschen in der natürlichen Einstellung hat. Für das naturalistische Weltbewußtsein besteht im strikten Sinn weder das Lebewesen noch die Person. Das Lebewesen und die Person werden für das naturalistische Weltbewußtsein insofern in Betracht gezogen, als sie als ein Stück der physikalischen Natur behandelt werden können.

III. Transzendentale Einstellung und transzendentale Überwelt

Wir haben bisher die Grundstruktur von zwei Arten der mundanen Welt in Betracht gezogen. Die Aufmerksamkeit des Subjekts, das in der mundanen Einstellung, sei es in der natürlichen, sei es in der naturalistischen, sein Leben führt, ist auf die weltlichen Gegenstände gerichtet: Dieses Subjekt hat zwar ein implizites Bewußtsein von der Existenz der mundanen Welt, aber es weiß nichts davon, daß die mundane Welt das noematische Korrelat des konstituierenden Bewußtseins darstellt und als solche eine bestimmte Struktur zeigt. Als eine notwendige Folge davon ist das Subjekt, das in der mundanen Einstellung sein Leben führt, nicht imstande, die Struktur der mundanen Welt bzw. des mundanen Weltbewußtseins zu enthüllen. Um die Struktur der mundanen Welt und des diese konstituierenden Bewußtseins zu enthüllen, muß man sich schon von den Schranken der mundanen Einstellung befreit haben. [8]

Dies besagt, daß wir in der bisherigen Betrachtung schon die mundane Einstellung verlassen haben und, um uns von den Schranken der mundanen Einstellung zu befreien, eine Maßnahme ergriffen haben. Es handelt sich dabei um den Vollzug der transzendentalen Reduktion.

Das Verdienst der transzendentalen Reduktion liegt vor allem darin, daß sie uns lehrt, daß die mundane Welt, wie sie vom Subjekt erfahren wird, bloß das relative Sein ist, das nichts anderes als das noematische Korrelat des konstituierenden Bewußtseins darstellt. Deshalb ermöglicht die transzendentale Reduktion, den relativen Seinscharakter der mundanen Welt zu begreifen und die Struktur des WeltHimmeltes allmählich zu enthüllen. Darüber hinaus ermöglicht sie uns, des Seins des konstituiernden Bewußtseins gewahr zu werden und dessen Struktur systematisch zu enthüllen. Durch die transzendentale Reduktion erweist sich das Bewußtsein, das die

---

[8] „Der natürliche Mensch und insbesondere der Naturforscher merkt diese Schranken nicht, er merkt nicht, daß alle seine Ergebnisse mit einem bestimmten Index behaftet sind, der ihnen bloß relativen Sinn anzeigt. Er merkt nicht, daß die natürliche Einstellung nicht die einzig mögliche ist, daß sie Blickwendungen offen läßt, durch die das absolute naturkonstituierende Bewußtsein hervortritt, in Beziehung auf welches vermöge der Wesenskorrelation zwischen Konstituierendem und Konstituiertem alle Natur relativ sein muß " (Hua IV, 179)

Welt bzw. die weltlichen Gegenstände konstituiert, als das absolute Bewußtsein, das als Bedingung der Möglichkeit von Welt ohne diese existieren kann. Das ist gerade der Sinn des Satzes, daß das konstituierende Bewußtsein „nulla ‚re' indiget ad existendum" (Hua III/1, 104).

Die These, daß das konstituierende Bewußtsein das absolute Bewußtsein ist, bedeutet aber, daß es das An-sich-Sein darstellt, das ohne die konstituierte Welt als das relative Sein bestehen kann. Die transzendentale Reduktion ist also nichts anderes als die Methode, das konstituierende Bewußtsein als das An-sich-Sein zu enthüllen. Die Aufgabe der transzendentalen Phänomenologie besteht darin, durch die Methode der transzendentalen Reduktion die Gesamtheit des An-sich-Seins zu enthüllen, die Husserl im Unterschied zur mundanen Welt als „die transzendentale Überwelt" oder als das transzendentale Monadenall bezeichnet.

Um die Aufgabe der Enthüllung der Grundstruktur der transzendentalen Überwelt zu bewältigen, muß ich in der Einstellung der transzendentalen Reduktion zuerst die ganzen Bewußtseinsgestalten, die in meinem Bewußtseinsstrom feststellbar sind, systematisch analysieren. Die transzendentale Überwelt besteht aber nicht allein aus meinem transzendentalen Subjekt, sondern auch aus den transzendentalen Subjekten sowohl anderer Mitmenschen als auch der Tiere und Pflanzen. Also nicht nur ich, sondern auch andere Mitmenschen, Tiere und sogar Pflanzen haben die transzendentalen Funktionen im weiteren Sinne und insofern haben sie auch ihnen eigenes An-sich-Sein.[9]

Darüber hinaus entwickelt Husserl in einem Manuskript noch die Lehre vom An-sich-Sein der materiellen Natur. [10] Danach sollte nicht nur die organische Natur, sondern auch die anorganische Natur, d.h. die materielle Natur, das An-sich-Sein haben. Die materielle Natur ist, transzendentalphänomenologisch betrachtet, kein totes Ding, sondern etwas Lebendiges, das sich im bloßen Schlafzustand befindet und unter Umständen in einen wachen Zustand übergehen kann. Eben deswegen kommt der materiellen Natur die ihr eigene Transzendentale Funktion im weitesten Sinne zu und insofern hat sie das An-sich-Sein. Bei dem An-sich-Sein der materiellen Natur handelt es sich um die materielle Natur, welche irrelativ auf das Regelsystem des sie konstituierenden Transzendentalen Lebens an sich aufgefaßt wird. In Transzendental-phänomenologischer Hinsicht betrachtet, ist das An-sich-Sein der materiellen Natur ein Glied der Transzendentalen

---

[9]Im Hinblick auf die Transzendentalität der Tiere heißt es an einer Stelle der *Krisis*-Abhandlung: „Und wie steht es mit den Tieren? Es erwachsen die Probleme der intentionalen Modifikationen, in denen allen diesen Bewußtseinsakten [...] ihre Weise der Transzendentalität zugewiesen werden kann und muß, eben als ‚Analogien' von uns."(Hua VI, 191)

[10]Es handelt sich dabei um das Manuskript B II 2 aus den Jahren 1907-1908. Die Lehre vom An-sich-Sein der materiellen Natur habe ich ausführlich behandelt in N.-I. Lee, *Edmund Husserls Phänomenologie der Instinkte*, 225ff.

Überwelt.

Das An-sich-Sein der Natur in diesem Zusammenhang darf aber natürlich nicht mit dem An-sich-Sein, das von Husserl im Rahmen der konstitutiven Analysen der Natur und des Geistes in den *Ideen II* ins Spiel gebracht worden ist, verwechselt werden. Dort ist die Rede von der „wesentlich unanschaulichen Natur-an-sich, einer intersubjektiv zwar theoretisch bestimmbaren, aber nicht direkt erfahrbaren, also nicht eigentlich beschreibbaren, durch keine unmittelbaren Erfahrungsbegriffe bestimmbaren Natur" (Hua IV, 207). Es handelt sich bei dieser Natur-an-sich ausschließlich um die „Natur der naturwissenschaftlichen Theorie", oder Cartesianisch gesprochen, um die „Natur einer reinen Intellektion"(Hua IV, 207) im Unterschied zur „Natur der Imagination."[11] Von dieser Natur-an-sich, also von der physikalischen Natur unterscheidet sich aber strikt das An-sich-Sein der Natur als ein Glied der Transzendentalen Überwelt. Denn die physikalische Natur hat kein absolutes Sein, sondern bloß ein relatives Sein, weil sie kein konstituierendes Sein, sondern eine konstituierte Gegenständlichkeit darstellt.

Mit der Entwicklung der Idee einer Transzendentalen Überwelt stellt sich natürlich die schwierige Frage nach der Methode der Transzendentalen Reduktion. In diesem Zusammenhang sei darauf hingewiesen, daß die Transzendentale Reduktion als die Methode der Enthüllung der Transzendentalen Überwelt sich nur schrittweise vollziehen läßt, weil die Transzendentale Überwelt nicht homogen ist, sondern, wie bereits erörtert wurde, aus strukturell verschiedenen Transzendentalen Regionen besteht, wie beispielsweise dem An-sich-Sein der Menschen, der Tiere, der Pflanzen und dem An-sich-Sein der materiellen Natur. Da sich die Transzendentale Reduktion in der Anfangsphase in Form einer egologischen Reflexion vollzieht, ist es klar, daß sie in sich die Reflexion als eine unentbehrliche Komponente enthält. Es ist aber nicht auszuschließen, daß sie im weiteren Vollzug notwendig in sich die Auslegung als seine Komponente haben muß. Es ist nun die künftige Aufgabe der Transzendentalen Phänomenologie, im Hinblick auf die Struktur der Transzendentalen Überwelt die konkreten Methoden der Transzendentalen Reduktion zu entwickeln. Es handelt sich dabei um die Aufgabe, die in den großen Problemzusammenhang der von Husserl erst in seiner späteren Schaffensperiode unternommenen Aufgabe der „Phänomenologie der phänomenologischen Reduktion"(Hua VIII, 164) gehört.

Durch das wiederholte Ins-Werk-Setzen der Transzendentalen Reduktion kann sich im Subjekt eine habituelle Einstellung etablieren, die Husserl im Unterschied zur mundanen Einstellung als die Transzendentale Ein-

[11] In diesem Sinn heißt es: „Das physische Ding ist ‚an-sich', und dieses An-sich ist naturwissenschaftlich nur eine formal-methodische Regel der Einheit, wonach jeder in der Einheit der Wechselverständigung Stehende ... die anschaulichen Dinglichkeiten seiner Umwelt ... konstruieren kann."(Hua IV, 376)

stellung bezeichnet. So wie die jeweilige mundane Einstellung in sich eine be-stimmte Form des Weltbewußtseins enthält, hat die Transzendentale Einstellung das ihr eigene Weltbewußtsein, das im Unterschied zum mundanen Weltbewußtsein als das Transzendentale Weltbewußtsein - im Sinne des Bewußtseins von der Transzendentalen Überwelt - bezeichnet werden kann. Es besteht also zwischen dem mundanen und dem Transzendentalen Weltbewußtsein eine strukturelle Ähnlichkeit.

Diese strukturelle Ähnlichkeit zwischen beiden Formen des Weltbewußtseins darf aber nicht darüber hinwegtäuschen, daß zwischen beiden ein großer Unterschied besteht. Während das mundane Weltbewußtsein als das die mundane Welt konstituierende absolute Sein immer dieser vorangeht und deren Grundstruktur im voraus bestimmt, ist das Transzendentale Weltbewußtsein nicht etwas, was der Transzendentalen Überwelt vorangehen und deren Struktur im voraus bestimmen kann. Gerade das Gegenteil trifft zu: Das Transzendentale Weltbewußtsein ist etwas, was gemäß der Struktur der Transzendentalen Überwelt erst allmählich gebildet werden kann. Dem oben erörterten schrittweisen Charakter der Transzendentalen Reduktion entsprechend kann sich das Weltbewußtsein nur schritt-weise bilden. Der Prozeß der wiederholten Transzendentalen Reduktion bedeutet also den Gang der Bildung des Transzendentalen Weltbewußtseins. Das ist gerade der Grund dafür, daß man nicht im voraus sagen kann, welche Gestalt und welche Komponente schließlich das Transzendentale Weltbewußtsein haben wird. Wegen dieses wichtigen Unterschiedes zwi-schen dem mundanen Weltbewußtsein und dem Transzendentalen Weltbe-wußtsein haben wir nicht versucht, zuerst die Struktur des Transzendentalen Weltbewußtseins zu erörtern und auf Grund dieser Erörterung die Struktur der Transzendentalen Überwelt zu enthüllen. Die Aufgabe der Transzendentalen Phänomenologie liegt darin, mit Hilfe angemessener Methoden der Transzendentalen Reduktion die Gesamtstruktur der Transzendentalen Überwelt und der Transzendentalen Einstellung systematisch zu enthüllen.

IV. Die Frage nach den Parallelismen von Welten als die Grundfrage der Phänomenologie

Ich habe nun vor, auf Grund der bisherigen Erörterung die eingangs erwähnte Finksche These näher zu bestimmen, indem ich das Verhältnis von verschiedenen Welten erörtere. Dabei geht es einerseits um das Verhältnis von mundanen Welten untereinander und andererseits um das Verhältnis von den mundanen Welten und der Transzendentalen Überwelt.

Ich will zuerst dem Verhältnis von der natürlichen Welt und der naturalistischen Welt nachgehen. In diesem Zusammenhang ist es wichtig, darauf aufmerksam zu machen, daß jedes Seiende als ein Glied der natürlichen Welt im Übergang von der natürlichen in die naturalistische Einstellung nicht aus dem Bewußtseinsfeld verschwindet, sondern als ein Glied der na-turalistischen Welt in einem neuen Gewand erscheint. Beispielsweise kann der Schreibtisch, an dem ich jetzt sitze und arbeite und der in der natür-lichen Einstellung gerade als ein Schreibtisch erscheint, in der naturalistischen Einstellung als ein physikalischer Gegenstand mit bestimmten physikalischen Eigenschaften erscheinen, die durchaus mathematisch bestimmbar sind. Ebenfalls wird mein Wahrnehmungserlebnis, das jetzt auf den Schreibtisch gerichtet ist und in der natürlichen Einstellung als meine personale Charaktereigenschaft erscheint, in der naturalistischen Einstellung nicht verschwinden, sondern es kann eben als ein Naturfaktum erscheinen, das auf meinen Leib als ein Naturfaktum fundiert oder von diesem kausal abhängig ist und als solches, wie andere Naturfakta in der naturalistischen Welt, seine mathematisch bestimmbaren Eigenschaften hat. Diese beiden Beispiele zeigen, daß zwischen der natürlichen Welt und der naturalistischen Welt ein Parallelismus besteht.

Freilich ist der Parallelismus zwischen der natürlichen und der naturalistischen Welt nicht der einzige, der im Hinblick auf die mundanen Welten feststellbar ist. Um dies zu zeigen, muß zuerst festgestellt werden, daß es außer der natürlichen und der naturalistischen Welt andere Formen der mundanen Welt gibt. Bei der Analyse der Entstehung der naturalistischen Welt aus der natürlichen Welt hat sich gezeigt, daß durch die Errichtung der habituellen Herrschaft der objektivierenden Intention gegenüber der nicht-objektivierenden Intention die naturalistische Einstellung bzw. die naturalistische Welt entsteht. Aber ein anderer Fall ist auch möglich, nämlich daß die nicht-objektivierende Intention gegenüber der objektivierenden Intention eine habituelle Herrschaft errichtet. In diesem Fall entstehen aus der natürlichen Einstellung verschiedene Formen der außertheoretischen Einstellung wie die ästhetische, die moralische, die religiöse Einstellung usw. und dementsprechend entstehen aus der natürlichen Welt verschiedene mundane Welten wie die ästhetische, die moralische, die religiöse Welt usw.

Es gibt also verschiedene mundane Welten einschließlich der natürlichen und der naturalistischen Welt. Im Hinblick auf die mundanen Welten ist es möglich, viele Parallelismen zu beobachten, die in jedem Paar von zwei mundanen Welten bestehen. Einer davon ist der oben erörterte Parallelismus zwischen der natürlichen und der naturalistischen Welt.

Gehen wir nun dem Verhältnis zwischen den mundanen Welten und der Transzendentalen Überwelt nach. Um dieses Verhältnis zu erläutern, möchte ich zuerst folgendes in Erwägung ziehen. Das Wahrnehmungserlebnis, das auf den Schreibtisch gerichtet ist und in der natürlichen Einstellung als meine Charaktereigenschaft, dann in der naturalistischen Einstellung als ein Naturfaktum mit bestimmten Dingeigenschaften erscheint, erweist sich in der Transzendentalen Einstellung als ein An-sich-Sein, weil es das Wahrnehmungsding konstituiert und ohne dieses, d.h. absolut, bestehen kann. Dies besagt, daß meine personale Charaktereigenschaft als ein Glied der natürlichen Welt und das ihr parallele Naturfaktum mit bestimmten physikalischen Eigenschaften als ein Glied der naturalistischen Welt zwei verschiedene Erscheinungen des An-sich-Seins des auf den Tisch gerichteten

Wahrnehmungserlebnisses darstellen. Allerdings ist es auch möglich, daß dieses An-sich-Sein durch die Einstellungsänderung ein Glied einer anderen mundanen Welt wird; dasselbe Erlebnis kann in der religiösen Einstellung als etwas aufgefaßt werden, das einen bestimmten religiösen Sinn hat. Daraus läßt sich schließen, daß die verschiedenen mundanen Welten die verschiedenen Erscheinungen derselben Transzendentalen Überwelt als der Gesamtheit des An-sich-Seins darstellen. Insofern ist es möglich, zwischen der Transzendentalen Überwelt und den verschiedenen mundanen Welten so viele Parallelismen wie die Zahl der mundanen Welten zu beobachten. Die Transzendentale Überwelt, die sich in der Transzendentalen Einstellung als das An-sich-Sein zeigt, kann also für die mundan eingestellten Subjekte verschiedene mundane Gesichter zeigen.

Abschließend möchte ich wieder auf die eingangs zitierte Finksche These zurückkommen. Mit E. Fink bin ich der Ansicht, daß die Grundfrage der Phänomenologie sich als die Frage nach dem Ursprung der Welt formulieren läßt. Die bisherige Analyse zeigt, daß die Frage nach dem Ursprung der Welt die Grundfrage der Phänomenologie und konkreter die Frage nach den Parallelismen zwischen den verschiedenen Formen der Welt bedeutet. Es handelt sich dabei im Grunde genommen um die Frage, die um das Spannungsfeld zwischen dem An-sich-Sein und den verschiedenen Gesichtern der Transzendentalen Überwelt kreist.

Noch einmal: Heidegger und Laotse

Otto Pöggeler

Laotse Martin Heidegger starb, 86 Jahre alt, am 26. Mai 1976. Im folgenden Jahr erschien der Sammelband *Erinnerung an Martin Heidegger*, hrsg. von Heideggers zeitweiligem Verleger Günther Neske in dessen Verlag. Der Band sammelt aufschlußreiche Erinnerungen jener, die mit Heidegger als Schüler, Freunde oder Gefährten zusammengetroffen waren. Die vertriebenen Schüler wie Hans Jonas oder Hannah Arendt fehlen; nur Herbert Marcuse berichtet über seine bald abbrechende Nähe zu Heidegger unter dem Titel „Enttäuschung." Vor allem dann, wenn Erinnerungen aus zweiter oder dritter Hand weitergegeben werden, verwirren sich oft die Daten und Fakten. So heißt es, Heidegger sei mit Martin Buber bei der Vorbereitung der berühmten Münchener Akademie-Vorträge *Die Sprache* auf der Mainau zusammengetroffen. Ein zweites Zusammentreffen habe Martin Buber vermieden: „Kampf zwischen zwei alten Männern, das ist nicht gut ... Und darin waren wir uns einig, daß dieser Kampf nicht zu vermeiden wäre." Dann wird von einem Zusammentreffen Heidegger-Buber in Altreuthe gesprochen; Heidegger habe am Abend alemannische Gedichte Hebels vorgetragen. Von einer Vorbesprechung in Bregenz ist auch die Rede. Buber mußte seinen Münchener Vortrag dann nachträglich halten (wegen des Todes seiner Frau). Doch diskutierte man in Jerusalem wie in Europa über das Zusammentreffen der Wege. Paul Celan z. B. sprach darüber mit der kranken Nelly Sachs in Stockholm. Als Adorno bei Buber wie bei Heidegger faschistoide Tendenzen fand, verwies Celan darauf, daß Adorno noch 1934 den romantischen Realismus eines Joseph Goebbels in der Vertonung von Gedichten Baldur von Schirachs gefunden habe.[1] Berichtet wird auch, daß Heidegger und Bultmann sich in Marburg wiedergetroffen hätten; die Fremdheit des einen gegenüber dem anderen wird mit dramatischen Formulierungen hervorgehoben. Der Briefwechsel Bultmann-Heidegger gibt da eine andere, nämlich die historische Sicht.[2]

Besonders ärgerlich ist eine ganz und gar phantastische Legende, die von den Freiburger Mitbürgern ihrem großen Philosophen zugedacht wurde. Sie erzählt davon, daß Edith Stein in der Kutte des Karmeliter-Ordens Heidegger in Freiburg aufgesucht habe, aber nicht einmal vorgelassen worden sei. Diese Unwahrheiten sind sofort von den Mitschwestern der Edith Stein korrigiert worden; die Sensationsmache hat sie trotzdem über den

---

[1] Vgl. *Erinnerung an Martin Heidegger.* Hrsg. von Günther Neske. Pfullingen 1977. S. 90 ff, 210, 240. Vgl. ferner Otto Pöggeler: *Spur des Worts. Zur Lyrik Paul Celans.* Freiburg/München 1986. S. 149 f, 247 f.

[2] *Der Briefwechsel* wird jetzt ediert von Klaus W. Müller und Andreas Großmann. Vgl. dazu meinen Vortrag Heidegger und Bultmann: *Philosophie und Theologie. Trierer Heidegger-Vorträge.* Hrsg. von Markus Happel. Im Druck.

Bericht des langjährigen chinesischen Lektors in Freiburg, Paul Hsiao, in den Gedenkband aufgenommen.[3] Muß man darum auch die Berichte Hsiaos über seine zeitweilige Hilfe für Heidegger bei dessen Bemühungen um Laotse verwerfen? Der Chinese Hsiao scheint für seine Bemühungen um Laotse eine besondere Naturnähe ins Feld führen zu können. Zwölf Stunden vor dem schrecklichen Luftangriff auf Freiburg im November 1944, so berichtet er, seien Menschen und Tiere in der Stadt unruhig geworden. Man habe dann jener Ente im Stadtgarten ein Denkmal gesetzt, die zwölf Stunden lang quakte, schnatterte und wild herumflatterte. Doch ein Bombenangriff sei keine Naturkatastrophe, die sich mit ersten Erschütterungen anmelden könne. „Das Denkmal für die Ente am Eingang des Freiburger Stadtgartens gibt nicht nur den Parapsychologen, ich meine, auch den Philosophen Rätsel auf." Hsiao sagt, er habe in Gesprächen mit Martin Heidegger die Freiburger Eindrücke wiederholt besprochen; doch Heideggers Meinung dazu wird nicht wiedergegeben.[4]

Hsiao gibt an, daß er Psychologie und chinesische Philosophie in Peiping studiert habe. Dann habe er in Mailand an der Katholischen Universität „scholastische Strenge" kennengelernt. Eine Übertragung Laotses ins Italienische erschien 1941. In Freiburg habe er 1942 Martin Heidegger kennengelernt, als Gasthörer an seinen „Seminaren" teilgenommen und ihm die Laotse-Übersetzung überreicht. Nach dem Kriege habe er sich mit Heidegger am Holzmarktplatz getroffen; Heidegger sei durch das Entnazifizierungsverfahren belastet gewesen. Von Heideggers Nationalsozialismus habe man in Freiburg „manches erzählt - nach dem Kriege mehr als während des Krieges." Hier wird dann die angebliche „rätselhafte Episode" mit Edith Stein eingeflochten. Doch nach dem Kriege habe Heidegger sich ungerecht behandelt gefühlt, und der Chinese, der seit seiner Jugend „viele Räuber-Romane und Helden-Geschichten gelesen" hatte, wollte gegen die Ungerechtigkeit kämpfen. Dabei sah er durchaus seine Grenzen: „Ich konnte die verantwortlichen französischen Offiziere nicht wie Schulknaben behandeln, obwohl viele von ihnen, wie die Herren in anderen Besatzungszonen, das verdient hätten." So griff der neue Held gegenüber Heidegger zurück auf ein Trostwort des Konfuzianers Meng-Tse: „Wenn der Himmel jemandem einen großen Auftrag erteilen will, wird er zunächst sein Herz und seinen Willen mit Bitterkeit erfüllen, seine Sehnen und Knochen zermürben, seinen Körper aushungern, seinen Leib mit großer Armut ausstatten, seine Unternehmungen verwirren, damit sein Herz angereizt, seine Natur gestärkt und seine Unzulänglichkeit zur Vollendung gebracht werde ..." Heidegger, „bewegt" von diesem Zitat, forderte den chinesischen Lektor auf, „mit ihm zusammen das Werk des Laotse ins Deutsche zu übertragen."

[3] Vgl. dazu Otto Pöggeler: Martin Heidegger und die Religionsphänomenologie. In: *Edith Stein Jahrbuch.* Band 2. Würzburg 1996. S. 15 ff.

[4] Vgl. *Erinnerung an Martin Heidegger.* S. 120. Zum folgenden vgl. S. 121 ff.

Hsiao war Heidegger 1946 wiederbegegnet in der Freude, daß man noch am Leben war. Die beiden trafen sich samstags in Heideggers Hütte oberhalb Todtnaubergs. Hsiao kam mit einem Motorrad und gab Heidegger von dem „unbezahlbaren Paket" mit Kaffee, Butter usf. mit, das er als „halber Alliierter" jede Woche ausgehändigt bekam. Von der gemeinsamen Arbeit berichtet Hsiao genauer: „Wir gingen bei der Übertragungsarbeit zunächst vom Text des Laotse nach Chiang Hsi-chang aus, der sich aus dem Vergleich von über 84 alten Texten ergeben hat und vorläufig als kritische Textausgabe betrachtet werden kann. Außerchinesische Übertragungen und Kommentare ließen wir beiseite. Als erstes nahmen wir uns die Kapitel über Tao vor, die ersichtlich die schwierigsten und wichtigsten sind. Durch die gründliche Gangart des Heideggerschen Denkens hatten wir am Ende des Sommers 1946 von den 81 erst 8 Sprüche bearbeitet. In etwa zehn Jahren wären wir vermutlich fertig geworden, vielleicht auch etwas früher, denn andere Kapitel sind nicht gar so verhüllt."

Heidegger fragte im wesentlichen „unablässig bohrend" nach dem Sinnzusammenhang im geheimnisvollen Wechselspiel der symbolischen Beziehungen. Nach dem Sommer 1947 aber wurde die Zusammenarbeit nicht fortgesetzt. Zwei Verse des 25. Kapitels hatte Heidegger sich in chinesischen Schriftzeichen als Wandschmuck schreiben lassen: „Wer kann das Trübe stillend allmählich klären? Wer kann die Ruhe bewegend allmählich beleben? " Als Hsiao mit einem „Freund aus der Industrie" Heidegger besuchte, diskutierte man Verse wie jenen aus dem 18. Kapitel: „Wird das große Tao verlassen, gibt es Humanität und Gerechtigkeit." Heidegger wies die Auffassung zurück, Laotse lehne zwar den Egoismus ab, wolle aber gerade dadurch „sein Ego vollenden." Er verwies auf den Satz des Augustinus: „Liebe und tue, was Du willst ... "

Andere Besucher aus dem Fernen Osten glaubten zu wissen, daß Heidegger den Zen-Buddhismus schätzte und in diesem Sinn eine präontologische Erfahrung mit „aesthetic" oder „poetic feeling" identifizierte. Chung-yuan Chang, der dieses schreibt, sagt auch: „I had heard that Heidegger was very interested in the *Tao Te Ching*, and in fact had a Chinese scholar helped him translate this ancient text into German." Der chinesische Gelehrte, längst in den USA lehrend, verwies in seiner englischen Übersetzung von Laotse beim Kommentieren auf Heideggers „neuen Weg des Denkens."[5] Ein besonders unzuverlässiger deutscher Bericht läßt Heidegger auch sagen, daß er die Zusammenarbeit mit Hsiao „nach dem achten Spruch aufgegeben" habe, da er immer mehr gelernt habe „wie entfernt und fremdartig die Sprachen und das Denken Asiens seien." Heidegger gedachte der langen Kontakte mit den Japanern, sagte aber auch: „Von Chinesen habe er in-

---

[5]Vgl. *Erinnerung an Martin Heidegger*. S. 69. Zum folgenden vgl. S. 102. Vgl. auch Otto Pöggeler: Westliche Wege zu Nishida und Nishitani. In: *Philosophie der Struktur - „Fahrzeug" der Zukunft? Festschrift für Heinrich Rombach.* Hrsg. G. Stener, M. Röhrig. Freiburg/München 1995. S. 95-108.

dessen mehr gelernt."

Heidegger sandte 1949 drei seiner Schriften, die neu aufgelegt worden waren, an Karl Jaspers: die Rede *Was ist Metaphysik?* mit Einleitung und Nachwort, den Vortrag *Vom Wesen der Wahrheit* und den *Brief über den Humanismus*. Karl Jaspers antwortete aus dem Sommerurlaub in St. Moritz: „Ich helfe mir etwa mit Erinnerungen an Asiatisches, zu dem ich all die Jahre gern gegangen bin, wohl wissend, nicht eigentlich einzudringen, aber auf eine wundersame Weise von dort her erweckt. Ihr ‚Sein,' die ‚Lichtung des Seins,' Ihre Umkehrung unseres Bezuges zum Sein in den Bezug des Seins zu uns, das Übrigbleiben des Seins selbst - in Asien glaube ich davon etwas wahrgenommen zu haben. Daß Sie überhaupt dahin drängen und, wie Ihre Interpretation von ‚Sein und Zeit' aussagt, immer gedrängt haben, ist außerordentlich." Jaspers betonte, er wolle aus dem Monolog und dem Nachreden der Monologe gegenwärtigen Philosophierens herauskommen. Er protestierte aber auch: ihm sei die Sprache nur Brücke, und so sträube er sich gegen die Auffassung von der Sprache als dem Haus des Seins. „Die Sprache ist doch im Mitteilen zur Aufhebung in der Wirklichkeit selbst zu bringen, durch Tun, Gegenwärtigkeit, Liebe. Ich könnte fast umkehrend sagen: Wo Sprache ist, da ist noch nicht oder nicht mehr das Sein selbst".[6] Heidegger nahm das Wort von den Monologen auf und erinnerte an Nietzche, für den Venedig als „Bild für die Menschen der Zukunft" aus „hundert tiefen Einsamkeiten" gebildet wurde. Heidegger berichtete dann: „Was Sie über das Asiatische sagen, ist aufregend; ein Chinese, der in den Jahren 1943-44 meine Vorlesungen über Heraklit und Parmenides hörte (ich las damals nur noch einstündig Interpretationen weniger Fragmente), fand ebenfalls Anklänge an das östliche Denken. Wo ich in der Sprache nicht einheimisch bin, bleibe ich skeptisch; ich wurde es noch mehr, als der Chinese, der selbst christlicher Theologe und Philosoph ist, mit mir einige Worte von Laotse übersetzte; durch Fragen erfuhr ich erst, wie fremd uns schon das ganze Sprachwesen ist; wir haben den Versuch dann aufgegeben." Trotzdem liege hier (im Übersetzen zwischen dem Europäischen und dem Ostasiatischen) etwas Erregendes, das wesentlich sei für die Zukunft. Die Anklänge an das Ostasiatische in seinen eigenen Schriften hätten „vermutlich eine ganz andere Wurzel." Seit 1910 begleite ihn „der Lese- und Lebemeister Eckehardt." Dieser und der Spruch des Parmenides von der Selbigkeit von Denken und Sein hätten sein Denken auf das gebracht, was dann wie eine Umkehrung des Verhältnisses von Denken und Sein aussähe. Doch gehe es um etwas ganz anderes, was dem Genannten vorausliege.

Das Johannes-Evangelium und der Erste Brief des Johannes sprechen vom Ruhen in der Liebe, die die Liebe Gottes mit der Nächstenliebe vereint. In seiner Augustinus-Vorlesung vom Sommer 1921 ging Heidegger auch ein

---

[6]Vgl. *Martin Heidegger/Karl Jaspers: Briefwechsel 1920-1963*. Frankfurt a. M. und München/Zürich 1990. S. 178 f. Zum folgenden vgl. S. 181 f.

auf die Erläuterungen des Augustinus zum Ersten Brief des Johannes. Er unterschied von der bloßen Liebe die eigentliche Liebe, die Wille zum Sein des Geliebten ist, eine Tendenz „auf das dilectum, ut sit." Offenbar las Heidegger Augustinus im Licht der Bernhardinischen Mystik, und so konnte er später die Formel bilden: „amo: volo ut sis." Diese Formel verband sich mit dem „Dilige et quod vis fac," das wir ebenfalls in der Augustinischen Auslegung des Johannes-Briefes finden. Von diesem Gedanken aus konnte Heidegger sich in Marburg mit Rudolf Bultmann treffen, der als christlicher Theologe die Nächstenliebe mit dem eigentlichen Selbstsein verband.[7]

Als Heidegger 1930 in Bremen seinen Vortrag über das Wesen der Wahrheit vortrug, verbiß sich eine Diskussionsrunde in die Frage, ob ein Mensch sich ganz in den anderen versetzen könne. Heidegger verlangte nach den Gleichnissen des Tschuang Tse, und der Hausherr konnte ihm die Bubersche Ausgabe holen. Am Gleichnis von der Freude der Fische machte Heidegger dann klar, daß der eine immer schon mit dem anderen da ist.[8] Bei der Interpretation von Hölderlins Rhein-Hymne im Winter 1934/35 zog Heidegger Nietzsches Mahnung heran: „Sei selig und thue dann, wozu du Lust hast." Bei Nietzsche birgt sich das Du aber nicht mehr in der christlichen Liebe; vielmehr drängt sich in einem Umsturz der Tradition die Lust als *voluptas* vor. Doch interpretiert Heidegger Nietzsche immer noch „augustinisch."

Als Martin Heidegger im WS 1936/37 die Reihe seiner Nietzsche-Vorlesungen begann, sollte Nietzsches Besinnung auf die Kunst noch durchaus zu dem führen, was man mit einer Formulierung, die von Heidegger gemieden wurde, eine „neue Mythologie" nennt. Doch schon das Jahr 1938 brachte die grundstürzende Einsicht, daß die Zeit dem, was Heidegger suchte, keinen Raum ließ. Nur kleine Anfänge einer anderen Zukunft ließen sich noch den ältesten Sprüchen der griechischen Denker oder den spätesten Fragmenten Hölderlins entnehmen. Die mystischen Motive der Armut und Gelassenheit, die im Nichts als der Leere das Sein vermuten lassen, hatten sich neu gemeldet, als Heidegger die Auseinandersetzung mit Nietzsche durch seine Arbeit über die seinsgeschichtliche Bestimmung des Nihilismus abschloß. War damit nicht der Weg dafür geöffnet, die abendländische Geschichte mit ihrem Anfang und anderen Anfang auf andere geschichtliche Zusammenhänge zu beziehen? Konnte über die Jahrtausende und die Kulturschei-

---

[7]Vgl. *Martin Heidegger: Phänomenologie des religiösen Lebens* (*Gesamtausgabe* Band 60). Frankfurt a. M. 1995. S. 291 f.

[8]Vgl. Heinrich Wiegand Petzet: *Auf einen Stern zugehen. Begegnungen und Gespräche mit Martin Heidegger 1929-1976.* Frankfurt 1983. S. 24. - Zum folgenden vgl. Martin Heidegger: Hölderlins Hymnen „Germanien" und „Der Rhein" (*Gesamtausgabe* Band 39). Frankfurt a. M. 1980. S. 286. - Zum Thema vgl. Otto Pöggeler: West-Östliches Gespräch: Heidegger und Lao Tse. In: *Heidegger and Asian Thought.* Ed. by Graham Parkes. Honolulu 1987. S. 47 ff; jetzt in Otto Pöggeler: *Neue Wege mit Heidegger.* Freiburg/München 1992. S. 387 ff.

den hinweg nicht das Denken, das mit dem Namen „Laotse" verbunden wird, Anstöße geben oder doch eine Bestätigung für den eigenen Weg?

Heidegger, so wird berichtet, liebte Bertolt Brechts *Legende von der Entstehung des Buches Taoteking auf dem Weg des Laotse in die Emigration*: als der Zöllner wissen wollte, wieso das Harte dem Weichen wie der Stein dem Wasser unterliege, schrieb Laotse beim Verlassen des Heimatlandes seine 81 Sprüche.[9] Heideggers Feldweg-Gespräche von 1944/45 suchten das Nicht-wollen der Gelassenheit; die Berufung auf Meister Eckhart mußte aber zugeben, daß der mittelalterliche Mystiker die Gelassenheit „noch innerhalb des Willensbereiches" dachte, den Heidegger verlassen wollte. Trug Laotse diese Gelassenheit nicht vor, ohne „humanistisch" auf die Person des Menschen oder gar auf einen persönlichen Gott als eine letzte Sicherung zurückzuweisen? Ließ das Nichts, in dem das Sein als abgründiges zu finden ist, sich nicht als das Leere denken und so als das Bewegende eines „Weges? " Die Feldweg-Gespräche fanden im Krug ein Beispiel für das, was gerade mit seiner Leere zu fassen vermag; der elfte Spruch des Laotse gab diesem Beispiel eine letzte Vertiefung. Laotse führte zu einem meditativen Denken, das nicht mehr Leistungs- und Herrschaftswissen und damit nicht mehr ein Angriff auf die „Natur" ist.

Als Heidegger 1950 in München den Bremer Vortrag *Das Ding* wiederholte, tat er es im Kreise von Heisenberg, den Brüdern Jünger und anderen bedeutenden Tagungsteilnehmern. Eine längere Diskussion mit Studenten führte hin zu Laotse, obwohl dessen Name nicht mit dem Beispiel des Kruges verbunden worden war.[10] Als Heidegger 1953 in München den Vortrag *Die Frage nach der Technik* hielt, sprach Werner Heisenberg über *Das Naturbild der heutigen Physik*; dabei berief Heisenberg sich auf Tschuang Tse, der einen Gärtner schon den Ziehbrunnen verwerfen läßt, weil diese Maschine dem Menschen ein Maschinenherz gäbe. Heideggers Freiburger Vorträge *Grundsätze des Denkens* von 1957 führten die Sätze über Identität, Differenz und Grund bis zu Hegels dialektischer Verknüpfung. Von Hölderlin und Novalis hieß es, daß sie in ihrer dichterischen Besinnung „noch erregter" von den „unausgeloteten" Tiefen der Dialektik angesprochen seien; Marx habe die weltgeschichtlichen Konsequenzen zu ziehen versucht. Die Weise, in der Hölderlin in seinem Gedicht *Andenken* das Lichte und das Dunkle beim Wein im Becher verbunden sieht, führte zum 28. Spruch des Laotse: „Wer seine Helle kennt, sich in sein Dunkel hüllt" (nach der Übersetzung von Victor von Strauß).[11] Als Heidegger sein Unterwegs-

---

[9]Vgl. Petzet (s. Anm. 8). S. 227. - Zum folgenden vgl. Martin Heidegger: Feldweg-Gespräche (*Gesamtausgabe* Band 77). Frankfurt a. M. 1995. S. 109.

[10]Vgl. Petzet (s. Anm. 8). S. 80. - Zum folgenden vgl. den Abschnitt über Heidegger und Heisenberg in Otto Pöggeler: *Schritte zu einer hermeneutischen Philosophie*. Freiburg/München 1994. S. 276 ff.

[11]Vgl. Martin Heidegger: *Bremer und Freiburger Vorträge* (*Gesamtausgabe* Band 79). Frankfurt a. M. 1994. S. 82, 94, 93. - Zum folgenden vgl. Martin

sein zur Sprache vom Bewegenden des Weges her zu fassen suchte, wurde ihm das Leitwort des dichterischen Denkens von Laotse, das Wort „Tao" oder „Weg," zum „Geheimnis aller Geheimnisse des denkenden Sagens." Ein Bremer Gespräch führte 1960 von Augustinus zurück zu Heraklit, verband dann Tschuang-Tses Gleichnis vom Glockenspielständer mit Klees Jenaer Rede über die moderne Kunst und führte so zu Heideggers Verbindung von Bild und Wort.

In seinen Gesprächen mit dem Psychiater Medard Boss, der auch über Indien geschrieben hatte, grenzte Heidegger sein Denken klar vom indischen Denken ab. Im indischen Denken gehe es um „das Aufgehen (Brahman) von Gelichtetheit an sich." Diese Gelichtetheit lichte sich selbst und alles, was in sie hervorkäme. Ähnliches vollziehe sich in der christlichen Mystik, wenn diese ein nunc stans erfahre als „einzige unwandelbare Gegenwart" ohne Vergangenheit und Zukunft. (Carl Friedrich von Weizsäcker hat diese Verbindung des Indischen und des Christlichen für Heidegger seinen Denkansatz beansprucht.)[12] Demgegenüber besteht Heidegger darauf, daß die Gelichtetheit im Menschen einen Hüter brauche, der endlich sei. Damit wird die Erde als Schon-gewesen-sein vor dem Menschen zugelassen; es gibt Sein oder Anwesen „auch ohne, unabhängig vom Menschen." Das Aufgehen der Gelichtetheit im Meditieren, das „Hellen," wird zurückbezogen auf das „Hallen"; das Wort, das gehört wird und nicht wie ein Bild zu umfassen ist, bekommt einen Vorrang. Wenn das östliche Denken den Menschen zurücknimmt in „die Grundnatur alles Seienden," dann ist dieses Denken immer noch ein „Mayaschleier." In diesem Schleier ist das Sein noch nicht zurückgenommen in das Ereignis. Unbeantwortet bleibt in diesen Gesprächen Heideggers Frage nach „Ostasien" und dem, was dort geschehe. Doch muß Heidegger resignieren: die „größte Lücke" in seiner Erörterung der Sprache sei, „daß die Möglichkeit einer zureichenden Erörterung der ostasiatischen Sprachen fehlt."

Als Ernst Jünger 1965 zu einer längeren Ostasienreise aufbrach, sandte Heidegger ihm den 42. Abschnitt des *Tao-te-king*: „Nicht zum Tor hinausgehen ..." An Bord des Schiffes schrieb Jünger dann an Heidegger, er werde auch dann, wenn er sich in ein Zimmer einschließe, wie ein französischer Vorgänger eine Reise durch das Zimmer beginnen. Besser sei es also, „die geistige Ruhe zu gewinnen und in ihr zu verharren, während der Raum sich bewegt." Jünger hätte sich für diese Auffassung auch auf den 26. Abschnitt des *Tao-te-king* berufen können.[13] Als Erhart Kästner in den „Byzantini-

---

Heidegger: *Unterwegs zur Sprache*. Pfullingen 1959. S. 198; vgl. ferner Petzet (s. Anm. 8) S. 65.

[12] Vgl. Carl Friedrich von Weizsäckers Selbstdarstellung, in: *Der Garten des Menschlichen*. München/Wien 2. Aufl. 1977. S. 594 ff. Vgl. ferner Martin Heidegger: *Zollikoner Seminare*. Hrsg. von Medard Boss. Frankfurt a. M. 1987. S. 224 f. Zum folgenden S. 223, 226, 230, 338, 316.

[13] Zum einzelnen vgl. Pöggeler: *Schritte zu einer hermeneutischen Philosophie*

schen Aufzeichnungen" *Aufstand der Dinge* gefragt hatte, ob Laotse im 15. Kapitel Trübwasser oder Quirlwasser meine, zeichnete Heidegger in seinem Dankbrief vom 30.7.73 gerade diese Überlegungen aus. Laotse blieb Thema gemeinsamer Überlegungen und ein Wegweiser, der allerdings auf unterschiedliche Lebens- und Denkwege verwies. Sicherlich hätte es Heidegger fern gelegen, wie der Dilthey-Schüler Georg Misch 1907/08 eine Weltreise zu unternehmen und dann in einer philosophischen Fibel die Leitworte der „metaphysischen" und vorwissenschaftlichen Philosophie wie Tao, Brahman, *logos* zusammenzustellen und zu interpretieren. Laotse blieb eine zeitweilige Hilfe auf dem eigenen Denkweg.

Laotse wurde für Heidegger vorübergehend zu einer Zuflucht; wurde er und überhaupt die mystische Tradition nicht auch zur Ausflucht vor der Bewältigung der eigenen geschichtlichen Verstrickungen? Natürlich mußte es Anstoß erregen, daß Heidegger in den Feldweg-Gesprächen von 1944/45 nicht die Verantwortung des einen vor dem anderen suchte und weiterentfaltete zu einer kommunikativen Ethik und Rationalität, sondern mit Meister Eckhart das Wort, das sich selbst verantwortet. Man muß sich aber hüten vor dem plötzlichen Fahnenschwenken mit großen Worten wie „Gerechtigkeit," das Laotse nach der schönen Legende gegenüber Konfuzius tadelte.[14] Jeder Denkansatz (bei Konfuzius wie bei Laotse) geht von einseitigen Akzentsetzungen aus, bleibt deshalb begrenzt und muß so zurückgestellt werden in ein übergreifendes, aber offenes Ganzes. Muß ein wirklichkeitsgerechtes Denken im 20. Jahrhundert gerade in Deutschland nicht auch fragen, wie die jüdische Mystik in den Vertreibungen und Ausrottungen zu bestehen suchte? Wird diese Frage ausgelassen, dann kann in der Tat der Griff nach Laotse zur Ausflucht werden.

Zweifellos steht Heideggers kurzer Versuch, mit Laotse in ein Gespräch zu kommen, in unserer heutigen Situation in einem neuen und anderen Kontext. Die Weise, wie Heidegger und z. B. auch Werner Heisenberg sich auf die taoistische Tradition beriefen, war aber wohl motiviert. Leitend war die Frage, wie die Natur in ihrer Eigenständigkeit und die Menschen in ihr vor dem Zugriff der universalen Technik in einer Zeit der Weltkriege und der Tendenzen zu einer alles nivellierenden Weltzivilisation zu retten seien. Heidegger hat schnell eingesehen, daß die Sprachbarriere auch mit Hilfe eines (längst europäisierten) chinesischen Lektors nicht zu überwinden sei. Offenbar hat er seine Arbeitsnotizen vernichtet. Ein später englischsprachiger Bericht von Hsiao grenzt die Zusammenarbeit mit Heidegger überhaupt auf

---

(s. Anm. 10). S. 274; zum folgenden vgl. zu Misch S. 17 ff. Zu Kästner vgl. Pöggeler: *Neue Wege* (s. Anm. 8). S. 109.

[14]Gleiches gilt gegenüber vorschneller Kritik an Heideggers mystischem Wortgebrauch; vgl. meine Bemerkungen in: Zerstörung des moralischen Selbstbewußtseins: *Chance oder Gefährdung? Praktische Philosophie in Deutschland nach dem Nationalsozialismus.* Hrsg. vom Forum für Philosophie Bad Homburg. Frankfurt a. M. 1988. S. 255.

das Jahr 1946 ein und bringt nur noch einen Brief Heideggers vom 9.10.47 bei mit dem Wunsch, die Gespräche möchten bald wieder aufgenommen werden. Der Brief bezieht sich auf den 15. Abschnitt des Taoteking, den Hsiao in chinesischen Zeichen für Heidegger auf Pergament geschrieben hatte, aber nach dieser Mitteilung so, daß gegen den Text selbst in die Mitte der acht Zeichen eingefügt wurde: „Des Himmels Tao."[15] Heidegger versuchte eine deutsche Wiedergabe: „Wer kann still sein und aus der Stille durch sie auf den Weg bringen (bewegen) etwas so, daß es zum Erscheinen kommt? / Wer vermag es, stillend etwas so ins Sein zu bringen? / Des Himmels Tao."

Heidegger nimmt auf, was vor mehr als 2000 Jahren in China gedacht wurde, als in einer Zeit politischer Wirren und dem Aufstand menschlicher Eigenmächtigkeit die Natur und das menschliche Leben in ihr in ihrem eigenen „Weg" gewahrt werden mußten. Wenn Heidegger das genannte Bewegen und den Weg zusammen sieht, dann vermischt er von der deutschen Sprache her, was im Chinesischen nicht zusammengehört. Er folgt einer Interpretationsweise, die in der langen Tradition der Kommentierung von Laotse neu ist: er trägt seinen eigenen Versuch, die abendländische Tradition von ihren Grundworten und von deren Zusammenspiel her aufzunehmen, in Laotse hinein. So fügt er Laotses Rede von Trübwasser und Quirlwasser in ein Wortfeld ein, dem er selber folgt, nämlich in den Zusammenhang von Stille, Bewegung, Weg, Erscheinen, Ins-Sein-bringen. Im Text Laotses ist die angesprochene Bewegung durchaus nicht unmittelbar auf den Weg zu beziehen, die gestillte Ruhe nicht auf Heideggers Rede von der Stille.

Nach dem abrupten Abbruch der Bemühungen um Laotse hat Heidegger gefordert, daß die Zwiesprache mit den Griechen und damit die Verständigung der abendländischen Tradition über sich selbst „Vorbedingung für das unausweichliche Gespräch mit der ostasiatischen Welt" werde. Damals sah Heidegger seine eigene Erörterung des Wesens der Sprache begrenzt durch die Unkenntnis der ostasiatischen Sprachen; so hoffte er auf ein künftiges west-östliches Gespräch, in dem sich die „einzige Quelle" für die unterschiedlichen großen Ströme der Sprachen melden könne.[16] Nicht von ungefähr sprach Heidegger diese Hoffnung gegenüber einem japanischen Gast aus. Inzwischen ist es soweit gekommen, daß der Austausch zwischen deutschen und japanischen Philosophen keine Einbahnstraße bleibt: auch jüngere deutsche Philosophen beherrschen die japanische Sprache und

---

[15] Vgl. *Heidegger and Asian Thought* (s. Anm. 8). S. 100 und 102.

[16] Vgl. Martin Heidegger: *Vorträge und Aufsätze.* Pfullingen 1954. S. 47; *Unterwegs zur Sprache* (s. Anm. 11). S. 94. - Zum folgenden vgl. Kah Kyung Cho: *Bewußtsein und Natursein: Phänomenologischer West-Ost-Diwan.* Freiburg 1987; Derselbe: Heidegger und die Rückkehr in den Ursprung. In: *Zur philosophischen Aktualität Heideggers* (Symposium der A. von Humboldt-Stiftung). Hrsg. von Dietrich Papenfuss und Otto Pöggeler. Band 3. Frankfurt a. M. 1989. S. 299 ff.

können deshalb ein wirkliches Gespräch führen. Das Gespräch mit China braucht seine Zeit. Doch hat Kah Kyung Cho nicht nur die nötigen philologischen Korrekturen an Heideggers vorschnellem Zugriff auf Laotse vorgetragen; er hat dabei auch die Sache, um die es Heidegger ging, in einer neuen Situation durchgehalten. Damit hat er Wege gebahnt, die in Zukunft ausgebaut werden müssen.

Antwort auf das Fremde: Grundzüge einer responsiven Phänomenologie

Bernhard Waldenfels

Das Antworten, von dem im folgenden die Rede sein soll, meint nicht bloß eine besondere Weise, wie wir uns anderen gegenüber verhalten können; es steht vielmehr für die genuine Art und Weise, in der uns Fremdes als Fremdes begegnet. Fremdheit und Response gehören zusammen, allerdings so, daß Fremdes uns herausfordert, indem es sich unserem Zugriff entzieht und indem es selbst noch das Verstehen überschreitet. Der fremde Anspruch, auf den wir antworten, und das Antwortereignis selbst bilden keine Korrelation wie Sinn und Intention, wie Noema und Noesis bei Husserl. Sie sind in keiner Einheit oder Ganzheit aufgehoben. Eine Phänomenologie, die davon ausgeht, daß wir dem Fremden stets etwas schuldig bleiben, auch wenn wir ihm gerecht zu werden versuchen, verwandelt sich in eine responsive Phänomenologie, die über eine Phänomenologie der Intentionalität ebenso hinausgeht wie über eine Hermeneutik der Texte.[1]

Was das Fremde angeht, so liegt auf der Hand, daß es als Gegenpart des Eigenen zu den hochaktuellen Problemen der modernen, post- oder hypermodernen Lebenswelt gehört. Man sollte allerdings nicht gleich von Mode reden. Es ist auch nicht damit getan, daß wir es Problemen einer Fremdenpolitik zurechnen, die durch die Öffnung nationaler Landesgrenzen und durch die Vermischung kultureller Lebensformen entstehen. Das Fremde ist kein bloßes Symptom einer zunehmenden Multi- und Interkulturalität. Phänomenologen können darauf hinweisen, daß die Fremderfahrung seit langem, von Husserl, Scheler, Heidegger und Schütz bis zu Sartre, Merleau-Ponty, Levinas und Derrida, zu den Grundthemen phänomenologischen Denkens gehört. Worte wie ‚Interkulturalität,' ‚Intersubjektivität' und ‚Interaktion' bleiben leere Worte, solange das ‚Inter', das ‚Zwischen' nicht eigens bedacht wird und solange man nicht zu einer Zwischensphäre vorstößt, die allen Zentrierungen zuwider läuft. Wenn der japanische Phänomenologe und Psychiater Bin Kimura dieses Zwischen mit dem japanischen Ki in Verbindung bringt, [2] dann zeigt sich, daß jenes erwähnte Zwischen selbst

---

[1]Dieser Aufsatz erschien zuerst in: B. Waldenfels und J. Därmann (Hg.), *Der Anspruch des Anderen. Perspecktiven phänomenologicher Ethik*, München: Fink 1998. Ich versuche im folgenden eine Brücke zu schlagen zwischen anfänglichen Überlegungen zum Fremden (vgl. *Der Stachel des Fremden*, Frankfurt/M. 1990) und neueren Überlegungen im *Antwortregister* (Frankfurt/M. 1994). Die Ordnungskonzeption, die der Bestimmung des Fremden als Außer-ordentlichem zugrunde liegt, habe ich in *Ordnung im Zwielicht* (Frankfurt/M. 1987) entfaltet.

[2]Ich beziehe mich auf Bin Kimura, *Zwischen Mensch und Mensch*, übersetzt und hrsg. von Elmar Weinmayr, Darmstadt 1995. Die Anspielungen auf den

noch eine interkulturelle Färbung annimmt. Der Weg von West nach Ost und der Weg von Ost nach West sind nicht ein und derselbe Weg, den wir in verschiedener Richtung durchlaufen, wie manche Weltkulturplaner meinen.

Schließlich ein Wort zum Motiv des Fremden im westlichen Denken. Es ist keineswegs so, daß dieses Motiv zum Grundbestand der abendländischen Philosophie gehört; das Fremde tritt erst spät in den Kernbereich des Denkens ein, ansatzweise im 18. und 19. Jahrhundert, in verstärktem Maße im 20. Jahrhundert. Daß das Fremde erst allmählich die Problematisierungsschwelle überschreitet, erklärt sich durch eine Mutation innerhalb des westlichen Denkens, für die zweierlei maßgebend ist: die Veränderung der neuzeitlichen Vernunftauffassung und die Veränderung der neuzeitlichen Subjektrolle.

Was das erste Moment betrifft, so hat sich gezeigt, daß alle *Ordnungen* an bestimmte *Grenzen* stoßen. Die Grenzen, die unserem Sehen, Sprechen oder Fühlen gesetzt sind, lassen sich nicht unendlich erweitern bis hin zu einem umfassenden Kosmos oder einer umfassenden Weltgeschichte, worin alles seinen Platz fände. Es gibt Sinn, aber kein Reich der Vernunft; es gibt Freiheiten, aber kein Reich der Freiheit. Ordnungen, die etwas *so* in Erscheinung treten und zum Ausdruck kommen lassen *und nicht anders*, erweisen sich als selektiv und exklusiv. Sie ermöglichen etwas, indem sie zugleich anderes verunmöglichen. Das ‚alles zugleich' weicht einer unaufhebbaren Inkompossibilität, einem Widerstreit auf der Ebene der Erfahrung, der tiefer gelagert ist als der Widerspruch, der auf der Ebene theoreti-scher und praktischer Stellungnahmen auftritt.

Unter den Voraussetzungen begrenzter Ordnungen macht sich das Fremde bemerkbar in Form eines Außer-ordentlichen, das auf verschiedene Weise an den Rändern und in den Lücken der diversen Ordnungen auftaucht. Was die veränderte Rolle des sogenannten Subjekts angeht, so verliert der Mensch, der sich lange als Zentrum der Welt betrachtete, seine beherrschende Stellung. Was wir sind, sind wir nie ganz und gar. Das ‚Subjekt', das allem, was ist, zugrundezuliegen schien und das sich als Ort oder Träger der Vernunft betrachtete, leidet unter einem *Selbstentzug*, der durch keinen reflexiven „Rückgang zu sich selbst" wettzumachen ist. Kurz gesagt: es gibt keine Welt, in der wir je völlig heimisch sind, und es gibt kein Subjekt, das je Herr im eigenen Hause wäre. Diese Art von ‚Götzendämmerung' konfrontiert uns mit einem radikal Fremden, das allen Aneignungsbemühungen zuvorkommt und das ihnen widersteht wie im Falle des fremden Blicks, der uns trifft, noch ehe wir uns dessen versehen.

---

japanischen Kulturbereich lassen sich mit entsprechenden Variationen auf andere fernöstliche Kulturen übertragen.

I. Der Ort des Fremden

Das Fremde, das derart aus dem Dunkel tritt, entpuppt sich als ein Phänomen besonderer Art, das nicht einfach dem *logos* der Phänomene gehorcht. Schon die Sprache zeigt, daß wir es im Falle des Fremden mit einem höchst komplexen Phänomen zu tun haben. Das deutsche Wort ‚fremd,' das in klassischen und modernen Sprachen vielfach nur mit verschiedenen Worten wiederzugeben ist, besagt erstens das, was außerhalb des eigenen Bereichs liegt (vgl. *externum, foreign, étranger*), zweitens das, was anderen gehört (vgl. *alienum, alien*), drittens das, was von anderer Art, also fremdartig, heterogen ist (vgl. *strange, étrange*). Unter diesen drei Aspekten von *Ort, Besitz* und *Art und Weise* ist der erste Aspekt ausschlaggebend für die Gesamtbestimmung des Phänomens. Fremdes ist nicht einfach ein Anderes, das - wie in Platons *Sophistes* - durch *Abgrenzung* vom Selben entsteht. Wenn wir zwischen Apfel und Birne oder zwischen Tisch und Bett unterscheiden, so werden wir schwerlich behaupten, daß eines dem anderen fremd ist. Das eine ist schlichtweg das andere des anderen, wenn wir es als dieses oder jenes bestimmen. Fremdes geht dagegen hervor aus einer gleichzeitigen *Ein* - und *Ausgrenzung*. Das Fremde befindet sich anderswo; es ist ähnlich wie Schlafen vom Wachen, Gesundheit von der Krankheit, Alter von der Jugend durch eine Schwelle vom jeweils Eigenen getrennt. Dabei steht keiner von uns jemals auf beiden Seiten der Schwelle zugleich.

Dies gilt auch etwa für die Geschlechterdifferenz und für kulturelle Unterschiede. Es gibt keinen neutralen ‚dritten Menschen,' der zwischen Mann und Frau unterscheiden könnte, da doch zunächst der Mann *sich* von der Frau und diese *sich* vom Mann unterscheidet. Ebenso gibt es keinen kulturellen Schiedsrichter, der europäische und fernöstliche Kultur äußerlich voneinander scheiden könnte, da Europäer zunächst *sich* von Asiaten und diese *sich* von Europäern unterschieden haben müssen, bevor ein Schiedsspruch erfolgen kann. Das Sichunterscheiden vom Fremden zeigt selbst vielerlei historische und kulturelle Varianten. So sind für Homer die Trojaner noch keine Unverständliches stammelnde ‚Barbaren,' Hektor findet durchaus einen Ehrenplatz neben Achill. Die Schwarzweißbetrachtung beginnt erst im Griechenland des 5. Jahrhunderts und ist nicht ohne eine bestimmte Monopolisierung des ‚Logos' zu denken. Die jahrhundertelange Abschirmung der japanischen Kultur gegen fremde Einflüsse, die bis zur Meji-Epoche andauerte, steht auf einem ganz anderen Blatt. Es gibt nicht ‚das Fremde,' sondern es gibt verschiedene Fremdheitsstile. Fremdheit bestimmt sich, wie Husserl sagen würde, okkasionell, bezogen auf ein jeweiliges Hier und Jetzt. Ein standortloses ‚Fremdes überhaupt' gliche einem ‚Links überhaupt' - ein monströser Gedanke, der Ortsangaben mit begrifflichen Bestimmungen vermengt.

Der Ort des Fremden erweist sich zudem als Ort besonderer Art. Er läßt sich nicht in ein Ortsnetz einzeichnen, in dem wir uns frei bewegen, da er nur über eine Schwelle hinweg, also im vollen Sinne gar nicht zu erreichen ist. Dementsprechend heißt es bei Husserl: Das Wesen des Fremden besteht in einer „bewährbaren Zugänglichkeit des original Unzugänglichen" (Hua I, 144). An dieser paradoxen Bestimmung ist entscheidend, daß Fremdes nicht - wie vielfach selbst bei Hermeneutikern üblich - als Mangel, als Defizit bestimmt wird, als handle es sich lediglich darum, daß uns etwas *noch nicht* oder *nicht mehr* bekannt ist, obwohl es an sich und in sich selbst erkennbar ist. Vielmehr gehören Abwesenheit, Ferne und Unzugänglichkeit zur Fremdheit als solcher, ähnlich wie im Falle der Vergangenheit, die nirgends anders faßbar ist als in ihren Nachwirkungen oder in der Erinnerung. Das Fremde befindet sich nicht anderswo, es bestimmt sich selbst als *Anderswo*, als Atopie, so wie Sokrates bei Platon als *atopos*, als ortlos und fremdartig erscheint. Fremdheit besagt, daß etwas oder jemand niemals völlig an seinem Platz ist.

Diese Fremdheit beginnt nicht außerhalb meiner selbst, sie beginnt in uns selbst in Form einer intrasubjektiven wie auch einer intrakulturellen Fremdheit. Es gibt nicht nur ein anderes, zweites Ich, ein *alter ego*, vielmehr gilt der Satz Rimbauds: „Ich ist ein anderer" (*Je est un autre*); das Ich ist nicht umstandslos als ‚erste Person' zu bezeichnen. Als geburtliches Wesen, das sich immer schon in einer Welt vorfindet, die es nicht geschaffen hat, das einen Namen trägt, den es von Anderen empfangen hat, und das sich in fremden Augen entdeckt wie in einem Spiegel, bin ich gezeichnet durch eine Kluft, einen Spalt, der verhindert, daß derjenige, der ‚ich' (*je*) sagt, jemals mit dem ausgesagten Ich (*moi*) zusammenfällt. Die Kontextualität eines Ich, das sich niemals völlig individualisiert und stets Züge eines namenlosen Niemand an sich trägt, [3] tritt in der größeren Variabilität japanischer Personalpronomina und in der schwächer ausgeprägten Personalität japanischer Satzformen deutlicher zutage als in den gewöhnlichen europäischen Formen der Ich-Rede.

In westlichen Sprachen läßt sich schwer ein Äquivalent finden für einen japanischen Wortwechsel wie: *nani shiteruno* (wörtlich: „Was machen ? ") - *ongaku o kiiterundayo* (wörtlich: „Musik hören"). [4] Wo ein Tun ist, da ist auch ein Täter, wie Nietzsche spöttisch bemerkt. Aber handelt es sich in diesen und ähnlichen Fällen um ein wirkliches Tun, wie die grammatische Form des aktiven Verbs suggeriert? Wenn Lichtenberg bemerkt: „*Es denkt* sollte man sagen, wie man sagt: *es blitzt*," so setzt auch er, als „guter Europäer," ein Fragezeichen hinter den Versuch, alles, was *mit mir* geschieht, *durch mich* geschehen zu lassen, als sei ich Herr selbst der Einfälle, die mir kommen. Die Fremdheit, die schon bei uns selbst, also auch in der

[3] Vgl. dazu M. Merleau-Ponty, *Le visible et l'invisible*, Paris 1964, S. 299, dt.: *Das Sichtbare und das Unsichtbare*, München 1986, S. 310.

[4] Der nach Geschlecht, Alter und Vertrautheit variierende Bezug zum Sprecher bzw. zum Gesprächspartner wird mit Hilfe der angefügten agglutinativen Elemente *no* bzw. *dayo* hergestellt.

Heimat beginnt, findet ihren prägnanten Ausdruck in einem Haiku des Dichters Bashō: „In Kyoto wohnend sehne ich mich, beim Schrei des Kuckucks, nach Kyoto." Der Schrei des Kuckucks mag noch so bekannt sein, er kann uns immer wieder aus dem Gewohnten herausreißen, solange wir bereit sind, uns überraschen zu lassen. Wer diese Fremdheit seiner selbst verkennt, findet überall nur dasselbe und sich selbst wieder, soviele Länder und Meere er auch bereist.

II. Intentionalität, Regularität und Responsivität

Ein Phänomen wie das Fremde, das sich nur zeigt, indem es sich dem Zugriff entzieht, könnte man als *Hyperphänomen* bezeichnen. Dies bedeutet nicht nur, daß das, was sich als dieses oder jenes, als Stuhl oder Lokomotive, als Mond oder Kirschblüte, als Junge oder Mädchen zeigt, stets mehr und anderes ist als das, als was es sich zeigt. Vielmehr ist es gerade das *Sich* des Sichzeigens, das nicht aufgeht in dem, *was* sich zeigt. Eine Malerei, die dieses Sichzeigen selbst im Bild sichtbar zu machen versucht, nimmt Formen einer „indirekten Malerei" an, wie Merleau-Ponty in seinem *Essay Das Auge und der Geist* schreibt. Sie macht Unsichtbares sichtbar, ohne es seiner Unsichtbarkeit zu berauben. Dies erinnert an den *Lob des Schattens* bei Junichiro Tanizaki; der Autor zeigt, wie die indirekte Beleuchtung, die in der japanischen Alltagskultur gang und gäbe ist, den Dingen ihre Ferne beläßt. Wie könnte eine Phänomenologie aussehen, die auf ähnliche Weise aufzeigt, was immer nur erscheint, indem es nicht selbst erscheint? Wie könnte eine Phänomenologie aussehen, die mit einer leibhaftigen Abwesenheit rechnet?

Eines scheint mir sicher, das Moment der *Intentionalität*, das Brentano in die Gegenwartsphilosophie eingeführt hat, das seit Husserl den Grundzug der Phänomenologie ausmacht und das sich auch in hermeneutischen und analytischen Theorien des Verstehens niedergeschlagen hat, ist für sich genommen, nicht in der Lage, dem Fremden als Fremdem Raum zu gewähren. Intentionalität besagt, daß *etwas als etwas* gemeint und *auf etwas hin* verstanden, also in einem bestimmten *Sinn* aufgefaßt oder behandelt wird. Da das Fremde auf diese Weise vorweg schon in einem bestimmten Sinn vorverstanden ist, wird es zum Teil eines Sinnganzen, selbst wenn dieses sich erst nach und nach und nie völlig enthüllt. Verstehen ist selbst eine Form der Aneignung, und zwar eine besonders sublime Form, weil sie den Anschein erweckt, das Fremde, oder wie es mit Vorliebe heißt, das Andere komme im wahren Verstehen als es selbst zum Ausdruck. Wer demgegenüber auf ein Fremdes pocht, das sich dem Verstehen entzieht, gerät, so scheint es, in die Falle des performativen Selbstwiderspruchs, da er in seiner Rede verständlich zu machen versucht, was er selbst als unverständlich hinstellt.

Nicht besser ergeht es dem Fremden, wenn es in das Räderwerk der *Regularität* gerät, wie es in sprachanalytisch geprägten Kommunikationstheorien geschieht. Gemessen an *Regeln, wonach* sich alles Reden und Tun richtet, erscheint die fremde Äußerung als *Fall eines Regelsystems*, dem sie ebenso unterworfen ist wie die eigene Äußerung. Diese Einebnung des Unterschieds zwischen Eigenem und Fremdem ändert sich selbst dann nicht, wenn man - wie es üblicherweise geschieht - eine offene und veränderliche Form der Regelhaftigkeit konzediert. Abweichungen von Regeln bleiben auf eine potentielle Regelbefolgung bezogen, wenn nichts anderes ins Spiel kommt als die bloße Abweichung von Regeln. Das Fremdartige erscheint so als das Vertraute von morgen.

Bei näherem Hinsehen findet man schon bei Husserl Ansätze zur Überschreitung jener umfassenden Sinnsphäre, die auf eigenen Intentionen und gemeinsamen Regeln beruht. Ich denke hierbei an Husserls Lehre von den Affektionen. Diese Lehre setzt sich allerdings aus heterogenen Bestandstükken zusammen, die aus verschiedenen Erbschaften, aus der aristotelischen, der kantischen so gut wie aus der fichteanischen stammen und die nicht ohne weiteres zusammenstimmen. Man kann zwischen einem *hyletischen*, einem *selbstbezüglichen* und einem *responsiven* Aspekt der Affektion unterscheiden.

(1) Innerhalb der statischen Sichtweise der *Ideen* I beschränken Affektionen sich auf die Bereitstellung eines Materials, aus dem Gegenstände gebildet und aufgebaut werden. Bei dynamischer Betrachtung geht das Material in eine Teleologie der Sinnbildung ein. Was gegeben ist, ist stets schon *als etwas* gegeben. Die pure Hyle erweist sich ähnlich wie die *materia prima* bei Aristoteles als bloßer Grenzbegriff.

(2) Die formgebende und zielgerichtete Bewegung bedeutet allerdings nur dann einen sinnhaften Prozeß, wenn das Erscheinen von etwas zugleich ein Sicherscheinen, ein Erscheinen für sich einschließt, wenn also die Ausrichtung auf etwas gleichzeitig auf sich selbst bezogen ist, anders gesagt: wenn das Affiziertsein mit einer Selbstaffektion einhergeht. Einen ‚ichfremden' Reiz kann es nur geben, wenn das Ich sich als affiziertes Ich selbst mit affiziert. Diese Selbstbezüglichkeit, die uns schon bei Aristoteles in der Form der *philautia*, bei Rousseau in der Form des amour de soi begegnet, taucht innerhalb der Phänomenologie in den verschiedensten Zusammenhängen auf, so etwa in Husserls Lehre von den Urimpressionen, auf die später auch Levinas zurückgreift, in der Analyse der zeitlichen Selbstaffektion, die Heidegger in seinem Kant-Buch vornimmt, in der hyletischen Phänomenologie von Michel Henry, die von einer Immanenz des Sichlebens und Sichempfindens ausgeht.

(3) Die Selbstbezüglichkeit hat allerdings zur Kehrseite eine Fremdbezüglichkeit; das ‚*Ich*fremde' ist zugleich ein ‚Ich*fremdes*.' Auf der dritten Ebene, die sich damit andeutet, kommen quasi-dialogische oder, besser gesagt, responsive Aspekte zum Zuge. Die Qualifikation der Affektion als responsiv trifft die Sache besser, weil diese Affektion mit ihrem Hiatus von Fremd- und Selbstaffektion noch auf keinen gemeinsamen Sinn zurückgreifen kann. Der Schmerz, der uns übermannt, hat als Schmerz keine Bedeutung, obwohl er nachträglich als Symptom einer leiblichen Störung und eines Körper-

defekts gedeutet werden kann. Vor allem in seinen Reflexionen zur Intersubjektivität spricht Husserl wiederholt von einer Af-fektion, einem An-tun, einem An-gang oder schließlich von Anruf und Appell. Das ‚Ichfremde' ist kein stummes Nicht-Ich, es ist auch noch kein anderes Ich, es ist das, wovon das Ich ausgeht, wenn es etwas als etwas und sich als sich selbst erfährt. Auch Heidegger, der dem ‚Ruf' des Gewissens und dem ‚Zuspruch' des Seins zunehmend Raum gewährt, bestimmt in seinen *Beiträgen zur Philosophie* die Erfahrung als ein „auf etwas stoßen": „Das Zu-stoßende, An-gehende, Af-fektion." [5]

Hier zeigen sich Spuren einer anderen Phänomenologie. Diese weisen hin auf eine Responsivität, in der die Sphäre eines intentional oder regelhaft konstituierten Sinnes überschritten wird. Der Überschritt vollzieht sich im Antworten auf einen *fremden Anspruch, der weder einen Sinn hat, noch einer Regel folgt*, der im Gegenteil geläufige Sinn- und Regelbildungen unterbricht und neue in Gang setzt. Das, *was* ich antworte, verdankt seinen Sinn der Herausforderung dessen, *worauf* ich antworte.

Das Fremde, das in einem fremden Anspruch zum Vorschein und zum Ausdruck kommt, verliert diese seine Fremdheit, wenn die *responsive Differenz* zwischen dem, worauf wir antworten, und dem, was wir antworten, eingeebnet wird zugunsten eines intentionalen oder regelgeleiteten Sinngeschehens. Die responsive Differenz verschwindet dann hinter einer *signifikativen* oder *hermeneutischen Differenz*, in der etwas als etwas aufgefaßt oder verstanden wird, und sie verschwindet hinter einer regulativen Differenz, wo etwas gemäß einer Norm behandelt wird.

Das Fremde als Fremdes erfordert eine responsive Form von Phänomenologie, die jenseits von Sinn und Regel beginnt, dort, wo etwas uns herausfordert und unsere eigenen Möglichkeiten in Frage stellt, bevor wir uns auf ein fragendes Wissen- und Verstehenwollen einlassen. Dem geläufigen Primat eines Fragens, das als Sachfrage direkt in ein Wissensstreben oder Wissenwollen einmündet oder als intersubjektive Anfrage indirekt dorthin führt, setzen wir keinen neuen Primat entgegen. Bloße Umkehrungen führen im allgemeinen nicht weiter.

Stattdessen bedarf es einer Gewichtsverlagerung und einer Umorientierung. Es wäre zu zeigen, daß der Kreislauf von Frage und Antwort, der auf eine Erfüllung von Intentionen oder Geboten abzielt, und daß die symmetrische Verteilung von Frage- und Antwortrolle, die mich den Anderen und diese mir gleichstellt, kurz gesagt: daß der Dialog eine Asymmetrie von Anspruch und Antwort voraussetzt. In jedem Sprechen liegt ein Versprechen, das dem Konsens eines Wechselgesprächs und dem Konformismus regelrechten Verhaltens entrückt ist. Das vielberufene „Gespräch, das wir sind," kommt aus der Ferne eines Fremden, dessen Anspruch jeder Partnerschaft vorausgeht.

---

[5] M. Heidegger, *Beiträge zur Philosophie*, GA 65, Frankfurt/M. 1989, S. 161.

III. Anspruch und Antwort

Im fremden Anspruch, der den Zielkreis der Intentionalität ebenso durchbricht wie den Regelkreis der Kommunikativität, tritt das Fremde in actu zutage. Dieser Anspruch bedeutet zweierlei, nämlich einen Appell, der sich an *jemanden* richtet, und eine Prätention, die sich *auf etwas* erstreckt. Das Eigenartige des fremden Anspruchs liegt darin, daß beide Formen des Anspruchs sich verquicken. Im Anspruch, den ich vernehme, erhebt sich ein Anspruch, der mir etwas abverlangt. Dieser situativ verkörperte Anspruch liegt jedem moralischen oder rechtlichen Ansprüch voraus. Die Frage, ob der Anspruch berechtigt sei oder nicht, setzt voraus, daß bereits ein Anspruch vernommen wurde. Wir erreichen hier einen Punkt *diesseits von Gut und Böse, diesseits von Recht und Unrecht.*

Die Moral zeigt hier ihren blinden Fleck.[6] Jeder Versuch einer Moralbegründung setzt bereits tatsächliche Ansprüche voraus, die als Ansprüche mehr sind als bloße Tatsachen. Der einfache Vorgang, daß jemand mich nach dem Weg oder nach meinem Namen fragt, wird dann zur Tatsache, wenn ich ihn als Tatsache behandle, etwa derart, daß ich beobachte, wie jemand mich fragt, daß ich festelle, daß jemand mich fragt, oder erzähle, daß jemand mich gefragt hat. Doch was zur Tatsache *wird, ist keine* Tatsache. Die Faktifizierung der fremden Frage kann nicht verhindern, daß ich von der Frage getroffen, daß ich in Anspruch genommen bin. Das Antworten beginnt nicht mit dem Reden über etwas, es beginnt überhaupt nicht mit dem Reden, sondern mit dem Hinsehen und Hinhören, das eine eigene Form der Unausweichlichkeit hat. Den Imperativ „Höre ! “ kann ich nicht hören, ohne auf ihn zu hören. Das Verbot „Hör nicht auf mich! “ führt zu dem bekannten *double bind*: Wie immer man darauf reagiert, man macht es verkehrt. Selbst das Weghören setzt ein Hören, das Wegsehen ein Sehen voraus, so wie Nietzsches Verachtung eine Form der Beachtung einschließt.

Das Antworten, das dem doppelgestaltigen Anspruch entspricht, nimmt ebenfalls eine doppelte Form an. Dem Anspruch auf etwas korrespondiert die Antwort (*answer*), die ich gebe. Sprechakttheoretisch gesprochen handelt es sich um den passenden Antwortgehalt, der die Leerstellen im propositionalen Gehalt der Frage oder der Bitte ausfüllt. Diese Form der Antwort behebt einen Mangel. Doch damit ist das Antworten keineswegs erschöpft. Dem Anspruch, der sich an mich richtet, entspricht ein Antworten (*response*), das keine Lücke füllt, sondern auf Angebote und Ansprüche des Anderen eingeht. Dieses Antworten, das gibt, was es nicht hat, sondern im Antworten findet und erfindet, unterscheidet sich von der gegebenen Antwort auf ähnliche Weise, wie die Verneinung sich von der negativen Aussage unterscheidet.

---

[6] Vgl. meinen Nietzsche-Aufsatz „Der blinde Fleck der Moral,“ in: *Deutsch-Französische Gedankengänge*, Frankfurt/M. 1995.

Die Verweigerung einer Antwort geschieht auf der Ebene des Aussageereignisses (*énonciation*), nicht auf der Ebene des Aussagegehaltes (*énoncé*). Das Geben einer Antwort erschöpft sich nicht in der gegebenen Antwort. Die gegebene Antwort kann unter Umständen von einem Antwortautomaten übernommen werden, der auf eine passende Anfrage passend reagiert. Für das Geben der Antwort gilt dies nicht, außer im Falle eines präfabrizierten Dialogs, wo Antworten lediglich ausgelöst oder abgerufen werden. Ein Automat, der nicht funktioniert, begeht keine Dienstverweigerung.

Ein deutliches Indiz für die erwähnte Verdoppelung der Antwort in Antwortereignis und Antwortgehalt findet sich darin, daß ich auf eine Frage durchaus mit einer Gegenfrage antworten kann, mit einer Antwort also, die das von einem anderen gesuchte oder erbetene Wissen gerade nicht beibringt. Keine Antwort ist bekanntlich auch eine Antwort. Wenn das gilt, so ist Antwort nicht gleich Antwort.

Das Antworten, das auf fremde Ansprüche eingeht, erschöpft sich keineswegs in sprachlichen Äußerungen. So gehen bei der Erfüllung einer Bitte oftmals fremde Rede und eigene Handlung ineinander über, so etwa wenn ich den gewünschten Handgriff tue. Man kann ferner mit Blicken provozieren und auf Blicke replizieren. Blickgefechte gehören zum Alltag einer Großstadt. Im Antworten verkörpert sich ein Ethos der Sinne, das von Grußritualen bis zu den Spielen der Liebe reicht. Der alte Satz: „Der Mensch ist ein Lebewesen, das Rede oder Vernunft hat,“ ließe sich umformen in den Satz: „Der Mensch ist ein Lebewesen, das Antworten gibt.“ Dabei müßte der Unterschied zwischen Mensch und Tier ebenso wie der zwischen Mensch und Maschine neu bedacht werden.

IV. Momente einer Antwortlogik

Die Responsivität als Grundzug menschlichen Verhaltens verlangt nach einer besonderen Art von *Antwortlogik*, die sich von der Logik intentionaler Akte, von der Logik des Verstehens oder von der Logik kommunikativen Handelns beträchtlich unterscheidet. Sie führt zu einer eigenen Form von responsiver Rationalität, einer Rationalität nämlich, die aus dem Antworten selbst entspringt. Vier Momente dieser Logik möchte ich abschließend skizzieren, um deutlich zu machen, wie traditionelle Themen im Lichte des Antwortens zu schillern beginnen.

Der fremde Anspruch, der mehr ist als Teil eines Ganzen oder als Fall eines Gesetzes, gewinnt eine eigentümliche *Singularität*. Diese Singularität tritt durchaus im Plural auf,[7] aber doch so, daß sie sich der Distinktion von Besonderem und Allgemeinem entzieht. Eine solche Singularität besagt nicht, daß etwas nur einmal vorkommt, wie etwa der gerade erklingende Ton

[7] Vgl. meinen Levinas-Aufsatz „Singularität im Plural,“ in: *Deutsch-Französische Gedankengänge, a.a.O.*

oder die begangene Straftat. Singularität besagt auch nicht, daß etwas sich als Einzelfall unter andere Einzelfälle einreiht.

Wir haben es nicht mit dem Individuum zu tun, das nach alter Auffassung unsagbar ist, weil es zum Saum einer alles bedeckenden Allgemeinheit gehört. Vielmehr handelt es sich um eine Singularität von Ereignissen, die als solche auftreten, indem sie von gewohnten Ereignissen abweichen und ein anderes Sehen, Denken und Handeln ermöglichen. Im Leben des Einzelnen wie im Leben ganzer Völker und Kulturen gibt es Schlüsselereignisse, ‚die sich nicht vergessen,' weil sie eine symbolische Ordnung einführen, Sinn stiften, eine Geschichte eröffnen, zu Antworten herausfordern, Verpflichtungen hervorrufen.

In diesem Sinne war die französische Revolution für die beteiligten Europäer keine Revolution unter anderen, und aus dieser Einzigartigkeit heraus wurde sie zum Kristallisationskern diverser Mythen und Riten. Erst mit den Augen eines Dritten betrachtet erscheint die französische Revolution neben der amerikanischen, der russischen oder der chinesischen als eine Revolution unter anderen, so wie das Kind, einmal erwachsen geworden, die Mutter als eine Frau neben anderen und den Geburtsort als einen Ort unter vielen betrachten lernt.

Der fremde Anspruch fällt ebenfalls nicht unter die Disjunktion von Tatsachen und Normen, von Sein und Sollen, die seit Hume und Kant das Feld der praktischen Philosophie beherrscht. Der Anspruch, der etwas zu sehen, zu hören, zu denken, zu tun und zu fühlen gibt, tritt auf mit einer *Unausweichlichkeit*, einer *necessitudo* im wörtlichen Sinne, die sich nicht aus allgemeinen Gesetzen ableitet, sondern als praktische Notwendigkeit zu den unumgänglichen Voraussetzungen unserer weltlich-sozialen Existenz gehört. Sie führt dazu, daß ich auf einen vernommenen Anspruch nicht nicht antworten kann, ähnlich wie ich laut Watzlawick *nicht nicht* kommunizieren kann; denn auch das Nichtantworten wäre eine Antwort.

Die doppelte Negation, die darin liegt, daß ich nicht nicht antworten kann, kennen wir aus der modallogischen Bestimmung der Notwendigkeit; [8] sie verweist auf Erfordernisse, die sich nur indirekt, nämlich als unumgängliche Voraussetzung bestimmter Erfahrungen fassen, nicht aber positiv herleiten lassen. Kant hat in ähnlichen Zusammenhängen von einem „Faktum der Vernunft," Husserl von der „Notwendigkeit eines Faktums" (Hua III, 109) oder von einem „absoluten Faktum", Sartre von einer „*nécessité de fait*" gesprochen. In dieser seiner Radikalität gleicht der fremde Anspruch traditionellen Instanzen wie Glücksstreben, Selbsterhaltungstrieb, kategorischer Imperativ und Freiheit, die - wenn es sie gibt - allesamt nicht zur Wahl stehen und sich allesamt einem Berechtigungsnachweis entziehen. Nach Auffassung Platons steht es nicht in unserer Macht, das Glück anzu-

[8] Der Satz „es ist notwendig, daß p" läßt sich mit Hilfe des Möglichkeits-Operators M wiedergeben als: „nicht M (nicht-p)."

streben, so wie für Kant es nicht in unserem Belieben liegt, ob wir auf das moralische Gesetz hören oder nicht.

Das, wovon unser Reden und Sagen ausgeht und immer schon ausgegangen ist, läßt sich nicht beobachten, beurteilen oder bewerkstelligen wie etwas, das vor unseren Augen und in unserer Hand liegt. Es tritt nur zutage, *indem* wir etwas sagen und tun. Es ist angewiesen auf eine indirekte Rede- und Mitteilungsweise, die dem Schweigen verbunden bleibt. Dies gilt auch für den Sog, der vom Fremden und speziell von einer fremden Kultur ausgeht. Gewiß spielen sich zwischen Kulturen auch Lernprozesse ab, sobald das Niveau eines 'interkulturellen Dialogs' erreicht ist. Doch einen Sog beherrscht man sowenig wie das Staunen oder die Manie der Liebe. Auf Beunruhigungen dieser Art kann man sich nur einlassen, oder man kann sich ihnen entziehen.

Singuläre Ereignisse treten nicht nur mit einem unausweichlichen Anspruch auf, sondern auch mit einer uneinholbaren *Nachträglichkeit*, die den Primat einer ursprünglichen Gegenwart untergräbt. Die Gegenwart ist nicht nichts, wie manche postmoderne Allesverflüchtiger meinen, aber sie begnügt sich nicht mit sich selbst. Das Antworten geschieht hier und jetzt, doch es beginnt anderswo. Die Nachträglichkeit führt laut Derrida dazu, daß das Ursprüngliche nur ‚ersatzweise' zum Vorschein kommt, nämlich gestützt auf Supplemente, die eine endlose Kette ‚originärer Wiederholungen' nach sich ziehen. Dieselbe Nachträglichkeit verweist auf jene traumatischen Unfälle, die laut Freud einzig in ihren Nachwirkungen faßbar sind, so etwa in der Kindheitsgeschichte des Wolfsmannes. Wollte man hier von kommunikativer Verzerrung reden, so würde man die Sache verharmlosen. Man übersähe auf diese Weise, daß die Einrichtung eines kommunikativen Feldes so wenig auf dem Weg kommunikativer Absprache geschieht, wie die Verfassung eines Landes nicht selbst von einem verfassungskonformen Akt eingeführt wird und ihre Befolgung nicht selbst in die Paragraphen der Verfassung Einlaß findet. Die Stiftung einer Ordnung ist ein Ereignis, das nicht Teil der Ordnung ist, die sie ermöglicht. Insofern hat jede Geburt, in der eine neue Welt sich eröffnet, Züge einer Wiedergeburt, da sie nur im nachhinein faßbar ist. Freiheit bedeutet in diesem Sinne die Fähigkeit, nicht schlechthin bei sich selbst, sondern anderswo anzufangen. Wer glaubt, bei sich selbst anfangen zu können, wiederholt nur, was schon ist; er fängt also gerade nicht an. Antwort bedeutet den Verzicht auf ein erstes - und somit auch auf ein letztes Wort.

Mit der zeitlichen Verschiebung von Anspruch und Antwort geht eine unaufhebbare *Asymmetrie* Hand in Hand, die den traditionellen Dialog, der auf gemeinsame Ziele ausgeht oder sich nach gemeinsamen Regeln richtet, unaufhaltsam aus dem Gleichgewicht bringt und auch moralische Gleichheitsforderungen wie die der Goldenen Regel hinter sich läßt. Wie Levinas zeigt, beruht die Asymmetrie nicht darauf, daß Rollen in einem bestehenden Dialog ungleichmäßig verteilt sind, sondern darauf, daß Anspruch und Antwort nicht auf ein Gemeinsames hin konvergieren.

Zwischen Frage und Antwort gibt es ebensowenig einen Konsens wie zwischen Bitte und Erfüllung. Sie prallen aufeinander wie zwei Blicke, die sich kreuzen. Das Eingehen auf einen fremden Anspruch und das Geschenk einer Antwort geraten erst dann auf die Bahnen eines wechselseitigen Gebens und Nehmens, wenn Eigenes und Fremdes im Lichte eines Dritten betrachtet werden, der Vergleiche anstellt und im Konfliktfall für einen Ausgleich sorgt.

Der Gesichtspunkt des Dritten, der Recht und Gerechtigkeit ermöglicht, ist auf gewisse Weise unentbehrlich. Sofern im Reden und Handeln immer schon wiederholbare Gestalten, allgemeine Regeln und Gesetze im Spiel sind, ist immer auch ein Dritter oder ein Drittes im Spiel. Doch indem der fremde Anspruch einem allgemeinen Gesetz unterworfen und derart gleich *gesetzt* wird, was nicht gleich *ist*, enthält Gerechtigkeit stets ein Moment der Ungerechtigkeit. Der Versuch, zwischen Eigenem und Fremdem eine endgültige Symmetrie herzustellen und beide einander gleichzumachen, gliche letzten Endes dem Versuch, Gegenwart und Vergangenheit, Wachen und Schlafen oder Leben und Tod in ein Gleichgewicht zu bringen, als könnte man die Schwelle, die eines vom anderen trennt, nach Belieben in beiden Richtungen überqueren. Das Fremde läßt dies nicht zu; es gleicht Einfällen, die uns kommen, Obsessionen, die uns heimsuchen, Träumen, aus denen wir nie völlig erwachen. Es entstammt einem unwiderruflichen Einst und Anderswo.

Wenn wir auf solche Weise das Antworten dem gegebenen Sinn und den bestehenden Regeln entrücken, dann müssen wir allerdings unterscheiden zwischen einem primär *repetitiven* oder *reproduktiven* und einem primär *innovativen* oder *produktiven* Antworten. Für das ordentliche, normale Antworten gilt, daß es Sinn hat und bestimmten Regeln folgt. Doch das gleiche gilt nicht für ein Antworten auf ungeahnte Ansprüche, das eine bestehende Ordnung durchbricht und die Bedingungen des Verstehens und der Verständigung mit verändert. Dort, wo die Ordnung der Dinge ins Wanken kommt, klafft ein Hiatus zwischen fremder Provokation und eigener Produktion. Wir stoßen hier auf das Paradox einer kreativen Antwort, das Merleau-Pontys Paradox eines kreativen Ausdrucks gleicht.[9]

Die Antwort ist als Antwort kreativ. Der Anspruch gehört nicht einer Ordnung an, in die das Antworten eingefügt oder der es unterworfen ist. Der Anspruch wird vielmehr erst zum Anspruch in der Antwort, die er hervorruft und der er uneinholbar vorausgeht. Das Antworten läuft somit über einen schmalen Grat, der bloße Hörigkeit und Willfährigkeit von Willkür und Beliebigkeit trennt. Wer auf fertige Antworten wartet, hat nichts zu sagen, weil alles *schon gesagt* ist. Wer umgekehrt redet, ohne zu antworten, hat auch nichts zu sagen, da es für ihn *nichts zu sagen* gibt. Wir erfinden,

---

[9] Vgl. „Das Paradox des Ausdrucks," in: *Deutsch-Französische Gedankengänge, a.a.O.*

was wir antworten, nicht aber das, worauf wir antworten und was unserem Reden und Tun Gewicht verleiht.

Literatur

Heidegger, Martin, *Beiträge zur Philosophie*, G.A. 65, Frankfurt/M. 1989.

Hussserl, Edmund, *Cartesianische Meditationen*, Husserliana I, Den Haag 1950.

Kimura, Bin, *Zwischen Mensch und Mensch*, übersetzt und hrsg. von Elmar Weinmayr, Darmstadt 1995.

Merleau-Ponty, Maurice, *Le visible et l'invisible*, Paris 1964. -Deutsch: *Das Sichtbare und das Unsichtbare*, übersetzt von Rejula Giuliani und Bernhard Waldenfels, München 1986.

Waldenfels, Bernhard, *Ordnung im Zwielicht*, Frankfurt/M. 1987.

Waldenfels, Bernhard, *Der Stachel des Fremden*, Frankfurt/M. 1990

Waldenfels, Bernhard, *Antwortregister*, Frankfurt/M. 1994.

Waldenfels, Bernhard, *Deutsch-Französische Gedankengänge*, Frankfurt/M. 1995.

Difference and Responsibility

Hwa Yol Jung

> Where there is no vision, the people perish. The scholars are the priests of that thought which establishes the foundation of the earth. – Ralph Waldo Emerson

> If we keep on speaking the same language together, we're going to reproduce the same history. – Luce Irigaray

> [T]he secret of man is the secret of his responsibility. – Václav Havel

I. Prologue

The concept of responsibility lives in the shadow of the hagiographic life of rights in the modern West. Western modernity has privileged rights while handcuffing and marginalizing responsibility. America, in particular, is the land of rights talk, and American political and legal thought has been enslaved to and by it. As Amy Gutman (1989: 338) recently points out, "[m]ost prominent political philosophers are now rights theorists." Today rights talk has invaded and colonized even the nonhuman world of nature: we speak of the "rights of nature" and "animal rights" as well as "civil rights" and "human rights." We are indeed possessed and compressed by rights talk. So-called "retreat" from or the "reclamation" of responsibility is a phantom expression because responsibility has never assumed conceptual prominence or strategic equity with rights in Western modernity.

The conceptual career of responsibility has been stagnant, taunted, and dismal. It has become suffused, infused, and confused with a person's "accountability" for his/her own conduct ever since it was first introduced in English and French in 1787 (see McKeon, 1957). Having been associated with personal, political, and legal reward and blame or punishment, responsibility has by and large become and still remains to be merely a sublimated correlative of rights (Card, 1987: 3) even for those who are concerned with the concept. Taking responsibility means standing behind, backing, or giving support to the substantive idea of rights (see Card, 1987: 5).[1]

[1] In the tradition of existential philosophy and phenomenology, Schrader (1960) attributes responsibility to the inner-directed formulation of existence. Dauenhauer's (1991) work is informative. It is useful particularly in that it distinguishes freedom as autonomous from freedom as relational. He (1991: xii) con-

I find it most ironic and incredible to discover that even the later writings of C. B. Macpherson (1985: 76-85), whose high reputation lodges in his single-minded and righteous critique of liberalism as possessive individualism (see Macpherson, 1962), appears to have succumbed to the language of rights when he suggests controvertibly if not incomprehensibly that we get further by treating "human rights" as "individual property rights" to promote, preserve, and reclaim both human dignity and the ecological balance of nature. Zygmunt Bauman (1993: 25), who considers Emmanuel Levinas as the most important moral philosopher of our century, too, falls unfortunately into the confusion between rights and responsibility on the one hand and between "having" and "being" on the other when he affirms:

> [m]oral responsibility is the most personal and inalienable of human possessions, and the most precious of human rights. It cannot be taken away, shared, ceded, pawned, or deposited for safe keeping. Moral responsibility is unconditional and infinite, and it manifests itself in the constant anguish of not manifesting itself enough. Moral responsibility does not look for reassurance for its right to be or for excuses for its right not to be. It is there before any reassurance or proof and after any excuse or absolution.

There is indeed a paramount and urgent need to rectify the name and concept *responsibility.*

This paper is conceived as a counterproposal to *Taking Rights Seriously* (1977) of Ronald Dworkin who has now become the chief spokesperson for the rights tradition of Hobbes, Locke, John Austin, and William Blackstone. "If someone has a right to something," Dworkin (1977: 269) asserts, "then it is wrong for the government to deny it to him even though it would be in the general interest to do so." The absolute and universal claim of rights talk begins with Locke's idea that *in the beginning* all the world was America and ends with Francis Fukuyama's recent apocalyptic and redemptive pronouncement that *in the ending* all the world will, if it has not already become, America.[2] In this paper I intend to unpack or deconstruct rights talk and explore the ethical and political discourse of responsibility as an alternative to it.

---

siders tyranny and anarchy as "the twin antitheses of responsible politics." May (1992) explores responsibility particularly from Sartre's social existentialism and the philosophical insights of Arendt. Most recently Derrida (1992) attempts to formulate responsibility with an accent on difference in the backdrop of the homogenizing logic of European modernity. They all lack the heteronomic structure which is found in Levinas.

[2]For a sharp critique of the "heavenly city" of Americocentric liberalism and of its universal commensurability of a global market, see John Gray (1994).

II. The Hegemony of Rights Talk and American Exceptionalism

Mary Ann Glendon's ***Rights Talk*** (1991) is the most scathing and serious critique of American liberalism as possessive individualism or what she calls "the American rights dialect," i.e., the American parochial language of the "*I's have it.*" "The American rights dialect," she (1991: 76) contends, "is distinguished not only by what we say and how we say it, but also by what we leave unsaid." As it has become absolutized and universalized, rights talk is the lightning rod of liberalism as possessive individualism because, as Annette Baier (1994: 232) concisely puts it, "the language of rights is the language of language users who are becoming conscious of themselves as individuals."

There is a revival of American exceptionalism — the revival of the heroic, self-reliant "frontier" individualism of Ralph Waldo Emerson which is indigenous to American soil whose two faithful "children" are Henry Thoreau who was a protestant individualist and naturalist and Walt Whitman who sang the "Song of Myself" and "Democratic Vistas." Interestingly, the revival of what I call American exceptionalism or — to use Jacques Derrida's (1992: 73) felicitous expression — "the irreplaceable ***inscription*** of the universal in the singular" at this juncture of American history would appear to be an expression of the American anxiety of European influence which, for nativists, litter the intellectual landscape of American academia: existentialism, phenomenology, hermeneutics, structuralism, poststructuralism, Marxism, critical theory, deconstructionism, postmodernism, and others.

Henry James, Sr. wrote that Emerson was an American John the Baptist, proclaiming tidings of great joy to the American Israel (see West, 1989: 9).[3] The Americanist Ihab Hassan (1996: 68) expands on James's description of American exceptionalism as vouchesafed in "a Puritan myth, deriving directly from God's Grace. This myth promised the New Jerusalem, the White City on the Hill, redemption from History. Later, in the more secular moment of the American Revolution, the myth assumed the fulfillment of the European Enlightenment, creating a society dedicated to life, liberty, and the pursuit of happiness."[4] Emerson's prophetic optimism for the future of the New World is quite unlike the European temperament of suspicion found in Marx, Nietzsche, and Freud. George Kateb has become an elegant spokesperson for both Emerson as a genius of American democratic politics and Emersonianism as a witness to American exceptionalism which

---

[3]See also Bercovitch (1975) for a hermeneutics of the New Jerusalem. West (1989: 9-41) singles out Emerson in the genealogy of American pragmatism.

[4]For a scathing critique of the connection between liberalism and the Enlightenment whose hegemonic grip leads to a global as well as Western shipwreck, see John Gray (1995), especially Chap. 10, "Enlightenment's Wake," pp. 144-84.

fashioned the American "intellectual Declaration of Independence" (Emerson, 1940a). The main title of his work *The Inner Ocean: Individualism and Democratic Culture* (1992) emulates Emerson's expression "internal ocean" in his seminal essay "Self-Reliance" (1940: 143) the kernel of whose message is the unwavering affirmation of individuality, that is, "the belief in the absolute integrity, spiritual primacy, and inviolable sanctity of the self" – to borrow the expression of the noted Americanist Sacvan Bercovitch(1993: 314). Kateb is unequivocal in claiming the overarching kernel of Emersonian self-reliance as democratic individualism, even as modern democracy when he (1995: 202) remarks: "Self-reliance is the soil and fruit and flower of modern democracy. If self-reliance is discredited, democracy is reduced. The status of Emerson is tied to the status of democracy."

Emerson envisioned the "nonconformist," rugged individual as the soul of the world as well as the moral center of the American way. What is new in him, Kateb (1992) emphasizes, is the ideal of democratic individualism which should not be confused with being "bourgeois" or "atomistic." The moral basis of Emerson's democratic individualism, according to Kateb (1992: 1), is the belief that "respect for individual rights is the best way of honoring human dignity, that is, the equal dignity of every individual." Human dignity is inseparable from individual rights: "To make rights anything but primary, even though in the name of human dignity, is to injure human dignity" (Kateb, 1992: 5). The nonconformist concern for individual dignity or rights in Emerson's ideal of self-reliance is not entirely new, however: it is the same concern for inviolable individuality articulated by Alexis de Tocqueville in the 1830s and later by John Stuart Mill. Let Emerson (1940: 143) speak for himself: ". . . now we are a mob. Man does not stand in awe of man, nor is his genius admonished to stay at home, to put itself in communication with the internal ocean, but it goes abroad to beg a cup of water of the urns of others men. WE MUST GO ALONE" (my capitalization). He made it perfectly clear that "in all my lectures, I have taught one doctrine, namely, *the infinitude of the private man*" (quoted in West, 1989: 28. My emphasis). Is he not speaking of the familiar American culture of narcissism – the narcissist being that individual who invests all of his attention and energy in himself/herself to the exclusion of others?

What is wrong with rights talk or the American rights dialect which has become the *lingua franca* of American political and legal thought? It is simply unbalanced or one-sided, that is to say, it is false and wrong when every want is translated into a right (see Elshtain, 1995a: 16) and compassion becomes defaced into and replaced by contempt (Lasch, 1995: 105). Unencumbered by responsibility or obligation, it is a fanatical conceit. Glendon, too, speaks of the "scotoma" of the American rights talk. To be sure, the goodness and badness of rights talk are in details. Since the time of Tom Paine who gallantly defended the "rights of man," rights talk has advocated the viewpoint of the victimized, oppressed, or disadvantaged including trees and animals (see Almond, 1993: 263). For example, the Rawlsian "original position" based imaginatively on the "veil of ignorance" can be viewed as an attempt to put every person including the disadvantaged on an equal footing. Nevertheless, rights talk may be faulted on a twofold account: first, it is ontologically misinformed and misconceived and secondly, it is, being egocentric, tantamount to the denial of the ethical in that there is no ethics involved in self-centeredness or in the pursuit of happiness as the maximization of one's self-interest. The ethical privileges the Other and is always other-directed.

III. The Embodied Aesthetic of Relationality

To be human is to be interhuman. Human existence is relational through and through. As human reality is social process, it is socially constructed: we are born into and construct the world as "multiple realities." Social existence is characteristic of, and quintessential to, the humanity of humankind. Good or bad, we are indeed condemned to social existence. Insofar as we are born of mothers, we are always already socially situated. The religious myth of immaculate conception is the most miraculous of all miracles because it defies the law of human coexistence. There is no self unencumbered by the surrounding environment both social and natural. Hannah Arendt (1958: 22) cannot be faulted when she declares that "[n]o human life, not even the life of the hermit in nature's wilderness, is possible without a world which directly or indirectly testifies to the presence of other human beings." However attractive and precious the terms *self-reliance, rights, autonomy,* and *independence* may be, they are disconnected with affiliation, association, and interdependence. Interdependence, that is, interdependence *cum* difference, cannot and must not be anathema to the human or cosmic condition of plurality.

In the beginning was the word, and it was called "Relation" that authors both thought and action in the co-presence of the self and the Other. As the basic root word or *Grundwort,* the Relation accompanies and corresponds to every human birth as a new beginning. Only where there is the Relation, is there the ethical. The ethical was born at the same time as the relational: they are born as twins. Like Jackson Pollock's paintings with a labyrinthine network of lines with uncountable intersections, the world is nothing but an interwoven web of relationships.

To put it simply: in the beginning was *primum relationis* (see Jacques, 1991: 115-61). In the world described in terms of the primacy of relation, we need to introduce new words, new concepts: "interbeing"[5] and

[5] "Interbeing" is the concept employed by the Vietnamese Zen Buddhist Thich Nhat Hanh (1993). It refers to the Buddhist teaching that in the universe nothing can exist by itself alone and that everything must "inter-be" with everything else. In sinic thought, it is called synchronicity.

"interdividuality."[6]

Alfred Schutz (1962: 53) defines the social construction of reality or "social reality" as "the sum total of objects and occurrences within the social cultural world as experienced by the common-sense thinking of men living their daily lives among their fellow-men, connected with them in manifold relations of interaction." Just as the world is not my private but already socialized world, my knowledge of it is from the start socialized as well by way of the "reciprocity" of individual perspectives or the "interchangeability" of individual standpoints. Likewise, moral philosophy itself is grounded in the natural experience of the life-world as socio-cultural world or what Charles Taylor (1989: 14) concisely calls the "affirmation of ordinary life." In his work on the phenomenology of morals, therefore, Maurice Mandelbaum (1955: 31) insists that the phenomenological approach is "eductive" rather than "deductive." "In other words," he (1955: 31) continues, "the phenomenological approach holds that the proper basis for any moral generalization, and for the confirmation which we rightfully demand for such a generalization, are to be found in an examination of the moral judgments which [ordinary] men [and women] make."

The body is the living site and the material condition of sociality. As the co-presence of the self and the Other, sociality is inconceivable without bodies-in-relation. It is made of fleshly connected selves, that is, it is intercorporeal. It is not trite to emphasize that we began only very recently to understand the weighty normative consequences of defining sociality in terms of intercorporeality on matters of life and death in humanity ranging from abortion to euthanasia, from sexuality to pornography, from incarceration and torture to capital punishment, from illness to health and medicine, etc. We particularly philosophers whose primary concern is allegedly the mind's I or Reason often forget or take for granted *the factum brutum* that the body is the active mode of being in the world and that it is the primordial location of the social (see Jung, 1996). The body is indeed a carnal interbeing. The most serious consequence of the Cartesian division of mind and body as two separate substances – one as *res cogitans* and the other as *res extensa* – is that it denies, and is incapable of justifying, the concept of sociality. The Cartesian *cogito* is totally unaware of the body as a social phenomenon. It takes the disembodied subject as the hostage of knowledge or – to borrow William James's expression (1909: 256) – it is "wedded to the decomposition of life." Its interiority is sealed from corporeal and thus worldly exteriority. Once the mind becomes a separate substance independent of and disconnected from the body, egocentrism or even solipsism is inevitable.

---

[6] "Interdividuality" is the neologism of René Girard (1987). I appropriate the term to emphasize the space of the betweenness (*inter*) without losing sight of "individuality."

The body (as flesh) is an intrinsically social phenomenon. Everything corporeal, every flesh, is social through and through: where there is no body, there is no sociality and no reality. To be social is to be intercorporeal. Only because of the body (as flesh) are we said to be visible and capable of relating ourselves first to other bodies and then to other minds. The body is our *social placement* in the world. Only in this sense, is the world said to be made of the same stuff as the body. In defining the social, the phenomenologist Erwin W. Straus favors the ontological primacy of the body over the mind when he (1966: 211) says that "the body of an organism is related to other bodies; it is a part of the physical universe. The mind, however, is related to one body only; it is not directly related to the world, nor to other bodies, nor to other minds." The mind becomes a relatum only because the body is populated in the world with other bodies. It is necessary that we exist as body, as flesh, in order to be social and thus ethical notwithstanding the ethics of the body itself. It stands to reason to conclude that there is not only the primacy of perception in everything we do and think but also there can be no "disembodied reason" insofar as perception is a "nascent *logos.*" Indeed the body is never an object among other objects but is a sentient subject or the subject of perception which is capable of "authoring" the world before "answering" it. Perception or the function of the body as flesh, in turn, is informed and "dilated" by the "ecological milieu" of culture.

Friedrich Nietzsche, who called himself a "physician" of culture, is a radically subversive thinker and as such occupies a unique place in the history of the aesthetic as a discourse of the body. His heroic philosophy of the body is indeed an *aesthetics of social existence.* Terry Eagleton (1990: 13) informs us that the body's opus is twofold. In the first place, the aesthetic (*aisthesis*) is born as a discourse of the body: it is intrinsically a carnal affair. In the second place, the aesthetic is the body's rebellion against the "tyranny of the theoretical" (*theoria*). It is no accident that he, who proposes in *Thus Spoke Zarathustra* (1959: 146) that "body am I entirely, and nothing else; and soul is only a word for something about the body," challenges and transgresses the speculative conumdrum of *theoria* and replaces it with *aisthesis.* By replacing specular *theoria* with participatory *aisthesis*, Nietzsche attempts to invert Platonism which seeks the eternal and heavenly ideas (*eidos*) radiated from the "mind's eye" and abandons the fleeing moments of earthly reality. In *The Birth of Tragedy*, his first major work, the young Tantric Nietzsche (1967: 52 and 141) valorizes music as the consummate aesthetic: "it is only as an *aesthetic phenomenon* that existence and the world are eternally justified" and that "only music, placed beside the world, can give us an idea of what is meant by the justification of the world as an aesthetic phenomenon." Only thinking *in, through, and with* the body, does Nietzsche offer an aesthetics of social existence. His ultimate and most trenchant criticism of the dominant Western tradition of philosophizing from Plato's *theoria* to Christian asceticism and Cartesian epistemocracy would be that it is a denial of sociality, it is elementarily and deeply anti-social.

IV. Difference as Relationality

Relation, subjectivity, and difference are intimately related and complementary but never oppositional terms (see Jacques, 1991). Plurality or a web of relationships, according to Arendt (1958: 175-76), initials the human condition. It means that we coexist with others in their otherness. As the existential condition of both action and speech, plurality has the twofold character of "equality" and "distinction." Without equality, on the one hand, we — those who are living, dead, and yet to be born — cannot understand or communicate with one another. Without distinction, on the other, we have no need to understand or communicate with one another; that is to say, we would need neither action nor speech. In order to preserve the conjunction and continuity of the acting subject with the plural world, Maurice Merleau-Ponty (1970: 40) proposes the idea of the "instituting subject":

> [i]f the subject were taken not as a constituting but an instituting subject, it might be understood that the subject does not exist instantaneously and that the other person does not exist simply as a negative of myself. What I have begun at certain decisive moments would exist neither far off in the past as an objective memory nor be present like a memory revised, but really between the two as the field of my becoming during that period. Likewise my relation to another person would not be reducible to a disjunction: an instituting subject could coexist with another because the one instituted is not the immediate reflection of the activity of the former and can be regained by himself or by others without involving anything like a total recreation. Thus the instituted subject exists between others and myself, between me and myself, like a hinge, the consequence and the guarantee of our belonging to a common world.

Difference is a distinct mark of sociality. But for difference, there would be no sociality. Without it human communication either in speech or in action is unnecessary because we would be able to understand one another completely. Difference is also the axial principium of postmodernism as a philosophical mood and style. What identity is to modernity, difference is to postmodernity. It is the notion of difference that makes all the difference between modernity and postmodernity. At the end of modernity lies the adventure of difference. There is a proliferation of the ideas of difference in postmodern thought: among the most prominent are Martin Heidegger's *Differenz* as *Unterschied*, Jacques Derrida's *différance*, Jean-François

Lyotard's *différend*, Levinas's heteronomy, Michel de Certeau's heterology, and Mikhail Bakhtin's heteroglossia.

Let us compare the "modernist" Georg W. F. Hegel and the "postmodernist" Heidegger on the question of the difference between identity and difference. In his eagerness to prove the teleology of history as the march of Reason, of world history or the end of historical progress, Hegel falls short of making his dialectics open-ended. History's final synthesis corresponds to the identity of identity and difference where the dialectics reaches or fulfills its telos. Gianni Vattimo (1993: 160) thus concludes that the Hegelian dialectics consummates the long metaphysical tradition of identity in Western philosophy. On the contrary, only respect for difference promotes the very idea of plurality or multiplicity as an end in itself or having no ending. Heidegger's *Differenz* as *Unterschied* offers a postmodern alternative to the cultural politics of identity. *Unterschied* doubles difference with the between (*Unter/schied*) that at once connects, preserves, and promotes difference and the relational (i.e., interbeing). Difference as dif/ference is capable of conserving the principle of complementarity in interhuman relationships. Nancy Julia Chodorow (1980) brings her psychoanalytical insight into the clarification of differentiation which is central to the security and promotion of a relational self. Differentiation even provides the basis of both spontaneity and autonomy. She (1980: 10-11) judiciously contends that "we are all to some degree incorporations and extensions of others. ... *Differentiation is not distinctness and separateness, but a particular way of being connected to others.* This connection to others, based on early incorporations, in turn enables us to feel that empathy and confidence that are basic to the recognition of the other as a self [and, I might add, of the self as an Other]" (italics original).

As postmodernity engenders the thinking of the body, sexed or otherwise, the feminist reclamation of the body is truly a postmodern event.[7] For postmodern feminism, the reclamation of the body and a search for difference are inseparable. It is wrong to say, as does Stanley Rosen (1989: 20), that postmodernism is "the Enlightenment gone mad" because it refers to the body reclaimed and restored, not Reason contradicted. Having "discovered" or "reinvented" the body, postmodern feminism seeks difference, not

---

[7]Rosi Braidotti (1994: 238) writes: "[i]n the feminist framework, the primary site of location is the body. The subject is not an abstract entity, but rather a material embodied one. The body is not a natural thing; on the contrary, it is a culturally coded socialized entity. Far from being an essentialistic notion, it is the site of intersection between the biological, the social, and the linguistic, that is, of language as the fundamental symbolic system of a culture. Feminist theories of sexual difference have assimilated the insight of mainstream theories of subjectivity to develop a new form of 'corporeal materialism' that defines the body as an interface, a threshold, a field of intersecting forces where multiple codes are inscribed." Thus far the most systematic formulation of corporeal feminism is found in Grosz (1994).

identity – that is, difference without separation and inferiority (i.e., positive heterology). Thomas Laqueur (1990: 62) elegantly sums up the reason for feminine resistance and hostility to the cultural politics of (masculine) identity:

> [i]n a public world that was overwhelmingly male, the one-sex [i.e., identity] model displayed what was already massively evident in culture more generally: *man* is the measure of all things, and woman does not exist as an ontologically distinct category. Not all males are masculine, potent, honorable, or hold power, and some women exceed some men in each of these categories. But the standard of the human body and its representations is the male body.

It is a supreme irony that philosophy or *philosophia* as the "love" (*philo*) of "wisdom" (*sophia*) has for long discredited the role of women in it. Indeed, it may be gynophobic.[8] The postmodern feminism of Luce Irigaray, who calls herself *une philosophe* and for whom the woman question is *the* philosophical issue of our time, incarnates the cultural politics of feminine difference. Her sexual difference is a species of Heideggerian difference (*Unterschied*) that promotes the primacy of relation and propagates "interbeing" or "interdividuality." Hers is not just a political position but also a systematic theory. The distinction between identity (the masculine self) and difference (the feminine Other) is most clearly drawn and defined in her *écriture féminine* where she unveils the "phallacy" of identity which is the philosophical root of denigrating women's way of thinking, knowing, and doing. She protests and argues against the phallocracy which claims that man is the measure of all things by refusing to recognize woman as an ontologically distinct category.

Luce Irigaray, Hélène Cixous, and Julia Kristeva are the influential trio of the French feminists of difference. Irigaray in particular proposes feminine difference as "a taste for intersubjectivity."[9] Sexual difference is a

---

[8]The work of Collin (1994) is the best summation of how to philosophize with feminine difference.

[9]Irigaray's taste for intersubjectivity for – that matter, I might add, the principal tenets of this essay – is indeed compatible with what Nicholson and Seidman (1995) call "social postmodernism." They (1995: 9) write programmatically: "it is possible for postmodern thinkers to focus on institutions as well as texts, to think about the interrelations of social patterns without being essentializing or totalizing, and to create constructive as well as deconstructive analyses of the social. The positive possibilities of postmodern theorizing can be matched, we believe, by constructive ideas about political action. Such ideas may seriously challenge and expand our ideas about how political change can take place. But, to transform present understandings of 'the political' is not equivalent to abandoning politics altogether. Rather, through the following essays we hope to begin the process of imagining what 'postmodern' social analysis can be and of how

substrate of radical alterity, of the otherness of the Other. But this feminine substrate is not just a figleaf hiding difference. Her feminist philosophy of sexual difference is indeed the "subversion of identity": it means to subvert the "malestream" domination and oppression of modern identity. Without difference, the very notion of subjectivity itself becomes for her undermined while without radical alterity, intersubjectivity becomes suspect. For its name sake, intersubjectivity is the meeting of two subjectivities with distinction wherein each subjectivity is different because it is unique. For Irigaray, there is neither "first" nor "second" in the feminist philosophy of sexual difference — with an obvious allusion to the "egalitarian feminism" of Simone de Beauvoir while accepting its existential thesis that one is not born but becomes a woman. Irigaray (1995: 11) contends that the issue of women's liberation has reached "beyond simply a quest for equality between the sexes."[10] The solution to men's exploitation of women must come only by way of sexual difference. Irigaray means to put a positive spin on feminine heterology. "Equality between men and women," she (1993b: 13) insists, "cannot be achieved without a *theory of gender as sexed* and a rewriting of the rights and obligations of each sex, *qua different*, in social rights and obligations." It is a matter of social justice, she maintains, to give cultural values to female sexuality and genealogy for the sake of balancing out the power of one sex over the other. In sum: Irigaray intimates the dialogical model of the two rather than the monological mode of the *one* — one is man and the other is woman who is "an autonomous and different subject" (*je* or I). The model of "equality" without sexual difference in which man and woman become homogenized or identical is a singular model of subjectivity which, as Irigaray contends, has been historically masculine and hierarchical – man on top and woman at bottom in patriarchy. Against privileging a universal model valid for all men and all women, Irigaray advocates the paradigmatic model of two autonomous and different subjectivities in order to ensure and promote inter/subjectivity (or interdividuality) – that is, to facilitate their cohabitation and dialogue. By so doing, Irigaray transverses gendered parochialism on the one hand and genderless universalism on the other. As she (1995: 11-12) writes forcefully:

> we must move on to the model of the two, a two which is not replication of the same, nor one large and the other small, but made up of two which are truly different. The paradigm of the two lies in sexual difference. Why there? Because it is there that two subjects exist who should not be placed in a hierarchical relationship, and because these two subjects share the common

'postmodern' political action can be understood."

[10]Irigaray's ontology and ethics of sexual difference are most systematically spelled out in her two works: *This Sex Which Is Not One* (1985) and *An Ethics of Sexual Difference* (1993a).

goal of preserving the human species and developing its culture, while granting respect to their difference.

V. Relationality and the Primacy of the Other

Alterity and relationality are born as twins. Alterity has already become "the topic of first philosophy" (Theunissen, 1984: 1). In the ethical, however, alterity is primary to the self. The ethical or ethics is always already social because it involves approval and disapproval. The absolute and universal claim of rights talk involves no ethics. For there can be no ethics involving the self alone without the Other or with the primacy of the self over the Other: in the ethical but not in the epistemological, egocentricity is a contradiction in terms or at best what Charles Taylor (1992: 16) generously calls "moral laxity." In the ethical the Other is the center of value.

Here I wish to appropriate Mark C. Taylor's neologism *altarity* (1987) to elevate alterity to a higher ground. What *différance* is to Derrida, "altarity"' is to Taylor.[11] The term *altar* comes from the Latin *altare* which signifies a higher place. Altarity refers to the inviolable sanctity of the other, not of the self. Thus the idea of altarity not only accentuates alterity as the otherness of the Other but also elevates the world of the Other and makes the reading of it an elevated text or intertext. The birth of heterocentricity is the ethical elevation of alterity to altarity. Altarity, in other words, is the ethical seat of responsibility if not the site of the ethical itself. In ethical relationships, *altarnation* – to use another neological variation – is the constant performance of moral rites by the dialogical reversal from one person to another. It is the "riteful" way of rotating transpositions of altarity. Only by way of altarity is an ethics possible in which the Other is not only not an alter ego but is primary to the self. In the ethics of altarity, responsibility as self-transcendence precedes freedom, for the former is other-directed while the latter is self-centered or egocentric. The ethical is the conception of the self whose center is "elsewhere" and "otherwise": the only ethical is a "responsible" self. Because each self is unique and thus different, responsibility is an untransferable moral performance (see Levinas, 1994: 95). From the standpoint of altarity, of responsibility, the very idea of *existence* has been profoundly misunderstood among its antagonists as well as its protagonists: as its etymology shows, what is really central to it is not the centrality but the *eccentricity* (ex-centricity) of the self toward the world of other people (*Mitwelt*) and other things (*Umwelt*). The

[11] "Altarity," Taylor (1987: xxviii) writes, "is a slippery word whose meaning can be neither stated clearly nor fixed firmly. Though never completely decidable, the field of the word 'altarity' can be approached through the network of its association: altar, alternate, alternative, alternation, alterity."

human as eccentric is a being who is compelled to direct himself/herself toward the outside world or what Levinas calls "exteriority." Thus the motto of existence must be: Do not go inside, go outside! Thus we need a new definition of existential authenticity as embodied eccentricity rather than disembodied egocentricity.

Let us consider Hannah Arendt's unforgettable discussion of Adolf Eichmann whose indifference to alterity – let alone altarity – resulted in unthinkably irresponsible acts. Eichmann's "thoughtlessness" or inability to think is identified by Arendt (1977) with the "banality of evil." By thoughtlessness she never meant it to be our inability to conceptualize abstractly or philosophically but our inability to judge or use common-sense judgments (*sensus communis*) to live our ordinary daily life as humans. It is seldom if ever noticed that by Eichmann's thoughtlessness Arendt meant his real *inability to think from the standpoint of an Other* (i.e., his inability to engage in *Fremdverstehen*). He never understood the notion that "I am an Other." Eichmann lost touch with others or became inflicted with cutaneous alagia, as it were. Incapable of thinking from the standpoint of an Other, thoughtlessness is tantamount to a "defacement" or an "effacement" of the Other: it is in essence the dehumanization of the Other, humanity's inhumanity to others. Eichmann's "banality of evil" is once again the reminder that the abolition of difference(s), of alterity is the price we must pay for the inhumane politics of cruelty, violence, and extermination.

Responsibility as self-transcendence rather than self-affirmation scales the philosophical depth and plateau of Levinas's ethics as first philosophy (*philosophie premiére*). His meditations on the primacy of the ethical and the heteronomic ethic of responsibility were inspired, according to his own admission, by the ancient heritage of Israel. He acknowledges that the prime importance of the ethical is the Jewish contribution to the history of Western philosophy, and he turns to Judaic texts for his heteronomic ethic of responsibility for illumination. For Levinas, Judaism is a parable, as it were, for the ethical. Although "Reason" and "Deed" go hand in hand, the former is the distinguishing characteristic of Greek thought, while the latter is that of Hebraic thought. One is preoccupied with immutable and totalizing *Being* in the arena of theory (the "I think"), while the other concentrates on mutable and infinite *Becoming* (movement) in the field of action (the "I do") (see Boman, 1960: 205-8). In hindsight, Heidegger's *ontology* and Levinas's *ethics* were on a collision course.

For Levinas, both heterogeneity and heterocentricity (i.e., heteronomy) enrich rather than impoverish the social and ethical life of the individual self. Phenomenologically speaking, responsibility refers to one's capacity to respond or answer to the call of the Other and it ends up with becoming one's ethical calling for others. Interestingly, in Hebrew, the "other" (*aher*) and "responsibility" (*ahariout*) share the same etymological root (see Chalier, 1995: 8). The speaking word in the life of a concrete individual person is a part of heteronomic dialogue. It is no accident that there is in German a familial circle of "word" (*Wort*), "answer" (*Antwort*), "to answer" (*antworten*), and "to be responsible for" (*verantworten*). Indeed, for Levinas, to be social is simultaneously to be ethical. Both sociality and ethicality can never be reduced to the regime of knowledge and truth. In writing his "Foreword" to Stéphane Mosès's recent study of Franz Rosenzweig, Levinas alludes to a deep crevice between Rosenzweig's heteronomic ethics and Hegel's abstract and totalizing logocentrism whose critique, I might add, can be traced in the modern West to Ludwig Feuerbach's paradigmatic discovery of Thou as the fountain of ethical life. Feuerbach's dialogical thinking abandons and refutes the monological thinking of a lone philosopher in isolation from the world.[12] The "new thinking" of Rosenzweig, too, is the anti-modern "idea of reducing everything back to *the self*" (Glatzer, 1953: 191). Levinas (1992: 19) draws our attention to Rosenzweig's teaching against modern logocentrism from Hegel to Habermas in which the Same absorbs the Other and absolute thinking is a thought thinking the identity of the same and the Other.

Altarity, it should be reiterated here, is the seat of responsibility if not the ethical itself. Heteronomy as the pragmatic "grammar of the Other" (see Dupuis, 1996: 158) is the heartland of Levinas's ethics as first philosophy – to use his own neologism – "meontology" which confirms ethics as the "negation" of ontology. It is heteronomy, i.e., the primacy of the Other which conditions and defines the ethical. For Levinas, language too is an instantiation of the ethical rather than, as Heidegger formulates it, the house of Being. Levinas (1987a: 52) declares that he is "radically opposed to Heidegger who subordinates the relation with the Other to ontology." No one, I think, is more daring than Levinas in challenging Heidegger by showing that the ethical cannot be inscribed or subscribed as a sequel to existential ontology.

Levinas's ethics as first philosophy stands independently of both ontology and epistemology. The ethical is for him neither ontological nor epistemological. There is no compromise between ethics and ontology or epistemology. The ethical is "otherwise than Being" or "beyond essence." As he (1982: 58) formulates it, "the social [i.e., the ethical] is beyond ontology." The *Da* of *Dasein* (Heideggerian category), according to Levinas (1994: 48) is not an ontological problem but already an ethical one. Zygmunt Bauman (1990: 16) is judicious in observing that Levinas's proposal for the primacy of ethics is "a scandal for [Heidegger's] ontology." Levinas (1982:

[12]Ludwig Feuerbach's Copernican discovery of "Thou" is iterated forcefully in the principle 59 of his "philosophy of the future" which was originally published in 1843. He (1966: 71) writes: "The single man for himself possesses the essence of man neither in himself as a moral being nor in himself as a thinking being. The essence of man is contained only in the community and unity of man with man; it is a unity, however, which rests only on the reality of the distinction between I and thou."

60) contends that "Knowledge is always an adequation between thought and what it thinks. There is in knowledge, in the final account, an impossibility of escaping the self; hence sociality [i.e., ethicality] cannot have the same structure as knowledge." Knowledge or the "I think" does not and cannot take place in the atmosphere of sociality; rather, it takes place in the absolute "solitude" of the ego. The ethical begins and ends with the social. Therefore, according to Levinas, sociality or ethicality cannot be reduced to the regime of knowledge and truth. The former is beyond the reach of the latter.

Levinas defines heteronomy as the primacy of the Other over the self in the ethical: the ethic of responsibility in interhuman relationship is always and necessarily heteronomic. For him, however, heteronomy necessary for the ethic of responsibility calls for an asymmetrical relationship: interhuman relationships are not the symmetrical plural of the I's. The I alone makes the ethical untenable. Indeed, it defaces or effaces the ethical. It is only the presence of the Other, alterity, that makes the ethical possible and necessary. For the ethical, it should be reiterated, is not self-centered obsession but self-transcendence.[13] Only by way of heteronomy or self-transcendence is an ethic possible in which, to repeat, the Other is not only not an alter ego but also is primary to the self. Thus Levinas maintains that plurality (sociality) is not a multiplicity of numbers, but is predicated upon a radical alterity of the Other. In the elevated ethic of alterity, in the ethic of altarity, responsibility does not negate but pre-

---

[13]In his *magnum opus, Totality and Infinity*, Levinas, (1969: 46) writes that "In subordinating every relation with the existent to the relation with Being the Heideggerian ontology affirms the primacy of freedom over ethics. To be sure, the freedom involved in the essence of truth is not for Heidegger a principle of free will. Freedom comes from an obedience to Being: it is not man who possesses freedom; it is freedom that possesses man. But the dialectic which thus reconciles freedom and obedience in the concept of truth presupposes the primacy of the same, which marks the direction of and defines the whole of Western philosophy." Viktor Frankl gives us a glimpse of responsibility as "self-transcendence" which deserves, I think, more than a passing comment. He was a survivor of a Nazi death camp and founded logotherapy, psychotherapy with a human face, as it were. Like Jonas's "new ethic of responsibility," logotherapy calls for the affirmation of life at all cost as opposed to the abnegation of life (nothingness) relying on Nietzsche's single dictum that "he who has a *why* to live can bear with almost any *how*." Like Levinas, more importanly, Frankl prompts and promotes an elegant way of formulating the concept of responsibility as "self-transcendence" which is "the cue to cure" the feeling that life is meaningless or worthless. By self-transcendence, Frankl (1985: 133) means the discovery and recovery of life's meaning by engaging in the world, in the other rather than one's own psyche. Self-transcendence is embodied in the idea of responsibility: "Freedom . . . is not the last word. Freedom is only part of the story and half of the truth. Freedom is but the negative aspect of the whole phenomenon whose positive aspect is responsibleness. In fact, freedom is in danger of degenerating into mere arbitrariness unless it is lived in terms of responsibleness."

cedes and contains autonomy: it is to heteronomy what autonomy is to egocentricity. Responsibility only decenters and consummates autonomy. Although responsibility without autonomy is a sham, autonomy alone is not sufficient to complete an ethic. Autonomy is ancillary but not contrary to responsibility, and not the other way around, simply because we can be autonomous without being responsible, but we can never be responsible without being autonomous. From the standpoint of heteronomic ethics, responsibility contains, but cannot be secondary and supplementary to, autonomy. "Existence," Levinas (1987b: 58) declares with Sartre in mind for whom hell is others, "is not condemned to freedom, but judged and invested as a freedom. Freedom could not present itself all naked. This investiture of freedom constitutes moral life itself, which is through and through a heteronomy." In Levinas, subjectivity is affirmed never for itself but for an Other (*pour l'autre*). It comes into being as heteronomic: "It is my inescapable and incontrovertible answerability to the Other that makes me an individual I" (Levinas and Kearney, 1986: 27). Consequently, the notion of responsibility that coincides with the ethical is, first and foremost, the confirmation of the "I," which is for Levinas the "meontological version of subjectivity." He (1982: 95) writes that responsibility is "the essential, primary and fundamental structure of subjectivity. For I describes subjectivity in ethical terms. Ethics, here, does not supplement a preceding existential base; the very node of the subjective is knotted in ethics understood as responsibility." Responsibility is the vulnerability of the self's all-consuming sensitivity to and compassion for the Other as a person. Since each subjectivity is unique and thus different from others, moreover, its responsibility is accordingly untransferable. Not only is responsibility untransferable but it is also nonreciprocal: as Levinas (1987b: 137) emphasizes in no uncertain terms, "responsibility is without concern for reciprocity: I have to respond to and for the Other without occupying myself with the Other's responsibility in my regard." Thus responsibility *for* others is an unconditional gift without the forethought of reciprocation. Responsibility without concern for reciprocity is — in the very words of Levinas (1988: 165) — "my call to help a person gratuitously in the asymmetry of the relation of *one* to the *other*."

The philosophical depth of Levinas's ethics as first philosophy is deeply scarred by the absence of its concern for the nonhuman world. It is most unfortunate and regrettable that in Levinas's ethics responsibility for the nonhuman world is unthought.[14] In this regard, the later Heidegger has a decisive edge over Levinas. Heidegger's *Gelassenheit* is a de-facto critique of the *Gestell* of modern technomorphic civilization whose *raison d'être* was initially justified and defended by Francis Bacon in advancing his anthro-

[14]Feminism, however, has taken seriously the ecological implications of caring as nonreciprocal responsibility. See, for example, Merchant (1996).

pocentric humanism in which the Promethean principles of *Herrschaftswissen* incorporate at once knowledge and power at the crossroads of utility.[15] John Llewelyn (1991: 144) judiciously notes that "Levinas is so preoccupied with doing justice to the human being that he fails to do justice to the nonhuman being, for despite his rare references to our responsibility 'for everything,' . . . Responsibility, Levinas maintains, is beyond nature, beyond *physis*, metaphysical."[16] In the postmodern age of ecology, the "greening" of the earth (*Gaia*) is and ought to be our foremost and ultimate concern and responsibility which calls for the question of *ethics as if the earth really matters.*

Václav Havel (1987), who read Levinas with care in his prison years (see Havel, 1989) and for whom responsibility is the master key that unlocks the secret of humanity in postmodern politics, is well aware of the ethical and political context in which "living in truth" embraces the impassioned sense of something profoundly wrong in the incredulous as much as unscrupulous disruption of the "natural order of things" (*Lebenswelt* or, as the Czech phenomenologist Jan Patočka calls it, *přirozený svět*) by spewing dark smoke that soils the heavens. For Havel, all nonhuman beings and things are entitled to have their distinct niches on earth and have, indeed, ethical standing; that is to say, they are intertwined with human conscience. The body as flesh, which is an element-like thing, is the living site of sociality. It actively places and engages us in the world with other people (*Mitwelt*) and other things (*Umwelt*). When I, with my wife and my friends, was visiting beautiful Cheju Island, which has been a Korean youthful honeymooners' paradise for sometime, I was deeply moved

[15]It is noteworthy that there is merit in Emerson's formulation of self-reliance that reproaches and jettisons our dependence on technology. Emerson (1940b: 167) writes: "The civilized man has built a coach, but has lost the use of his feet. He is supported on crutches, but lacks so much support of muscle. He has a fine Geneva watch, but he fails of the skill to tell the hour by the sun. A Greenwich nautical almanac he has, and so being sure of the information when he wants it, the man in the street does not know a star in the sky. The solstice he does not observe; the equinox he knows as little; and the whole bright calendar of the year is without a dial in his mind. His note-books impair his memory; his libraries overload his wit; the insurance-office increases the number of accidents; and it may be a question whether machinery does not encumber; whether we have not lost by refinement some energy, by a Christianity, entrenched in establishments and forms, some vigor of wild virtue." Stanley Cavell (1981: 131) perceptively notes an affinity between Heidegger's notion of poetic dwelling or what Heidegger calls *Gelassenheit* and Emerson's proposition that "[a]lways our thinking is a pious reception."

[16]It is appropriate to recognize the importance of the work of Professor Kah Kyung Cho (1987). It belongs to the needed species of philosophizing called comparative philosophy that lays the ontological or, more daringly, "metaphysical" foundation that glues transcendental human consciousness (*Bewußtsein*) and nature (*Natursein*, *physis*).

and struck by the inscription in both Korean and Chinese ideograms that read "Shin To Bul Yi" – "body and land (or soil) are not two," that is, they are one – at the entrance of a botanical garden. Gilles Deleuze and Félix Guattari (1994: 85-113), too, map out the conceptual contours of "geophilosophy" in which the earth is not just one element among others (air, fire, and water) but is that all-encompassing element which "brings all the elements in a single embrace" and without which all life-forms are unsustainable. It may be said that ecophilosophy in its holistic content and method is the "geophilosophy" par excellence for the simple reason that it is concerned with the quintessential question of how to dwell properly on earth.[17] In his attempt to create an "ethico-aesthetic paradigm" in opposition to a scientific one, furthermore, Guattari (1995: 119-20) raises a weighty and timely question:

> [t]he ecological crisis can be traced to a more general crisis of the social, political and existential. The problem involves a type of revolution of mentalities where they cease investing in a certain kind of development, based on a productivism that has lost all human finality. Thus the issue returns with insistence: how do we change mentalities, how do we reinvent social practices that would give back to humanity – if it ever had it – a *sense of responsibility*, not only for its own survival, but equally for the future of all life on the planet, for animal and vegetable species, likewise for incorporeal species such as music, the arts, cinema, the relation with time, love and compassion for others, the *feeling of fusion* at the heart of cosmos? (my emphasis)

In the final analysis, the ethics and politics of responsibility are required to appease nature's mutiny called the ecological crisis which is always silent and stoic but deadly.

VI. Feminine Difference and the Ethic of Caring

We would be remiss if we leave out from our discussion caring as the primordial type of responsibility. Caring-centered analysis confirms the feminist contention that the personal is also political. Since care is a participial

---

[17]See Haar (1993) on how to dwell properly on earth which is a deeply Heideggerian question. Jung (forthcoming) also deals with the overarching question of ecophilosophy or geophilosophy as a postmodern issue. Geomancy is an integral part of ecophilosophy or "geophilosophy." For the unique contribution of Korean geomancy to geophilosophy, see Choi (1984 and 1997). Here I also wish to acknowledge my gratitude to the President of Minumsa Publishing Co. in Seoul, Mr. Maeng-Ho Park, for arranging in August, 1997 a dialogue between Dr. Choi and me on the nature of Korean geomancy, body politics, and "ecopiety" which will be published in a forthcoming issue of *Hyundai Sa Sang*.

act, the term *caring* is preferred. What "being" is to "becoming," "care" is to "caring." Unfortunately, however, being like becoming is a participial gerund whereas care is not. Caring refers to that social or, more specifically, consociational process which is active, nonreciprocal, nontransferable, and unfinished. It is, therefore, the consociational prototype of responsibility.

Caring, which is always tender and involves corporeal and spiritual intimacy, is the ethical site of feminine distinction, i.e., of "gynesis" (Jardine, 1985). Enshrined in altarity, caring privileges feminine – particularly maternal – experience as "a different reality" (see Whitebeck, 1983).[18] Hans Jonas (1984: 39) maintains that "parental responsibility" toward children, which is nonconsenting and nonreciprocal, is "the archetype of all responsible action." This elementary type of responsibility, according to him, "fortunately requires no deduction from a principle, because it is powerfully implanted in us by nature or at least in the childbearing part of humanity," i.e., maternal humanity. Maternal or gynocentric responsibility, in other words, is inherently "selfless care" (see Jonas, 1984: 39).

In the academic discourse of the American feminist movement, Carol Gilligan's *In a Different Voice* (1982) birthed and unearthed the ethic of caring as the privileged marker of uniquely feminine experience and distinction and thus held forth a radical departure from or an interruption of traditional ethics and even politics.[19] Her search for "a different voice" which echoes Irigaray's *écriture féminine* and Arendt's human plurality (see Baier, 1994: 294-312) is altogether a modest but paradigmatic proposal: it claims itself to be only one of many different voices within and without feminism. It makes no absolute or universal claims. Gilligan's "different voice" seriously entertains the Gadamerian hermeneutical possibility that the other may be right.[20]

Gilligan's "different voice" is the voice of *parler-femme*. It is a distinct gynolect which is distinctively heteronomic. The term *voice* in a journey to discover "ways of making connection in the face of difference" (Gilligan,

---

[18]The ethic of caring as the prototype of responsibility that privileges feminine experience may be called phenomenological. Cf. Mandelbaum (1955: 31): "The phenomenological approach utilizes moral experience in another way. Its method is eductive rather than deductive. Its essential methodological conviction is that a solution of any of the problems of ethics must be educed from, and verified by, a careful and direct examination of individual moral judgments."

[19]Lawrence A. Blum (1980) proposes "a new conception of the moral self" based on sympathy and compassion for the well-being of others which is meant to be an alternative to both Kantianism and utilitarianism. It is high time for us to pay serious attention to Scheler's (1954) phenomenological ethics of sympathy. Poole (1991) regards gender as the basis of two different conceptions of morality and argues for the feminine formulation of morality for a geniune concern for others.

[20]In 1989 Hans-Georg Gadamer stated (see Grondin, 1994: 124) that "[t]he possibility that the other person may be right is the soul of hermeneutics."

Lyons, and Hanmer, 1989: 10) is inserted for a definite purpose. In the first place, it carries with it what Lyn Mikel Brown and Gilligan (1992) call the "harmonics of relationship" which may be likened to the language of Nietzsche's aesthetics and body politics. By centering on voice, they mean to accent the idea that relationship is an embodied event in which voice connects rather than separates psyche and body. Unlike vision or sight which is spectatorial, voice is participatory. "Voice," Brown and Gilligan (1992: 20) declare, "is inherently relational – one does not require a mirror to hear oneself – yet the sounds of one's voice change in resonance depending on the relational acoustics: whether one is heard or not heard, how one is responded to (by oneself and by other people)." In the second place, voice carries with it the dynamic sense of intimacy and proximity. It is connected to consociational relationships or relationships of intimate beings – family members, relatives, friends, and neighbors – in which participants share each other's temporal contiguity and spatial proximity.

This is also Levinas's ethical language of responsibility with an accent on the face or interface without confrontation (without "in your face!"). For him, the body matters and the face matters deeply. For that very reason, Ludwig Wittgenstein (1980: 23e) calls the face "the soul of the body" which is totally exposed or, according to Levinas (1994: 158), defenselessly naked. As a voice, the face speaks intimately, indeed. As a dialogue is an exchange of two voices, it is also interfacial and cannot be otherwise. The ethic of caring, unlike Kantian and utilitarian ethics, is an ethic with a human face.

With the intent of making connection in the face of difference which resembles Irigaray's model, Gilligan contends that Lawrence Kohlberg's influential psychology of human moral development, which has been well received and endorsed by such philosophers as John Rawls and Jürgen Habermas, is prejudiced and flawed in method and substance and as such fell far short of the universal moral point of view he purports to advance and promote. There is indeed a continental divide between Gilligan and Kohlberg. Gilligan (1982: 19) sums up women's moral orientation which is a radical departure from its male counterpart as formulated by Kohlberg:

> the moral problem arises from conflicting responsibilities rather than from competing rights and requires for its resolution a mode of thinking that is contextual and narrative rather than formal and abstract. This conception of morality as concerned with the activity of care centers moral development around the understanding of responsibility and relationships, just as the conception of morality as fairness ties moral development to the understanding of rights and rule.

In opposition to Kohlberg's focus on abstract rights and formal rules for the development of moral conduct, Gilligan centers her ethical concern around concrete relationships and responsibility. While rights are self-centered, caring is heteronomic. The ethic of caring is a relational ethic for the sake of the Other which is self-transcending. To reiterate: heteronomy alone is the site of caring (as responsibility) if not the ethical itself. In this context, it is worth noting that there are the "caring" and the "justice" perspectives: one is coded as feminine, while the other is tagged as masculine (see Clement, 1996). Some feminists contest that the ethic of caring tends to perpetuate feminine stereotypes, while others attempt to reconcile the ethic of caring with the ethic of justice. First, however, the ethic of caring as primary responsibility (see Jung, 1995) is in stark contrast to the ethic of justice for no other reason than that justice is generally viewed as a correlative of rights because it is a fair and symmetrical distribution of rights to every citizen on an equal footing where none will under the "veil of ignorance" start with an unfair advantage. In this respect, justice is a selfsame species of rights. Levinas is an exception to the general rule. For him, justice is aligned not with rights but with responsibility when he (1994: 45) emphasizes: "[i]t is the responsibility for the other that determines the legitimacy of the state, that is, its justice." Second, the ethic of caring uses feminine difference as a "resource" (Young, 1996: 127) for constructing a paradigmatic moral theory. The fact that the ethic of caring as responsibility engendered by women or embodying "gynesis" cannot be faulted or devalued. The fault lies in the fact that the ethic of caring has been devalued and marginalized because it is *engendered* primarily by women.[21]

It is noteworthy that neither Heidegger in *Being and Time* (1962) nor Michel Foucault in his suggestive title *The Care of the Self* (1986) is fully aware of caring as self-transcendence, that is, as an ethical notion. For Foucault, on the one hand, care is a matter of self-indulgence although it intensified social relations and binds a system of reciprocal obligations (cf. Smart, 1995: 104-7). It is a "technique of self" (*technique de soi*). Heidegger, on the other, defines human existence (*Dasein*) itself as care (*Sorge, cura* which is a feminine category) in his seminal work *Being and Time*. Invoking the old Latin fable of Hyginus, he (1962: 198) intimates that human existence is inspirited with care which shapes *homo* with its body (*corpus*) as the gift of *humus* (earth). However, his conception of care is marred by being self-centered (*eigentlich*) and thus care authenticates only existential autonomy but not responsibility as self-transcendence. Erich Fromm (1956: 1) perceptively observes that most people see the issue of love primarily as that of *being loved* rather than that of *loving*, of one's capacity to love – that is to say, love is receiving or taking rather than active giving.

[21] "Care," Tronto (1993: 180) stresses, "is not a parochial concern of women, a type of secondary moral question, or the work of the least well off in society. Care is a central concern of human life. It is time that we began to change our political and social institutions to reflect this truth." Goodin (1985 and 1988) vigorously defends the welfare state and institutional responsibility to protect the "unheavenly city" of the "vulnerable" (the human and the nonhuman).

Thomas Moore's work *Care of the Soul* (1992) has been the steady diet for the American popular psyche. It broaches the "self-centered" consolation of care as the nourishment of the individual soul which reflects the American culture of narcissism. Confession, too, is self-serving and part of the *reductio ad insanitatem* of American narcissism (see Hughes, 1993: 13). In the language of "pop-therapeutics" in American "talkshowology," you have to love yourself first in order to love another person! Have we ever thought that it is wrong to say that understanding the self helps to understand others rather than the other way around – that is, understanding others helps to understand the self? The caring self is the relational self for whom the Other is primary. It cannot be a "technique of self." In the words of Gilligan (1986: 252), the relational or dialogical self *alone* that joins "the self with the other and the other with the self" points to the way of opening up "a new understanding of morality and love."

Kateb (1995: 172) likens Emerson to Foucault in holding the idea that only by taking oneself seriously does one take the world seriously. In an interview shortly before his death, Foucault (see Bernauer and Rasmussen, 1988: 7 and Kateb, 1995: 172) exemplified Socrates as "truly the man who cares for others." "A city in which everyone would be correctly concerned for self," Foucault (Bernauer and Rasmussen, 1988: 7 and Kateb, 1995: 172) continues, "would be a city that would be doing well, and it would find therein the ethical principle of its stability. . . . One must not have the care for others precede the care for self. *The care for self takes moral precedence in the measure that the relationship to self takes ontological precedence*" (my emphasis). For Kateb, however, Emerson is more radical, more preoccupied and consumed than Foucault with the idea of identity as discipline, that is, "Foucault ends where Emerson begins and ends" (Kateb, 1995: 172).

On the one hand, it is ironic that Foucault who is reputed to be a philosopher of difference and discontinuity identifies himself with, and returns to, the philosophical politics of identity and continuity. He may be able to free himself from Heidegger as his old nemesis, but unable to shake him off as his new mimesis. Confession, whether it be Augustinian, Rousseauan, or Foucauldian, is auto/biographic and thus necessarily self-centered: confession prolongs the "use of pleasure": the principle of pleasure and that of care are in one and the same continuum. William E. Connolly is wrong, I think, when he (1991: 57) declares that "Foucault offers rudiments of a constructive general theory . . . when he speaks of a new subjectivity and the cultivation of care for difference through strategies of critical detachment from the identities that constitute us." On the contrary, Foucault dissolves difference into identity and fails to transgress the cultural politics of identity and reach the promised land of difference, of heterotopia. In this regard, he ceases to play the agonistic "jester" against the "priest" when he converts the paradox of difference into the disciplinary rule of identity.

On the other hand, Emerson is a "genius" of American culture and politics who is preoccupied with the seminal thought of self-reliance, the "mental" side of which is primary to its "active," social side. Self-reliance accords the primacy of *vita contemplativa* over *vita activa.* Emersonian self-reliance disfigures and anaesthetizes sociality as the co-presence of the self and the other. Emerson issues a stern warning not to mortgage ourselves to and for others. As Kateb (1996: 31) points out, "it is most itself when it is a method of intellect rather than a way of being or acting in the world. ... [I]t is the steady effort of thinking one's thoughts and thinking them through. It is intellectual independence, reactive and responsive self-possession." Although it rejects the acquisitive and consumerist idea of self-centeredness, Emerson's self-reliance is a plea for the cultivation of the philosophical culture of identity in conscripting others to become "like me": the homogenizing logic of self-reliance exorcises sociality. It is indeed dedicated to the decomposition of interactive social life. It is a self-enclosed circle that has no intersection, no interconnection. Emersonian self-reliance promotes the production and reproduction of the Same, of identity politics. It may be likened to the self-destroying, entropic uroboros biting and eventually consuming its own tail and body. What Maurice Merleau-Ponty (1973: 205) said of Jean-Paul Sartre may also apply to Emerson for whom there is only a plurality or multiplicity of unconnected individuals whose social world is "a sheaf of irreconcilable perspectives" which is held together only by the "heroism of the I."

To sum up: neither Emerson nor Foucault has any sense or knowledge of care primarily as "taking care of others." For Emerson, one's self-reliance can only "help elicit the *self-reliance* of another" (Kateb, 1995: 138). For Foucault, who, too, uses the expression self-reliance (1986:100), care has exclusive reference to "taking care of oneself" which can only inspire others to take care of themselves. He (1986: 100) considers, for example, medicine (or medicare) as a way of defining "a way of living" that is "a reflective mode of relation to oneself, to one's body, to food, to wakefulness and sleep, to the various activities, and to the environment." Diatetics as "*curatio corporis*," too, refers to paying "vigilant attention" to one's own body (Foucault, 1986: 103). He is unaware of or refuses to consider the body as the embodied locus of relationality.

William E. Connolly's ambitious, agonistic project in *Identity\Difference* (1991) of resolving the political paralogy of identity and difference is relevant to our discussion here. It contains a critique of Kateb's democratic individualism rooted in Emerson's self-reliance by appropriating Foucault, Heidegger, and Nietzsche whom Kateb calls the faithful intellectual heir of Emerson. Connolly (1991: 91) contends that "democracy reaches its highest level of achievement when agonistic respect is folded into its politics." While he agrees with Kateb's *ethic* of individuality, he faults Kateb's "minimalist" politics or "apolitics" of liberal individuality. He (1991: 83) puts it bluntly: "*this theorist of liberal individuality offers an ethic of individuality in lieu of a political theory of individuality*" (italics original). The issue is not, I think, the question of ethics or political theory. Rather, it is the question of how both ethics and political theory are constructed.

Connolly's political paralogy intends not to play the old game of "identity/difference." Instead, it intends to play the new game of "identity\difference" with a marked accent on the "back slash" for the purpose of, I suspect, transgressing or reversing the modern primacy of identity over difference in the direction of the postmodern primacy of difference over identity. Although he refuses – after the fashion of Nietzsche, Heidegger, Foucault, Lyotard, Deleuze, and Derrida – to be "an identity junkie" (Jan Clausen's expression), Connolly falls short of radicalizing the philosophy of difference. He (1991: 67) acknowledges and understands well the double bind of identity and difference: "identities function to convert differences into otherness and otherness into scapegoats created and maintained to secure the appearance of a true identity. To possess a true identity is to be false to difference, while to be true to difference is to sacrifice the promise of a true identity." However, he fails to put identity under erasion or elision. Norman O. Brown once proposed to resolve the question of identity by "losing" it. Caught in the deadlock of identity and difference, Connolly also fails to comprehend or get a handle on the double meaning of Heidegger's (*Differenz* as) *Unterschied* (dif/ference) that connects rather than separates (see also Chodorow, 1980). Heterology (the idea of otherness) for Connolly appears negative. Difference as a postmodern event is invented to discover the way of "curing" that is, "taking care of" the identity addiction of modernity. In other words, Connolly can neither *unmake* the politics of modern identity nor *make* the politics of postmodern difference. By failing to radicalize difference as *Unterschied*, he is not cognizant of the heteronomic structure of ethical and political responsibility. Like Emersonian self-reliance, Foucauldian care, Nietzschean ressentiment, and Freudian guilt, (self-)responsibility is for Connolly inner-directed and self-centered: they are all *selfsame*. It would be unfair to say that Connolly (see 1996: 202-3) is not unaware of Levinas. Although he derives his inspiration from Nietzsche's "nontheistic ethic of pluralization" (as well as Foucault's agonistic thought) rather than Levinas's "divinely sanctioned morality of plurality," he is fully aware of Levinas's call for alterity and responsibility. It would be fair, however, to conclude that Connolly, in the end, is ignorant of Levinas's heteronomy, Levinas's heteronomic ethic of responsibility, and its paradigmatic implications for politics in transgressing and surpassing *both* the ethics *and* the political theory of so-called "democratic individuality."

VII. Responsibility and the Politics of Civility

Richard J. Bernstein (1994) highly recommends Hans Jonas's "command performance" in the timely construction of a much-needed ethic of responsibility which purportedly transcends all traditional anthropocentric ethics. Bernstein raises a series of challenging questions as well as objections concerning Jonas's formulation of responsibility. By making parental responsibility archetypical, Bernstein contends that Jonas denigrates the importance of the reciprocal type of responsibility among equals or equal adults. The paradigm of parental responsibility will make reciprocal political responsibility "paternalistic." "An adequate normative account of politics and political responsibility," Bernstein (1994: 846) objects, "must also recognize the centrality of mutual reciprocal responsibility that can (and ought to) exist among participants in a democratic political community." The feminine ethic of care has been subjected to the same kind of criticism that Bernstein raises against Jonas.

Bernstein's criticism, however, misses the following two points. First, Bernstein forgets that the personal is also political (see Tronto, 1996). Second, both forms of responsibility — parental and reciprocal — have the same heteronomic structure. Both ontogenetically and phylogenetically, one precedes the other: parental responsibility is primary, while reciproal responsibility, which I call "altarnation," is secondary. This means neither that one is better than the other nor that the latter is "paternalistic" (in a pejorative sense) rather than autonomous, self-reliant, or self-sufficient. The concept of public welfare, too, has unduly and unfairly been subjected to criticism and attack in recent years which includes claims of alleged flaws in the character of its recipients. As the aim of public welfare is to *take care of* the underprivileged or the "vulnerable" (both human and nonhuman), it has the same heteronomic structure of the ethic of caring.

The real question, I think, is why good samaritans or altruists have increasingly become victimized in the land of rights talk which is tied to choices, contracts, and entitlements. Kristen Renwick Monroe's recent work *The Heart of Altruism* (1996) has a decisive bearing on the ethic of caring as responsibility which, as a paradigmatic moral theory, is an *altarnative* to rights talk. It is deeply heartening when the kind face of compassion transfigures and prevails upon the nasty face of contempt and cruelty. Monroe attempts to answer James Q. Wilson's (1993: 245) cogent question: "If rights are all that is important, what will become of responsibilities?" Altruism may not be "a strong beacon light" but is "a small candle flame" that is capable of dispelling the darkness and warming our soul once it is brought close to our heart and cupped in our hands (see Wilson, 1993: 251). Both altruism and the ethic of caring are heteronomic: one refers to relationships of "consociates" (*Mitmenschen*), while the other concerns the "anonymous" relationships of "contemporaries" (*Nebenmenschen*) who share one another's temporal contiguity of the "now" but not spatial proximity.

Altruism lands a mortal blow to the cherished tradition of "rational choice theory" whose center is "economic rationality" – a part of rights talk. Wilson echoes Monroe when he claims (1993: 238) that "the teachings of the heart deserve to be taken as seriously as the lessons of the mind."[22] Economic rationality in rational choice theory is based on the premise that "rational man" is one who chooses to maximize his/her own self-interest, "enlightened" or otherwise. He/she is a self-centered person, while the altruist is heteronomic. The altruist has the natural disposition and propensity to linking himself/herself to others through "a shared humanity." In essence, the "heart of altruism" refutes the twofold character of rational choice theory: (1) rationality and (2) choice. Neither rationality nor choice explains the good deeds of altruists. As Monroe (1996: 216) emphasizes, altruists are left with "no choice in their behavior toward others. They are John Donne's people. All life concerns them. Any death diminishes them. Because they are part of mankind."

The reverse side of altruism may be found in Eichmann's "banality of evil" where blind obedience was mistaken as Kantian "obligation" or "duty." Arendt's report on Eichmann's "banality of evil" drew severe criticisms from all quarters including her friend and colleague Jonas. For Arendt, however, the "banality of evil" does not absolve Eichmann's crimes against humanity because she appeals to the "ethics of consequences" ("responsibilities") rather than Kantian ethics of intention and principles.[23] Arendt's "verdict" relies on the "actuality" of what Eichmann did. For her, he is guilty of committing crimes against humanity because "politics is not like the nursery; in politics obedience and support are the same" (Arendt, 177: 279). He and he alone is "guilty" and "responsible" for what he actually did. Arendt condones no "collective guilt" or "collective responsibility" simply because "where all, or almost all, are guilty, nobody is" (Arendt, 1977: 278).

So far I have discussed the informal, primary dimensions of the ethic of responsibility in caring and altruism. The formal, secondary dimension of responsibility is connected directly with the politics of civility in two specific but integrally related ways: (1) against violence and (2) for democratic deliberation.

1. The late political philosopher Judith N. Shklar (1984: 44) once proposed that "liberal and humane people ... would, if they were asked to rank the vices, put cruelty first. Intuitively they would choose cruelty as the worst thing we do." Indeed, it is a "black hole" in the humanity of humankind. Cruelty, in all forms of its manifestation, results from disrespect

---

[22]Since altruists under discussion by Monroe (1996) include rescuers of Jews in Nazi Europe, worth noting is Lyotard's (1988: 179) challenge to Hegelianism that embodies the logocentrism of European modernity: "Everything real is rational, everything rational is real: 'Auschwitz' refutes [this] speculative doctrine."

[23]Merleau-Ponty (1969: xl) notes that "Max Weber refuses to choose between an 'ethics of responsibility' [*la morale de la responsibilité*], which does not judge according to the intention of the action but according to its consequences, and an 'ethics of faith' or 'conscience' [*la morale de la foi*], which places value on the unconditional respect for ends regardless of consequences."

for (the Other's) difference based on the anti-hermeneutical principle that the Other is never right. No doubt, violence — whether it be war, revolution, or capital punishment — is a form of cruelty, the ultimate form of cruelty. It is in principle an irresponsible act because it aims at the obliteration of the Other (both human and nonhuman) from the face of the earth. It is indeed the total, complete effacement of the Other. As Mona Ozouf (1988: 12) puts it well, violence (revolution) is "the price to be paid for the abolition of differences," of alterity, of altarity which signifies each person's dignity as a human being. Violence is a result of failure to acknowledge the worth of the Other in the life and death struggle of recognition – to use the gratuitous language of Hegel.[24] It results from the absolute and universal affirmation and claims of the self against the Other that violate the basic principle of human plurality based on difference.

The language of violence as well as rights talk tends to absolutize and universalize the human condition. They speak the language of identity at the expense of the language of difference. For in the absolute and universal, the other becomes exactly the same as the self (see Stocker, 1976: 219). Leszek Kolakowski (1968: 9-37) once pointed out that there is an ageless antagonism between a philosophy that perpetuates, and a philosophy that questions, the absolute and universal. It is the antagonism between the "priest" with "the garrote of catechism" and the "jester" (or "fool") with "the needle of mockery." The priestly finds solace in the stability and immobility of an established system, while the jesterly thrives on destabilizing and resisting it (i.e., it is "heresiarchal"). One relies on the politics of identity and the other fosters the politics of difference.

Notwithstanding the claim of violence as the only way of transforming history and politics, nonviolence, too, is entitled to the remaking of history and politics. Albert Camus (1956) justifies the cause of nonviolent rebellion against violent revolution in the name of tolerance, of difference and humanity. "Rebellion at grips with history," he (1956: 277) asserts, "adds that instead of killing and dying in order to produce the being that we are not, we have to *live and let live* in order to create what we are." The rebel as a nonviolent person readily acknowledges the dialogical interplay between the *ethical* principle of culpability and the *epistemological* principle of fallibility, whereas the (serious, too serious) revolutionary as a violent person thrives on the monologic of inculpability and infallibility. Epistemological dogmatism and moral absolutism contradict the essence of the dialogical principle of coexistence that always and incessantly recognizes the zone of ever present, porous *ambiguity* between doubt and certainty. In the final analysis, ambiguity is an unavoidable condition of human pluraity

[24]For the implications of Hegel's thought concerning recognition and violence, see Hoffman (1983). The best phenomenological work on violence as war is found in J. Glenn Gray (1959).

or peaceful coexistence with others.

2. The recognition of and respect for difference calls for democratic deliberation in the ever dangerous presence of violence as the act of effacing the otherness of the Other. Deliberation is the "moral equivalent" of violence. As the French *différend* in particular, of which Jean-François Lyotard (1988) makes judicious use, implies disagreement (and dispute), difference gives rise to disagreement whose conflict is resolved by a "parliamentary" method. It is no mere accident that the parliamentary system of government is also called a "responsible government." In perpetuating dialogue, democratic deliberation is indeed a "talking cure" for politics, which is also a politics of civility. For, to paraphrase Alfred North Whitehead slightly, civilization is the victory of persuasion over violence.

Just as difference is a permanent condition of humanity, "moral disagreement is a permanent condition of democratic politics." So ably argue Amy Gutman and Dennis Thompson in their recent work *Democracy and Disagreement* (1996: 9). They argue, however, neither for the ethic of responsibility nor against violence which are perfectly compatible with, and even enhance, their formulation of the ethics and politics of deliberative democracy. Gutman and Thompson (1996: 91) argue that "[a] deliberative democracy governed by reciprocity flourishes neither in a society of self-centered citizens nor in a society of saints."[25] Presumably because in a society of self-centered or self-righteous citizens there would be no possible agreement or compromise based on genuine reciprocity, while in a society of morally perfect persons, no occasion would arise for disagreement. A deliberative democracy allows that disagreement which is deliberative but not adversary. Rights talk is incompatible with deliberative democracy because it is deliberate but not deliberative, it knows no language of compromise (cf. Glendon, 1991: 9). Emerson's unflinching commitment to self-reliance makes every citizen a prisoner of his/her own truth in living his/her life in splendid isolation from others. Deliberative democracy is necessary and possible because we are neither truthfully self-righteous nor saintly. The principles of deliberative democracy, Gutman and Thompson argue, offer a way of reading and judging public policies more defensible than those of either utilitarianism, or libertarianism, or egalitarianism which, despite their differences, share in common the conception of what is morally correct prior to and independently of democratic deliberation. By contrast, democratic deliberation is a search for answers constrained by constitutional principles, which are themselves determined and developed through deliberation. Deliberative democracy is deliberative through and through.

[25] Significant synonyms for "deliberative" in the contemporary discussion of political theorists are "discursive," "communicative," and "dialogical." See particularly Benhabib (1996) and Young (1996). Particulary Young's "communicative model" plays on difference.

Without question, reciprocity is for Gutman and Thompson the "leading principle" of deliberative democracy. By maintaining moral integrity but not moral arrogance or dogmatism, the virtue of "mutual respect" fosters the principle of reciprocity that facilitates accommodation, compromises, or mutually acceptable terms. Parenthetically, Gutman and Thompson's principle of reciprocity couched in "mutual respect," I think, answers in part if not wholly Bernstein's critique of Jonas for being "paternalistic" or his lack of concern with the reciprocal dimension of political responsibility.

Arendt, for whom speech or "talking cure" has a special, "riteful" place in the human condition, argues that the *altarnative* to violence – including anti-colonial revolution argued for by Franz Fanon and supported by Sartre — is not nonviolence but power. Power does not come out of "the barrel of a gun." Nonetheless, she (1958: 200) argues that "[p]ower is actualized only where word and deed have not parted company, where words are not empty and deeds not brutal, whereas words are not used to veil intentions but to disclose realities, and deeds are not used to violate and destroy but to establish relations and create new realities." As "action in concert," power then has the character of "potentiality" (*potentia, dynamis,* or *Macht*) rather than of unchangeable and measurable substance. Power as a political concept and as the faculty of action is the human capacity to transform the world and, as she put it, create new realities. Action or political action is distinguished from the *necessity* of labor and the *utility* of work. Unlike her mentor Heidegger whose *Dasein* is characterized by death or mortality, Arendt defines the *initium* of action, which is the fountain of human capacity to create new realities, in terms of the facticity of birth or natality. "Philosophically speaking," Arendt (1972: 179) emphasizes, "to act is the human answer to the condition of natality. Since we all come into the world by virtue of birth, as newcomers and beginnings, we are able to start something new; without the fact of birth we would not even know what novelty is, all 'action' would be either mere behavior or preservation." Since human action is irreversible, that is, what is done cannot be undone, moreover, we actors can only forgive or be forgiven. On the other hand, equally because human action – unlike "behavior" – is unpredictable, we can only promise or be promised. Because action is unpredictable, politics is the adventurous art of the impossible as well as the possible.

VIII. Epilogue

In conclusion: this paper contends that social existence is the basic condition of humanity. By social existence, I mean an ensemble of multiple relationships anchored securely in bodies-in-relation, i.e., intercorporeality which had almost always been taken for granted or rejected until it has been reclaimed by postmodern, corporeal feminism. Plurality is marked by difference, by alterity. But for alterity, there would be no plurality, no relationality. Altarity elevates the Other to the altar of interhuman relationships without defacing or emasculating but only decentering the self. It alone engenders the heteronomic ethic of responsibility inscribed in postmodern feminism and its ethic of caring and Levinas's ethics as first philosophy. All of them judiciously appropriate difference as a bountiful resource for constructing and promoting the ethic of responsibility as first philosophy. The ethic of responsibility reclaims and continues the Copernican revolution of social thought initiated by Ludwig Feuerbach: what geocentrism is to egocentrism, heliocentrism is to heterocentrism. Feuerbach invented the "new thinking" of responsibility which has a riteful place in the study of politics because what is political is ethical. In his attempt to initiate a "responsibile politics" by integrating ethics and politics, Václav Havel (1991: 395) speaks of politics hopefully as the art of the impossible or heterotopia, that is, the art of improving ourselves in the world of difference (cf. Elshtain, 1995b). We may even agree with Arendt (1990: 83) that ethics is primary to politics because "[j]ust as eating is not life but the condition of living, so living together in the polis is not the good life but its material condition." The ultimate rationale for politics as ethics is that "it is not good to be alone" (Arendt, 1990: 103). Indeed, the ethical is ubiquitous and overarching because it is related to everything we do and think.

This paper further contends that the ethic of responsibility is an "altarnative" to rights talk and that it should become — as Hans Jonas (1989: 166) puts it – "the center of morality." A Confucian would say that the only exemplary and proprietary rights are rites.[26] The ethic of responsibility calls for "downsizing" rights talk – to use the current language of the American corporate world. It would, however, be foolhardy for anybody to dump the Bill of Rights in the rubbish-bin of political, social, and economic thought. I only suggest that we tone down the cadences of rights talk because it has reached the point of eutrophication that destroys a web of interdependence and diversity.

To repeat once again: what autonomy is to modernity, responsibility is to postmodernity.[27] It is not the "sleep of reason" but the lack or absence

---

[26]De Bary (1991) contends that the trouble with Confucianism in China is symptomatic of the world in trouble today. He speaks of the Confucian notion of self-cultivation, for example, is not the cult of the self but the cultivation of "correlative responsibility." In Tu, Hejtmanek and Wachman (1992), Confucian humanism is said to emphasize "communicative rationality," and it is concerned with "human rites" rather than "human rights." In saying "Adieu" to Levinas, Derrida (1996: 2) remarks that the word *droiture* ("straightforwardness" or "uprightness"), which is akin to the Confucian *rite* (ritefulness), comes from Levinas's teaching. It means "to speak straight on, to address oneself directly to the other, and to speak for the other whom one loves and admires, before speaking *of* him." The center of Levinas's thought lies in the "unlimited" and "unconditional" ethics of responsibility which precedes and exceeds freedom. Responsibility is "ethics beyond ethics." And yet death silences and dissolves responsibility.

[27]Descombes (1993: 148) considers autonomy as the "veritable content" of

of altarity that produces monsters and monstrous deeds. The future of difference will make the heteronomic ethic of responsibility the pillar of heterotopia. The ethic of responsibility as self-transcendence subverts the obsession of the modern West with the sovereignty of the self, self-reliance, or narcissistic absorption, i.e., the ethic of autonomy. The noble idea of self-reliance or independence may be a necessary but not a sufficient condition for the postmodern geopolitics and geoculture of interdependence in the world becoming increasingly a global village. We must not be mesmerized by the power and rhetoric of autonomy, independence, or self-reliance. As the "responsible self" refutes the atomized and collectivized self as a theoretical abstraction and chimera, the ethic of responsibility is a hopeful *altarnative* to both liberal individualism today and the totalitarian politics of bygone years. In the ethic of responsibility neither the individual nor the collectivity – the "two [contradictory] sovereigns" of European modernity, as Keith Tester (1992) calls them – is sovereign. As it knows no language of compromise, however, the ethical and political Esperanto of rights is indeed unpromising and uncompromising for the future. The ethic of responsibility heralds and celebrates the dialogical principle of a consummate community where the caring individual self is enfleshed with the cared Other. Notwithstanding the conviction of Emerson – the champion of "democratic individualism" – that the self-reliant individual knows no discontent because one has "infinite resources" for oneself, for oneself alone, Michael J. Sandel is poignant when he (1996: 338) contends forcefully that it is "the loss of mastery and erosion of community that lie at the heart of democracy's discontent." Responsibility-centered ethics is imperative for the future survival and preservation in perpetuity of the earth which shelters and nurtures humanity and nature in myriad ways. It is a paradigmatic way of thinking and doing – the way of a new phoenix, as it were, rising from the ashes of the past. By cultivating the habits[28] of the heart as well as the mind, the heteronomic ethic of responsibility opens a new threshold for philosophizing politics for generations yet to come. How right Emerson was when he (1979: 120) said in 1841 that without vision the people would perish and that we intellectuals are "the priests of that thought which establishes the foundations of the earth"! Now the old "priestly" vision of Emersonian self-reliance or rights talk must give way to the new "jesterly"

---

modernity. Tester (1993: 125) asserts that "the central problem which runs through the relationships and categories of post-modernity is the question of responsibility.... They [the inhabitants of post-modernity] should be also responsible for the very possibility of the future of Man and Nature alike."

[28]Bourdieu's (1990) "*le sense pratique*" includes *habitus* which is eminently practical and spontaneous as well as embodied. He (1990:57) writes that "the *habitus* is what enables the institution to attain full realization: it is through the capacity for incorporation, which exploits the body's readiness to take seriously the performative magic of the social...."

and cosmopolitan vision of responsibility which will "green" the land and people of the entire globe as well as the United States.

References

Almond, Brenda. 1993. "Rights," in *A Companion to Ethics*, ed. Peter Singer. Oxford: Blackwell, pp. 259-69

Arendt, Hannah. 1958. *The Human Condition*. Chicago: University of Chicago Press

Arendt, Hannah. 1972. *Crises of the Republic*. San Diego: Harcourt Brace Jovanovich

Arendt, Hannah. 1977. *Eichmann in Jerusalem: A Report on the Banality of Evil*, rev. and enl. ed. New York: Penguin Books

Arendt, Hannah. 1990. "Philosophy and Politics," *Social Research*, 57: 73-103

Baier, Annette. 1994. *Moral Prejudices*. Cambridge: Harvard University Press

Bauman, Zygmunt. 1990. "Effacing the Face: On the Social Management of Moral Proximity," *Theory, Culture and Society*, 7: 5-38

Bauman, Zygmunt. 1993. *Postmodern Ethics*. Oxford: Blackwell

Benhabib, Seyla. 1996. "Toward a Deliberative Model of Democratic Legitmacy," in *Democracy and Difference*, ed. Seyla Benhabib. Princeton: Princeton University Press, pp. 67-94

Bercovitch, Sacran. 1975. *The Puritan Origins of the American Self*. New Haven: Yale University Press

Bercovitch, Sacran. 1993. *The Rites of Assent*. New York: Routledge

Bernauer, James and David Rasmussen (ed.). 1988. *The Final Foucault*. Cambridge: MIT Press

Bernstein, Richard J. 1994. "Rethinking Responsibility," *Social Research*, 61: 833-52

Blum, Lawrence A. 1980. *Friendship, Altruism and Morality*. London: Routledge and Kegan Paul

Boman, Thorlief. 1960. *Hebrew Thought Compared with Greek*. Philadelphia: Westminster Press

Bourdieu, Pierre. 1990. *The Logic of Practice*, trans. Richard Nice. Stanford: Stanford University Press

Braidotti, Rosi. 1994. *Nomadic Subjects*. New York: Columbia University Press

Brown, Lyn Mikel and Carol Gilligan. 1992. *Meeting at the Crossroads*. Cambridge: Harvard University Press

Camus, Albert. 1956. *The Rebel*, trans. Anthony Bower. New York: Alfred A. Knopf

Card, Claudia. 1987. "Intimacy and Responsibility: What Lesbians Do." Working Papers Series 2, No. 10. Madison: Institute for Legal Studies

Cavell, Stanley. 1981. *The Senses of Walden*. San Francisco: North Point Press

Chalier, Catherine. 1995. "The Philosophy of Emmanuel Levinas and the Hebraic Tradition," in *Ethics as First Philosophy*, ed. Adriaan T. Peperzak. New York: Routledge, pp. 3-12

Cho, Kah Kyung. 1987. *Bewusstsein und Natursein*. Freiburg: Alber

Chodorow, Nancy Julia. 1980. "Gender, Relation, and Difference in Psychoanalytic Perspective," in *The Future of Difference*, ed. Hester Eisenstein and Alice Jardine. Boston: G.K. Hall

Choi, Chang-Jo. 1984. *Han Kook ui Pung Su Sa Sang*. Seoul: Minumsa

Choi, Chang-Jo. 1997. *Han Kook ui Ja Saeng Pung Su*, Vol. 1. Seoul: Minumsa

Clement, Grace. 1996. *Care, Autonomy, and Justice*. Boulder: Westview Press

Collin, Françoise. 1994. "Philosophical Differences" (trans. Authur Goldhammer), in *A History of Women in the West*, Vol. 5: *Toward a Cultural Identity in the Twentieth Century*, ed. Françoise Thébaud. Cambridge: Harvard University Press, 261-96

Connolly, William E. 1991. *Identity\Difference*. Ithaca: Cornell University Press

Connolly, William. 1996. *The Ethos of Pluralization*. Minneapolis: University of Minnesota Press

Dauenhauer, Bernard P. 1991. *Elements of Responsible Politics*. Dordrecht: Kluwer

De Bary, Wm. Theodore. 1991. *The Trouble with Confucianism*. Cambridge: Harvard University Press

Deleuze, Gilles and Félix Guattari. 1994. *What Is Philosophy?*, trans. Hugh Tomlinson and Graham Burchell. New York: Columbia University Press

Derrida, Jacques. 1992. *The Other Heading*, trans. Pascale-Anne Brault and Michael Naas. Bloomington: Indiana University Press

Derrida, Jacques. 1996. "Adieu" (trans. Pascale-Anne Brault and Michael Naas), *Critical Inquiry*, 23: 1-10

Descombes, Vincent. 1993. *The Barometer of Modern Reason*, trans. Stephen Adam Schwartz. New York: Oxford University Press

Dupuis, Michel. 1996. *Pronoms et Visages*. Dordrecht: Kluwer

Dworkin, Ronald. 1977. *Taking Rights Seriously*. Cambridge: Harvard University Press

Eagleton, Terry. 1990. *The Ideology of the Aesthetic*. Oxford: Blackwell

Elshtain, Jean Bethke. 1995a. *Democracy on Trial*. New York: Basic Books

Elshtain, Jean Bethke. 1995b. “A Performer of Political Thought: Václav Havel on Freedom and Responsibility, ” in *Theory and Practice* (Nomos 37), ed. Ian Shapiro and Judith Wagner DeCew. New York: New York University Press, pp. 464-82

Emerson, Ralph Waldo. 1940a. “The American Scholar,” in *The Complete Essays and Other Writings of Ralph Waldo Emerson*, ed. Brooks Atkinson. New York: Modern Library, pp. 45-63

Emerson, Ralph Waldo. 1940b. “Self-Reliance,” in *The Complete Essays and Other Writings of Ralph Waldo Emerson*, ed. Brooks Atkinson. New York: Modern Library, pp. 145-69

Emerson, Ralph Waldo. 1979. “An Oration,” in *Nature, Addresses, and Lectures*, ed. Robert E. Spiller and Alfred R. Ferguson. Cambridge: Harvard University Press, pp. 120-37

Feuerbach, Ludwig. 1966. *Principles of the Philosophy of the Future*, trans. Manfred H. Vogel. Indianapolis: Bobbs-Merrill

Foucault, Michel. 1986. *The Care of the Self*, trans. Robert Hurley. New York: Pantheon Books

Frankl, Viktor E. 1985. *Man's Search for Meaning*, rev. ed. New York: Washington Square Press

Fromm, Erich. 1956. *The Art of Loving*. New York: Harper and Row

Gilligan, Carol. 1982. *In a Different Voice*. Cambridge: Harvard University Press

Gilligan, Carol. 1986. “Remapping the Moral Domain: New Images of the Self in Relationship,” in *Reconstructing Individualism*, ed. Thomas C. Heller, Morton Sosna, and David E. Wellbery. Stanford: Stanford University Press, pp. 237-52

Gilligan, Carol, Nona P. Lyons, and Trudy J. Hanmer. 1989. *Making Connections*. Troy: Emma Willard School

Girard, René. 1987. *Things Hidden Since the Foundation of the World*, trans. Stephen Bann and Michael Metteer. Stanford: Stanford University Press

Glatzer, Nahum N. 1953. *Franz Rosenzweig*. New York: Schocken Books

Glendon, Mary Ann. 1991. *Rights Talk*. New York: Free Press

Goodin, Robert E. 1985. *Protecting the Vulnerable*. Chicago: University of Chicago Press

Goodin, Robert E. 1988. *Reasons for Welfare*. Princeton: Princeton University Press

Gray, J. Glenn. 1959. *The Warriors*. New York: Harcourt, Brace

Gray, John. 1994. “After the New Liberalism,” *Social Research*, 61: 719-35

Gray, John. 1995. *Enlightenment's Wake*. New York: Routledge

Grondin, Jean. 1994. *Introduction to Philosophical Hermeneutics*, trans. Joel Weinsheimer. New Haven: Yale University Press

Grosz, Elizabeth. 1994. *Volatile Bodies*. Bloomington: Indiana University Press

Guattari, Félix. 1995. *Chaosmosis: An Ethico-Aesthetic Paradigm*, trans. Paul Bains and Julian Pefanis. Bloomington: Indiana University Press

Gutman, Amy. 1989. "The Central Role of Rawl's Theory," *Dissent*, 36: 338-42

Gutman, Amy and Dennis Thompson. 1996. *Democracy and Disagreement.* Cambridge: Harvard University Press

Haar, Michel. 1993. *The Song of the Earth*, trans. Reginald Lilly. Bloomington: Indiana University Press

Hassan, Ihab. 1996. *Between the Eagle and the Sun.* Tuscaloosa: University of Alabama Press

Havel, Václav. 1987. *Living in Truth*, ed. Jan Valdislav. London: Faber and Faber

Havel, Václav. 1989. *Letters to Olga*, trans. Paul Wilson. New York: Henry Holt

Havel, Václav. 1991. *Open Letters*, trans. Paul Wilson. New York: Alfred A. Knopf

Heidegger, Martin. 1962. *Being and Time*, trans. John Macquarrie and Edward Robinson. New York: Harper

Hoffman, Piotr. 1983. *The Human Self and the Life and Death Struggle.* Gainesville: University Presses of Florida

Hughes, Robert. 1993. *Culture of Complaint.* New York: Warner Books

Irigaray, Luce. 1985. *This Sex Which Is Not One*, trans. Catherine Porter. Ithaca: Cornell University Press

Irigaray, Luce. 1993a. *An Ethics of Sexual Difference*, trans. Carolyn Burke and Gillian C. Gill. Ithaca: Cornell University Press

Irigaray, Luce. 1993b. *Je,Tu, Nous*, trans. Alison Martin. New York: Routledge

Irigaray, Luce. 1995. "The Question of the Other" (trans. Noah Guynn), *Yale French Studies*, No. 87: *Another Look, Another Woman*, ed. Lynne Huffer, pp. 7-19

Jacques, Francis. 1991. *Difference and Subjectivity*, trans. Andrew Rothwell. New Haven: Yale University Press

James, William. 1909. *A Pluralistic Universe.* New York: Longmans, Green

Jardine, Alice A. 1985. *Gynesis.* Ithaca: Cornell University Press

Jonas, Hans. 1984. *The Imperative of Responsibility.* Chicago: University of Chicago Press

Jonas, Hans. 1989. "Ontological Grounding of a Political Ethics: On the Metaphysics of Commitment to the Future of Man, " in *The Public Realm*, ed. Reiner Schürmann. Albany: State University of New York Press, pp. 154-66

Jung, Hwa Yol. 1995. "Body Politics and Caring as Responsibility," *Social Science and Policy Research*, 17: 81-114

Jung, Hwa Yol. 1996. "Phenomenology and Body Politics," *Body and Society*, 2: 1-22

Jung, Hwa Yol. Forthcoming. “The Greening of Postmodern Ethics: The Ethical Question of Reinhabiting the Earth,” in *Postmodern Ethics*, ed. Hugh Silverman. New York: Routledge

Kateb, George. 1992. *The Inner Ocean: Individualism and Democratic Culture*. Ithaca: Cornell University Press

Kateb, George. 1995. *Emerson and Self-Reliance*. Thousand Oaks: Sage Publications

Kolakowski, Leszek. 1968. *Toward a Marxist Humanism*, trans. Jane Ziekonko Peel. New York: Grove Press

Laqueur, Thomas. 1990. *Making Sex*. Cambridge: Harvard University Press

Lasch, Christopher. 1995. *The Revolt of the Elites and the Betrayal of Democracy*. New York: W. W. Norton

Levinas, Emmanuel. 1969. *Totality and Infinity*, trans. Alphonso Lingis. Pittsburgh: Duquesne University Press

Levinas, Emmanuel. 1987a. *Collected Philosophical Papers*, trans. Alphonso Lingis. Dordrecht: Martinus Nijhoff

Levinas, Emmanuel. 1987b. *Time and the Other*, trans. Richard A. Cohen. Pittsburgh: Duquesne University Press

Levinas, Emmanuel. 1988. “Useless Suffering,” in *The Provocation of Levinas*, ed. Robert Bernasconi and David Wood. New York: Routledge, pp. 156-67

Levinas, Emmanuel. 1992. “Foreword,” in Stéphane Mosès, *System and Revelation*, trans. Catherine Tibany. Detroit: Wayne State University Press, pp. 13-29

Levinas, Emmanuel. 1994. *Outside the Subject*, trans. Michael B. Smith. Stanford: Stanford University Press

Levinas, Emmanuel and Richard Kearney. 1986. “Diaglogue with Emmanuel Levinas,” in *Face to Face with Levinas*, ed. Richard A. Cohen. Albany: State University of New York Press, pp. 13-33

Llewelyn, John. 1991. *The Middle Voice of Ecological Conscience*. New York: St. Martin's Press

Lyotard, Jean-François. 1988. *The Differend*, trans. Georges Van Den Abbeele. Minneapolis: University of Minnesota Press

Macpherson, C.B. 1962. *The Political Theory of Possessive Individualism*. New York: Oxford University Press

Macpherson, C.B. 1985. *The Rise and Fall of Economic Justice and Other Essays*. New York: Oxford University Press

Mandelbaum, Maurice. 1955. *The Phenomenology of Moral Experience*. Glencoe: Free Press

May, Larry. 1992. *Sharing Responsibility*. Chicago: University of Chicago Press

McKeon, Richard. 1957. “The Development and the Significance of the Concept of Responsibility,” *Revue Internationale de Philosophie*, 11: 3-32

Merchant, Carolyn. 1996. *Earthcare*. New York: Routledge

Merleau-Ponty, Maurice. 1969. *Humanism and Terror*, trans. John O'Neill. Boston: Beacon Press

Merleau-Ponty, Maurice. 1970. *Themes from the Lectures at the Collège de France*, trans. John O'Neill. Evanston: Northwestern University Press

Merleau-Ponty, Maurice. 1973. *Adventures of the Dialectic*, trans. Joseph Bien. Evanston: Northwestern University Press

Monroe, Kristen Renwick. 1996. *The Heart of Altruism*. Princeton: Princeton University Press

Moore, Thomas. 1992. *Care of the Soul*. New York: Harper and Collins

Nhat Hanh, Thich. 1993. *Interbeing*, rev. ed. Berkeley: Parallax Press

Nicholson, Linda and Steven Seidman (ed.). 1995. *Social Postmodernism*. New York: Cambridge University Press

Nietzsche, Friedrich. 1959.*The Portable Nietzsche*, ed. and trans. Walter Kaufmann. New York: Penguin Books

Nietzsche, Friedrich. 1967. *The Birth of Tragedy*, trans. Walter Kaufmann. New York: Random House

Ozouf, Mona. 1988. *Festivals and the French Revolution*, trans. Alan Sheridan. Cambridge: Harvard University Press

Poole, Ross. 1991. *Morality and Modernity*. New York: Routledge

Rosen, Stanley. 1989. *The Ancients and the Moderns*. New Haven: Yale University Press

Sandel, Michael J. 1996. *Democracy's Discontent*. Cambridge: Harvard University Press

Scheler, Max. *The Nature of Sympathy*, trans. Peter Heath. New Haven: Yale University Press

Schrader, George A. 1960. "Responsibility and Existence," in *Responsibility*, ed. Carl J. Friedrich. New York: Liberal Arts Press, pp. 43-70

Schutz, Alfred. 1962. *Collected Papers*, Vol. 1: *The Problem of Social Reality*, ed. Maurice Natanson. The Hague: Martinus Nijhoff

Shklar, Judith N. 1984. *Ordinary Vices*. Cambridge: Harvard University Press

Smart, Barry. 1995. "The Subject of Responsibility," *Philosophy and Social Criticism*, 21: 93-109

Stocker, Michael. 1976. "Agent and Other: Against Ethical Universalism," *Australian Journal of Philosophy*, 54: 206-20.

Straus, Erwin W. 1966. *Phenomenological Psychology*. New York: Basic Books

Taylor, Charles. 1989. *Sources of the Self*. Cambridge: Harvard University Press

Taylor, Charles. 1992. *The Ethics of Authenticity*. Cambridge: Harvard University Press

Taylor, Mark C. 1987. *Altarity*. Chicago: University of Chicago Press

Tester, Keith. 1992. *The Two Sovereigns*. New York: Routledge

Tester, Keith. 1993. *The Life and Times of Post-Modernity*. New York: Routledge

Theunissen, Michael. 1984. *The Other*, trans. Christopher Macann. Cambridge: MIT Press

Tronto, Joan C. 1993. *Moral Boundaries.* New York: Routledge

Tronto, Joan C. 1996. "Care as a Political Concept," in *Revisioning the Political*, ed. Nancy J. Hirschmann and Christine Di Stefano. Boulder: Westview Press, pp. 139-56

Tu, Weiming, Milan Hejtmanek, and Alan Wachman (ed.). 1992. *The Confucian World Observed.* Honolulu: East-West Center

Vattimo, Gianni. 1993. *The Adventure of Difference*, trans. Cyprian Blamires with Thomas Harrison. Baltimore: Johns Hopkins University Press

West, Cornel. 1989. *The American Evasion of Philosophy.* Madison: University of Wisconsin Press

Whitebeck, Caroline. 1983. "A Different Reality: Feminist Ontology," in *Beyond Domination*, ed. Carol C. Gould. Totowa: Rowman and Allanheld, pp. 64-88

Wilson, James Q. 1993. *The Moral Sense.* New York: Free Press

Wittgenstein, Ludwig. 1980. *Culture and Value*, trans. Peter Winch. Chicago: University of Chicago Press

Young, Iris Marion. 1996. "Communication and the Other: Beyond Deliberative Democracy," in *Democracy and Difference*, ed. Seyla Benhabib. Princeton: Princeton University Press, pp. 120-35

How the Japanese "Edition" of 'Bewußtsein und Natursein' was born

Kiyoko Shimizu

The story of the Japanese translation of Professor Cho's *Bewußtsein und Natursein* is closely knit with the experience of my personal awakening and commitment to a cause that I now hold most precious. Until I had the fortune to meet Cho *sensei* (teacher) in 1990, I grew up in an atmosphere in which Korea was so far away from the daily reality of my life. The only memory I had of the Korean War that broke out when I was ten years old was a scene in a picture showing impoverished people salvaging metal scraps from war ruins. Some years later, in preparation for the high school entrance examination, I had to hammer into my memory the obviously important lesson taught in the social study class that the Korean War greatly contributed to Japan's economic boom. This superficial image of the neighboring country was shaken one day, however, when the high school teacher of world history described the background of the conflict of powers surrounding the Korean peninsula and the enormous suffering of Korean people. At that point I began to realize how shamefully little we knew about our own recent past.

Subsequently my eyes were also opened to the plight of the second generation Koreans in Japan through *The Meaning of Living*, a book by Koh Sa-myung who grew up himself in Japan. I became skeptical of the way young people in Japan were educated, especially with regard to lessons to be learned from history. Then my turbulent years in college from 1960 began with student protest against the U.S.-Japan Security Treaty which eventually led to the cancellation of President Eisenhower's visit to Japan. But when such student activism accomplished little and the organized student movement fell apart, I began to ponder about my future and finally decided to study philosophy.

In my choice of this "thinking" profession, I was probably influenced to a certain extent by my mother who was a devout Christian and who gave me in my early years knowledge of the Bible. At first I was drawn to the study of German Idealism, to Kant's moral philosophy known as "Rigorism". However, after going through the rebellious phase of youth by joining the anti-establishment rallies which were the fashionable political agenda of the day, the limits of the introvert *Gesinnungsethik* of Kant became all too clear to me. I then turned toward his philosophy of history, looking for ideas more closely in touch with concrete reality. An inevitable corollary of my emergent sense of reality was the awareness of the position of women in Japanese society. This coincided with the newly rising interest in the feminist literature during the seventies, when Simone de Beauvoir's *The Second Sex* and Betty Friedan's *The Feminine Mystique* touched off an explosive enthusiasm in Japan, even while the protests surrounding Vietnam War and civil rights movement were spreading a worldwide sentiment for the emancipation of all oppressed people.

In the eighties, it was my good fortune to have encountered the work of the renowned Jewish philosopher Hannah Arendt. Arendt was an ideal combination of Kant and feminism, even though with her creative extension of Kant's theory of *judgment* to the domain of political and moral philosophy she remained rather detached from any recognizable feminist movement. But her imaginative interpretation of Kant was so congenial to me that I momentarily felt I could rewrite her thought in my own idiom. When I was thus projecting my own lifework along the line of Arendt's political philosophy, I was to meet yet another extraordinary teacher in April of 1990. Cho sensei arrived in Osaka on the invitation of the Japan Society for the Promotion of Science. Though he stayed only one semester, his erudite public lectures and many incisive comments at colloquy sessions, all delivered in impeccable Japanese, left a lasting impact on all those who listened to him. He spoke to the audience who came from various parts of the Kansai area on such topics as "Phenomenological Approach: an Eastern View", "Heidegger and Lao Tzu", "Beyond the Philosophy of Consciousness", "Heidegger and the Oriental Thinking", among others.

Cho sensei was not just a highly reputed guru of European philosophy. It was readily apparent that he had squarely positioned himself as an *Asian* who is committed to the heritage of the classical Eastern philosophy, and yet he moved with absolute ease and persuasiveness in interpreting the recondite thought of the likes of Husserl and Heidegger. I felt smitten by the expansive scale of his philosophy that bridged East and West. But I also saw a certain continuity between Hannah Arendt's adopted position, that of a *Conscious Pariah* and the way Cho sensei's cosmopolitan learning outstripped all chauvinistic egocentrism without sacrificing the inner stability of his Koreanness. Thus my encounter with Cho sensei was a further confirmation of my fascination with Arendt as a philosopher who thinks and lives *in principle* the life of a "world citizen". It is this principle that has become also the guiding spirit of my life. What is more, I enjoyed the personal guidance of Cho sensei as well after he carefully read my Japanese articles on Arendt and gave me valuable advice and encouragement. And I in turn wished earnestly to learn from his philosophy and decided, with his help, to read his *Bewußtsein und Natursein* in the original German.

Initially, I had only hoped to understand for myself some chapters of the book. In this attempt, we never actually met in person, but chose to use the telephone in the evening hours to clarify the meaning of some difficult passages. There were many such hour-long conversations, and yet progress was slow. As the time of Cho sensei's departure drew near, I found myself having barely finished the translation of one chapter entitled "Ecological Suggestibility in Heidegger's Later Philosophy". The weight of this chapter seemed to me appropriate for publication as a self-contained article in the collection of theses of the Otemon-Gakuin University. Once we agreed to bring this chapter to print, the thought of publishing the whole book in Japanese became irresistible, and before I knew it, I had accepted head-on this sheer daunting challenge.

In retrospect, this was indeed an undertaking I could not have mastered all by myself. Even the one chapter I first managed to publish at Otemon required a good deal of help from colleagues of Osaka University who were familiar with the difficult and often impossible language of Heidegger. I therefore set out to contact one by one my Japanese colleagues who heard Cho sensei's lectures and were, so to speak, still fresh under his spell. Soon the number of willing participants in this team-translation grew to eight, including myself. Among them, my younger colleague at Otemon, Professor Hiroshi Yamamoto, bore the brunt of what turned out to be a grueling marathon that lasted nearly two years. He not only set the tone for a rigorous and meticulously accurate translation, but coordinated, together with me, the individual translating efforts of all members and gave the final touch by adding an "Exposition" at the end of the volume.

Not to be forgotten, though, was the fact that Cho sensei himself was deeply involved in the process, as the translated Japanese drafts were continuously faxed to him for validation or correction. Bridging the gulf between a highly stylized philosophical German language and the scholarly Japanese diction trying to capture the original nuance required no small feat of imagination. Few direct, verbal translations turned out to be useful. What ensued was therefore a work fit to be labeled "the Japanese edition" of *Bewußtsein und Natursein*, for which the original author became a member of the translating team. In some cases, the author revised or updated the text, and translators supplemented their own separate notes, to make the book virtually the latest and more complete edition. During those two years, our team met to discuss and compare individual notes at regular intervals, and at its twelfth session, Professor Cho visited us in Osaka to finalize the draft before it was turned over to the publisher. The manuscript was accepted by the Hosei University Press and printed as a volume in the prestigious *Universitas* Series. It was September 1994, when finally our unswerving dedication to scholarship, years of perseverance and the spirit of international cooperation bore its fruit, and *Ishiki-to Shizen* was born. In purely human terms, it was a heart-warming experience. It has bonded the spirits of many people, far beyond the circle of translators. As for the scholarly merit of this publication, Professor Yamamoto should be given the word. Below is a slightly modified excerpt from his "Expository Summary" which he wrote for the Japanese readers.

I have already mentioned briefly that the echo of Professor Cho's *Bewußtsein und Natursein* had reached even the artists' circle in Germany. Several reviews I have at hand show that this book received extremely positive evaluations worldwide. Without going into details, the measure of repercussions of *Bewußtsein und Natursein* can be readily guessed from the fact that Hans-Georg Gadamer and Manfred Riedel have quoted Cho's work many times in their articles. Particularly the second chapter of the book, in which Heidegger's later philosophy was shown by the author to have developed ecologically significant ideas, stirred up quite a response, and yet its true merit lies rather in Cho's shrewd distinction of Heidegger's own call for the "guardianship of *Being*" from the popular ecologist argument for the "protection of *nature*". Since the author's Introduction contains a summary account of each chapter, I shall mainly focus on the overall theme and flesh out what is meant by the book title, "Consciousness and Nature".

In "The Age of World Picture", Heidegger sums up the essential characteristic of the modernity of the West in "the transformation of the very essence of man himself into the *subject*". Through this interpretation, Heidegger points out two interdependent problems. One of which concerns the Western view of nature, and the other that of man. *Subject* is that which has positioned itself at the center of all the relations. Having "thrust" (ject) himself at the basis (sub) of all entities, man has now become the subject who no longer comports receptively (vernehmen) toward the entities as they manifest themselves, but sets them up before his view (vor sich stellen), re-presenting them as something that stands over against himself, namely, as *object*. To that extent, world or nature as the totality of entities becomes reduced to a "picture" (Bild), posited in front of the subject through its "re-presenting" act. Such a reduction of world to a mere world-view, or understanding the "true" being of nature basically in terms of its progressive physico-scientific conceptions, would be none other than what Heidegger decries as the "forfeiture of the naturalness of nature"

Along with this re-presentation of nature that took hold of the modern West, man inevitably establishes himself as the re-presenting subject, a thesis that found its clearest formulation in the famous "*Cogito, ergo sum*" of Descartes. But this is precisely what Heidegger is referring to when he speaks of the rise of the "metaphysics of subjectivity" in the modern era. This subjectivation of man as "conscious being" (Bewußtsein) has brought about not only the objectivation and "depotentiation" of nature. In Heidegger's view, the origin of the "death of God" can also be traced to the relativization of the "Absolute", inasmuch as the *transcendence* of God has been brought down to being a *correlate* of the finite consciousness of man. But more pointedly, overarching over these two major transformations of the modern age, and giving it its unique brand of planetary scope, is the third and most widespread phenomenon of *technology*.

Regarding this problem, Heidegger says in "The Technology and the Turn" that modern technology, in contradistinction to the conventional, arranges and takes stock of the totality of entities solely as a "reserve" (Bestand) that is at man's disposal. Man's access to all the entities under this exclusively self-centered viewpoint preempts the way in which the entities could reveal themselves *as they are.* Not that such a forcible "setting up" of things is not indeed primordially rooted in the very possibility of "bringing forth" (poiesis) of nature itself. But it is a way in which the *essence* of nature gets rather covered up. Herein lies the danger of modern technology. For technology is the thought that has lost touch with Being, which only is worthy of thought, and has become transformed to a calculating and dominating reason. Descartes typically illustrates this shift of thinking in his *Discourse on the Method* (Part 6): "By knowing clearly the power and operation of fire, water, wind, stars and heaven, and all other physical bodies that surround us, we can apply them to appropriate use. In this way we discover a practical philosophy which enables us to become the master and possessor of nature".

The ascendancy of modern technology, however, has its roots in a much more distant past. It is the short-sightedness of modern critics who take issue with the phenomenon of technology without realizing that it is merely the *consequence* of something that has preceded it and thereby determined it. Heidegger sees such a determining effect in the early Greek philosophy, especially at the juncture when man's relation to Being is interpreted in terms of his *having Logos* (Aristotle). In the more primordial encounter of man with Being, i.e. during the Pre-Socratic period, however, thought (*Logos*) belonged to Being (*physis*). And the reawakening of this sense of man's being-in-the-world as *responsive* dwelling, by heeding to the *call* of Being, is what constitutes the message of Heidegger's much discussed *turn* or reversal. Such renunciation of the will to dominate necessarily entails man's altered relation to technology, in whose original meaning, *techne*, the essence of *art* is to be retrieved. To *reverse* and to turn around the danger of the present technological age does not imply, therefore, to refuse flat-out any use of technology. Instead of going against the modern technology, the more thoughtful path to go would be to help "bring forth" (poiesis) the truth of Being through the means of *techne* as art. The poetic "bringing forth" of the truth of Being goes also hand in hand with the ecologically significant attitude of man towards nature, namely, guarding and fostering things instead of lording over them. In this manner, Heidegger's later philosophy articulates his *turn* away from the traditional logocentrism toward *physis*-centeredness, away from technological toward *poetic* thinking. Little wonder that this bold line of Professor Cho's Heidegger interpretation caught the attention of German artists in Munich and Saarland and as a result a special symposium was arranged in 1989[1] to which he was invited as keynote speaker.

Though Heidegger in all appearance sought to prepare for this reversal of the metaphysics of subjectivity by a re-appropriation of the early

[1] *Natur, Technik und Kunst*, Internationale Symposion, Oct. 20-21, 1989, Kunstgalerie Saarbrücken

thought of the Pre-Socratic philosophers, it is another highlight in Cho's work which demonstrates that there was an old *Eastern* connection in Heidegger's path. We know that the noted Heidegger scholar Otto Pöggeler underwrote Professor Cho's special contribution to this aspect of Heidegger scholarship. Where until recently such a connection to Zen Buddhism was openly suggested, there in reality were no more than some fleeting impressions of affinity, more in style than in substance, of his thought with Zen Buddhism. With Taoism and with Lao Tzu in particular, however, Heidegger ventured into a greater speculative depth, and even surmised, in the "primary word" *Tao*, a common origin of "Saying" that is older than Logos, Physis and Moira. To this attempt of Heidegger to span East and West may the subtitle of Professor Cho's book, *Phenomenological East-West-Divan* very well be alluding. But Cho's book was, as suggested by the perceptible echo of the title of Goethe's collection of poems[2], in which he transcended the Eurocentric provincialism of his time, not simply an interpretive case study of someone else's East-West synthesis, even if that someone happens to be Heidegger. What Professor Cho presents here is nothing less than a living testimony of his own global perspective, an original undertaking to *poetically* burst through the conventional barrier between two worlds held to be unbridgeable, and show, in the spirit of finely discerning phenomenological exhibition, that a constructive dialogue between East and West is possible.

Not only would the breadth of scale encompassed by the whole work inspire the readers. The rich tableaux of themes are as fascinating as they are enlightening. The author traces the origin of "depotentiation of nature" to the emergence of the idea of "transcendence" in Christianity (an event Nietzsche described as "the greatest misfortune"), sets the Taoist notion of nothingness side by side with that of the Negative Theology, and unravels the connection between the narrowly consciousness-centered reading of human existence and the grammatical structure of Indo-Germanic languages in which the *subject* plays such a privileged role. Moving to the domain of aesthetic experience, he brings the leading Taoist concept of *kojol* to bear upon its representative counterpart in Zen Buddhist tradition, *sabi*, and augments the Husserlian theme of the "anonymously functioning subjectivity" with his own exploration of the phenomenon in the field of literature. All this makes the lecture of this book a memorable, riveting experience.

As shown in Professor Yamamoto's aptly rendered summary, Cho sensei has presented in this volume some of the most weighty and intriguing issues of phenomenology. But from his treatment of those issues exudes such a

[2]Karsten Harries gave a background account of this subtitle, and hinted at the similar intention Cho had with Goethe. See "Phenomenology Beyond the Spirit of Revenge", in *Research in Phenomenology*, Winter 1990, p.275ff.

suggestive power that we are bound to think continuously about them in the days and years ahead. Needless to say, I have benefited a great deal professionally by actively working together with the author in the making of this Japanese edition. But my gain was also significant from the human side of this professional encounter. It is true that I have developed interest for and became involved in human rights issues in general and women's rights in particular, largely on my own account. Nevertheless, had it not been for Cho sensei's guidance, the Himmel of my problem awareness and the scope of international exchange would not have widened so markedly. I owe him, for instance, my valuable acquaintance with Korea's noted women leaders. Hyo-Jae Lee and Jeong-Ock Yoon are two of the Christian feminist leaders I now know first hand. I learned to admire their personal integrity, indefatigable spirit of independence and upright judgment. Theirs is a world I could not have had the privilege of knowing, if I had been confined to my home country. I have learned to look at the thorny issues affecting the relationship of our two nations from the vantage point of an *Asian*. Some German thinkers and political leaders who stood tall as *Europeans* may be looked upon as models. Through my study of Arendt, I became interested in her relationship to her two teachers, Heidegger and Jaspers. About Heidegger, who erred so egregiously in his political judgment, and to whom Arendt nevertheless had a close personal tie, enough is known today, though still much more remains controversial. Unlike him, Jaspers stood, with his stalwart conscience of an "Europäer", head and shoulder above average Germans. If I have compared previously Cho sensei's cosmopolitan trait to the type of *Conscious Pariah* that Hannah Arendt represented, I can say now even more confidently that he has about him this touch of fatherliness which Arendt must have felt too in her relation to Jaspers. Professor Cho always put my professional interest first, and paved my way to visit the New School for Social Research in New York and the Library of Congress for my further research on Arendt. He also arranged my appearance at several colloquy sessions in the United States. I, for my part, feel fortunate to have done my share in providing him with a window of opportunity to see Japan critically and fairly, and to maintain his professional contact with Japanese colleagues.

Finally, I must come back to my colleagues, without whose help and advice I could not have finished this arduous task. Professor Yamamoto and the rest of the translating team deserve all the credit for their utterly selfless dedication. Nor can I forget the valuable criticisms, generous comments and encouragement I received from Professors Gunshi Satomi, Kohei Mizoguchi of Osaka University and many others, from the moment when I started cautiously to translate a chapter of the book in a ground breaking effort. My most sincere appreciation is due them all.

Heidegger's Phenomenological Archeology of Language

Seung-Chong Lee

Philosophy is actually homesickness. - Novalis -

I. Formal Science and Archeology

Here is one way of looking at *language*: language is the set of its well-formed formulas. The set of well-formed formulas of language is determined by a fiat of its creator. Usually he does this by specifying (1) a set of symbols (the alphabet of his language) and (2) a set of formation rules determining which sequences of symbols from his alphabet are well-formed formulas of his language. As the language is constructed by its creator, it can thus be changed according to his needs.

Here is another way of looking at language: language is a phenomenon of human life. Language is understood in terms of (1) the context in which it is used and (2) the actions into which it is woven. Like human life and historical tradition, language is what has been handed down to us. We therefore have to accept it as it is, and adapt ourselves to it.

Here is one way of looking at the *meaning* of language: language acquires meaning when its components – symbols or well-formed formulas – are assigned a set of objects. This process of assigning meaning to language is what is called interpretation. Interpretation cannnot but depend on the interpreter's intentions and purposes. However, those intentions and purposes can always be diverse and what is more, there is always room for unintended interpretation. It can be said that meaning is determined by interpretation rather than intention. Therefore surplus interpretation is always possible. This is a philosophical lesson of the Löwenheim-Skolem theorem.

Here is another way of looking at the meaning of language: the meaning of a word is its use in the language. Meaning and use are inseparable. As human beings are the ones making use of language, the meaning of language begins and ends in men. There is no surplus meaning beyond human beings.

Here is one way of looking at the *inquiry* into language: the inquiry begins with the formalization of natural language. In this process, which is furthermore formally systematized, natural language is replaced by formal language when necessary. Formal language is systematized by specifying a deductive apparatus for it. A deductive apparatus for a formal system is given (1) by laying down by fiat that certain well-formed formulas of the formal language are to be axioms of the formal system, and (2) by laying down by fiat a set of transformation rules that determines which relations between the well-formed formulas of the formal language are relations of immediate consequence in the formal system. Proof theory is a theory of formal languages with deductive apparatuses. It is the syntax of formal languages. The semantics of formal languages is called the model theory. The model theory is a theory of interpretations of formal languages. A model of a formula of a language is an interpretation of the language for which the formula comes out true. Many important concepts such as logical consequence and validity are defined by the truth within the model. The semantics of the well-formed formulas based on the model theory is supported by the semantics of possible worlds. The model of formal language which has modal operators such as $\Box$ and $\Diamond$ (representing necessity and possibility, respectively) consist of the set of objects called the possible world. Thus, truth is relativized not only by the model but also by the model's possible worlds.

Here is another way of looking at the inquiry into language: the inquiry needs to question the historicity and the context-dependence of language. Language is the totality of what has been handed down to us through history. Everything about human life is melted down in language. And we are born within this totality. It is also within this totality that we learn and use language. Therefore, ironically speaking, we are not the ones using the language to communicate. Instead, it is language which is utilizing us and speaking through us. Language can be understood in two ways: as a medium for the historical world of beings to make itself known to human beings, or as a means for human beings to understand and describe the historical world of beings. The world's Himmel of meaning opens up to men through language. In this light, understanding language as a mere formal system is a distortion of the essence of language. The task of formalization that separates language from the context of its use freezes the historicity and temporality in language. The interpretation that understands meaning by separating it from language makes it difficult to disclose the world that is embedded in language. The semantics of the possible world that attempts to understand meaning by relating it to the possible worlds forgets the fact that human beings are beings-in-the-world who exist only in this world. The possible world is not a truly independent world by itself. Instead, it is only a shadow of this world that is fabricated based on the human understanding of the world.

The goal of discussing such opposing views is not simply to distinguish the science of formal language from the philosophy of natural language. Rather, our goal is to focus on Heidegger, the owner of the most unique and indepth voice among the minority that criticized the theory of formal language which lead the 20th century. In the pairs of contrasting views discussed above, the latter ones are those of Heidegger.

Heidegger did have contemporaries that seemed to hold similar philosophical position to his. Further, there were also philosophers that seemed to be the forerunners of his philosophical methods. Wittgenstein and Strawson can be seen as Heidegger's fellow thinkers in that they criticized formal language from the perspective of natural language. [1] Other noticeable resemblances to Heidegger's method are found in the analysis and synthesis of Pappus, in Kant's transcendental deduction, and Husserl's phenomenology. All three thinkers share the common search for language's condition and presupposition. However, when Heidegger set out to track down language's historicity and its roots in the history of philosophy, no longer were Wittgenstein and Strawson successful in catching up with him. Heidegger argued that when one traces the condition and presupposition of language down to man's circumstances in actual life and historical beings in general – rather than to logical inferences and epistemological postulates –, the analysis/synthesis, the transcendental deduction, and the phenomenological reduction presented by Pappus, Kant and Husserl respectively, posed as nothing but potential hindrances which Heidegger tried to overcome.

According to Heidegger, language is a relic of archeology. The language of philosophy is an archeological relic that reflects the thoughts and lives of the ancient Greeks. This is so because philosophy traces its roots to ancient Greece and the language of philosophy was also formed in that era. Like everything else that exists on the face of the earth, language is also something handed down from the past. Of course, today's language is far from the original form it started out to be. Time and history have transformed and reinterpreted language along its journey in time. We can find traces of this history and tradition in our language. Since we can not travel back in time, our only means of understanding this history and tradition is through the correct interpretation of these relics.

Heidegger demonstrates that our own thoughts are not cut off from the tradition of the past. He does this by tracking down and reconstructing the etymological roots or more specifically, the Greek roots of the language we use today. Just like an archeologist who investigates and interprets the relics, Heidegger rediscovers the concepts used in philosophy and listens to the historical meanings and stories behind each concept. For the next 2,000 years since they first appeared during the ancient Greek era, these concepts have contributed in disclosing "Being" to man in every period, according to the period's method. Furthermore, he reflects on the basic concepts of the pre-Socratic philosophers, such as *aletheia*, *logos* and *moira*. These are concepts based on a naive and sound starting point, and are free from the tradition of theoretical analysis that was preserved throughout the Sophists, Socrates and Plato. By reflecting on these concepts, Heidegger attempts to figure out what thinking was before Being was forgotten; in those times when the disclosure by language did not distort Being.

[1] See my "Untimely Meditations: Wittgenstein and Heidegger as Critics of Mathematical Logic," in *History and Phenomenology*, edited by the Korean Society for Phenomenology, Seoul: Philosophy and Reality Press, 1999.

II. Causality, Logic and the Understanding of Meaning

We explain and understand the given phenomena. In the tradition of German hermeneutics, explanation and understanding were contrasted as the methodology of natural science and the methodology of human science. In natural science, explanation translates into causal explanation. The phenomena of the natural world are interwoven with each other in terms of causal relationships. Although the debate as to whether this relationship is deterministic or not remains controversial, [2] none of the phenomena that we understand or know about the natural world is beyond the control of the causal relationship. An explanation about a phenomenon is only possible by showing the phenomenon prior to it, which is the cause of the latter one. However, it is important to note that, as Davidson pointed out, mere presentation of the causal relationship does not imply justification (Davidson 1982, p. 331). Unlike the indication of cause, the task of justification is a logical and linguistic job. In short, one proposition is justified by none other than another proposition. If the justification is logically incomplete or probabilistic, it is called induction. On the other hand, if the justification is logically complete, it is called deduction or proof. While the relationship between one phenomenon and another in the natural world is one of causal sequence, the logical relationship between one proposition and another in language is one of justification.

With this in mind, then, what is the relationship between the world and language? First, there are two types of theories concerning this subject. One is that of Wittgenstein and Carnap which sees the structure of the world as logical. The other is Putnam and Kripke's theory which observes that, the meaning of language is bestowed by the causal relationship between language and the world. These are cases where the structural relationship of language has been applied to the world, or the world's structural relationship to language. However, these views are not without faults.[3] They have two things in common: they commit the mistake of overlooking the fact that language and the world belong to different catagories and of presupposing the homogeneity and isomorphism of these two factors in question. By doing so, they seem to have committed either the fallacy of category mistake or the fallacy of premise smuggling.

A more influential theory than logical isomorphism or causal theory of meaning between language and the world is the referential theory of meaning. This theory argues that language acquires its meaning by referring to the world. This theory also presupposes the correspondence between lan-

---

[2]See my "Quantum Mechanics and EPR Debate," in Young-Hwan Oh (ed.), *Science and Metaphysics*, Seoul: Free Thought Press, 1993.

[3]See Newton Garver and Seung-Chong Lee, *Derrida and Wittgenstein*, Philadelphia: Temple University Press, 1994, Ch. 2.

guage and the world. However, the correspondence cannot mean that the components of language are at one-to-one correspondence relationship to the components of the world because the components of language and the world are organically interrelated to the whole they belong to which are "language and the world." For example, the word "red" presupposes the language and the grammar that have color concepts as its components. The color "red" also presupposes the object that is red and the color spectrum. This presupposition is also applicable when words are set up to refer to the objects. When we point at a red pencil and say to a child "This is tove," our words fail to determine what tove means. To the child, tove could signify anything from red, wood, pencil, hardness and much more (Wittgenstein 1958, p. 2). The child cannot know the point of view from which we are speaking about the object. This suggests that referring cannot be the source of meaning because referring presupposes a lot more primordial things. And also because meaning seems to originate not so much from the referring as from those presuppositions.

The discussion so far does not refute the referential theory of meaning. It only shows that the referential theory is an incomplete theory. When we refer to the world through language, we are attempting to disclose certain aspects or modes of the world through a certain point of view. When we say, "this is ...," we are calling out to the foreground that which the phrase is referring to and is, at the same time, within our visual space. With this, the rest of our visual space fades into the background. Furthermore, when we say, "... is red," we come to observe that which is called out in this manner from the point of view of color. The other aspects, such as the fact that it is made of wood and is a pencil, fade into the background. Since the words that form a sentence are vocative codes that bring out a certain aspect or point of view of the world, sentences – be it declarative sentences, interrogative sentences or negative sentences – are all fundamentally vocative.

Heidegger distinguishes that which is called out through language as "being," and the background of that which is called out as "Being." If being is an individual, Being is the whole. An easy way to understand this relationship is to compare Being to the waves of a vicious coastal area and beings to the foam that is produced and then swept away with the waves. If being occupies a position, Being is the system of co-ordinates. Just as the called out foreground presupposes its background, being presupposes Being. The act of calling out the world through language is possible through the interactive totality of beings and Being. It is through this totality that language discloses not only beings, but also their background which is Being. The meaning of language is also found in the disclosure of such Being through the use of language. Heidegger says:

> Being is that which is not a being and does not belong to beings ... What is not accessible to direct representing and thought:

> that is the genuine background. (Heidegger and Fink 1970, p. 123)
>
> ... usage is thought as essential presencing in Being itself. (Heidegger 1950a, p. 367; English trans. p. 53)

The limitations of the current theories of meaning are that they try to relate the world and language on the Himmel of being after the disclosure has taken place and not through language's disclosure process itself. As a result, the theories are only interested in the disclosed foreground and overlook the fact that the foreground acquires meaning in harmony with its background.

This is also true in the case of the traditional correspondence theory of truth that is based on the referential relation between language and the world. In order for a proposition to fit a fact and to be true, the fact itself must be disclosed first. However, the traditional correspondence theory of truth regards disclosure as a natural thing and does not questions it at all. On this matter, Heidegger criticizes as follows:

> However, the fact must show itself to be fact if knowledge and the proposition that forms and expresses knowledge are to be able to conform to the fact; otherwise the fact cannot become binding on the proposition. How can fact show itself if it cannot itself stand forth out of concealedness, if it does not itself stand in the unconcealed? (Heidegger 1950b, p. 38; English trans. p. 51)

The locus of meaning is the use of language by human beings. Human being's Himmel of meaning determines his ways of understanding Being, and vice versa. The language of a pantheist discloses Being as pious and this piety gives meaning to his language. The language of greedy businessmen discloses Being through electricity, furniture and material goods and it is only usefulness which determines the Himmel of meaning. To the businessman, the piety of Being is meaningless or is a value beyond his realms of interest and understanding. The question of what is meaningful and what is not, is directly related to his understanding of the world and the orientation of his practice. For instance, the difference between a poet's language and a scientist's language and their sphere of meaning is interrelated with the difference of their understandings of the world and their modes of description.

Now we know that the relationship between the world and our language is not that of correspondence or of referring, nor of causal relations, but rather, it is the formation of meaning through the calling process. The diverse aspects of this "calling" imply the diversity of Being in the world. Since human beings are the only ones that use language, only we are concerned about Being that is disclosed through language. Human beings are the shepherds of Being and the ones who can decipher the codes that are given to us by Being. In this light, Heidegger was displeased with the idea of language being defined before its use as in theoretical science. This is because definition strictly limits and tightly regulates the wide range of possibilities by which language can disclose the world. Moreover, Heidegger believed that it is better to have less of such limitations and restrictions because this width of freedom is equal to the broadness by which Being can disclose itself (Heidegger 1959, p. 113). This also explains the reason why he devoted himself to the study of the language of poetry which was full of metaphors. It is for the same reason that the way and width of our thoughts should not be restricted by any kind of pre-established methodology whatsoever (Heidegger 1959, p. 105).

Traditionally, referring and correspondence have been regarded as the criterion for meaning and truth. After pointing out that the concepts of referring and correspondence are incomplete and insufficient as the criterion for meaning and truth, Heidegger declares that truth is unconcealment. Truth is not discovered by the contrast between the language and the world related to it, but by the unconcealment of Being through language. Heidegger argues that *aletheia*, the ancient Greek concept for truth, holds the meaning of such unconcealment. If to traditional philosophy, truth was the property of a proposition that correctly described the given world, to Heidegger, truth was the event of the unconcealment of Being through language. However, it is unclear how Heidegger solved the problem of whether this unconcealment was the right kind of unconcealment or not. Since not all unconcealment can be the right kind of unconcealment, should not there be a standard to evaluate the appropriateness of unconcealment? Some might criticize that such questioning is based on the traditional way of attempting to use correspondence as a basis for understanding truth. We believe, however, that the concept of truth as right and wrong is still a useful one and that there is no reason for us not to use it in evaluating whether the unconcealment has been done rightly.

III. A Philosophical History of Oppression

Heidegger points out that the diverse disclosures of Being through language have been distorted by a one-sided monopoly of a certain kind of method. This method is none other than the understanding of the world in terms of the linguistic artifact called theory. The theoretical point of view is a product of the Freudian oppression that is applied onto Being's richness. The colonization and displacement of the natural language by formal language is part of the last steps of the theory-oriented philosophy (Heidegger 1959, p. 110). However, according to Heidegger, the emergence and development of theory, is an unavoidable fate of human history that dates back to the ancient Greeks 2,000 years ago.

According to Heidegger (Heidegger 1959, p. 165), the ancient Greeks did not have a word for language. To them, language was *logos*. Then, what is *logos*? *Logos* means order. In other words, language is the embodiment of order. [4] In ancient Greece, *logos* was the order of language as well as the order of the world. [5] The Greek belief that the universe is orderly is reflected on the word *cosmos*, which means both universe and order. The Milesian school, which marks the starting point in the history of western philosophy, questions the *arche* of all creation. This shows that they were already presupposing an attitude to explain all things by reducing them to something fundamental. The struggle to search for a constant order in an uncertain world can be regarded as the manifestation of the will survive in an often hostile world. It is also the effort to give some kind of eternal meaning to life and the universe and to obtain some understanding of both. This kind of will and struggle leads to Plato's dichotomy of the world and human beings. The phenomenal world that includes the human body along with the opinion (*doxa*) of human beings about this world, holds the property of contingency which is restricted by time and space. On the other hand, reality and human being's rational cognition (*episteme*) of it are classified as something beyond time and space holding the property of necessity. Human beings complete themselves by overcoming the given restrictions of time and space, and by understanding reality in a rationally intuitive way. If the uncertainty of life can be said to contribute to the temporality of life, which is accompanied by the changes of becoming and destruction, then it is possible to say that human life is completed by the constancy that is gained by transcending life's temporality and the properties that accompany it.

Escape from the uncertain phenomenal world is possible by freezing the temporality and historicity of the phenomenal world that we live in. Heidegger sees this as the first oppression that appears in the history of western philosophy. With this background, the task of observing the real world from a theoretical point of view finally becomes possible. (*Θεωρεῖν*, the Greek root word for "theory," originally meant "to see.") However, we, who are the ones looking at the real world, are no longer a concrete self possessing a body. We exist neither in the phenomenal world nor in the real world. In short, we are not beings-in-the-world in any sense for we have already transcended the phenomenal world and are confronting and observing the

[4]The tradition of identifying the *logos* as order with language is observed in the writings of Wittgenstein. "In fact, all the propositions of our everyday language, just as they stand, are in perfect logical order" (Wittgenstein 1961b, 5.55563); "it is clear that every sentence in our language "is in order as it is" " (Wittgenstein 1967, §98).

[5]Such thoughts have also been carried through all the way to young Wittgenstein. See my "The Life of Identity," in Sang-Hwan Kim (ed.), *Philosophical Studies on Media*, Seoul: Nanam, 1998.

real world from the outside. There is nothing between us and the real world except the relationship of seeing. Also, we are not allowed any sort of specific practice other than seeing. In addition, because we do not belong anywhere, we do not have any kind of practical interest nor any purpose. Perhaps it would be more precise to say that all interests and purposes were eliminated the instant man escaped from the phenomenal world. Heidegger perceives the restrictions of human behavior and the elimination of human interests and purposes as the second oppression. Further, he argues that freezing the temporality and historicity from the world and eliminating human behavior, interests and purposes, are in short, acts of stripping away the very world in which we live in. This is true because there no longer exists the time and space for the world to become the world and there remains no existing human beings. The third oppression is none other than the oppression of the world itself.

Modern philosophy is often identified with epistemology. Nevertheless, Heidegger believes that modern philosophy has also made a contribution to ontology. Although Descartes' proposition, "I think, therefore I am," emphasizes the primacy of rational thought over Being, it can also be interpreted as endowing a certain kind of ontological status to the rational cognition (thought) that has been unable to find its place ever since the ancient times (Heidegger 1957, p. 24). Modern epistemologists believed that each of the ideal representations that constituted the mind had an independent standing. Thus, they believed that it was possible for an ideal representation to be individually understood and used without any supporting contextual background. To Hume, the mind, after all, was nothing more than a bundle of separate representations. His skepticism began with his query as to how such a bundle could obtain an ontological status like an "I" as the thinking subject.

Nonetheless, despite Hume's skepticism, the task of the ontological construction of the mind is still continued today. According to cognitive science and the philosophy of language of our times, the mind is a software in which reason intuits and thinks of the world. The realization of such software in an incomplete hardware – the body –, constitutes human being. Or it can also be said that law is the software that is realized in an unstable hardware, which is matter. This realization constitutes the phenomenal world. By the same token, language is the expression of mental representations that re-present the world. If the meaning of language is language's software, then the spoken and written language are the hardware that embodies it. Theories such as the mind-body dualism of Descartes, the functionalist philosophy of psychology that is based on computer metaphor, and the theory of mental representation of language all build up abstract and theoretical views about human beings, language, and the world ignoring the concrete human being, the life-world and the ordinary use of language.

IV. Heidegger's Dictionary

Philosophy in the traditional sense begins with the epoche of a concrete phenomenal world. Ever since we started considering the escape from the phenomenal world as our mission, the world ceases to "appear" to us. The history of philosophy is the history of the forgetfulness and oppression of Being of the world that should have appeared. On the one hand, Heidegger sees this as a natural thing, and on the other hand, he sees this as a huge case of putting the cart before the horse. Let us find out what the two sides of the forgetfulness of Being are.

Breathing is the main biological source of life. But usually we are not conscious of its importance. It is not until we face some sort of breathing disorder that we realized it. Similarly, it is light that allows us to see the world but we can not see light itself. We realize the importance of light only after we are deprived of it. A fish or a worm would react similarly to the deprivation of water and soil, which are indispensible to each.

Being is disclosed in various ways through us. We experience numerous phenomena in our daily lives. Phenomenon in Chinese, *Hyun-Sang*, is the composite of such a temporal moment as presence (*Hyun*) and of the being (*Sang*). In other words, phenomenon means the state in which being is disclosed through temporality. The events that we experience are precisely the events of disclosure. However, usually, we recognize neither this disclosure nor the event that makes it possible. We only recognize the disclosed being, or the correlation of meaning between the disclosed being and us. Not only do we forget that Being is an on-going, $Be + ing$ event, but we also reify Being as being. Yet, Being is not an object. By arguing that Being is nothingness, Heidegger opposes the act of reifying Being (Heidegger 1929). The reasoning that Being is equal to Nothing is readily implying that Being is not an object ($No + Thing$).

In the same way, in language, we do not give our attention to Being and the "be" that is equivalent to the event of its disclosure. The "be" is very common and is used in many different ways. The Greek root word for "be," *einai*, is a polysemy that can be used in various ways as the following: i) as the copula "be," ii) as the quantifier "exist," iii) as the equivalence "is the same as," and finally, iv) as the truth-claim "is true." In short, i) predication, ii) existence, iii) equivalence, and iv) the idea of truth originate from one language and one root (Khan 1973; 1976; 1986). It is just that we do not recognize such diverse disclosures and their source.

In this light, the forgetfulness of Being of which Heidegger takes notice occurs naturally in our daily lives. To borrow his words, Being discloses and hides itself at the same time (Heidegger 1977, p. 337). And this is Being's fate. Thus, the forgetfulness of Being that has been observed throughout the history of philosophy might not be something unnatural. Nevertheless, the forgetfulness of Being is not such an innocent and harmless matter. In fact, it is subjected to a dangerously intentional distortion, which promotes the sorts of oppressions that were discussed earlier.

One distinctive feature of the phenomenal world that has been disclosed, is that it holds a complex relationship of meaning with human beings. Human beings that are thrown into this world strive to adapt themselves to it. Then they actively project their purposes and interests upon the world. Human beings are practical beings who use the world as a tool to accomplish their purposes and interests. Heidegger calls the aspect of the world that we encounter in terms of practical care and equipmental totality, "the readiness-to-hand" (*Zuhandenheit*) of the world. It is in this relationship of readiness-to-hand that human beings and the world are entangled into one. Futhermore, Heidegger suggests that man is the central subject of such entanglement and calls him *Dasein.* Heidegger says the following:

> Self and world belong together in the single being, the Dasein. Self and world are not two beings, like subject and object, or like I and thou, but self and world are basic determination of the Dasein itself in the unity of the structure of being-in-the-world. (Heidegger 1975, p. 422; English trans. p. 297)

Just as light and air are not readily recognized, the equipmental entanglement or readiness-to-hand between the world and us in our daily life world often goes unnoticed. We are only devoted to accomplishing the purposes and interests that are meaningful to us and recognize the readiness-to-hand only after we are deprived of it. And this is when the structure of ready-to-hand entanglement between the world and us is finally disclosed in its totality. However, if the readiness-to-hand is destroyed and this state of destruction is prolonged in a thorough manner, we end up separating the world from our Himmel of meaning and interests and further objectifying the world in a fragmental manner. Heidegger calls this fragmentary aspect of the world that we encounter in terms of observation and reification, "the presence-at-hand" (*Vorhandenheit*) of the world.

If the world that is seen from the perspective of the readiness-to-hand is a set of monads with windows, then the world seen from the perspective of the presence-at-hand is a set of windowless monads. This is so because while the readiness-to-hand emphasizes the equipmental totality amongst components of the world in terms of $\tau\acute{\epsilon}\chi\nu\eta$ by relating it to human being's practical interests, the presence-at-hand isolates the components of the world from their contextual background and emphasizes them in terms of $\Theta\epsilon\omega\rho\acute{\iota}\alpha$. Further, while the monads with windows are entangled with each other in the world seen under the species of temporality, windowless monads, which are abstract objects that transcend temporality, are related only extensionally in terms of *ex post facto* logic that is imposed by the theory that sees the world under the species of eternity. Traditional philosophy often sees the world through the eyes of the presence-at-hand that has broken away from our Himmel of meaning and interests and considers this world as a neutral and objective world. Traditional philosophy also argues that since the Himmel of meaning and interests distorts the world's objectivity and is merely a product of human subjectivity, it should be duly eradicated. However, this would only be an example of putting the cart before the horse. Heidegger demonstrates this by presenting the following example: (Heidegger 1953. p. 111)

> Imagine looking down at a city from an observation platform. The view before our eyes is a combination of the city's features and our perspective of it. What we see is not a representation of the city but a presentation of the city that is disclosed from our perspective. Our perspectives and points of view are not subjective schemes distorting the city's original features but indispensable windows that the city needs in order to disclose its features to us. Therefore, a city that is free from our perspective and view and that is entirely objective cannot be. Just as well, a map or photograph of the city would just be another perspective of it and it would not be in any kind of privileged position in comparison to our views.

Traditional philosophy describes the world's readiness-to-hand as deficiency and subjectivity and the world's presence-at-hand as sufficiency and objectivity. This implies that it is not until we have transcended the readiness-to-hand and reached the presence-at-hand that we are able to see the world in a correct way. Nevertheless, Heidegger believes that it is the other way around. He sees the presence-at-hand as being derived from the lack of components that make up the readiness-to-hand. This lack begins with the oppressive epoche of the world that is intersubjectively related to human beings and that constitutes the background of the presence-at-hand. The fragments of Being that have seceded from the intersubjective net of meaning between the world and human beings, lose their significance and position, and become mere objects of contemplation. In the same way, the fragments of language that have broken away from the ready-to-hand net of meaning embedded in language, become mere symbols that have lost their significance and position. Theories are those that have been constructed under the hypothesis that these symbols and objects form an extensional correspondence. Within the perspective of the formal system, the meanings and functions of language and theory are arbitrarily imposed through an artificial point of view called interpretation. However, the extensional correspondence between the symbol and the object is only a distortion of the event in which language discloses the world and of the readiness-to-hand interrelation that is created in this process between the world and human beings. Therefore, the theory that is produced by the presence-at-hand is only a secondary thing, unable to describe the reality of the world. A transcendental reality that is free from the concrete context of life, is nothing more than a fantasy made from the ascension of the abstract and the deficient. The world appears before human beings not through the theory but through history and time.

V. Standing on the Himmel of Archeological Meaning

Heidegger's contribution to philosophy can be found in his disclosure and criticism of the limitations of traditional philosophy within its boundaries. Another philosopher who caught up with Heidegger, though later, is Wittgenstein. Yet, unlike Heidegger, Wittgenstein has a past of having been obsessed by the thoughts of traditional philosophy. We can see his fascination with traditional philosophy in one of his early writings:

> The usual way of looking at things see objects as it were from the midst of them, the view *sub specie aeternitatis* from outside. In such a way that they have the whole world as background. Is this it perhaps – in this view the object is seen *together with* space and time instead of *in* space and time? (Wittgenstein 1961a, p. 83)

Traditional philosophy regards the world that is seen from *sub specie aeternitatis* as the world in its totality. That world, however, is one that human beings do not live in. *I* am deprived of the world, for *I* am only watching the world from the outside. And through this, *I* am deprived of myself.

> There is no such thing as the subject that thinks or entertains ideas. (Wittgenstein 1961b, 5.631)

> This is the way I have travelled: Idealism singles men out from the world as unique, solipsism singles me alone out, ... and so on the one side nothing is left over, and on the other side, as unique, the world. (Wittgenstein 1961a, p. 85)

Yet, from Heidegger's point of view, the world that is left as unique is only an abstract one and not a life-world. It is nothing but an ideological shadow of the world.

After a 10-year gap following his completion of the *Tractatus Logico-Philosophicus*, Wittgenstein returned to the community of philosophers in 1929. In that same year, he expressed his sympathy for Heidegger's philosophy to the members of the Vienna Circle. If we suppose that the year 1929 marks the division between the earlier and later period of Wittgenstein's philosophy, this holds many suggestions. As it is well known, in his latter term, Wittgenstein's view on language regards meaning as that which is disclosed through the use of language. He considered our act of using language in one way or another as meaning's ultimate Himmel. This Himmel is not some sort of epistemological foundation, but a form of life of human beings which includes the acquisition of skill and its application. The content of life that corresponds with the form of life is what Wittgenstein calls the language-game. Language-game is the whole, consisting of language and the actions into which it is woven (Wittgenstein 1967, §7). The basis in which meaning is produced is this concrete language-game and the total sum of the games is the culture and mode of life that human beings carry on. In the same manner as Heidegger, Wittgenstein compares language to a tool. It is without doubt that regarding language as a tool is what makes Wittgenstein regard the world from a readiness-to-hand perspective.

Wittgenstein, like Heidegger, sees language from a historical point of view. According to him, the problems of philosophy are diseases caused by the misuse of language.

> The sickness of a time is cured by an alteration in the mode of life of human beings, and it was possible for the sickness of philosophical problems to get cured only through a changed mode of thought and of life, not through a medicine invented by an individual. (Wittgenstein 1978, p. 132)

Wittgenstein uses the case of religion to explain the relationship between the use of language and the mode of life. According to Wittgenstein, the significance of the language of religion transcends its literal meaning and is disclosed through the life and practice of a religious person. The language of religion regulates the religious man's life and behavior. It also works as an evaluational and self-reflectional principle in his life and his behavior. This is the way a religious person uses the religious language. In other words, this is the grammar of religious language and the nature of the certainty of one's religious beliefs.[6]

Unlike Wittgenstein, Heidegger looked out for the possibility of the right use of language, not in religion but in art, especially in poetry. According to Heidegger, Homer's epic poems and the lyric poetry of Hölderlin and Rilke are representative languages of the ages they belonged to. They disclose the world in a new and realistic manner. Likewise, Heidegger's interest in language begins with the philosophical interest of the disclosure of Being. Moreover, his philosophy of language is archeological, as emphasized earlier in this paper. Language is an antique historical relic that holds the necessary code to disclose and interpret the hidden Being. Heidegger tells us the archeological stories of the forgotten Being which he rediscovered in language. Although Wittgenstein also firmly maintained his interest in the historicity of language and philosophy, his version of the history of philosophy is a product of his ingenious reconstruction of the effective-history

[6]See my "The Language and Grammar of Religion," *Proceedings of the Korean Philosophers Associations*, 1995.

that was embedded in the works of several of his contemporary philosophers such as Frege, Russell and Moore. Hence, Wittgenstein's history of philosophy is always an anonymous one. Wittgenstein is merely criticizing the fictitious philosophical history that he has produced based on the natural inclination of human thinking.

On the contrary, Heidegger sets to excavate the actual history that holds the insight into the history of philosophy. His archeological excavation is critical and deconstructive in that it attempts to closely examine the closure of history. In addition, he retraces his deconstructive and archeological interests to the presocratic philosophy which was the heroic period in the history of western philosophy that Wittgenstein failed to reach due to his ignorance and indifference to the actual history of philosophy. There, *logos* is no longer reason and truth is no longer a contrast. There, *logos* is an event of understanding and gathering Being of the beings (Heidegger 1953, p. 171), and truth is an event where gathered Being is disclosed. In short, the correct and original meaning of the philosophical language that Heidegger was trying to restore is that which was hidden in the times before Plato who marked the Big Bang of the history of philosophy. However, this does not mean that the history after Plato's Big Bang was worthless. Over the 2,000 years or so of the long history that we human beings have experienced, Being has been steadily disclosing and hiding itself in various ways. It is just that we have been so obsessed by the light of the transcendental truth, that we have resulted in forgetting the historical roots and failing to correctly recognize Being, and thus depreciating it.

Heidegger opened a previously unexplored Himmel to us. This is the Himmel of the historical meaning in the present perfect progressive tense that his archeological philosophy of language excavated. Our task is to figure out how to best unfold the Himmel of meaning in the progressive form of the present and the future that he left incomplete. Yet, we are not the only ones responsible for this unfolding task. As a matter of fact, history is responsible for the unfolding of the present and the future for we are sediments of our history. And it is because history is melted in our language, that Heidegger's phenomenological archeology of language is much needed for exploring it. We no longer speak the language or speak of the language. We speak through language and our words return to language. This readily means that we speak through history and return our words to history. And according to Heidegger, such method of speaking is called dialogue (Heidegger 1959, p. 141). Not theory but dialogue, not a calculated thought based on methodology but the participation between the past, the present and the future through their dialogue with history, is the alternative mode of thinking that will allow us to trace our history through the present and the future. Heidegger puts this into practice by holding a dialogue with the history of philosophy that he rediscovered using his archeological philosophy of language as a tool.

References

Davidson, D. (1982) "Empirical Content," reprinted in LePore(1986).

Garver, N. and Seung-Chong Lee. (1994) *Derrida and Wittgenstein.* Philadelphia: Temple University Press.

Heidegger, M. (1929) "Was Ist Metaphysik?," reprinted in Heidegger 1976.

Heidegger, M. (1950a) "Der Spruch des Anaximander," reprinted in Heidegger 1977: Trans. D. Krell and F. Capuzzi. "The Anaximander Fragment," *Early Greek Thinking.* New York: Haper and Row, 1975.

Heidegger, M. (1950b) "Der Ursprung des Kunstwerkes," reprinted in Heidegger 1977: Trans. A. Hofstadter, "The Origin of the Work of Art," *Poetry, Language, Thought.* New York: Harper and Row, 1971.

Heidegger, M. (1953) *Einführung in die Metaphysik.* Tübingen: Niemeyer, 1983.

Heidegger, M. (1957) *Sein und Zeit.* Tübingen: Niemeyer.

Heidegger, M. (1959) "Aus einem Gespräch von der Sprache," reprinted in Heidegger 1985.

Heidegger, M. (1975) *Die Grundprobleme der Phänomenologie.* Frankfurt am Main: Klostermann: Trans. A. Hofstadter, *The Basic Problems of Phenomenology.* Bloomington: Indiana University Press, 1982.

Heidegger, M. (1976) *Wegmarken.* Frankfurt am Main: Klostermann.

Heidegger, M. (1977) *Holzwege.* Frankfurt am Main: Klostermann.

Heidegger, M. (1985) *Unterwegs zur Sprache.* Pfullingen: Neske.

Heidegger, M. and E. Fink. (1970) *Heraklit.* Frankfurt am Main: Klostermann.

Kahn, C. (1973) *The Verb "Be" in Ancient Greek.* Dordrecht: Reidel.

Kahn, C. (1976) "Why Existence Does Not Emerge as a Distinct Concept in Greek Philosophy?" *Archiv für Geschichte der Philosophie*, vol. 58.

Kahn, C. (1986) "Retrospect on the Verb 'To Be' and the Concept of Being," in Knuuttila and Hintikka 1986.

Kim, Sang-Hwan. (ed.) (1998) *Philosophical Studies on Media* (Korean). Seoul: Nanam.

Knuuttila, S. and J. Hintikka. (eds.) (1986) *The Logic of Being: Historical Studies.* Dordrecht: Reidel.

Lee, Seung-Chong. (1993) "Quantum Mechanics and EPR Debate," (Korean) in Oh 1993.

Lee, Seung-Chong. (1995b) "The Language and Grammar of Religion," (Korean) *Proceedings of the Korean Philosophers Associations.*

Lee, Seung-Chong. (1998) "The Life of Identity," (Korean) in Kim 1998.

Lee, Seung-Chong. (1999) Untimely Meditations: Wittgenstein and Heidegger as Critics of Mathematical Logic," in *History and Phenomenology*, edited by the Korean Society for Phenomenology, Seoul: Philosophy and Reality Press.

LePore, E. (ed.) (1986) *Truth and Interpretation: Perspectives on the Philosophy of Donald Davidson.* Oxford: Basil Blackwell.

Oh, Young-Hwan. (ed.) (1993) *Science and Metaphysics* (Korean). Seoul: Free Thought Press.

Wittgenstein, L. (1958) *The Blue and Brown Books.* Oxford: Basil Blackwell.

Wittgenstein, L. (1961a) *Notebooks 1914-1916.* Ed. G. H. von Wright and G. E. M. Anscombe. Trans. G. E. M. Anscombe. Oxford: Basil Blackwell.

Wittgenstein, L. (1961b) *Tractatus Logico-Philosophicus.* Trans. D. Pears and B. McGuinness. London: Routledge and Kegan Paul.

Wittgenstein, L. (1967) *Philosophical Investigations.* 3rd edition. Ed. G. E. M. Anscombe and R. Rhees. Trans. G. E. M. Anscombe. Oxford: Basil Blackwell.

Wittgenstein, L. (1978) *Remarks on the Foundations of Mathematics.* Revised edition. Ed. G. H. von Wright, R. Rhees, and G. E. M. Anscombe. Trans. G. E. M. Anscombe. Cambridge, Mass.: MIT Press.

„Logik der Philosophie" in der Philosophie Nishidas

-insbesondere über die Logik der „Negativität" in seiner späteren Denkperiode-

Yoshihiro Nitta

> „Was sich ausdrückt, muß so gestaltet sein, daß seine Verhältnisse zwar durchaus erscheinen, daß sie aber zugleich nicht erscheinen, d.h. daß sie sich selbstverneinend erscheinen." (Nishida, GW. XI, 197)

I. Einleitung

In diesem Artikel möchte ich die „Logik der Philosophie" dem späten Denken in der Philosophie Nishidas entnehmen und die darin enthaltene Problematik untersuchen. Für den Zweck, die Eigentümlichkeit des Standpunktes des späten Denkens hervorzuheben, erwähne ich zunächst mehrere Phasen seines Denkens in der früheren Periode und bestätige, daß die Logik der Philosophie Nishidas bereits in seinem frühreren Denken im Grunde festgelegt war. Als die erste Phase wurde der „Beginn von der reinen Erfahrung," von der aus die Bildung alles Wissens beginnt, in seiner ersten Schrift „Über das Gute" erklärt. Dann wird die zweite Phase, nämlich die Tatsache, daß die Struktur des Selbstgewahrens schon in der Erfahrung selbst funktioniert, in seinen Aufsätzen in „Anschauung und Reflexion im Selbstgewahren" festgestellt. In der dritten Phase wird die Logik, die in dem Grund des Entstehens des Wissens wirkt, durch den Begriff des „Ortes" in verschiedenen Artikeln in der Periode des „Ortes" untersucht. Seine Frage und sein Interesse in der jeweiligen Periode, die durch die obigen Grundbegriffe thematisiert werden, haben eine starke Beziehung zu den Grundzügen der jeweiligen Periode.

Zunächt in der ersten Phase läßt sich das gemeinsame „Problemsbewußtsein von der Philosophie in der Zeit" von etwa dem Ende des 19. Jahrhunderts bis zum Anfang des 20. Jahrhunderts, nennen. Mit einem Wort wird das mit der Betonung der Eigenschaft der Theorie des Wissens, die der Begriff der „Erfahrung" hat, bezeichnet. Die Welt aller theoretischen Wissenschaften hat „lebendige Erfahrung" in ihrer Basis des Theoretisierungsaktes. Die Welt der Wissenschaft wird erst durch die idealisierende Verselbständigung der Momente, die bereits in der Erfahrung selbst artikuliert werden, konstituiert. Diese Akzentuierung auf den Begriff der Erfahrung Ende des 19. Jahrhunderts und zu Anfang dieses Jahrhunderts entspricht der Grundhaltung des Denkens Nishidas in dieser Periode. In diesem Sinne kann man sagen, daß der Beginn der Gemeinsamkeit zwischen seiner Fragestellung und der der damaligen Zeit bereits in dieser Periode feststellbar ist.

In der zweiten Periode wird die Funktion des ,,Selbstgewahrens" im Grund der Erfahrung durch die kritische Übernahme des Begriffs des Bewußtseins in der modernen Philosophie entdeckt. Die Einsicht von Fichte, der das Wesen des Ichs in der ,,Tathandlung" sieht, wird in die Struktur der willentlichen Aktivität des Lebens übertragen, die aus dem aktiven Wesen des Ichs stammt. Dies ist eines der gemeinsamen Interesse des philosophischen Denkens in der damaligen Zeit, das in der Entwicklung der Wissenslehre der Lebensphilosophie, z.B. in dem früheren Konzept Diltheys, in der ,,Breslauer Ausarbeitung" erscheint. Bei Nishida wird dies als die Wirkung des ,,Selbstgewahrens," die die Funktion des Selbst-Wiederscheinen des Lebens als Wille ist, diskutiert. Das läßt sich als eine Art des Versuchs der ,,Konfrontation mit der modernen Zeit" nennen, die Überlieferung von der Bewußtseinsphilosophie in der westlichen Neuzeit in ihm eigentlicher Art kritisch zu vermitteln und sich zu eigen zu machen.

Ferner in der dritten Phase wird die Logik seiner Philosophie als die ,,Logik des Ortes" begründet, indem Nishida sich frontal und kritisch dem Grundstandpunkt der Logik der westlichen Wissenschaft seit Aristoteles gegenüberstellt. Dabei diskutiert er, indem er die logische Struktur der Satzform ,,S ist P" als methodischen Leitfaden nimmt und nicht in Richtung auf das Subjekt wie bei Aristoteles, der in dem Pol dieser Richtung das Individuum erreicht, sondern in Richtung auf das Prädikat verallgemeinert und schließlich im Grenzfall dieser Verallgemeinerung ,,den Ort des Nichts" erreicht.

Nishidas Logik, die das fundamentale Thema seiner Philosophie ausdrückt, das in der Entwicklung seines früheren Denkens allmählich ihr klares Bild bekam, wird im Satz ,,das Selbst spiegelt sich in sich selbst" und im Begriff ,,die Selbstbestimmung des Allgemeinen" formuliert. Bereits in ,,Über das Gute" ist das selbe Konzept in der vorläufigen Form, ,,die selbstentwickelnde Erfahrung" am Werk. Aber deutlich wird dieses Konzept durch die Betrachtung der Funktion des Selbstgewahrens, die der thematische Begriff in den Artikeln über ,,das Selbstgewahren" ist. Genauer wird ,,die Selbstbestimmung des Allgemeinen" als ,,die sich selbstgewahrende Selbstbestimmung des Allgemeinen" ausgedrückt. Somit wird in dem Artikel über den ,,Ort" das Verhältnis vom ,,Spiegelnden und Gespiegelten" als ,,die Selbstbestimmung des Ortes," nämlich als die Selbstbestimmung, wo sich der Ort an sich spiegelt, hinsichtlich dessen Logik untersucht. Auf diese Weise wird im früheren Denken Nishidas der reflektierende Weg genommen, der sich von der Beschreibung der reinen Erfahrung in die Logik der Selbstbestimmung des Ortes vertieft hat. Schließlich erreicht seine Reflexion die Dimension des intellektuellen Selbstgewahrens als die allerletzte Dimension der Reflexion, wo die Selbstbestimmung des Allgemeinen ,,die

Selbstbestimmung des Ortes des Nichts" genannt wird. Für die Gewinnung des methodischen Wegs für das Herabsteigen in die mit der Bewußtseinsdimension unerreichbare Dimension wird das phänomenologische Begriffspaar „Noesis und Noema" durch seine eigene Interpretation und im Sinne des Grenzbegriffs gebraucht. Insofern bedient er sich einer Methode, die den Bewußtseinsbegriff annimmt und gleichzeitig das Durchbrechen seines Grundes ermöglicht.

Die Logik des „Spiegelns und Gespiegelten" wird auf sein späteres Denken direkt übertragen. Aber in dem späteren Denken wird der Bewußtseinsbegriff nicht mehr angenommen, wie dies mit vom Titel „Vom Hergestellten zum Herstellenden" ausgedrückt wird, sondern vom Standpunkt des Begriffs der Handlung versucht Nishida die Struktur der „Selbstbestimmung des Allgemeinen" in dem Ereignis „der Selbst-Bildung der geschichtlichen Welt" zu erblicken. Die sich Selbstgewahrende Selbstbestimmung nimmt ihre Formulierung in „der sich ausdrückenden Selbstbestimmung" und somit wird die konkrete, handelnd-bildende Seite der handelnden Anschauung betrachtet und die Einsicht in den Charakter der absoluten Tatsächlichkeit durch die sich selbstgewahrende Reflexion gewonnen.[1]

So wird das Gleiche, nämlich „das sich Spiegeln an sich selbst" in der früheren und späteren Periode verschieden formuliert. In der späteren Periode wird es als das dynamische Ereignis in der wesentlich konkreteren und wirklicheren Ebene als in der früheren Periode aufgefaßt. D.h. von der etwas statischen strukturellen Analyse zurück, wird die Konkretheit, die die Beschreibung der Erfahrung in „Über das Gute" hat, zurückgewonnen, um in die Wirklichkeit, in der die Logik lebendig wirkt, hineinzudringen. Er versucht nämlich die Struktur des Verhältnisses, „des sich Spiegeln in sich selbst" als „der Sache des Denkens," „der gelebten Erfahrung" entsprechend, emporsteigen zu lassen. Das wird der Tatsache entnommen, daß besonders der Begriff des Lebens (aber im Sinne des Ereignens als des Handelns) in der gewichtigen Bedeutung geäußert wird. Nishida sagt, „Das echte Leben entsteht als die Selbstbestimmung der sich ausdrückenden Welt." Das, was im Denken der sich ausdrückenden Selbstbestimmung geäußert wird, bedeutet, wie später gezeigt wird, daß die Welt als Selbst-Verneinung entsteht. Hier wird „die Logik der Negativität," die im Wort „Ausdruck" enthalten ist, untersucht und es wird gezeigt, auf welche Weise die Logik der Negativität in der Grundstruktur der Beziehung des Menschen auf die Welt konkret funktioniert. Und hier tritt das Ausdruck „die Selbstidentität des absoluten Widerspruchs" als das Wort auf, das den problematischen Charakter dieser Funktion ausdrückt. Das Ereignis, das diese Logik der Negativität durchzieht, nämlich die Erfahrung des Men-

---

[1] Vgl. Y. Nitta, Aktualität der Philosophie Nishidas – Erfahrung und Reflexion in seiner früheren Periode, in: *Die Frage nach der Philosophie Nishidas*, hrsg. v. Sh. Ueda, (japanisch) Tokyo 1990.

schen als die Funktion der Negation selbst, ist ,,die handelnde Anschauung." Hier geschieht die Selbstbestimmung der geschichtlichen Welt als die handelnde Anschauung in der handelnden Anschauung selbst. Einzelheiten sollen später erneut diskutiert werden.

Sicher findet man im späteren Denken mehrere, spekulativ klingende Wörter und Begriffe, die von Hegels Dialektik übernommen zu sein scheinen, wie z.B. ,,die geschichtliche Welt," ,,das dialektische Allgemeine." In diesem Sinne kann man nicht negieren, daß die philosophische Begriffe, die das Zeitbewußtsein der bestimmten und speziellen Zeit (des 19. Jahrhunderts) abspiegeln, unmittelbar übertragen werden und sie der Auseinandersetzung der heutigen Wissenschaftslehre nicht entsprechen können. Auch von der Zeit bedingt ist, daß Nishida unerwartete logische Gedankensprünge macht. Aber die dynamische Kraft seines Denkens, die solche Bedingtheit aus der Zeit durchbricht und übersteigt, kann beweisen, daß seine Frage sich, der Sache selbst entsprechend, bewegt.

Diese Frage hat auch heute die Wirkungs-kraft, die in dem Grund der Erfahrung des Menschen geschehende Beziehung auf die Welt zu hinterfragen. Vielmehr ist heute wird endlich klar geworden, was ,,die Sache des Denkens," die Nishida durchdenken wollte, ist. Besonders beachtenswert ist, daß er in seinem späteren Denken einerseits die Systemtheorie, die sich auf die Ergebnisse von der Wissenschaft des Lebewesens und der auf der Theorie der Verdinglichung basierenden Kulturtheorie beruht, sozusagen, vorwegnimmt und andererseits den Gedanken des ,,abhängigen Entstehens" des Mahayana-Buddhismus als die Logik des Realen unmittelbar, frontal einführt; aber im früheren Denken hat er vielmehr mit der von der damaligen Zeit bedingten Auseinandersetzung gegenüber der europäischen Philosophie begonnen und seine eigene Logik durch die methodische Annahme der Logik der europäischen Philosophie gebildet.

Es ist kaum zu übersehen, daß er dadurch den Ort, wo die Logik der Vergegenständlichung der Einzelwissenschaften entsteht, zu verdeutlichen und gleichzeitig die Logik der unvergegenständlichbaren Dimension zu untersuchen und somit den Weg der der Sache selbst entsprechenden Vereinigung der beiden Richtungen durchzuführen versucht hat. Dies gibt uns deutliche und aufschlußreiche Hinweise auf die Problematik, auf welche Weise die philosophische Frage nach dem Verhältnis zwischen ,,Leben und Logik," zwischen ,,Leben und Wissen des Menschen" entwickelt werden kann, die heute zu einer zur alle Menschen umfassenden und dringenden Frage geworden ist.

II. Die sich ausdrückende Selbstbestimmung der Welt

II-1. Die handelnde Anschauung

Die Selbstbestimmung der geschichtlichen Welt ist mit dem Begriff des Lebens verbunden, wie sie auch die Selbstbestimmung des geschichtlichen Lebens genannt wird. In diesem Fall wird der Begriff des Lebens von dem Begriff des Lebens im biologischen Sinne, der im Sinne seines Verhältnisses zur Umwelt aufgefaßt wird, unterschieden und der Begriff des Handelns wird miteinbegriffen. Nishida faßt Handlung zunächst als die herstellende Handlung auf, durch die der Leib des Menschen mit einem Werkzeug etwas herstellt, nämlich eine kreative Handlung, die zwischen dem Leib und der Umwelt zustandekommt. Zweitens schließt sie in sich „das Sehen" ein und sie vereint sich mit diesem Sehen. Diese Sachlage wird so ausgedrückt: „Es gibt keine Handlung ohne Sehen" (Nishida, „Logik und Leben" in: „Kitaro Nishida Philosophische Abhandlung II," hrsg. v. Shizuteru Ueda, S. 201. Ab hier abgekürzt: „Ab. II"; Zitate aus dem Gesamtwerk von Nishida werden mit „GW" angegeben.) und sie wird somit „die handelnde Anschauung" genannt. Aber dies bedeutet nicht nur, daß das Herstellen gleichzeitig das Sehen des Hergestellten ist, sondern auch, daß das Herstellen selbst der Akt des Ausdrucks ist. In diesem Sinne wird die handenlde Anschauung der Akt der *sich ausdrückenden* Bestimmung genannt.

Die Handlung bei der handelnden Anschauung bedeutet zunächst, daß der Leib des Menschen Dinge mit einem Werkzeug herstellt, nämlich daß der Mensch mit seinen Händen Werkzeuge herstellt und Dinge mit Werkzeugen herstellt. Das Werkzeug kann aber unabhängig vom Leib sein und somit ein Ding sein. Das verdinglicht umgekehrt den Leib und macht ihn zum Werkzeug. Daher haben wir den Leib als Werkzeug. Das Verbindende zwischen dem Leib und dem Werkzeug ist nämlich die Technik. Wenn das Handeln Herstellung und die Handlung Sehen ist, „ist die Herstellung das Sehen." Auf diese Weise entsteht der enge Zusammenhang zwischen Sachlagen wie Leben, Handeln, Herstellen und Anschauung.

Nun wird in Wirklichkeit solch ein Akt des herstellenden Ausdrucks als Akt des Selbstausdrucks der geschichtlichen Welt, nämlich als die sich ausdrückende Selbstbestimmung der geschichtlichen Welt bezeichnet. Daher ist die handelnde Anschauung nichts anderes als das Durchführen des Ausdrucks der Welt als die sich ausdrückende Selbstbestimmung der geschichtlichen Welt. Wenn die geschichtliche Welt der bildende Akt und der bildende Akt das Sehen ist, ist die Selbstbestimmung der geschichtlichen Welt das Erscheinen der Dinge als Formen. Das Erscheinen der Formen ist nämlich die sich ausdrückende Selbstbestimmung.

Unser Sehen der Dinge ist, „daß die Welt sich selbst bildet." Das wird auch so ausgedrückt: „Die Welt bestimmt sich selbst, während sie nichts bestimmt. Das heißt nämlich, daß die geschichtliche Natur sich selbst technisch bildet. Die Kultur ist eine Kontinuität solcher Natur. Wir existieren als der sich ausdrückende Leib des Aktes in solcher Welt.“ (Ab. II. S. 211) Dies bedeutet eben, daß das Selbst als „das Element der Arbeit der kreativen Welt“ in die Selbst-Bildung der geschichtlichen Welt eingegliedert ist. Dazu wird folgendes gesagt: „Die Technik gehört nicht nur zum Subjekt, sondern sie bedeutet, daß das Ich ins Ding eintritt. Die Wirkung der Dinge wird zur Wirkung des Ichs.“(Ab. II. S. 202) Unser leibliches Selbst ist schließlich das Element des Selbst-Ausdrucks der geschichtlichen Welt. D.h. das Ich verneint sich selbst in der handelnden Anschauung und läßt die Welt ausdrücken.

Die Grundbedeutung, die Nischida in der handelnden Anschauung sieht, liegt in der Kreativität; d.h. „das echte Leben muß in sich das absolute Nichts enthalten.“ Die handelnde Anschauung ist sicher der Akt des Ausdrucks der Welt selbst, der in der Weise geschieht, daß das Ich sich verneint und dadurch die Welt entstehen läßt, aber der Akt des Ausdrucks ist gleichzeitig das Sehen des Ausdrucks. Denn „die Welt wird auf dem Standpunkt der handelnden Anschauung zum Ausdruck des Lebens.“ Daher kann das Leben erst im Ausdruck „das Selbst als das Leben sehen.“ In diesem Fall ist also das Wissen des Selbst durch das Medium des Ausdrucks nichts anderes als „Selbst-Evidenz des Lebens.“ Alles, was oben gesagt wird, wird im folgenden Satz zusammengefaßt: „Die Selbst-Evidenz des Lebens ist der Ausdruck des Selbst, die Bildung des Selbst und das Sehen des Selbst in der handelnden Anschauung.“ (Ab.II. S. 297.) Wie ich bereits erwähnt habe, wird "das Selbst-Spiegeln in sich selbst“ im früheren Denken Nishidas hier als der Ausdruck des Selbst der Welt genannt. Nun ist die Struktur der Selbstverneinung, nämlich „das Enthaltensein des Nichts in sich selbst“ weiter zu erforschen.

II-2. Die Logik der absolut widersprüchlichen Selbstidentität

Was bedeutet eigentlich, daß das Ausdrücken, wenn die Welt sich ausdrückt, die Verneinung des Selbst sei? Wenn es gesagt wird, daß „das echte Leben als die Selbstbestimmung der sich ausdrückenden Welt entsteht,“ nämlich daß die ausdrückende Selbstbestimmung eben die Selbstverneinung ist, wird das in der letzten Betrachtung so gezeigt, daß das Ich sich selbst verneint und somit die Welt in Erscheinung auftritt. Aber „das Verneinen des Selbst“ allein verbleibt noch in der Verneinung des individuellen und leiblichen Selbst. Das, was unter dem „Enthalten des Nichts in sich selbst“ gemeint ist, bedeutet in Wirklichkeit, daß das formlose Leben durch die Selbtverneinung sich selbst als Form erscheint.

Eben eines der Grundworte in der späteren Periode des Denkens Nishidas „die absolut widersprüchliche Selbstidentirät“ drückt die Sachlage „des Enthaltenseins des Nichts in sich selbst“ begrifflich aus. Hier ist das Gefüge ihrer selbstverneinenden Struktur ein zentrales Problem. Wie oft bemerkt wurde, ist es in der Tat fragwürdig, ob der Begriff „Widerspruch,“ der im Wort „die widersprüchliche Selbstidentität“ enthalten ist, treffend oder unpassend ist; [2] die Sachlage dieses Wortes ist vielmehr das gegenseitig verneinende und voneinander abhängige Verhältnis der einander gegenüber Seienden. Dieses voneinander abhängige Verhältnis bedeutet, daß die in der gewöhnlichen Logik gegenseitig Verneinenden und Ausschließenden ins ineinander eindringende und miteinander bedingende Verhältnis im Standpunkt der Handlung eintreten. Die Funktion der Negativität, die beide Momente zerreißt, bringt die Bewegung hervor, die beide in der Weise, den Satz des Widerspruchs durchbrechend, verbindet. Diese Sachlage hat mit der gegenwärtigen Philosophie, besonders mit der Phänomenologie den gemeinsamen Grund dessen, was durch die Betrachtung in die fundamentale Struktur der Erfahrung erörtert wird.

Nishida betrachtet diese Sachlage als eine Wechselbeziehung, die zwischen den einander Gegenüberstehenden wie zwischen Selbst und Umwelt, Einheit und Vielheit, Ich und Du in der Handlung entsteht. Zunächst steht Selbst und Umwelt in einer sich gegenseitig verneinenden Beziehung wie die zwischen dem Hergestellten und dem Herstellenden. In der Handlung ist „das Gegebene" schon „das Hergestellte" und „das Hergestellte" ist deswegen „hergestellt," weil es gerade verneint wird. Das Verhältnis von Umwelt und Selbst ist solch ein sich verneinendes Verhältnis, das als ein widersprüchlich gegenüberstehendes Verhältnis zwischen beiden Richtungen, Leib und Ding, betrachtet wird.

Ich möchte hier einen sehr bekannten Abschnitt aus Nishidas spätem Aufsatz „Logik des Orts und religiöse Weltanschauung" zitieren. „Unser Selbst ist das Wirkende. Was ist das Wirken? Es wird in der Wechselbeziehung zwischen Dingen gedacht. Was für eine Beziehung ist sie? Wenn es Wirken genannt wird, muß es eine sich gegenseitig verneinende Beziehung, in der das Eine das Andere verneint und das Andere das Eine verneint, geben. Jedoch kann die bloße wechselseitig verneinende Beziehung nicht das Wirken genannt werden. Die wechselseitige Verneinung muß gleich die wechselseitige Bejahung sein. Es muß so sein, daß beide (das Eine und das Andere) stets ihre Eigenheit haben und das wechselseitig Gegenüberstehen und Verneinen die wechselseitige Verbindung und Bildung einer Form ist und umgekehrt das Aufeinander-beziehen, das Einander-verbinden und die Bildung einer Form stets die wechselseitige Gegenüberstellung und das wechselseitige Verneinen ist."(Ab.III. S. 302.) Dieser Abschnitt ist wegen

---

[2] Z. B. Yamauchi weist darauf hin, daß die Logik von Nishida nicht durch den Begriff „des Widerspruchs" von Hegel zutreffend ausgedrückt werden kann, sie vielmehr die Logik des dem Osten eigenen Denkens von „gleich und ungleich" ist und diese Logik in Ausdrücken wie „Entsprechung" oder „Gegensatz" am Werk ist. Vgl. T. Yamauchi: Die Logik von gleich und ungleich. 2. kritische Betrachtung und Ergänzung der Grundbegriffe von Philosophie Nishidas, in: *Philosophie der Neigung*, (japanisch) Tokyo 1993. Aber es ist fragwürdig, ob die Sachlage, die der Logik Nishidas entspricht, nur durch die dem östlichen Denken eigentlichen Logik ausgedrückt werden kann oder nicht.

der hegelschen Färbung, die die in dieser Periode Nishidas auftretende Terminologie hat, leicht mißverständlich. Jedenfalls wird mit dem Ausdruck „wechselseitig" behauptet, daß die wechselseitig Verneinenden wechselseitig einander verbinden. Aber das bedeutet nicht bloß, daß beide aufgehoben werden, sondern daß bei der Bildung einer Form die Selbstverneinung des Formlosen in der Weise der wechselseitigen Verneinung beider gegenüberstehenden Momente sich ereignet.

II-3. Verdinglichung und „Bewußt-Werden": die Theorie der Annäherung zur Grenze

Nishida sagt, wenn man diese wechselseitig verneinende Beziehung in der Richtung des Limes auffaßt, nämlich wenn diese gegenüberstehende Beziehung, der Idee entsprechend, extrem gedacht wird, geschieht „das Auftreten der einander widersprechenden, ausschließenden Welt des Gegenübers." Hier entstehen verschiedene Welten des Wissens (der Ort des Seins) .

Wenn man jedes Beziehungsglied von Umwelt und leiblichem Selbst an der Grenze denkt, wird dies einerseits in „der Richtung der Verdinglichung" und andererseits in „der Richtung der Verleiblichung (des Bewußt-Werdens) „durchgeführt. Über "die Verdinglichung" wird folgendes gesagt: „Wenn das Ich zum Ding wird, geht das Ich sich selbst verloren. An dieser Grenze verschwindet das Ich einmal. .... Wenn der Leib zum Ding wird, d.h. wenn das Ich verloren geht, wird die Welt instrumental. Wenn die Welt total instrumental gedacht wird, ist sie die mechanische Welt."(Ab.II, S. 209) Das ist natürlich keine letzte Grenze dieser Richtung, aber in dieser Richtung auf das Limes wird die mechanische Welt aufgestellt. Denn die Welt des Zeichens kommt in der noch gründlicheren Annäherung an die Phase des Limes zustande.[3] Von dieser Theorie der Annäherung an das Limes ausgehend, wird, wie später erwähnt wird, eine genetische Betrachtung über das Entstehen der sogenannten wissenschaftlich-theoretischen Welt möglich. Diese Sichtweise hat eine Überschneidung mit der Einsicht der husserlschen Phänomenologie, in der die Entstehung der neuzeitlichen Wissenschaft in der Richtung auf die Idealisierung betrachtet wird.

Andererseits wird über die „Verleiblichung" oder „das Bewußt-Werden" folgendes behauptet. „In der Richtung, daß man Dinge zu seinem Leib werden läßt, gehen Dingen verloren. Am Limes wird es zur Welt des Bewußtseins. Ein Ding als Instrument zu haben, das bedeutet umgekehrt, den Leib als Instrument zu haben und ihn in der Handlung zu sehen. Den Leib

[3]Nach Nishida muß die Entstehung der Welt des Zeichens daraufhin betrachtet werden, daß in der handelnden Anschauung außerhalb dem Herstellen mit dem Instrument auch der Akt der Bezeichung enthalten wird. Wie es später erwähnt wird, die mechanische Welt, der Richtung des Ichs des Bewußtseins entsprechend, zur Grenze der Welt des Zeichens gebracht wird. Vgl. dazu K. Nishida, Logik und Leben, in: Ab. II, (japanisch) Tokyo 1988.

ständig nur als Instrument zu haben, das ist nämlich, der Annäherung an die Grenze entsprechend, die Abscheidung des Selbst vom Leib; hier wird das Selbst zum bloß sehenden Selbst. Hier wird das Ich des Bewußtseins gedacht."(Ab.II., S. 210.) Im in dieser Richtung entstehenden Reich des Bewußtseins ist „der Gegenstand nur das Gespiegelte" und er ist kein Ausdruck im echten Sinne, sondern bloß semantisches, daher immanentes Sein. In diesem Sinne bleibt das Reich des Bewußtseins „die abstrakte Selbstbildung der Welt" ; es ist keine ausdrückende Selbstbildung der Welt. Das Bewußtsein ist die unkreativ handelnde Anschauung, die nur den Schatten des Dinges spiegelt.

Nun entspricht aber dieser Richtung des Denkens die mechanische Welt als sein Gegenstand. In Nishidas Betrachtung über „die Verdinglichung" und „das Bewußt-Werden" findet man eine negative Seite der Einseitigkeit (Selbstblindheit) der methodischen Abstraktion, die in der Phänomenologie gezeigt wird, und eine positive Seite, daß dieses Denken so weit zugelassen wird, insofern es als eine Methode auf dem Grund des Wissens ihrer sachlichen Herkunft bewußt durchgeführt wird. Z. B. in der Verdinglichung gibt es eine Seite, nämlich das Glauben des An-sich-Seins in der natürlichen Einstellung und die andere Seite, nämlich „das methodische Denken als die Idealisierung, die als die Thematisierungsarbeit bestimmt gedacht wird. In diesem letzteren Sinne wird das Entstehen des pluralen Seins des Ortes so wie die Welt des Zeichens oder die Welt des Bewußtseins ermöglicht. Das, was er das Reale nennt und in der Wirklichkeit der geschichtlichen Welt als ein Moment eingeschlossen ist, ermöglicht die Einsicht der abstrakten Abscheidung dieser Art. Ohne methodische Reflexion wird diese Einsicht zur verscheidenen dogmatisch-philosophischen Behauptung.

Von dem Standpunkt der handelnden Anschauung gesehen, ist das Abstrakte eigentlich keine sogenannte Abstraktion, die vom Konkreten getrennt wird, sondern das Moment des Konkreten selbst. In diesem Sinne wird die sich ausdrückende Welt, die in der kreativen Richtung durch die Selbstverneinung zustande kommt, gegenüber dem kreativen Akt abstrakt bezeichnet und an solcher Grenze entsteht die Welt des Zeichens. Daher gehört die sich ausdrückende Welt zur handelnden Anschauung selbst, eben durch die Verneinung dieser Anschauung. Nishida sagt: „Die wirklich konkrete Welt, die kreative Welt ist notwendigerweise die Welt, die in sich das unendliche Selbst-Ausdrücken und die unendliche Abstraktion enthält. Die abstrakteste, unanschaulich anzusehende Wissenschaft, Physik ist der Selbst-Ausdruck des konkretesten Realen im Bereich des Zeichens."(Ab. III. S. 252). Auch das Wissen der Naturwissenschaft basiert auf der handelnden Anschauung. Dazu sagt Nishida: Eine bestimmte Welt bestimmt sich selbst und das ist ein Axiom. D.h. das Wissen der Naturwissenschaft entsteht als das Sein des Ortes. „Das Axiom der einzelnen Wissenschaften ist eine speziale Form der Logik der kreativen Anschauung," (Ab. III. 256) auch so formuliert Nishida. Jedoch „entwickelt sich unser Wissen nicht nur in diese Richtung. Das Axiom selbst muß reflektiert werden," nämlich auf dem Standpunkt der Anschauung der Welt „muß das Axiom selbst verfeinert werden." D.h. das Axiom muß in die Konkretheit der handelnden Anschauung zurückgebracht und dessen sachliche Herkunft festgestellt werden.

II-4. Die wechselseitige Bestimmung der Zeit und des Raumes: Kritik an der Logik der neuzeitlichen Wissenschaft

Nishida kritisiert sowohl die mechanistische Anschauung der Natur und der darauf beruhenden Theorie der Erkenntnis als auch die dem gegenüberstehende teleologische Einsicht der Natur deswegen, weil beide die von der konkreten Basis abgeschiedene, abstrahierte Theorie und insofern die ideologisch einseitige Theorie ist. Denn das Wirken der handelnden Anschauung ist die wechselseitige Bestimmung zwischen Subjekt und Umwelt. Wenn nur die Seite, daß die Umwelt das Subjekt bestimmt, einseitig betrachtet wird, kommt die mechanistische Richtung zustande, und umgekehrt, wenn nur die Seite, daß das Subjekt die Umwelt bestimmt, einseitig betrachtet wird, entsteht die teleologische Richtung. Es ist doch selbstverständlich, daß der Mechanismus und die Teleologie die zwei repräsentativen Theorien der Weltinterpretation in der neuzeitlichen Wissenschaft sind. Nach Nishida ist der Mechanismus eine Theorie, die behauptet, daß das Eine „im Verhältnis der Vielheit" erscheint, nämlich daß es als „das Eine der Vielheit" erscheint, und die Teleologie nimmt den Standpunkt der Logik an, nach der das Eine die Vielheit vereinheitlicht, nämlich das Eine als „die Vielheit des Eines" erscheint.

Nishida versucht im Grunde diese zwei gegenüberstehenden Richtungen auf das gegenüberstehende Verhältnis von Zeit und Raum zu reduzieren und die Logik dieses Verhältnisses zu erhellen. Nach dem rein formalen Gesichtspunkt ist der Raum „die Form der homogenen Koexistenz" und die Zeit ist die Art und Weise des ständig verschwindenden Flusses, nämlich „die Form einer synthetischen Vereinheitlichung des Heterogenen." Wenn man die Funktion der zwei Ordnungsformen Zeit und Raum betrachtet, ist die Nähe zum Denken von Bergson leicht festzustellen. Nach Nishida bedeutet „das Eine der Vielheit" daß die einender gegenüberstehende Vielheit in der Art und Weise, hinsichtlich der räumlichen Richtung nebeneinander zu koexistieren, in eins ist. Wenn die Welt nur räumlich gedacht wird, entsteht die mechanistisch gesehene Welt, in der alles für das gleichzeitige Sein gehalten wird. Im Gegensatz dazu bedeutet „die Vielheit des Einen", daß die Vielheit im Fluß der Zeit miteinander deckt und den Gegensatz auflöst. In dieser Richtung entsteht die zweckmäßige Welt, in der das ganzheitliche Eine als die Einheit der Vielheit konsitituiert wird, wie bei einer Zelle im biologischen Sinne des organischen Lebens. Aber auch wenn die Welt in diesem Sinne dynamisch, in der Entwicklung aufgefaßt wird, ist sie immer noch eine biologische Welt und sie entspricht nicht der handelnden Welt.

Demgegenüber bleibt die Aktivität des Lebens als der Akt der Selbstbildung der geschichtlichen Welt ungleich wie das biologische Leben. Insofern sie die Selbstbildung ist, die der Handlung gemäß, d.h. „vom Hergestellten zum Herstellenden," entsteht, beziehen sich die Vielheit und die Einheit nur wechselseitig bestimmend und somit wird das sich ausdrückende Verhältnis zwischen der individuellen Vielheit und der weltlichen Einheit gebildet. Gerade weil die Welt sich durch den herstellenden Akt des Menschen ausdrückt, „verbindet sich das Leben beim Leben des Menschen mit dem Grund des Leben."(GW. XI. S. 308)

Der Mechanismus ist die Logik des Gegenstandes und bildet die Erkenntnis durch die Art, der vorgegebenen Vielheit die Einheit zu geben. Die Teleologie ist die Logik des Werdens und bildet den Prozeß durch die Entwicklung des Ganzen auf ein bestimmtes Ziel. Im Gegensatz zu beiden tritt die dritte Logik auf, die als die Logik der von einender Abhängigen und gleichzeitig in Gegensatz zueinander Stehenden die Logik der absolut widersprüchlichen Selbstidentität ist, die in der handelnden Anschauung am Werk ist. Das sachliche Fundament dieser Logik, d.h. die Grundstruktur der abhängigen Beziehung von denen, die in ihrem Wesen in Gegensatz zueinander stehen und in der handelnden Anschauung entstehen, ist nämlich die Art und Weise der wechselseitigen Verschränkung zwischen Zeit und Raum.

Auf welche Weise ereignet sich dann diese wechselseitige Vermittlung? Nach Nishida ist die Vergangenheit schon vergangen, dennoch ist sie nicht vergangen. Die Zukunft ist noch nicht gekommen, dennoch ist sie bereits in der Gegenwart da. (Vgl. Ab.III. S. 9) Dieses „Gleichzeitig-Sein" solcher unendlichen „Vergangenheit und Zukunft" entsteht im „räumlichen Verhältnis des Zeitlichen." Das bedeutet, daß die Gegenwart sich selbst bestimmt. (Vgl. Ab.II. S. 282) Auf dem Grund solcher Struktur des „Sich-Entfallens" wird die Selbstbestimmung der absoluten Gegenwart oder die Kontinuität der Diskontinuität behauptet. Ferner wird das Verhältnis von der Bildung und dem Ausdruck, wie oben gezeigt, durch das wechselseitig verneindende und zueinander gehörige Verhältnis zwischen Zeit und Raum erörtert. In diesem Fall wird ein anderer Ausdruck, nähmlich das wechselseitige Verhältnis zwischen Innen und Außen, gebraucht.[4] „Die Zeit hat sich selbst im Raum, und das Innen nennt sich selbst das Außen, so lautet der Ausdruck."(GW. XI. S. 341) Das bedeutet auch die sich ausdrückende Selbstbestimmung, in der das Selbst sich selbst spiegelt. Im Gergemsatz dazu, wenn „der Raum sich selbst an der Zeit hat, das Außen das Innen ist,"(ebd.) wird die Seite, die sich selbst transzendiert und bildet, gezeigt. Das von einander abhängige Gestehen von beiden Momenten, Zeit und

[4]Das wechselseitg abhängige Ereignis muß nicht im Sinne „der verräumlichten Zeit (nach Bergson)," sondern als „Zeit-Spiel-Raum" (nach dem späteren Heidegger) verstanden werden.

Raum ist nämlich die Selbstbestimmung der absoluten Gegenwart und das Entstehen des Verhältnisses von der Bildung und dem Ausdruck.

II-5. Selbstbestimmung des Einzeldinges und wechselseitige Bestimmung von Einzeldinge

Die handelnde Anschauung ist ohne weiteres eine leibliche und poietische Aktivität einzelner Menschen. Aber sie als die sich ausdrückende Selbstbestimmung der Welt ereignet um die Achse der Negativität. Diese Negativität ist sowohl die sich ausdrückende Selbstbildung durch die Selbstnegation des Aktes des Lebens als auch das Wirken der Negativität des einzelnen Subjekts, das das Subjekt des einzelnen Menschen als das Element der Aktivitäten in sich einschließt. Dazu sagt Nishida, ,,Das Selbst-Entsthung durch die absolute Negation des Anderen schließt in sich notwendigerweise die absolute Negation des Selbst ein."(Ab. III. S. 223.) Dies ist, wie oben gezeigt, die Struktur der Selbstnegation, die ins Wirken der Selbstbildung der Welt verwirklicht wird. ,,Das Wirken unseres Selbst ist das Wirken des Selbst aber zugleich der selbstbildende Akt der Welt. Wenn auf diese Weise die Welt und das Selbst wie eins wirken, nenne ich dies die handelnde Anschauung."(GW. XI., S. 191.)

Das Entstehen der Selbstbildung der Welt in dem Akt des Ausdrucks ist das Entstehen des ausdrückenden Verhältnisses von dem Einen der Welt und der Vielheit einzelner Dinge. Das heißt das Einzelding spiegelt die Welt, und für Nishida heißt es, daß die Welt sich an dem Einzelding spiegelt. Über dieses Denken des Aspekts sagt er, ,,Unser Selbst als ein ausdrückender Punkt der Welt bildet die Welt dadurch, daß es die Welt an sich selbst ausdrückt. Der Ausdruck der Welt an sich selbst muß die Subjektivierung der Welt an sich selbst."(GW. XI. S. 377.) Dies wird auch mit dem Wort, ,,der eine Standpukt des Selbstausdrucks der Welt" oder ,,der selbstbildende Fokus der Welt" (Ab.III. S. 307), ferner ,,der Standort, in dem die Welt sich spiegelt," oder ,,ein Mitglied der Selbstbestimmung der Welt" bezeichnet. Ein Mitglied bedeutet natürlich einer von mehreren. Ein Aspekt kann eigentlich kein Aspekt sein, wenn er keine unersetzbare Selbstheit und umgekehrt keine Pluralität hat.[5] Insofern das Einzelding den Charakter des Aspekts hat und die Welt in sich spiegelt, läßt sich die Struktur des Verhältnisses befinden, nämlich das voneinender abhängige Verhältnis mittels der wechselseitigen Neagtivität zwischen dem Einen und dem Anderen, d.h. das Verhältnis der widersprüchlichen Selbstidentität auch zwischen einzelnen Dingen. Das Einzelding spiegelt die Welt. Das wird daher gleichzeitig die wechselseitige Bestimmung zwischen dem einen Einzelding und dem anderen Einzelding genannt. Nishida sagt, Einzeldinge

[5]Über die Aporie dieses Aspekts vgl. Y. Nitta, Selbstheit und Anderesheit, in: *Phänomenologie des Anderen*, hrsg. v. Y. Nitta u.a. (japansich) Tokyo 1982.

sind wechselseitig „zusammengehörig“.[6] Das bedeutet nichts anders als die wechselseitige Abhängigkeit mittels der Negativität.

III. Die Faktizität des Selbstgewahrens und die Logik der Philosophie

III-1. Die absolute Faktizität des selbstgewahrenden Realen

Nach Nishida hat die Welt die Realität gegenüber dem, was sie negiert. Der Selbstausdruck der Welt ist die Bildung des Seins des Ortes und die Welt hat die Realität im Gespiegelten, nämlich im Selbst-Bild. D.h. „das Gespiegelte“ ist nicht bloß ein Schatten und es hat „seine eigene Selbstheit.“ Dasselbe wird anderes ausdrückt: „Ohne den Selbstausdruck gibt es keine Realität der Welt“ oder „Im Sein des Ortes ist das Phänomen gleich das Reale. Dabei muß das Moment, daß die Negation versteht sich als das Selbstgewahren, enthalten sein. Das nennt Nishida, daß das ausdrückende Element selbstgewahrlich wird. Dazu sagt er im Zusammenhang mit dem Verhältnis von Zeit und Raum folgendes:

> Wir wissen, daß das Wirkende im unseren Selbstgewahren sich selbst, das Wirken des Selbst weiß. Nein, das Wirken ist das Wissen und das Wissen ist das Wirken. Hier ist schon die Zeit räumlich und wirkt sich als die Selbstbestimmung des durch die Zeit begründeten Raums. Das Selbst intendiert sich selbst in sich unendlich und die Tiefe des Selbst ist darin begründet, daß das Innen das Außen ist. Die Tiefe des Selbst ist die Tiefe der Welt. Von dem Bereich der Intention allein tritt der Akt selbst niemals hervor ... Bei dem Selbsgewahren ist unser Selbst bereits im Außen. (GW. XI, S. 346.)

Durch die Negation läßt die Welt sich als Form in Erscheinung auftreten. Das ist nichts anderes als die Struktur des Selbstgewahrens des Realen, in der das Reale sich in sich selbst spiegelt. Das bedeutet notwendigerweise, daß der Akt des Spiegelns sich in der handelnden Anschauung wirkt und gleichzeitig sich der Akt des Wissens vom desselben wirkt.

Nishida spricht davon, „daß es das Verstehen selbst als die Sache des Selbst enthalten muß.“(Ab. III, S. 189.) Die Struktur des Selbstgewahrens des Realen ist eben „das von sich selbst Verstandene“ als die absolute Faktizität. Wie er sagt, „daß unser Selbst die absolute Faktizität in der geschichtlichen Welt ist,“ ist sie die Faktizität, daß das Selbstgewahren der Welt in unserem Selbst ereignet und gleichzeitig das Selbstgewahren dieser

[6] Auch Heidegger gebraucht das Wort „Zusammengehörigkeit,“ wenn er das wechselseitig zugehörige, durch die Negativität so wie „ontologische Differenz“ vermittelte Verhältnis ausdrückt.

Tatsache selbst ist. Dieses Selbstgewahren ist das der Welt und auch das des Einzeldinges deswegen, weil „unser Selbst sich als Einzelding solcher Welt gewahrt." Davon spricht Nishida kurz und bündig: „Wenn die Welt sich gewahrt, gewahrt sich unser Selbst."(Ab. III, 262.)

Andererseits wird es behauptet: „das Selbstgewahren ist es, abgründig zur absoluten Sache zu werden." Die selbstgewahrende Tatsache ist in diesem Sinne jeweils absolut und abgründig. Das Abgründig-Sein des Selbstgewahrens ist nichts anderes als das, daß „die selbstgewahrende Tatsache die Bewegung des selbstverneinenden Selbsterscheinung," die „von einer Sache zu der anderen Sache," „von einer Form zu der anderen Form" ständig ereignet, ist. Mit anderen Worten ist "das, was sich selbst im Ausdruck des Selbst hat," nämlich „das, was sich selbst nur durch das absolute Andere hat," unmittelbar das, „was durch das Verschwinden lebt." Der hier bemerkbare Gedanke über das momentane Geborenwerden und Verschwinden der abgründigen Tatsache läßt sich erblicken, daß er mit der Einsicht über das Sein von dem sogenannten „jijimuge (von Ereignis zu Ereignis ohne Störung)" der Kegon-Schule, nämlich dem Gedanken von „engi (das abhängige Entstehen)" des Mahayana-Buddhismus einen gemeinsamen Grund hat.

III-2. „Die Rationalisierung des Nicht-Rationalen"

Nishida hat keine metaphysische Fragestellung nach dem Grund als die Frage nach dem Hintergrund der Welt. Daher entsteht bei seinem Denken keine Kehre des Denkens, die dem Ereignis, „dem Scheitern der metaphyschen Frage nach dem Grund" im Nihilismus Europas entspricht. Denn Nishida nimmt seinen Ausgangspunkt in der absoluten Faktizität der Erfahrung und versucht das Entstehen und die Struktur der urtümlichen Erfahrung, ohne sich von der Erfahrung zu trennen, zu untersuchen. Der Vertiefung des Schrittes seines Denkens entsprechend wird es versucht, vom Geschehen der Welt als dem Ereignis des selbstverneinenden Erscheinens der Welt selbst stets in der Erfahrung selbst zu reden, ohne die Welt für das An-Sich-Sein zu halten oder sie hinter ihr zu transzendieren. In welcher Stelle sieht Nishida selber den philosophischen Standpunkt solchen Denkens des Seins? Auf welche Weise wird die Frage der Philosophie in „die Bewegung der selbstverneinenden Selbstbildung der Welt" eingefügt? Nun zum Schluß möchte ich der Logik der Struktur der Sebstreferenz der Philosophie bei Nishida nachgehen.

Zunächst ist seine folgende Aussage zu bemerken, daß die Richtung der selbstgewahrenden Reflexion gegenüber der kreativen Richtung als der handelnden Anschauung steht. Die Philosophie als die selbstgewahrende Reflexion beruht auf der selbstgewahrenden Anschauung des kreativen Selbst und sie muß auf dem Grund der handelnden Anschauung da sein. „Die kreative Anschauung ist die Selbstreflexion der Vernunft selbst. Letztlich beruht die Philosophie so wie das wissenschaftliche Wissen nicht auf der handelnden Anschauung des poiesischen Selbst, sondern auf der Anschauung der kreativen Selbst."(GW. X, S. 561.) Dazu sagt er auch: „Unser Wissen ist in der Richtung der handelnden Anschauung stets wissenschaftlich und in der Richtung der gewahrenden Anschauung stets philosophisch."(GW. X, S. 563.)

Über die Aufgabe, die Nishida in seiner Philosophie erfüllen wollte, habe ich in meinen anderen Artikeln folgendes geschrieben: „Nishidas Denken ist der Versuch, die gesamte Struktur zwischen den beiden Polen, nämlich einerseits dem Standpunkt des wissenschaftlichen Denkens, das an der Grenze des Ortes des Seins entsteht, und andererseits dem Standpunkt der Religion, wo man sich in der Richtung des Nichts, das in keiner absoluten Bestimmung erfassbar wird, in seinem Erlebnis versenkt, konsequenterweise als die Sache des Denkens, d.h. auf dem Standpunkt des selbstgewahrenden Handelns, sehen zu lassen."[7]

Dieser Versuch stammt daraus, daß Nishida die Rolle der Philosophie in „der Rationalisierung des Nicht-Rationalen" sieht. Wir können uns daran erinnern, daß bereits in seiner früheren Periode der „Logik des Ortes" die Logik der Philosophie als eine solche „Rationalisierung des Nicht-Rationalen" charakterisiert wurde.[8] Aber in der späteren Periode wird diese Charakterisierung sowohl auf die handelnde Anschauung als auch auf die selbstgewahrende Anschauung angewendet. [9]

In dem ersten Fall ist die handelnde Anschauung „die Rationalisierung des Nicht-Rationalen"; dies bedeutet das Wirken des Selbstspiegelns in den verschiedenen Dimensionen und die Rationalisierung ist schließlich nichts anderes als das Entstehen der „Form." In dem zweiten Fall ist die selbstgewahrende Anschauung eben die Anschauung, die Ort und Stelle vom Innen weiß, in dem das Nicht-Rationale rationalisiert wird, und diese „Rationalisierung des Nicht-Rationalen muß als die Rationalisierung", als die Arbeit der Philosophie, „die Rationalisierung des Nicht-Rationalen selbst zu logisieren", verstanden werden. Die Logik der Philosophie selbst thematisiert nicht nur die Logik der „Rationalisierung des Nicht-Rationalen," sondern erst wenn das Denken der Philosophie selbst als die Rationalisierung des Nicht-Rationalen durchgeführt wird, kann die Philosophie die Rationalisierung des Nicht-Rationalen bei sich beweisen und die Logik der Selbstreferenz vorlegen.

In diesem Fall muß die Philosophie zunächst die selbstverneinende Struktur der Selbstbildung der Welt in verschiedenen Erscheinungen hervorheben und diese Struktur als die Logik, die die Art und Weise der „Rationalisierung des Nicht-Rationalen" erhellt, zeigen und somit die Arbeit, den

---

[7]Vgl. Y. Nitta, Wissenschaftlichkeit der Philosophie Nishidas, in: *Für das Lernen der Philosophie Nishidas*, hrsg. v. K. Ohmine (japansich) Tokyo 1996.

[8]Vgl. meinen Aufsatz in der Anmerkung 1.

[9]Z.B. sagt er „z.B. unser Leib ist das Organ für die Rationalisierung des Nicht-Rationalen."

Standpunkt verschiedener Selbstbildungen zu begründen, durchführen. Zum zweiten muß sie die Struktur, die in der Selbstbildung selbst wirkt, durch die eigene Arbeit erblicken und somit die logische Struktur der „Rationalisierung des Nicht-Rationalen" selbst untersuchen. Die erste Aufgabe ist eine wissenschafstheoretische Aufgabe, „die Bildung des Ortes des Seins" zu untersuchen. In dieser Aufgabenstellung findet man Nishidas Haltung, den wissenschaftlichen Raum der neuzeitlichen Wissenschaften in Europa aufzunehmen, und die Möglichkeit dieser Aufnahme. Im Zusammenhang mit der gegenwärtigen Gedanken ist die Überschneidung mit der Wissenschaftstheorie, dem theoretischen Feld allgemeiner Kulturtheorie und ferner der heutigen Systemtheorie zu bemerken. Sie ist mit anderen Worten die Richtung der mehrdimensionalen und mehrschichtigen Theorie des Wissens.

Die zweite Aufgabe liegt darin, von der Grundfrage aus, die danach fragt, auf welche Weise das Formlose eine Form annehmen kann, erneut zu fragen, auf welche Weise das Unsagbare sagbar wird; das ist die Frage nach der Dimension, wo die Logik der Philosophie entsteht. Nach Nishida liegt sie in der Richtung, in der danach gefragt wird, auf welche Weise die Logik des Selbstgewahrens selbst sagbar ist. Wahrscheinlich liegt hier der Ort, wo die Logik der Philosophie Nishidas mit der Frage nach „der Logik des Verhältnisses," „der Vernunft und ihrem Anderen" in dem deutschen Idealismus, die sich im urtümlichen Entstehen des Denkens wirkt, überschneidet und der Logik der Differenz, die sich in der Vertiefung des Denkens der Phänomenologie in Erscheinung tritt, begegnet. Diese Frage ist auch mit der Frage gebunden, wo die Grenzen der Philosophie liegen, insofern sie die Frage nach dem Wissen bedeutet, und sich von Kunst und Religion unterscheidet. Obwohl das Wissen so sehr mehrdimensional und mehrschichtig ist und seine geschichtliche Wandlung erfährt, hat es sein Problem, das das fundamentale, unter solcher Wandlung wirkende Gefüge betrifft, insofern Wissen als Wissen bleibt. Dazu werde ich mich in einem anderen Artikel äußern.

Es ist am Nishidas Denken sehr klar abzulesen, daß die oben erwähnten zwei Richtungen als Momente, die zu einer Sache des Denkens gehören, synthetisch problematisiert werden. Das ist für das heutige Denken besonders zu bemerken, denn sie betrifft die Frage nach der Sache, die neu herausgearbeitet werden muß. Diese einheitliche Sache ist nämlich, daß die zwei Sachen, der Akt des Beziehens des Menschen auf die Welt und der Akt des Beziehens der Welt auf den Menschen, in Wirklichkeit sich als das Eine ereignet. Nishidas Frage fordert das heutige Denken auf, so daß die Erfahrung des Menschen als eine solche Sache erneut gedacht werden muß.

Über den Philosophiebegriff des 19. Jahrhunderts und seine Auswirkung auf die Gegenwart

Ernst Wolfgang Orth

Wenn wir von der Philosophie des 19. Jahrhunderts sprechen, so ist es zunächst und auf den ersten Blick gar nicht so eindeutig, auf welche philosophischen Arbeiten wir uns beziehen sollen. 1939 schrieb Karl Löwith in seinem japanischen Exil in Sendai im Vorwort seines Buches ‚Von Hegel zu Nietzsche‘ folgende zwei Sätze: „Hegel und Nietzsche sind die beiden Enden, zwischen denen sich das eigentliche Geschehen der Geschichte des deutschen Geistes im 19. Jahrhundert bewegte" und „Erst das 20. Jahrhundert hat das eigentliche Geschehen des 19. Jahrhunderts deutlich und deutbar gemacht."[1]

Man kann diesen beiden Sätzen zustimmen und doch eine bestimmte Einseitigkeit in Löwiths Betrachtungsweise konstatieren, eine Betrachtungsweise, die ja sehr wirksam geworden ist. Sind wirklich Hegel, der Däne Kierkegaard, Marx und Nietzsche die wichtigsten Figuren der deutschen Philosophie des 19. Jahrhunderts und die wichtigsten Quellen ihrer Auswirkung auf Philosophie und Wissenschaften über Deutschland hinaus? Wo bleiben in diesen Überlegungen eigentlich die großen Vertreter der akademischen Philosophie, z.B. Adolf Trendelenburg (1802-1872), Rudolf Hermann Lotze (1817-1881), Wilhelm Dilthey (1833-1911), Franz Brentano (1838-1917) und die frühen Neukantianer von Friedrich Albert Lange (1828-1875) über Kuno Fisher (1824-1907), Eduard Zeller (1814-1908) bis zu Aloys Riehl (1844-1924) und Hermann Cohen (1842-1918)? Wo bleibt eine Figur wie Wilhelm Wundt (1832-1920), der die systematische Philosophie und die empirischen Wissenschaften als Physiologie und Psychologie gleichermaßen bearbeitet? Ganz zu schweigen von so wirkungsvollen, wenn auch heute weitgehend ungekannten Philosophen wie Johann Friedrich Herbart (1776-1841) und Jakob Friedrich Fries (1773-1843)? Immerhin gab es im 20. Jahrhundert wiederholte Herbart-Renaissancen (in der Pädagogik) sowie eine Neu-Friessche Schule,[2] die im sogenannten kritischen Rationalismus der Popper-Schule wieder aufgegriffen wird.

---

[1]Karl Löwith, *Von Hegel zu Nietzsche. Der revolutionäre Bruch im Denken des 19. Jahrhunderts. Marx und Kierkegaard*, Zürich 1941, Stuttgart[5] 1964, S. 7.

[2]Zu Herbart vgl. E.W. Orth: Johann Friedrich Herbart als Philosoph des 19. Jahrhunderts. In: *Die Albertus-Universität zu Königsberg und ihre Professoren. Aus Anlaß der Gründung der Albertus-Universität vor 450 Jahren*, hrsg. von Dietrich Rauschning u. Donata v. Nerée, Berlin 1995, S. 137-151. Für Fries ist auf die Forschungsarbeit von Lutz Geldsetzer und Wolfram Hogrebe zu verweisen.

Löwith hat sein Buch, das 1941 in erster Auflage in Zürich erschienen ist, seinem Lehrer Edmund Husserl gewidmet, bei dem er übrigens 1922 ein Seminar über Lotze besuchte.[3] Edmund Husserl aber, der mit seiner Phänomenologie die Philosophie auf neue Grundlagen stellen, ja sie allererst in ihrer wahren Gestalt inaugurieren wollte, greift nicht auf Hegel oder Kierkegaard, Marx oder Nietzsche zurück, sondern dann doch eher auf Trendelenburg, Lotze, Dilthey und ausdrücklich zumal auf Brentano.[4] Trotzdem ist Löwiths Art des Zugriffs auf das 19. Jahrhundert nicht verfehlt. Denn es ist jene akademische Philosophie, in welcher sich das vorbereitet, was man - mit Marxens Floskel - die ‚Verweltlichung oder auch die Verwirklichung der Philosophie' nennen mag. Die Philosophie wird zur Kulturphilosophie, zur Anthropologie oder zur Kulturanthropologie. Die entsprechende Terminologie wird von der akademischen Philosophie des 19. Jahrhunderts durchaus vorbereitet, um dann im 20. Jahrhundert ihre eigentliche Wirkung zu entfalten. Es geht dem 19. Jahrhundert in einer durchaus kritischen Haltung gegenüber der Metaphysik - wenn auch nicht bei gänzlicher und durchgehender Ablehnung derselben - um die bedingten Möglichkeiten einer Rationalisierung der Menschenwelt, gerade auch mit Blick auf die modernen Entwicklungen dieser Menschenwelt, freilich im Zusammenhang ihrer konkreten Geschichte. Die ‚Welt des Menschen' ist aber das, was wir Kultur nennen.

Wenn Löwith die „philosophische Geschichte des 19. Jahrhunderts im Himmelte der Gegenwart ‚umschreiben' "will"[5], „um im Lichte der Gegenwart die epochale Bedeutung einer in Vergessenheit geratenen Episode zu erhellen"[6], so folgt er durchaus - ob wissentlich oder nicht - einer Betrachtungsweise, die wir bei Philosophen wie Trendelenburg, Lotze und zumal bei Dilthey ausdrücklich am Werke sehen. Wir haben es mit dem paradoxen Sachverhalt zu tun, daß den unakademischen Philosophien von Kierkegaard, Marx und Nietzsche ihr authentischer Indiziencharakter, theoretisch, eigentlich erst von der akademischen Philosophie zugesprochen wird - und zwar in dem Maße, als diese akademische Philosophie die Gegenwart des Menschen in der Welt - als Menschenwelt - philosophisch zu bestimmen sucht und als die Hauptaufgabe der Philosophie herausstellt. Es ist Kants Bestimmung der ‚Philosophie dem Weltbegriffe nach', die im 19. Jahrhundert in der akademischen Philosophie Schule macht.[7]

---

[3]Vgl. Karl Schuhmann, *Husserl-Chronik. Denk- und Lebensweg Edmund Husserl*, Den Haag 1977, S. 259.

[4]Vgl. die einschlägigen Arbeiten des Verfassers.

[5]Löwith, a.a.O., S. 7.

[6]Löwith, a.a.O., S. 8.

[7]Den ‚Weltbegriff' betonen Lotze und Dilthey im Anschluß an Kant ausdrücklich und damit auch die anthropologische Perspektive, unter der schon Fries die ‚neue' Vernunftkritik gesehen hatte. Die ‚Kultur' wird auch von Wilhelm Wundt thematisiert.

Besonders deutlich wird dies bei Dilthey, der Anfang der siebziger Jahre von der „großen Krisis der Wissenschaften und der europäischen Kultur" spricht.[8] Diese Krisis meldet sich vor allem in dem vielberufenen ‚historischen Bewußtsein' des 19. Jahrhunderts zu Wort. Was Dilthey mit ‚historischem Bewußtsein' meint, wird allerdings erst richtig verständlich, wenn man seine These beachtet: „Nur aus dem Verständnis der Gegenwart kann das rechte philosophische Wort... hervorgehen".[9] Und auch Lotze geht es um das Verständnis der Gegenwart des um Weltorientierung bemühten Menschen, wenn er 1857 schreibt: „Nach einer so langen Entwicklungsgeschichte der Philosophie, die alle möglichen Standpunkte mehr als einmal entdeckt und wieder verlassen hat, gibt es kein Verdienst der Originalität mehr, sondern nur noch das der Genauigkeit. Abzuleugnen, daß die ganze Vergangenheit auf uns gewirkt hat, und die am meisten, in deren Verlauf wir selbst noch verwickelt sind, würde ebenso fruchtlos als töricht sein."[10] Es geht hier bei Lotze nicht um die bloße Vergangenheit; es geht um die Adjustierung der Gegenwart; denn in den ‚Streitschriften' ringt Lotze um einen neuen Wissenschafts- und Philosophiebegriff - gegen die Systemwut des deutschen Idealismus.

Die Gegenwart aber, um die es hier geht, ist die Gegenwart der Kultur, d.h. die Welt des Menschen, des Menschen, der sich geschichtlich verwirklicht, indem er sich und seine Wirklichkeit in die Zukunft zu tragen sucht, d.h. sich *vergegenwärtigt*. An diese Kulturgegenwart und an diese Gegenwart des Geistes - mit der Frage, wie sie denn möglich und zu gewährleisten sei - knüpft die Philosophie im 19. Jahrhundert gleichsam ihr Schicksal, als Frage nach der Gegenwart der Philosophie. Das ‚geschichtliche Bewußtsein,' der ‚historische Sinn' sollte nicht voreilig mit genauer Kenntnis des Historischen verwechselt werden. Es handelt sich um das durchschnittliche Bewußtsein, sich in tatsächlichen Entwicklungen zu befinden, das auch einen Philosophen wie Edmund Husserl, der nicht beansprucht, ein professioneller Historiker zu sein, mehr und mehr prägt.

Die Philosophie des 19. Jahrhunderts ist das Ergebnis einer Krise, einer Krise, die man positiv als eine ‚Aufbaukrise' und durchaus nicht als einen Zusammenbruch charakterisieren mag.[11] Kants stolzes Wort, daß die Philosophie der Theologie nicht länger die Schleppe nachtragen müsse, sondern der Theologie (als einer Wissenschaft unter anderen) die Fackel voraustra-

---

[8]Vgl. Clara Misch (Hrsg.): *Der junge Dilthey. Ein Lebensbild in Briefen und Tagebüchern 1852-1870* (1933), Stuttgart& Göttingen,1960, S. VII.

[9]Vgl. Dilthey, GS VIII, S. 190, aus 1898. Heideggers, schon in den frühen Vorlesungen propagierte ‚Auslegungen des Heute' darf hier angeschlossen werden.

[10]R.H. Lotze: Streitschriften. In Bezug auf Prof. I.H. Fichte's Anthropologie, Leipzig 1857, S. 5.

[11]Zum Terminus, Aufbaukrise vgl. Karl Bühler: *Die Krise der Psychologie* (1927), Stuttgart^3 1965, S. 1.

gen dürfe,[12] markiert einen allgemeinen Umbruch, der allerdings erst im 19. Jahrhundert mit all seinen Auswirkungen zu begreifen und zu bewältigen war, ja in den nachkantischen Jahrhunderten erst Sinn erhält.

Denn was bedeutet die vermeintlich befreiende Überwindung der These, daß die Philosophie ‚ancilla theologiae' sei? Diese These hatte im Mittelalter eine durchaus positive Bedeutung, die sich bis ins 17. Jahrhundert auswirkte. Die Theologie war ja keine Einzelwissenschaft, sondern die Rahmen bildende, umsichtig organisierte Einsicht und Gewißheit, daß der fragmentarische Menschengeist mit allen Bemühungen um Rationalisierung seines Handelns und Erkennens in einem göttlichen Geist und göttlichen Sein aufgehoben ist. Der Rationalismus des 17. Jahrhunderts hat diesem Gedanken in Gestalten wie Descartes und Leibniz, aber auch bei empiristischen Denkern wie John Locke eine beeindruckende und moderne Form gegeben. Wenn das 18. Jahrhundert sich gegen die Vorherrschaft der Theologie wendet, so ist das zunächst ein Kampf gegen die Bevormundung durch die institutionalisierte Kirche, resp. die institutionalisierten Kirchen, sowie ein Kampf um die Verfeinerung szientifischer, an der Erfahrung orientierter Methoden. Und methodisches Denken war ja von der Theologie nicht grundsätzlich ausgeschlossen worden. Vor allem wird nun aber seit dem späteren 18. Jahrhundert die Theologie selbst zunehmend als Einzelwissenschaft verstanden, die ihre universalen Orientierungsansprüche ex definitione nicht länger aufrechterhalten darf.

Für einen Weltaugenblick lang - nämlich in der europäischen Philosophie der Aufklärung, in der Kantischen Philosophie und ihrer Weiterbildung im deutschen Idealismus - wird aber gerade jener aus der alten Theologie ererbte Universalismus auf die angeblich theologiefreie Philosophie übertragen, die nun in einem umgreifenden Souveränitätsanspruch das ganze Pathos universaler Wissenschaftlichkeit auf sich zieht, um die ganze Kultur zu bestimmen. Die Philosophie ist die Wissenschaft überhaupt, die Wissenschaft schlechthin. Und die Wissenschaft ihrerseits ist die Kirche der modernen Welt.[13]

Mag nun auch die Philosophie nicht mehr länger der Theologie die Schleppe nachtragen, sondern ihr und allen anderen Einzelwissenschaften die Fackel voraustragen; in Wirklichkeit sah sich die Philosophie im 19. Jahrhundert bald in der Lage, bloß noch der Schleppenträger der positiven Wissenschaften zu sein. Es ist dieses Paradox der Philosophie, frei zu sein und gleichzeitig von den Ansprüchen positiver Einzelwissenschaften gefordert und herausgefordert zu werden, dem Philosophen wie Trendelenburg, Lotze und Dilthey sich stellen mußten. Die Wissenschaftlichkeit der Philosophie schien abgewandert in die Einzelwissenschaften. Ja, die Wirkungen

---

[12] I. Kant: Der Streit der Fakultäten (1798), Akad. Ausg. VII, S. 28.

[13] Deshalb polemisiert Nietzsche 1873 in seiner Ersten Unzeitgemäßen Betrachtung gegen David Friedrich Strauß.

der Philosophie sind verborgen in diesen Einzelwissenschaften bis hin zur Anonymisierung der Philosophie selbst; ein Vorgang, der sich am deutlichsten bei Dilthey belegen läßt, in dessen Werk Philosophie sich allfällig als *Besinnung* manifestiert. Diese Besinnung aber kann sich methodisch jeweils nur als historische, psychologische, biologische und hermeneutische Betrachtungsweise vollziehen. Diltheys Floskel von der ‚Philosophie der Philosophie‘ [14] aus 1907 ist Ausdruck für die Schwierigkeit, das, was ‚philosophische Einstellung‘ ist, zu fixieren. Das läuft darauf hinaus, daß derjenige, der gerade zuletzt über Philosophie spricht, jene ‚Philosophie der Philosophie‘ für sich in Anspruch nehmen kann. Der jüngere Neukantianer Richard Hönigswald wird im Hinblick auf diesen Vorgang in unserem Jahrhundert positiv von der ‚Ubiquität der Philosophie‘ sprechen.[15]

Heideggers leicht mißverständlicher Satz „Die Wissenschaft denkt nicht“[16] bestätigt durchaus diesen Befund, zumal wenn man ihn im Lichte seines Aufsatzes aus den späten sechziger Jahren versteht: ‚Das Ende der Philosophie und die Aufgabe des Denkens.‘[17] Der Satz von 1954 wird im Lichte des Titels von 1969 verständlich: nicht nur die Wissenschaft denkt nicht, auch die Philosophie verfehlt das Denken als ‚ein freies Fragen des rein auf sich gestellten Daseins,‘ wenn sie bloß Disziplin ist. Der gemeinsame rationale Kern dieser Heideggerschen Thesen vom Nicht-Denken der Wissenschaften und dem Ende der Philosophie besteht darin, daß das philosophische Denken sich nicht zureichend in einer Disziplin institutionalisieren läßt, nicht einmal in einer Disziplin namens Philosophie. Als institutionalisierte Universalwissenschaft hat die Philosophie keineswegs das Monopol auf das Denken, ebensowenig wie die stets unter bestimmten Bedingungen arbeitenden Einzelwissenschaften ein solches Monopol beanspruchen dürfen.

Aber nach dieser Einsicht muß umgekehrt vermutet werden, daß philosophisches Denken sich jeweils, ohne daß es auch nur unter diesem Namen auftritt, in den Einzelwissenschaften lebendig zu Wort melden kann; dann nämlich: wenn solche Einzelwissenschaften aus eigener Arbeit auf Probleme stoßen, die den Rahmen festgefügter Disziplingliederungen sprengen. Helmuth Plessner empfiehlt zu diesem Zweck die bewußte ‚Entsicherung‘ als ‚Grenzforschung.‘[18] Und in der Tat ereignet sich solche Aufsprengung im 20. Jahrhundert in vielfacher Weise, wenn sogenannte philosophische

---

[14] Vgl. Dilthey, *Gesammelte Schriften* VIII, S. 269.

[15] Vgl. Richard Hönigswald: Die Systematik der Philosophie aus individueller Problemgestaltung entwickelt, I. Teil, *Schriften aus dem Nachlaß*, Bd. IX, Bonn 1976, S. 150 f.

[16] Martin Heidegger: *Was heißt Denken?*, Tübingen 1954, S. 4.

[17] Martin Heidegger: *Zur Sache des Denkens*, Tübingen 1969.

[18] Vgl. E.W. Orth: Helmuth Plessners Anthropologiekonzeption und sein Begriff von Wissenschaft und Philosophie. In: Jürgen Friedrich/Bernd Westermann (Hrsg.): *Unter offenem Himmelt. Anthropologie nach Helmuth Plessner*, Frankfurt/Berlin 1995, S. 67-74.

Probleme aus ganz unphilosophischen Wissenschaften oder selbst auch aus anderen Kulturbereichen aufbrechen. Dies muß durchaus nicht nur als ein ganz neues Phänomen angesehen werden, wenn man sich daran erinnert, daß das vieldeutige Verb *philosophein* im antiken Griechenland offensichtlich früher auftrat als das stabilisierte Substantiv *philosophia.*

Diese erneute Entsubstantivierung und Verbalisierung der Philosophie im 19. Jahrhundert deutet sich durch die Erfindung oder Forcierung neuer Disziplinen an, die gleichermaßen philosophisch sein und den Einzelwissenschaften dienen wollen, sowie sich methodologisch mit der Arbeit der Einzelwissenschaften zu verknüpfen suchen. Solche offenen Disziplinen sind die seit Beginn des 19. Jahrhunderts bis in die rezente Gegenwart wirkenden Forschungsrichtungen wie ‚Erkenntnistheorie,' ‚Wissenschaftstheorie' sowie ‚Wissenschaftskunde,' ‚Weltanschauungslehre,' auch ‚Ideologie' sowie ‚Phänomenologie' und ‚Hermeneutik.' Sie können durchaus auch auf das Prädikat ‚philosophisch' verzichten. Folgerichtig wird Aloys Riehl in seinem ‚Philosophischen Kritizismus' 1876 eine Möglichkeit des Ausgleichs suchen und schreiben: „Die Philosophie ist nicht die Gesamtwissenschaft ..., wohl aber ist sie die Allgemeinwissenschaft, oder die Wissenschaftslehre, die sich als solche von den Einzelwissenschaften bestimmt unterscheidet, ohne doch aus dem Zusammenhang mit diesen herauszutreten."[19] Das Problematische dieses Zusammenhangs scheint allerdings bei Riehl im Vergleich zu anderen Bemühungen des 19. Jahrhunderts durchaus noch unterschätzt zu werden.

Denn *erstens* gibt es für die Einheitlichkeit der Wissenschaftslehre gemäß der oben genannten offenen Disziplinen durchaus verschiedene Perspektiven. Sie kann erkenntnistheoretisch, wissenschaftstheoretisch (d.h. methodologisch), wissenschaftskundig (d.h. wissenschaftsgeschichtlich), Weltanschauungen analysierend (oder ideologisch resp. mentalitätsgeschichtlich) sein, oder auch phänomenologisch und hermeneutisch. *Zweitens* verknüpfen sich die genannten Disziplinen von vornherein auf die vielfältigste Weise mit speziellen einzelwissenschaftlichen Methoden und Erkenntnisgehalten. So verbindet sich die *erkenntnistheoretische* Betrachtungsweise als Bewußtseinstheorie mit psychologischen und logischen Fragen bis hin zu sozialwissenschaftlichen und biologischen Himmelten.

Die *Wissenschaftstheorie* knüpft an die speziellen Verfahrenstechniken der empirischen Einzelwissenschaften und der (mathematisierten) Logik an; die *Wissenschaftskunde* und Wissenschaftsgeschichte an die Geschichtswissenschaft und an die Mentalitätsgeschichte, die ihrerseits zu Fragen der *Weltanschauung* und der *Ideologie* führt. Die *Hermeneutik* hat ihre Vorlagen in Problemen der Textauslegung und der Ausdruckskunde bis hin zur Semiotik und Sprachphilosophie; und schließlich sucht die *Phänomenologie*

---

[19] Aloys Riehl: *Der philosophische Kriticismus und seine Bedeutung für die positive Wissenschaft*, 1. Bd., Leipzig 1876, Leipzig[3] 1924, S. 2.

wieder ihren Anhalt an einer eigentümlichen Psychologie und an der durchaus ontologischen Konzeption eines Erscheinungsmodells, das seinerseits noch diskussionsbedürftig ist.

Was die Entwicklung des Titels ‚*Erkenntnistheorie*' betrifft, zu dessen historischer Erforschung in der jüngsten Zeit Klaus Christian Köhnke Wichtiges beigetragen hat,[20] so ist er schon zu Beginn des 19. Jahrhunderts bei Ernst Reinhold virulent, um dann 1831 bei Eduard Beneke, 1847 bei I.H. Fichte und 1862 als Titelbegriff bei Eduard Zeller aufzutauchen.

Wissenschaftstheorie als ‚Theorie der Wissenschaften' wird 1840 in Trendelenburgs ‚Logischen Untersuchungen' ausdrücklich zum Fundamentalbegriff der Philosophie. Nicht erst die Neukantianer (vor allem mit Hermann Cohen) gehen von dem ‚Faktum der Wissenschaften' als Kulturtatsache aus. Das tut und empfiehlt schon Trendelenburg. ‚Wissenschaftskunde' als Wissenschaftsforschung ist schon in den fünfziger Jahren des 19. Jahrhunderts ein Grundanliegen von Rudolf Harms und dann bei seinem späteren Berliner Nachfolger Wilhelm Dilthey, der Thomas Kuhns Konzept einer Wissenschaftsforschung (von 1962) längst vorweggenommen hat.

Der bei Kant in spezieller Bedeutung, an einer bestimmten Stelle in der ‚Kritik der Urteilskraft' (§26) auftauchende Terminus ‚*Weltanschauung*' wird spätestens seit Trendelenburg zu einem leitenden Begriff. Bei Lotze finden wir ihn eher in der terminologischen Gestalt von ‚Weltansicht' und ‚Weltansichten.' Die Verknüpfbarkeit des Titels mit dem *Ideologie*begriff, nicht im Sinne Marxens, sondern des seit Ende der neunziger Jahre des 18. Jahrhunderts wirkenden Franzosen Destutt de Tracy, ist noch zu erforschen. Nicht erst bei Dilthey, sondern schon bei Trendelenburg und seinen Schülern (Adolf Kym) zeigt sich, daß das Weltanschauungsproblem Fragen der Wissenschaftslehre und der Analyse anderer Kultursysteme - wie Kunst, Literatur und Religion - notwendig verbindet.

Wichtig ist hier die 1854 erschienene Schrift des Trendelenburg-Schülers A.L. Kym: ‚Die Weltanschauungen und deren Konsequenzen,' in welcher wir auch schon eine frühe Differenzierung zwischen Natur- und Geisteswissenschaften finden. (A.L. Kym: *Die Weltanschauungen und deren Konsequenzen*, Zürich 1854, S. 64.) Dabei ist die Forcierung des Begriffs ‚Weltanschauung' als eines Hauptthemas der Philosophie weder im Sinne eines ‚weltanschaulichen' Dogmatismus noch als voreilige Ideologiekritik zu verstehen. Vielmehr liegt die anthropologische Einsicht zugrunde, daß der Mensch prinzipiell und strukturell die Eigenheit hat, immer schon Ansichten, Anschauungen von der Welt zu bilden, die sich in moderner Zeit vornehmlich als Wissenschaft und Wissenschaften manifestieren, die aber auch in Gestalt anderer Kulturformen auftreten - als Religion, Kunst, Lite-

[20] Vgl. Klaus Christian Köhnke: Entstehung und Aufstieg des Neukantianismus. Die deutsche Universitätsphilosophie zwischen Idealismus und Positivismus, Frankfurt 1986. Hier finden sich auch wichtige bibliographische Hinweise.

ratur, Politik usw. Diese menschliche Eigenheit wurde im 20. Jahrhundert von Max Scheler mit dem Titel ‚Weltoffenheit' belegt. Die These, daß für die Analyse möglicher menschlicher Orientierungsleistungen vom Faktum der Wissenschaften auszugehen sei, kann damit erweitert werden: es muß von allen möglichen Fakten menschlichen Weltverständnisses ausgegangen werden, auch von vor- und außer-wissenschaftlichen. Im 20. Jahrhundert wird der jüngere Neukantianer Ernst Cassirer mit seiner ‚Philosophie der symbolischen Formen' genau diese Betrachtungsweise empfehlen und durchführen.[21]

Mit ‚*Hermeneutik*' und ‚*Phänomenologie*' erhalten zwei ältere Termini eine neue Bedeutung im 19. Jahrhundert, um sich zu philosophischen Fundamentalbegriffen auszuweiten und zu vertiefen, die uns im 20. Jahrhundert zu Husserl und Heidegger führen, aber nicht nur zu ihnen. Man muß Diltheys bekannte Rolle für die Entwicklung der modernen Hermeneutik nicht besonders betonen; weniger bekannt ist der Beitrag Lotzes für den Begriff - nicht so sehr für den Terminus - Phänomenologie. Lotzes Erscheinungslehre als Lehre von jener Instanz, der überhaupt etwas erscheinen kann, hat immer noch unterschätzte Nachwirkungen für die Philosophie des 20. Jahrhunderts. Tendelenburg und Lotze wirken ihrerseits auf Franz Brentano, dessen Verdienst es ist, den älteren Terminus Phänomenologie, dem er freilich wie Dilthey den Begriff der ‚deskriptiven Psychologie' vorzieht, gleichsam an Husserl weiterzureichen. An die neugefaßte Bestimmung der ‚Phänomenologie' wird Husserl im 20. Jahrhundert das Programm einer neuen Philosophie knüpfen. Er übernimmt dabei den Begriff der Intentionalität - ebenfalls von Brentano -, um ihn entscheidend zu vertiefen und zu differenzieren. Dabei wird es in Zukunft zu fortwährenden Wechselbeziehungen zwischen Hermeneutik und Phänomenologie kommen.

Die Komplexität dieser Orientierungslage im 19. Jahrhundert könnte Anlass zu einem Skeptizismus sein, wie wir ihn heute am Beispiel der Postmoderne und des Poststrukturalismus finden. Für die akademische Philosophie des 19. Jahrhunderts ist - bei aller Einsicht in den Aspektreichtum der Philosophie- und Wissenschaftskultur - gleichwohl das Bemühen charakteristisch, solche Vielfalt von Motiven und Perspektiven rational diskussionsfähig zu halten - im Rahmen einer lebensfähigen und praktizierbaren Kultur. Das zeigen Werke wie die 1840 bis 1870 in drei Auflagen erschienenen ‚Logischen Untersuchungen' von A. Trendelenburg und das zwischen 1856 bis in die zwanziger Jahre dieses Jahrhunderts in sechs Auflagen erschienene dreibändige Werk Rudolph Hermann Lotzes ‚Mirkokosmus. Ideen zur Naturgeschichte und Geschichte der Menschheit. Versuch einer Anthropologie' (3 Bde. 1856/58/64). Obwohl Trendelenburg seine ‚Logischen Untersuchungen' als wissenschaftstheoretische Untersuchungen zugleich auch

[21] Vgl. E.W. Orth: *Von der Erkenntnistheorie zur Kulturphilosophie. Studien zu Ernst Cassirers Philosophie der symbolischen Formen*, Würzburg 1996.

als Fundamentalphilosophie und Metaphysik bezeichnet und obwohl Lotze zwei ‚Metaphysiken' geschrieben hat, versuchen doch beide, eine von der Erfahrung isolierte und durch vorausgesetzte Formbegriffe festgelegte Metaphysik zu verabschieden. Im Mittelpunkt ihres Denkens steht der Bezug auf die Tatsächlichkeit. Freilich wird diese Tatsächlichkeit entschiedener durchdacht und erwogen, als es in den formierten Empirismen der Fall ist. Denn solche Tatsächlichkeit steht immer unter der Perspektive, daß sie Tatsächlichkeit für eine andere, eigentümliche Tatsächlichkeit ist, nämlich den orientierungsbedürftigen und orientierungsfähigen Menschen. Deshalb arbeitet Trendelenburg ‚über den letzten Unterschied der philosophischen Systeme' (1847), eine Abhandlung, die entscheidende Auswirkungen auf Diltheys Konzeption von Weltanschauungstypen hat; und deshalb diskutiert Lotze die Möglichkeit einer Wirklichkeitslehre am Beispiel von ‚Ansichten,' die über die Wirklichkeit geschichtlich vorliegen.

Neben ihrer Kritik an der Philosophie Hegels, der für beide ein großer Philosoph bleibt, steht bei Trendelenburg und Lotze die Auseinandersetzung mit Herbart, dessen Konstruktionen zwar kritisiert werden, dessen Rolle aber für die Eröffnung eines über den deutschen Idealismus hinausführenden Weges der Erfahrungsanalyse gewürdigt wird. Die unterschwellige Wirkung der Herbartschen Philosophie, die im 19. Jahrhundert zunächst eine bemerkenswerte Aufnahme in Österreich fand, ist heute noch sowohl bei Freud als auch bei Heidegger nachweisbar. Der Mechanismus des Psychischen als eines Systems der ‚Hemmung,' ‚Förderung' und ‚Verdichtung' von Vorstellungsmassen ist formal prägend für Freuds psycho-analytisches Modell. Der Herbartsche Begriff der ‚Störung' wirkt nach in Heideggers Gedanken der ‚Störung des Bewandtniszusammenhangs' als eines Motivs der Entfaltung des verstehenden Daseins. Auch die Geschichtlichkeit der Metaphysik als ein fundamentales Geschehen wird bereits von Herbart betont. Herbarts Formel ‚soviel Schein soviel Sein' ist im 20. Jahrhundert nicht nur für die Phänomenologie zur stillen Devise geworden.

Besonders aber einige jüngere Vertreter aus der Herbart-Schule gewinnen eine entscheidende Bedeutung für die philosophischen Aufgabestellungen des 20. Jahrhunderts: Heymann Steinthal (1823-1899) eröffnet mit seinen Studien zur Sprachwissenschaft neue Methoden für eine konkretere Erfahrung des menschlichen Geistes - mit der gleichzeitigen Möglichkeit rationalerer Stukturierung. Er greift dabei auch auf das Werk Wilhelm von Humboldts zurück.[22] Moritz Lazarus (1824-1903) bearbeitet neben einer Erforschung des Verhältnisses von ‚Erscheinung' und ‚Seele' das Problem der Mentalitätsgeschichte unter dem Titel ‚Über die Ideen in der Geschichte'

[22]Die Humboldt-Renaissance führt aber zu einer entscheidenden Vertiefung der sprachphilosophischen Interessen im 20. Jahrhundert - mit einer Vorwegnahme des sogenannten ‚linguistic turn.'

(1865).[23] Beide wirken außer-ordentlich stark auf Dilthey. Zwischen 1860 und 1890 erscheinen zwanzig Bände ihrer ‚Zeitschrift für Völkerpsychologie und Sprachwissenschaft,' in welcher Hermann Cohen 1871 seine erste Neukantische Arbeit publiziert, die sich mit Kuno Fischers und Adolf Trendelenburgs Streit über die Apriorirtät des Kantischen Raumbegriffs befaßt. Die ‚Zeitschrift für Völkerpsychologie' kann auch als ein erster Reflex europäischer Selbstkritik angesehen werden, als ein Aufbrechen des Problems, das man heute unter dem Titel ‚Euro-Zentrismus' und ‚Logo-Zentrismus' behandelt.

Es wäre eine reizende Aufgabe, zu zeigen, mit welcher kritischen Umsicht und mit welch präzisem und konkretem Erfahrungsbezug vor allem Trendelenburg und Lotze in ihren jeweiligen Werken, den ‚Logischen Untersuchungen' und dem ‚Mikrokosmus,' eine zusammenhängende und bilanzierende Besinnung auf all jene verschiedenartigen Motive versucht haben. Das ist im einzelnen innerhalb eines begrenzten Essays jedoch nicht möglich. Trendelenburgs ‚Logische Untersuchungen' sind durchaus keine Logik im spezielleren Sinne, weder in dem der damaligen noch in dem der heutigen Logiken. Und auch Lotzes ‚Mikrokosmus' ist keine Anthropologie als Disziplin. Logische, resp. anthropologische Fragestellungen dienen hier eher als eine Art Fluchtpunkt für eine grundlegende Diskussion möglicher Orientierung. Es handelt sich eher um Erwägungen über die Tragfähigkeit wissenschaftlicher Projekte überhaupt.

Trendelenburg stellt dabei die Begriffe von ‚Bewegung' und ‚Zweck' in den Mittelpunkt. Von hier aus versucht er das Kategorienproblem, das er an anderer Stelle - ausgehend von Aristoteles - historisch gründlich untersucht hat, in seinen gegenwärtigen Möglichkeiten zu bestimmen. In der zweiten und dritten Auflage der ‚Logischen Untersuchungen' findet man so auch folgerichtig eine Anwendung dieser Kategorialforschung. Trendelenburg setzt sich hier auf der Grundlage einer differenzierten Handhabung des Zweckbegriffs mit der damals neuen wissenschaftlichen Richtung des Darwinismus - vor allem mit dessen deutschen Vertretern - auseinander. Es gelingt Trendelenburg, einen positiven, empirischen und methodischen Darwinismus, den er bei Darwin selbst sieht, von einem verkehrten und parametaphysischen zu unterscheiden, wie man ihn im sogenannten deutschen Monismus vorfindet (z.B. bei Ernst Haeckel). Trendelenburgs Handhabung des Zweckbegriffs muß man als eine ganz entscheidende Vorbereitung für die Entwicklung des Sinnbegriffes ansehen, wie er bei Philosophen wie E. Cassirer oder H. Plessner im 20. Jahrhundert ausgearbeitet wird.

Lotzes philosophisches Grundmotiv ist das, was er die ‚geistige Regsamkeit' nennt, mit welcher er zunächst die Fähigkeit des Menschen zu beschrei-

[23]Zur Rolle dieser Geschichtskonzeption und ihrer impliziten Auswirkung im 20. Jahrhundert vgl. Karl-Heinz Lembeck: Platon in Marburg. Platonrezeption und Philosophiegeschichtsphilosophie bei Cohen und Natorp, Würzburg 1994.

ben versucht, Erscheinungen erscheinen zu lassen. Diese ‚Regsamkeit‘ ist aber bereits in jedem organischen Leben, im Organismus, angelegt. Aus diesem Grundmotiv der Regsamkeit entwickelt Lotze die Begriffe ‚Wirkung‘ und ‚Wechselwirkung‘, den er in den verschiedensten Bereichen der Wirklichkeit - gleichsam in unterschiedlichen Aggregatzuständen - zu bestimmen versucht. Fundament jeder Wirkung und Wechselwirkung ist die lebendige Wirksamkeit und Leidensfähigkeit des erlebenden Menschen. Trotz des Eigenwertes des Geistigen, den Lotze fordert, kann er damit so doch etwas wie das Projekt einer ‚Mechanik der Gesellschaft‘ - also eine Soziologie - empfehlen, ähnlich wie Trendelenburg die empirische Forschung Darwins im Rahmen seines eigenen Zweckdenkens positiv zu würdigen wußte.

Der Mensch ist für Trendelenburg und für Lotze das Wesen, das nicht nur die Natur zu erkennen sucht, sondern auch innerhalb dieser Natur steht, obwohl die letzte Bestimmung seines Erkennens und seines Wollens keinem Naturalismus zugänglich ist. Es sind diese Thesen, die im 20. Jahrhundert auf Philosophen wie Max Scheler, Ernst Cassirer, Helmuth Plessner und Arnold Gehlen wie Herausforderungen gewirkt haben, auf die sie neue Antworten zu geben versuchten, ohne sich den Rahmenbedingungen, die das 19. Jahrhundert gesetzt hat, eigentlich entziehen zu können.

Man kann auch ganz gegenwärtige Betrachtungsweisen und Problemstellungen bei Trendelenburg und Lotze erkennen - sowohl was die Formulierung der Probleme als auch ihre Diskussion betrifft. Ich will zum Abschluß zwei solcher Problemtypen - in heutiger Terminologie - nennen:

1. die Unterscheidung von Metawissenschaft und Basiswissenschaft,

2. die Unterscheidung von universalem Diskurs und Diskurspluralität bis hin zum gegenseitigen Ausschluß der Diskurse.

1. Bei der Unterscheidung von Metawissenschaft und Basiswissenschaft handelt es sich darum, daß unsere wissenschaftliche Forschung und unser wissenschaftlicher Disput sich in zwei Richtungen bewegen. Man beansprucht *einmal* die Möglichkeit, die Wissenschaften umgreifend mit Hilfe strukturierender Funktionsenergien zu umfassen und zu beurteilen. Solche Funktionsenergien manifestieren sich in den Fähigkeiten, die wir mal ‚Reflexion‘ mal ‚Besinnung‘ nennen. Das Modell solcher Funktionsenergien und seine Begründung, die meist zirkuläre Selbstbegründung ist, nennt man gerne Metawissenschaft. Die Instrumentierung erfolgt oft durch elaborierte Logiken. Man beruft sich zum anderen auf paradigmatische Sachverhalte oder Einstellungen, aus denen sich fundierend und genetisch alle übrigen Wissenschaften verständlich machen lassen. Als solche paradigmatische Basen können z.B. u.a. das ‚Biologische‘ und das ‚Ökonomische‘ dienen. Den Typ einer solchen paradigmatischen Wissenschaft nennen wir Basis-Wissenschaft. Beide Typen - Basis-Wissenschaft und Meta-Wissenschaft - verbinden sich nicht selten wechselweise bis zur Unkenntlichkeit der Einzelmomente. Ein prominentes Beispiel für eine solche Verbindung von Basis-

und Meta-Wissenschaft ist im 19. Jahrhundert die Handhabung der Psychologie als Erkenntnistheorie.

Bereits Trendelenburg und Lotze haben erkannt, daß die Alternative ‚Basis-Wissenschaft - Meta-Wissenschaft' als echte Wahlmöglichkeit gar nicht besteht, sondern daß die Spannung beider Orientierungstypen ausgehalten werden muß und dauernd durch die Forschung neu zu adjustieren ist. Im 19. Jahrhundert wurde dies vor allem an der scheinbar ausweglosen Gegenüberstellung von Idealismus und Naturalismus, resp. Materialismus diskutiert.

2. Die Gegenüberstellung eines universalen, umfassenden Diskurses und der Vielfalt sich gegeneinander ausschließender Diskurse können wir heute sehr sinnfällig in Philosophien wie der Frankfurter Schule einerseits und dem Poststrukturalismus etwa Lyotards andererseits studieren. Auch diese Alternative ist in der akademischen Philosophie des 19. Jahrhunderts - bei Trendelenburg, Lotze und Dilthey - gründlich durchdacht worden. Ich erinnere hier an die Analysen der Weltanschauungen und Weltansichten. Die Erforschung dieser Problematik im 19. Jahrhundert hat aber gerade zur Relativierung der genannten Alternative geführt, so daß sie heute eher veraltet scheint, auch wenn sie unverdrossen wiederholt wird.

Der 16. Deutsche Kongreß für Philosophie, der im September 1993 in Berlin stattfand, hatte den Titel ‚Neue Realitäten. Herausforderung der Philosophie.' Ob es sich bei der ‚Herausforderung der Philosophie' um einen genitivus subjectivus oder einen genitivus objectivus handelt, läßt die bloße Lektüre des Titels offen. Auf dem Hintergrund der Philosophie des 19. Jahrhunderts kann man allerdings hinsichtlich sogenannter neuer Realitäten die Frage stellen: Kennen wir eigentlich schon die alten Realitäten? Und wenn wir sie kennen - was heißt es eigentlich, Wirklichkeit aufzufassen und zu erkennen? Welche Rolle spielt dabei beispielsweise die Zeitlichkeit des menschlichen Bewußtseins und Erlebens, d.h. der menschlichen Erfahrung, die sich stets in den Kategorien von Bewegung, Regsamkeit, Wechselwirkung und Zweckhaftigkeit entfaltet? Es ist offenkundig, daß beispielsweise Husserls Analysen der immanenten Zeitlichkeit, der kontinuierlichen Synthesis des Wahrnehmungsbewußtseins und der immanenten Teleologie der Bewußtseinssphäre sowie der Erfahrung als noematischer Sinnbildung an diese Kategorien anschließen.

Was der Anspruch von Wirklichkeitsverständnis bedeutet, das hat die akademische Philosophie des 19. Jahrhunderts mit einer Gründlichkeit und Subtilität bearbeitet, daß es sich auch noch im ausgehenden 20. Jahrhundert lohnen würde, darauf wieder zurückzukommen; zumal dieses 20. Jahrhundert ohnehin - ob es dies merkt oder nicht - von dem 19. Jahrhundert in ganz außerordentlicher Weise beeinflußt und geprägt ist.

Quantum Phenomenology

Harry P. Reeder

I. Introduction

The early twentieth century was an exciting time in both philosophy and physics. In some interesting ways the developments of physics and the phenomenological philosophy paralleled each other. Research in both physics and philosophy led from the taken-for-grantedness of the givenness of things in ordinary perception to talk of new sorts of objects, objects requiring new modes of looking, new modes of thinking, and new senses of "*die Sachen selbst.*"[1] This essay will explore these parallels and place them in their historical contexts, in order to show that phenomenology, far from being the unscientific idealism which is its all-too-common interpretation,[2] is in fact a rigorous scientific philosophy[3] whose development was demanded by the relevant evidence, just as quantum mechanics is the result of rigorous scientific development demanded by relevant evidence. In both cases, the new evidence led to profound and far-reaching questions, with implications for both epistemology and ontology. In particular, the development of the notion of 'quantum' in physics has some interesting parallels with the development of a new sort of "empirical evidence" in phenomenol-

---

[1]For a helpful discussion of *die Sachen selbst* in Husserl, see John Sallis, "The Identities of the Things Themselves," in Kah Kyung Cho, ed., *Philosophy and Science in Phenomenological Perspective*, (Phaenomenologica, no. 95), (Boston: Martinus Nijhoff, 1984), pp. 183-194. I thank Denny Bradshaw for his comments on a draft of this essay.

[2]See, e.g., Paul Ricoeur, *Husserl: An Analysis of His Philosophy*, (Northwestern University Studies in Phenomenology and Existential Philosophy), (Evanston, IL: Northwestern University Press, 1967), pp. 24, 82-85.

[3]Charles W. Harvey argues that, " ... the entire development of Husserl's thought can be read as an attempt to achieve this theoretical understanding of natural science and its objectivistic achievements." *Husserl's Phenomenology and the Foundations of Natural Science*, (Series in Continental Thought), (Athens, OH.: Ohio University Press, 1989), p. 8. See also Theodore J. Kisiel, "Phenomenology as the Science of Science," in Joseph J. Kockelmans and Theodore J. Kisiel, *Phenomenology and the Natural Sciences: Essays and Translations*, (Northwestern University Studies in Phenomenology and Existential Philosophy), (Evanston: Northwestern University Press, 1970), pp. 5-44.

ogy, which Husserl calls "categorial"[4] or "eidetic intuition,"[5] or as Richard Cobb-Stevens calls it, "discernment of essence."[6] This evidence, Husserl argues, can be achieved only through a transcendental-phenomenological methodology. This is one of Husserl's most radical and contested claims. The present argument attempts to establish that Husserl's transcendental phenomenology is in fact an empirically demonstrated feature of the understanding of the world.

Are we arguing that there is no difference between phenomenology and quantum mechanics? Of course not – they are different fields of investigation (different parts of a regional ontology). Nonetheless, they are both examples of scientific thinking, and it is to the interesting epistemological, methodological, and ontological parallels between these two parts of science that we are drawing attention. Central to these parallels is a fundamental change in the understanding of "empirical evidence," and the "subjective" and "objective" elements of scientific research in both scientific and philosophical thought in the twentieth century.

Developments in quantum mechanics led scientists to a sort of crisis in understanding the relations between physical theory and the world, calling into question such basic scientific ideas as the notions of "particle," "wave," and "causation." In phenomenology, Husserl showed that the world of everyday experience, the *Lebenswelt*, had become so intertwined

---

[4]Edmund Husserl, *Logical Investigations*, 2 vols., tr. J. N. Findlay (New York: Routledge & Kegan Paul, 1970), Vol. II, p. 832; Husserl, *Logische Untersuchungen*: Zweiter Band, Zweiter Teil, ed. Ursula Panzer, (Husserliana, XIX/2), (The Hague: Martinus Nijhoff, 1984), p. 731. Hereinafter cited as *LI*. See also Husserl, *Cartesian Meditations: An Introduction to Phenomenology*, tr. Dorion Cairns, (The Hague: Martinus Nijhoff, 1970), p. 78; Husserl, *Cartesianische Meditationen und Pariser Vorträge*, ed. S. Strasser (Husserliana, I), (The Hague: Martinus Nijhoff, 1973), p. 111, hereinafter cited as *CM*; and Husserl, *The Idea of Phenomenology*, tr. Wm. P. Alston and George Nakhnikian, (The Hague: Martinus Nijhoff, 1964), p. 56; Husserl, *Die Idee der Phänomenologie : Fünf Vorlesungen*, ed.Walter Biemel, (Husserliana, II), (The Hague: Martinus Nijhoff, 1973), p. 71.

[5]*CM*, p. 72; Hua. I, p. 106. See also Husserl, *Ideas Pertaining to a Pure Phenomenology and to a Phenomenological Philosophy: First Book; General Introduction to a Pure Phenomenology*, tr. Fred Kersten, (Edmund Husserl: Collected Works, II), (The Hague: Martinus Nijhoff, 1982), p. 186; Husserl, *Ideen zu einer reinen Phänomenologie und phänomenologischen Philosophie. Erstes Buch, Allgemeine Einführung in die reine Phänomenologie*, ed. Karl Schuhmann, (Husserliana III, 1 and 2), (The Hague: Martinus Nijhoff, 1976), III/1, p. 175. Hereinafter referred to as *Ideas*.

[6]Richard Cobb-Stevens, "Husserl on Eidetic Intuition and Historical Interpretation," *American Catholic Philosophical Quarterly* LXVI, no. 2(1992), pp. 261-275. I prefer this phrase because it reflects the fact that in phenomenology "intuition of essence" is an achievement based in careful attention to intersubjective method, rather than some sort of immediate "presentation," a widespread misinterpretation of Husserl which sees his phenomenology as merely a form of Cartesianism.

with scientific ideas that it had led to a crisis – a crisis of humanity's self-understanding in the face of an increasingly estranged and estranging view of the world of nature.[7] Husserl demonstrated that the relationship between scientific and "ordinary" ideas led to a self-concealing "scientism."[8] Just as Husserl was led to a hermeneutic of scientific knowledge,[9] physicists were led philosophically to re-evaluate ordinary experience and its relation to scientific data, laws, and theories.[10]

Insofar as phenomenology arose from Husserl's concerns with "theory of science" (*Wissenschaftslehre*)[11] and was a sustained attempt to develop a "philosophy as a strict science,"[12] Husserl's phenomenology may be characterized as, amongst other things, philosophy of science. As a philosophy of science, at the methodological level, phenomenology includes a philosophy of physics. Both phenomenology and physics are the result of rigorous and far-reaching studies into *die Sachen selbst*, the former at the level of the interplay between concepts, experience, and self-understanding, and the latter at the level of using theory and experiments to understand nature.

---

[7] Husserl, *The Crisis of European Sciences and Transcendental Phenomenology: An Introduction to Phenomenological Philosophy*, tr. David Carr, (Evanston, IL: Northwestern University Press, 1970), §§5-6, pp. 11-18; Husserl, *Die Krisis der europäischen Wissenschaften und die Transzendentale Phänomenologie: Eine Einleitung in die phänomenologische Philosophie*, ed. Walter Biemel, 2d ed., (Husserliana, VI), (The Hague: Martinus Nijhoff, 1976), pp. 9-14. Hereinafter cited as *Crisis*. Cf. Theodore J. Kisiel, "Phenomenology as the Science of Science," p. 44; and Theodore J. Kisiel, "Husserl on the History of Science," in Joseph J. Kockelmans and Theodore J. Kisiel, *Phenomenology and the Natural Sciences: Essays and Translations*, (Northwestern University Studies in Phenomenology and Existential Philosophy), (Evanston: Northwestern University Press, 1970), pp. 68-90, p. 76; and Joseph J. Kockelmans, "The Mathematization of Nature In Husserl's Last Publication, Krisis," in Joseph J. Kockelmans and Theodore J. Kisiel, *Phenomenology and the Natural Sciences: Essays and Translations*, (Northwestern University Studies in Phenomenology and Existential Philosophy), (Evanston: Northwestern University Press, 1970), pp. 45-67, especially pp. 47-48.

[8] Joseph J. Kockelmans notes that what Husserl calls 'objectivism' is today often called "scientism." Both refer to the view that natural science is the one proper way to approach all questions of nature and humanity. "The Mathematization of Nature In Husserl's Last Publication, Krisis," p. 47.

[9] Theodore J. Kisiel, "Husserl on the History of Science," pp. 70, 83-84.

[10] Heisenberg, *Physics and Beyond: Encounters and Conversations*, (World Perspectives, Vol. XLII), (N.Y.: Harper & Row, 1971), Ch. 10, pp. 117-124, Ch. 20, pp. 237-247.

[11] *LI, I, p. 60; Hua. XVIII, p. 26.*

[12] See Edmund Husserl "Philosophy as Rigorous Science," in *Phenomenology and the Crisis of Philosophy*, tr. Quentin Lauer, (N.Y.: Harper & Row, 1965, pp. 71-147; Husserl, *Aufsätze und Vorträge* (1911-1921), eds. Thomas Nenon and Hans Rainer Sepp, (Husserliana, Bd. XXV), (Dordrecht: Martinus Nijhoff Publishers, 1987), pp. 3-62. First published as "Philosophie als strenge Wissenschaft," *Logos*, I (1910-11), pp. 289-341.

As such, physics and phenomenology are very different forms of investigation. Nonetheless, both have required methodological decisions based on seemingly paradoxical evidence. And both led to views of the world that many find challenging, in large part because they require new methodologies to deal with new sorts of evidence, methodologies that raise serious philosophical questions.

The immediate background of quantum physics was a growing concern among physicists that experimental results stemming from the nineteenth century and the beginning of the twentieth century were strikingly paradoxical, demanding explanations that seemed to elude explanation by the theories and methods of classical physics. The results seemed to indicate that light came in the form of particles, particles that traveled in trajectories that could be affected by magnetic fields.[13] Nevertheless, there were also experimental results that seemed to establish that light took the form of waves, which could interfere with each other in ways well understood from wave theory.[14] Surely, they thought, light cannot be both a wave and a particle; in fact, nothing can have such properties. Tables and chairs, rocks and sound, cannot be both waves and particles. Why, or how, could light be any different? Surely, the line of thought went, a scientific method that led us to understanding the composition of tables, chairs, rocks and sounds, should not lead to objects that defy such theories. Thus, a primary concern of the early theorists of quantum physics was, "the search for a consistent means of linking the everyday world of the laboratory with the strange new world of the minuscule atom."[15]

The immediate philosophical background of phenomenology was the turn-of-the-century groundswell of positivism, with its insistence upon limiting philosophy to the methods of natural science. This view grew in popularity despite bitter disputes in the nineteenth century with thinkers like Dilthey,[16] who insisted that philosophy, like all the *Geisteswissenschaften*, requires a different method, because it deals with human beings that cannot be reduced to natural objects. After a serious attempt to work within descriptive psychology in founding mathematics,[17] Husserl came to agree

---

[13]For a very clear and non-technical account of this, see Tony Hey and Patrick Walters, *The Quantum Universe*, (Cambridge: Cambridge U. Press, 1987), Ch. 1, pp. 1-12. A more technical, but still relatively clear, version can be found in Ch. 1, pp. 1-37 of Jim Baggott, *The Meaning of Quantum Theory*, (Oxford: Oxford University Press, 1992).

[14]Emilio Segr; *From X-Rays to Quarks: Modern Physicists and their Discoveries*, (San Francisco: W.H. Freeman & Co., 1980), p. 150.

[15]David C. Cassidy, "Heisenberg, Uncertainty, and the Quantum Revolution," *Scientific American*, May, 1992, pp. 106-112, see p. 106.

[16]See. e.g., Wilhelm Dilthey, *Selected Works, Volume I: Introduction to the Human Sciences*, eds. Rudolf A. Makkreel and Frithjof Rodi, (Princeton, N.J.: Princeton University Press, 1989), pp. 66-72.

[17]Edmund Husserl, *Philosophie der Arithmetik: Psychologische und logische*

that humans could not be reduced to natural objects, and in fact launched an all-out attack upon the naturalistic metaphysical assumptions underlying positivism in general and psychologism in particular.[18] Surely, Husserl thought, human consciousness is not just another "thing" in the world in the same way as natural objects such as tables, chairs, and atoms. Husserl's deliberations on this problem led to his famous "paradox of subjectivity," according to which human subjectivity is both a subject for the world, and an object in the world.[19] And what about numbers and logical forms? Surely, they, too, must differ from both natural objects and consciousness. However, Husserl was determined to find the foundations of logic and mathematics[20], seeing that they are principles of the foundation of the sciences, and that the current positivistic methodologies of the sciences cannot establish this foundation because of unquestioned prejudices and assumptions, assumptions that kept thinkers from pursuing the phenomenological

---

Untersuchungen. (Husserliana, XII), (The Hague: Martinus Nijhoff, 1970).

[18]This was a major argument of the Prolegomena to Husserl's *LI.* Husserl's attacks upon psychologism stem in part from the fact that he had championed the view himself in his researches in and for his *Philosophie der Arithmetik.* See *LI,* I, pp. 42-43; Hua. XVIII, pp. 6-7.

[19]See *Ideas,* §53, pp. 124-127; Hua. III/1, pp. 116-118; *Crisis,* §§53-54, pp. 178-186; Hua. VI, pp. 182-190. See also Brett Jackson, "Critique of De Boer and the Paradox of Subjectivity," *Journal of the British Society for Phenomenology,* 18, no. 1(Jan., 1987), pp. 38-48. Jackson defends Husserl's interpretation of the paradox, replying to critiques by Theodore De Boer (*The Development of Husserl's Thought,* tr. Theodore Platinga, (The Hague: Martinus Nijhoff, 1978), Paul Ricoeur (*Husserl: An Analysis of His Philosophy,* tr. Edward Ballard and Lester Embree, (Evanston: Northwestern University Press, 1967), pp. 4, 10, 88-89), Roman Ingarden (*On the Motives Which Led Husserl to Transcendental Idealism,* tr. Arnor Hannibalsson (The Hague: Martinus Nijhoff, 1975), pp. 58, 62, 65), Leszek Kolakowski (*Husserl and the Search for Certitude,* (New Haven: Yale University Press, 1975), pp. 69-73), and James Collins (*The Existentialists,* (Chicago: Henry Regnery Co., 1952), pp. 34-37). James C. Morrison ("Husserl's *Crisis*: Reflections on the Relationship of Philosophy and History," *Philosophy and Phenomenological Research* 37(March 1977), pp. 312-330) argues that Husserl is still too Cartesian to overcome the paradox. John Burkey ("Descartes, skepticism, and Husserl's hermeneutic practice," *Husserl Studies* 7(1990), pp. 1-27) interprets Husserl as beyond Descartes in the sense that, "Transcendental subjectivity makes no appearance in the world; only human subjectivity is both a subject for the world and an object in the world," p. 14.

[20]See Husserl, *Formal and Transcendental Logic,* tr. Dorion Cairns, (The Hague: Martinus Nijhoff, 1969), Introduction, pp. 1-17; Husserl, *Formale und Transzendentale Logik: Versuch einer Kritik der logischen Vernunft,* ed. Paul Janssen, (Husserliana, XVII), (The Hague: Martinus Nijhoff, 1974), pp. 5-21, hereinafter cited as FTL; Husserl, *Experience and Judgment: Investigations in a Genealogy of Logic,* ed. L. Landgrebe, tr. J.S. Churchill and Karl Ameriks, (Evanston, IL: Northwestern University Press, 1973), pp. 11-13; Husserl, *Erfahrung und Urteil: Untersuch. zur Genealogie der Logik,* ed. L. Landgrebe, (Hamburg: Claassen & Goverts 1948), pp. 1-4, hereinafter cited as *EJ/EU.*

direction of research that is required to solve the problem empirically.

The following discussion will focus upon seven interrelated themes in both quantum physics and phenomenology: new research puzzles, new types of objects of investigation required to solve these puzzles, new methodological processes required to identify and investigate the new objects of investigation, shifts in language and meaning required by the new methods and discoveries, a re-thinking of normative theories (especially mathematics) and their roles in scientific methodology, the "new place" for the observer in the scientific system, and the ontological implications of the new researches. These seven interrelated themes help to show a remarkable methodological similarity of twentieth-century developments in both physics and phenomenological philosophy.

II. New Puzzles

In both physics and phenomenology new puzzles were brought to light by scientific and philosophical developments in the nineteenth and early twentieth centuries. In physics, the study of light uncovered both particle-like and wave-like behavior of light passed through single and double slits in an opaque barrier and recorded on photographic plates beyond the slits. Light passing through a single slit propagates like individual particles hitting a photographic plate placed behind the slit, opposite from the light source. This was taken to be clear evidence that the long-standing battle was over between scientists believing that light was a particle and those believing it to be wave-like, with the former scientists having been vindicated. However, other related experiments passed light to a photographic plate after passing through two slits-and this light propagated in a classic wave-like pattern. Having been confirmed and re-confirmed, these experiments left physics in a quandary. The natures of particles and waves are both well-understood and quite distinct. Unable to reject either form of experimental evidence, physicists were clearly puzzled. Nothing in classical physics had prepared them for these paradoxical results. As will be seen below, many other baffling features emerged in the experiments of quantum mechanics, features that led to the questioning of many foundational assumptions of classical physics, such as the objective determinacy and locality of physical objects.

By the late nineteenth century, the success of the natural sciences had had a tremendous influence upon Western culture generally, and upon its philosophy in particular. The rise of positivism had led more and more philosophers to decide that the (one) method of empirical science should be the test of all philosophical questions, at least in the long run.[21] The

[21] Auguste Comte, *Introduction to Positive Philosophy*, ed. and tr. Frederick Ferré, (Indianapolis: Hackett Publishing Company, 1988), pp. 12-14. Hereinafter referred to as IPP.

development of positivism has not been without its ironies. Many recognize Hume's "mitigated" sceptical philosophy[22] as an important historical root of logical positivism. Hume nonetheless had a wider notion of evidence than was adopted by the positivists. Hume recognized both "inward sentiments" and "outward sentiments," appealing to evidence that came to be called "private" and "public," respectively, in the twentieth century. Some positivists, however (especially Carnap and Neurath) had come to reject appeals to "inner" or "private" evidence, assuming that such appeals would soon be replaced by scientific studies of the brain.[23] Comte had urged earlier that introspective findings should not even be considered by serious philosophers: "I must be content with indicating the principal consideration which proves clearly that this pretended direct contemplation of the mind by itself is a pure illusion."[24]

Despite this "outward focus" of positivism, with its resultant behavioristic trend, Brentano, an empirical psychologist,[25] sought in the late nineteenth century to re-instate the importance of inner phenomena, although insisting that they are intrinsically and essentially related to "objects" through *intentionality.*[26]

Husserl, a student of Brentano, undertook to establish the foundation of logic and mathematics in descriptive (empirical in Brentano's sense) psychology.[27] The results of this investigation he published as *Philosophie der Arithmetik.*[28] However, despite many important results that can be retained from this work, Husserl concluded that this enterprise could not be

---

[22] *An Enquiry Concerning Human Understanding*, ed. Eric Steinberg, (Indianapolis: Hackett Publishing Company), p. 11.

[23] See, e.g., Rudolf Carnap, "Psychology in Physical Language," in A.J. Ayer, ed., *Logical Positivism*, (Library of Philosophical Movements), (N.Y.: Free Press, 1959), 165-198, in which Carnap sets out ". . . to establish the thesis that *every sentence of psychology may be formulated in physical language*," p.165. (Originally published in *Erkenntnis* III(1932/33).

[24] Comte, IPP, pp. 20-22, quote from p. 20.

[25] Franz Brentano, *Psychology from an Empirical Standpoint*, Ed. Oskar Kraus, Eng. Edition Ed. Linda L. McAlister, (International Library of Philosophy and Scientific Method), (N.Y.: Humanities Press, 1973). (First published in 1874.) It should be noted here that the conception of an "empirical psychology" was very much under discussion at this historical point; some empiricists would resist calling Brentano an empiricist because of his focus on intentionality. Nonetheless, he and many of his students saw his work as a furthering of the cause of an empirical psychology.

[26] Ibid., p. 89.

[27] For Husserl's debt to Brentano, see *Crisis*, p. 298; Hua. VI, p. 346.

[28] See note 17, above. For an insightful critical discussion of the relation between Husserl's research in the *Philosophie der Arithmetik*, and its relation to his later phenomenology, see José Huertas-Jourda, *On the Threshold of Phenomenology: a Study of Edmund Husserl's Philosophie der Arithmetik*, Ph.D. Dissertation, New York University, 1969.

fulfilled. In order to deal with the essentially normative and non-sensory nature of the presentation of logical and mathematical form, Husserl recognized that a new form of evidence – evidence of a *new empirical kind* – was required. These further insights led to his rejection of psychologism in volume I of the *Logical Investigations*, and to his development in volume II of a new methodology, called "phenomenological reduction," to ground formal or essential elements of logic and mathematics in human experience.[29] In essence, Husserl, like twentieth-century physicists, was led by evidence to see the need to extend the traditional methodology (in Husserl's case positivism) to a point where the ruling methodology itself seemed to be challenged by its own application.

III. New Objects

The objects uncovered in physics were doubly paradoxical. Not only were results obtained that were at best puzzling and at worst self defeating, but these results were derived through the careful application of well established methodologies of classical physics. The struggle to find an interpretation for these new data led to frank discussion of a fundamentally new type of object. Researchers for a time used the metaphorical word "wavicle," eventually calling this new form of things "quanta," to refer to objects that seemed to be *both* particles and waves. In addition to acting both like particles and waves, quantum objects also exhibit even stranger properties, such as "objective indefiniteness, objective chance, objective probability and nonlocality."[30]

Perhaps the strangest objects in the quantum universe are virtual particles, the force-transferring objects (bosons) and the objects that are not even there-but then are there, and then again are not there. These short-lived quantum particles challenge our understanding of what an "object" is more than any others. According to Heisenberg's uncertainty principle, not only can we not determine a quantum particle's precise position and momentum, the particle cannot *have* both properties at the same time. A more technical explanation of the uncertainty principle is:

> Briefly put, the uncertainty principle states that the simultaneous measurement of two so-called conjugate variables, such as the position and momentum of a moving particle, entails a necessary limitation on precision. The more precise the measurement of position, the more imprecise the measurement of the momentum, and vice versa. In the most extreme case, absolute precision of one variable would involve absolute imprecision regarding the other. This indeterminacy is not the fault of

[29] *LI*, Investigations V-VI.

[30] Abner Shimony, "The Reality of the Quantum World," *Scientific American*, January, 1988, pp. 46-53, see p. 50.

> the experimenter: it is a fundamental consequence of quantum equations and a feature of every quantum experiment.[31]

This has startling implications for the understanding of the "void" of space between planets, stars, galaxies, galaxy clusters, etc. In fact, because of the Heisenberg uncertainty principle there cannot, after all, be a void:

> So in empty space the field [actually fields in the plural, such as gravitational and electromagnetic fields] cannot be fixed at exactly zero, because then it would have both a precise value (zero) and a precise rate of change (also zero). There must be a certain minimum amount of uncertainty, or quantum fluctuations, in the value of the field. One can think of these fluctuations as pairs of particles of light or gravity that appear together at some time, move apart, and then come together again and annihilate each other. These particles are virtual particles like the particles that carry the gravitational force of the sun: unlike real particles, they cannot be observed directly with a particle detector. However, their indirect effects, such as small changes in the energy of electron orbits in atoms, can be measured and agree with the theoretical predictions to a remarkable degree of accuracy.[32]

Space has measurable physical properties:

> Space is not just the nothing between the earth and the stars. Nor is it simply the void between the electron and the atomic nucleus. It is a ubiquitous medium more resilient than rubber, more rigid than steel.[33]

The virtual particles seem not only to challenge our understanding of being, but also our understanding of the central theme of all scientific

---

[31]Cassidy, "Heisenberg, Uncertainty, and the Quantum Revolution," p. 106. According to the Copenhagen interpretation of quantum mechanics, the inability of achieving measurements of the conjugate variables (an epistemological claim) had the ontological implication of making such claims about quanta impossible. Some went further claiming that this was the way the quanta *really are* (an ontological claim). Early in the discussion, the "ontological irrelevance" of such (unprovable) claims was by no means accepted by all.

[32]Stephen Hawking, *A Brief History of Time: From the Big Bang to Black Holes*, (N.Y.: Bantum Books, 1988), pp. 105-106, my interpolation. See also Jonathan J. Halliwell, "Quantum Cosmology and the Creation of the Universe," *Scientific American*, December 1991, pp. 76-85, esp. p. 79; and Kip Thorne, *Black Holes & Time Warps: Einstein's Outrageous Legacy*, (Commonwealth Fund Book Program), (N.Y.: W.W. Norton & Company, 1994), pp. 430-431.

[33]Russell Ruthen, "Catching the Wave," *Scientific American*, March, 1992, pp. 90-99, quote from p. 90. See also John Gribbon, In *Search of Schrödinger's Cat: Quantum Physics and Reality*, (New York: Bantum Books, 1984), p. 201-202.

problems and discoveries, that "everything that happens, happens due to a cause." We will return to these issues in Section VII, below.

In philosophy, Husserl discovered that he could not ground the normative systems of mathematics and logic in descriptive psychology because of certain hidden "sensationalist"[34] presuppositions in scientific method as currently understood. Husserl came to see that a foundation of logic and mathematics was achievable, but only with a widening of the concept of "empirical evidence," one that recognized in experience the presentation of objects of consciousness that went beyond the presentations of the "outward" senses. Similarly, the appearance of eide in conscious acts of knowing raised ontological as well as epistemological questions. Like the physicists, Husserl had discovered that a foundational understanding of the law-like nature of science required a new openness toward "the things themselves." To refer to this wider form of empirical evidence, Husserl took the traditional term "intuition" and modified it to expand the Kantian concept (standing for a sensory perception) into a non-sensory "eidetic intuition," a new name for a newly discovered form of lived evidence.[35]

Like the quantum physicists, once Husserl was willing, because "forced by empirical evidence,"[36] to accept these new types of objects, he became more and more willing to accept the further experimental results resulting from their "empirical" (in both cases in a new, widened sense of the word) researches. In physics this led to the discovery of a whole range of quantum "particles," quantum forces, and measurable quantum effects. In phenomenology, the insight into eidetic intuition in logic and mathematics in the *Logical Investigations* led Husserl fairly quickly to see the much wider philosophical implications of this new sort of object, as published in the *Ideas*, and developed throughout his phenomenological career.

---

[34] *Crisis*, p. 298; Hua.VI, p.346.

[35] Of course, Husserl's eidetic intuition relates rather directly to many philosophical insights of the philosophic tradition, from Plato's *eidei* to Locke's abstraction of general terms. What is new in Husserl is the development of a method that facilitates the identification and description of eidetic objects in a way that does not restrict one to an ontological prejudice about what sort of object it is.

[36] Of course, because of the possibility of *ad hoc* interpretations, one can always cling to old ways of dealing with new evidence, as noted by both Popper and Kuhn. See Karl Popper, *Objective Knowledge: An Evolutionary Approach*, (Oxford: Oxford University Press, 1975), pp. 15-16, 192-194, 294-295; and Thomas S. Kuhn, *The Structure of Scientific Revolutions*, 2d ed., (International Encyclopedia of Unified Science), (Chicago: University of Chicago Press, 1970), pp. 77-80). Nonetheless, in the cases under investigation the belief in the "promise" of the new way of thinking about "seeing" the data led to important results. I am not ready to accept either Kuhn's incommensurability thesis (with its resultant radical relativism), or Popper's critical realism without knowing subjects, but to develop these arguments would take us too far afield from the present investigation.

IV. New Methods

As quantum physics and phenomenology developed, they required of their practitioners a shift in methodological focus. In both cases theoretical questions about the interplay of theories, objects, and methods of investigation resulted in a consciously more active (and thus, up to a point, rationalistic) role for the minds of investigators. In addition, the relation between scientific and philosophical research and everyday experience had to be reconsidered, albeit in different directions. In physics, researchers gradually accepted the famous Copenhagen interpretation of quantum mechanics, which essentially denied that the laws and phenomena of atomic physics could be discussed in the same terms as ordinary experience, because at the quantum level the world appears very different. Claims are only permitted *given* the researchers' observations and the particulars of their experimental apparatus.[37] The gap between physics and everyday thinking quickly grew so wide that laymen were discouraged from trying to grasp the new physics, with its more and more mathematical and counterintuitive models. Although "popular" versions of relativity and quantum physics appeared, scientists stressed the misleading nature of the analogies with everyday experience. Relativistic time was explained in terms of the "twin paradox," and quantum "wavicles" were called *quanta*, described as "localized energy waves," or "wave packets,"[38] even though quantum waves are extended infinitely in space-time until reacted upon by another particle.[39]

In quantum physics, the active role of the mind in forming theories, hypotheses, and models took to the forefront, leaving behind the more traditional empiricist claim that hypotheses somehow spring from theory-free data.[40] Experiments in quantum physics led leading physicists into discussions of ontology and epistemology, as they struggled to deal with the "fit" (or, perhaps better, lack of fit) between quantum mechanics and everyday experience.[41]

In phenomenology, Husserl saw the new method called the transcendental-phenomenological reduction as arriving at a new kind of object (*eidos*). In the process, Husserl changed the restrictive, "outward" sensory bias of the empirical tradition after Hume, and came to see greater and greater

---

[37] See Cassidy, "Heisenberg, Uncertainty, and the Quantum Revolution," p. 106, and also Shimony, "The Reality of the Quantum World," p. 52.

[38] Jim Baggott, *The Meaning of Quantum Theory*, pp. 25-26.

[39] See Shimony, "The Reality of the Quantum World," pp. 46-47.

[40] See, e.g., Francis Bacon, *The Great Instauration*, Part II, *The New Organon; or, True Directions concerning the Interpretation of Nature*, aphorism xi, p. 95, in Edwin A. Burtt ed., *The English Philosophers from Bacon to Mill*, (N.Y.: Modern Library, 1967).

[41] *Heisenberg, Physics and Beyond, pp. 40-41.*

epistemic and ontological implications of Brentano's focus upon the intentionality of conscious experience. Philosophically, empirical researchers after the Enlightenment had decided to follow a path restricted — either methodologically or ontologically — to sense data for its "empirical input." Husserl's attempt to found logic and mathematics upon the intentionally reflected data of sensation and of day-to-day introspection failed precisely with regard to the normative nature of logic and mathematics. Sense data can be found to be erroneous or misleading by future sense data (of course, organized and interpreted through theory); such a source cannot found the *a priori* and normative role that is required for the practical *use* of logic and mathematics in science and in everyday life.[42] Rather than give up the idea of such a normative function altogether, as is done in various forms of scientism, objectivism, pragmatism, naturalism, and "post-modernism,"[43] Husserl saw that such a foundation was possible, as long as one adapted the empirical method to include the relevant new form of data, the *eidei*, or objects of categorial or eidetic intuition.[44] Husserl actually could claim, and did claim, to be following in the empirical tradition while at the same time widening the notion of "empirical data." Thus, Husserl claimed his phenomenology to be a truer form of empiricism than that of many of his predecessors.[45] In the process, Husserl developed a radical new post-modern sense of both rationalism and empiricism through a descriptive method founded in the empirically discovered intentional nature of consciousness, in which the (inward) subject and the (outward) objects presented in lived experience are intentional correlates[46] or transcendental correlates.[47] The rationalistic element of phenomenology appears in its openness to the evident "reality" (in a sense to be clarified in a new form of regional ontology), of general, or universal objects of consciousness, a sense that Husserl gradually modified and qualified between his early and late thought. To be accurate, it should be noted that Locke tried to hold on to

---

[42] This is a central argument of the Prolegomena to the *Logical Investigations.*

[43] "Post-modernism" is a very vague phrase these days, usually used to refer to a plethora of more or less related forms of sceptical relativism. This is the sense in which it is being used here. Below, Husserl's thought will be characterized as a form of "post-modernism" (using the phrase more historically and programmatically than is often the case), a form that is neither sceptical nor relativistic, at least in the usual senses of the terms.

[44] Husserl regarded himself as a positivist up until the *Ideas.* See Edmund Husserl, *Introduction to the Logical Investigations*, tr. P.J. Bossert and C.H. Peters, ed. Eugen Fink, (The Hague: Martinus Nijhoff, 1975), p. xv, n. 14. See also *LI*, I, p. 226; Hua. XVIII, p. 231; *Crisis*, §§60-62, pp. 211-219, §§69-72, pp. 235-265; Hua. VI, pp. 215-222, 238-269; and *Ideas* (Kersten tr.), §§69-75, pp. 156-170; Hua. III/1, pp. 144-158.

[45] *CM*,§61, pp. 141-148; Hua. I, pp. 168-174.

[46] *CM*, p. 37; Hua. I, p. 75.

[47] *Crisis, p.181; Hua. VI. p.184*

a version of this rationalistic notion of "general ideas" through his theory of abstraction,[48] a theory that was roundly criticized by both Berkeley and Hume.[49] Both Berkeley's and Hume's critiques, along with Locke's view, all appealed to an "inspection of the mind,"[50] a view that came to be rejected by subsequent empiricists in their migration toward behaviorism.

The method Husserl claimed to be necessary properly to uncover the eidetic foundations of science, perception, the world, and indeed, all of human experience, is the transcendental-phenomenological reduction, especially the *eidetic reduction*,[51] achieved through a "free variation in phantasy,"[52] a method related both to Plato's dialectical training for uncovering the "world of being"[53] and Locke's theory of abstraction. Using the imagination, and the logic of parts and wholes developed in Husserl's *Logical Investigation* III, the conscious mind isolates and describes the objects of eidetic intuition, the *eidei* or essences of things. The use of imagination is another somewhat rationalistic feature of the phenomenological method, a method partially anticipated by Descartes in his argument to show that the concept of "substance" must be innate.[54] For Husserl, however, the description of the objects called "eidei" present to consciousness in conscious "acts" is fuller and more highly articulated.[55] In particular, Husserl's eidetic descriptions include an account of how the presentation of eidei differs from, yet can be related to, sensory instances of the eide.[56] An essential feature of the experience of eide is the experience of "and so on," when the phantasizing mind recognizes the lack of need further to instantiate or exemplify the eidos, that is, when "enough variation is enough" to grasp the ideal object.[57] The phenomenological reduction is not something that happens all at once. For one thing, holding conscious acts in retention in order to submit them to phenomenological description requires painstak-

---

[48] John Locke, *An Essay Concerning Human Understanding*, Collated and Annotated by Alexander Campbell Fraser, Vol. II, (N.Y.: Dover Publications, Inc., 1959), Book III, Chapter III, pp. 14-31.

[49] George Berkeley, *The Principles of Human Knowledge: with other writings*, ed. G.J. Warnock, (London: Wm. Collins Sons & Co., Ltd. 1962, pp. 47-63. David Hume, *A Treatise of Human Nature*, ed. L.A. Selby-Bigge, (Oxford: Oxford University Press, 1888), Book I, Part I, Sect. VII, pp. 17-25.

[50] Berkeley, *The Principles of Human Knowledge*, pp. 50-52.

[51] Husserl, *CM*, §34, pp. 71-72; Hua. I, pp. 103-106.

[52] *CM*, pp. 70-72; Hua. I, pp. 104-106.

[53] Plato, *Phaedo*, 78d-79d.

[54] René Descartes, *Discourse on Method and Meditations on First Philosophy*, tr. Donald A. Cress, (Indianapolis: Hackett Publication Co., 1980), pp. 64-67.

[55] On the distinction between "acts" and "objects" in consciousness, see *LI*, II, §§46-47, pp. 786-792; Hua. XIX/2, pp. 673-681.

[56] *LI*, I, p. 339; Hua. XIX/1, p. 113.

[57] Husserl, EJ, §87b, p.342; EU, pp. 412-413. For a very helpful discussion of the "and so on," of eidetic intuition, see Cobb-Stevens, "Husserl on Eidetic Intuition and Historical Interpretation" pp. 267-268

ing concentration, training, and relative freedom from interruption. Also, the ability to "bracket out" or "put out of play" our ordinary naive realist and naive empiricist modes of thinking about the objects of consciousness is something that develops over time – hours, weeks, months, years[58] and not something that happens only once, or at once. For another thing, the running through of free variations in imagination takes time, longer and shorter time for different forms of objects of conscious acts. Far from being infallible or incorrigible, eidetic variation, like almost any other conscious process, is subject to difficulties, vagaries, and outright mistakes. [59] A faulty focus on the laws of wholes and parts can also lead to mistakes in eidetic intuition. Discernment of essence, then, is much more methodologically controlled than were traditional introspective claims by rationalists and empiricists alike. The new "data" of eidetic insight are thus bound by the need for careful correlation of insights, not just over time, but also over "public" control through the publication and discussion of one's results for others to experience and to test. [60]

V. Shifts in language

In both physics and phenomenology, the new developments of the early twentieth century required researchers also to alter the very language of research. [61] In both cases researchers started out adapting old terms to the new meanings, but then increasingly found it necessary to invent neologisms to account for some of their results. Quantum physicists began to use the metaphorical term "wavicle" to refer to the objects of investigation, such as light, which experimentally produce both wave-like and particle-like behavior. [62] However, as research progressed, more and more objects were discovered to behave in similar ways, so that the word "quantum" came to be used more and more frequently. Because of the non-continuous "quantum-leap" nature of sub-atomic behavior, and the recognized importance of various mathematical constants such as Planck's constant, the sub-atomic world came to be talked about as a "quantum world," in which "quanta" behave in ways completely different from the ordinary, macroscopic, perceptual

---

[58] Husserl, *Introduction to the Logical Investigations*, p. 57.

[59] Husserl, *Introduction to the Logical Investigations*, p. 56.

[60] See Harry Reeder, "hermeneutics and Apodicticity in Phenomenological Method," *Southwest Philosophy Review*, Vol. 6 no. 2, (July, 1990), pp. 43-69.

[61] For instance, see Ch. 11, pp. 125-140 in Heisenberg, *Physics and Beyond.*

[62] Paul Ricoeur has developed a powerful theory of metaphor to explain the way in which language-users use the very grammar of their own languages to modify its logic to accommodate new meanings. See, e.g., *The Rule of Metaphor: Multi-disciplinary studies of the creation of meaning in language*, tr. Robert Czerny with Kathleen McLaughlin and John Costello, SJ, (Toronto: University of Toronto Press, 1977).

world. As research progressed, researchers shifted more and more from altering traditional terminology (e.g., wavicle) to neologisms such as "quark," "up," "down," "charm," and "color." The new terms seemed necessary to the researchers to represent the radically new and different nature and behavior of the denizens of what had come to be called "the quantum world," and to stress its radical differences from objects in the perceptual world. Further such technical terms as the "position," "velocity," and "path" of quantum particles were re-defined to fit the results of quantum experiments. Even the ordinary word for the "picturable" (*schaulich*) nature of one's theoretical account of observed experimental data in terms of a simple sketch was challenged by Heisenberg, in order to counter Schrödinger's critique of discontinuous particle physics as "essentially irrational and *unschaulich*."[63]

Phenomenology, too, at first relied as often as possible upon traditional terms, modifying their meanings contextually to adapt to newly discovered layers of *Erlebnisse*.[64] This program largely characterizes Husserl's writings, although, to be sure, he used neologisms (e.g., "protention")[65] where he felt the novelty of his discoveries required it. However, as Husserl found out (much to his dismay) his "linguistic conservatism" resulted in a prevailing trend of misunderstanding and rejection of his work by his contemporaries. He realized that this was the result of philosophers reading his works without performing the necessary cognitive activities upon which they are based.[66] This, in part, led Heidegger to strive to re-describe phenomenological results in terms of a radically new form of language, which uses traditional terms in new ways (e.g., *Dasein*), but more and more often using neologistic emendations of language (e.g., *Da-sein, In-der-Welt-Sein, Sein-zum-Tode*) to force readers radically to break with ordinary ways of thinking, speaking about, and "seeing" the world and man's relationship to it.[67]

It is important to stress the fact that such new manifestations of language are related to, but different from, the sorts of linguistic change manifested in fiction and poetry. Whether one is metaphorically straining a traditional term by saying "my love is a red, red rose," or inventing a whole new race

---

[63] Cassidy, "Heisenberg, Uncertainty, and the Quantum Revolution," p. 110.

[64] Edmund Husserl, *LI*, Vol. 1, p. 194; Hua. XVIII, p. 193.

[65] Husserl, *The Phenomenology of Internal Time Consciousness*, tr. J.S. Churchill, ed. Martin Heidegger, (The Hague: Martinus Nijhoff, 1964), p. 58; Husserl, *Zur Phänomenologie des inneren Zeitbewusstseins* (1893-1917), ed. Rudolf Boehm, (Husserliana, X), (The Hague: Martinus Nijhoff, 1966), p. 35.

[66] See Husserl, *Ideas: General Introduction to Pure Phenomenology*, tr. W. R. Boyce Gibson, (N.Y.: Collier Books, 1962), pp. 5-22; and Husserl, *Introduction to the Logical Investigations*, tr. P.J. Bossert and C.H. Peters, ed. Eugen Fink, (The Hague: Martinus Nijhoff, 1975), pp. 55-60.

[67] Martin Heidegger, *Being and Time*, tr. John Macquarrie and Edward Robinson, (San Francisco: Harper and Row, 1962); Heidegger, *Sein und Zeit*, 6th ed., (Tübingen: Max Niemeyer, 1986).

of fictional beings in a fictional world of phantasy or science fiction, the poets and creative writers deal at best only metaphorically with what "really" happens in the world.[68] In physics and phenomenology the new ways of talking are tied to the "real" world (in some suitably vague sense) in methodologically precise ways, through performing empirical experiments. In this sense, both in physics and in phenomenology the new ways of speaking are carefully tailored to represent "the things themselves," although taking this phrase in different manners.

VI. A changed role for normative systems

Quantum physics developed a new conception of the link between mathematics, theory, and observation. Traditionally, researchers thought that nature itself reflected a "geometric" and "mathematical" design of the universe.[69] The view that one mathematics and one (Euclidean) geometry are the systems "truly in the world" came into severe challenge at the turn of the twentieth century.[70] By the present, non-Euclidean geometries and non-base-ten arithmetics have been found to be more and more useful than the traditional systems in interpreting some scientific results. In the development of quantum mechanics, rival methods of calculating and characterizing physical systems were sometimes chosen more by their ease of use than by their accuracy. Indeed, some different methods of calculation even came to be seen as equivalent.[71] In 1949, Richard P. Feynman discovered that "the space-time description of a positron moving forward in time is *exactly* equivalent to the same mathematical description of an electron

[68]The use of the words "only" and "really" here is not meant to denigrate the importance of literature and poetry. Indeed, Ricoeur argues that fiction provides the "free variation in phantasy" of the concept of "self" through which children learn what a self is. Paul Ricoeur, *Oneself as Another*, tr. Kathleen Blamey, (Chicago: University of Chicago Press, 1992).

[69]This view stems from the sixth century, B.C., when the Pythagoreans believed the world to be made of numbers. This view has had an enormous impact on the history of science, with Plato analyzing the world as made of particles in the shape of the five rational solids, Aristotle's belief that heavenly motions must be perfect and spherical, and Kepler and Newton thinking that they were uncovering God's geometric and mathematical design of the universe.

[70]To be sure, Euclid's geometry had its detractors in post-Aristotelian classical thought, but ironically these challenges were lost to the West between roughly the eighth and the thirteenth centuries. The retrieving of lost post-Aristotelian philosophy from the Arabs, beginning in the twelfth century, in fact spurred Western thinking on to the scientific revolution and the enlightenment. See DeLacy O'Leary, D.D., *How Greek Science Passed to the Arabs*, (Boston: Routledge & Kegan Paul, 1979), and DeLacy O'Leary, D.D., *Arabic Thought and its Place in History*, (London: Routledge & Kegan Paul, 1939).

[71]See, e.g., Heisenberg, *Physics and Beyond*, p. 71; and Cassidy, "Heisenberg, Uncertainty, and the Quantum Revolution," p. 109.

moving backward in time along the same track in the Feynman diagram."[72] These shifts in the understanding of the relationship between mathematics and physical systems have shifted quantum physics from understanding the "fit" between them as more or less one-to-one to the more fluid concept of a mathematical "model."[73] In this sense, quantum mechanics has made physicists (and subsequently other scientists) much more astute in both epistemological and ontological understanding of their work and their results. As Patrick Heelan put it:

> Quantum mechanics was a new kind of physical theory. In the first place, it determined the possible range of values of its own variables, which classical theory left – except in exceptional cases – to factual observation. In the second place, it allowed the calculation not merely of the ideal norm (or expectation value) of sets of concrete data, which was the aim of classical deterministic theory, but also the manner of distribution of individual instances about the expectation value.[74]

In contrast to the scientific revolution, when philosophers thought they were finding in nature "God's mathematical design of the cosmos," in quantum mechanics mathematics came to be seen more and more as a heuristic tool in the design and interpretation of experiments. The new emphasis on the heuristic nature of mathematics in physics led Einstein to conclude not that observations somehow "dictate" theories, but that, "It is the theory which decides what we can observe."[75] Mathematics itself came to be seen by some as a construction or operation of humanity.

Husserl broke through to phenomenology in the attempt to found logic and mathematics on human experience. This was, in some senses, quite a break with the philosophic past, which had taken the relation between mathematics and science to be driven by ontological truth, or, by Kant and Kantians, as a transcendental truth of human experience. (This is not, however, to say that Husserl's phenomenology cannot be characterized as a new form of transcendental philosophy.)[76] The very attempt to find an empirical foundation for the normative systems of science raised a great

---

[72] John Gribbon, *In Search of Schrödinger's Cat*, p. 187.

[73] Heisenberg (*Physics and Beyond*, p. 76) notes that the Copenhagen group reached the conclusion that "they must abandon all attempts to construct perceptual models of atomic processes." Cf. Ibid., p.71.

[74] Patrick A. Heelan, *Quantum Mechanics and Objectivity: A Study of the Physical Philosophy of Werner Heisenberg*, (The Hague: Nijhoff, 1965), p. 33.

[75] As reported by Heisenberg, *Physics and Beyond*, p. 63.

[76] See Husserl, *CM*, p. 1; Hua. I, p. 43; Husserl, *Crisis*; and Nathan Rotenstreich, "Variations of Transcendentalism," in Kah Kyung Cho, ed., *Philosophy and Science in Phenomenological Perspective*, (Phaenomenologica, no. 95), (Boston: Martinus Nijhoff, 1984), 171-181.

many questions in both epistemology and ontology.[77] Trying to avoid the errors of traditional metaphysics, Husserl resisted ontological claims in order to work out phenomenology as an epistemological philosophy,[78] but by the end of his life he had seen more and more need to account for the ontological implications (and grounds) for phenomenological philosophy,[79] a theme to which we will return in Section VII, below. Meanwhile, in trying to work out the epistemology of phenomenology and its method of phenomenological reduction, Husserl was thrown back upon the importance of ordinary experience ("naive," or pre-scientific and pre-philosophical, in Husserl's sense) of the *Lebenswelt.* Husserl was led to consider the origin and development of mathematics in science also as a cultural and historical problem in a rigorous attempt to re-think the "fit" between normative, *a priori* systems and their *a posteriori* application, especially in science.[80] Thus, Husserl re-evaluated the roles of logic and mathematics both in the foundations of science (*LI, Crisis*) and in the development of Western culture and philosophy (*Crisis*). However, unlike quantum theorists, who were addressing problems at different methodological levels, Husserl found that the grounding of the normative systems of logic and mathematics could be achieved only in the "experiments" of eidetic reduction.

VII. The observer as part of the system observed

One of the reasons that experiments in quantum mechanics were so hard to interpret had to do with the incredibly small size of the phenomena observed. They simply cannot be "seen." The puzzling particle-wave duality of quanta led physicists to realize that in their experimental observations they were bringing about noticeable effects in the observed quantum phenomena. To observe quanta required experimenters to interact with tools of observation which were either quanta themselves, like photons of light or sub-atomic particles such as electrons or protons, or much larger objects such as photographic plates, slitted barriers, etc.[81] They gradually came

[77]An earlier attempt by Mill impressed Husserl very much. J.S. Mill, *A System of Logic: Ratiocinative and Inductive, being a Connected View of the Principles of Evidence and the Methods of Scientific Investigation*, (London: 1843).

[78]The program in the *Ideas.*

[79]See *Crisis*, §51, pp. 173-174; Hua. VI, pp. 176-177; and *CM* §§59-60, pp. 136-141; Hua. I, pp. 163-168.

[80]*Crisis*, Part II, §§8-9, pp. 21-59, and Appendix V, pp. 353-378; Hua. VI, pp. 18-60, 365-386. See also Kockelmans, "The Mathematization of nature In Husserl's Last Publication, *Krisis.*"

[81]On the philosophical implications of our inability to "see" objects except through elaborate, theory-laden machines, see Hacking, Ian, "Do We See Through A Microscope?" in Baruch A. Brody and Richard E. Grandy eds., *Readings in the Philosophy of Science*, 2d. ed., (Englewood Cliffs, N.J.: Prentice Hall, 1989),

to see that the very methods they used to bring about observed quantum effects affected the behavior – even the apparent particle-wave "nature" – of the quanta themselves. In the quantum world, objects apparently "can exist in an ambiguous state until a measurement is made," and these sorts of features have since been demonstrated at the macroscopic level.[82] As a result, the traditional belief that science uses only "objective" (neutral, non-subjective, non-causally interfering) methods of investigation was itself questioned. By positioning the observers and the observing methods, apparati, and conditions within the framework of the "causal system" of the quantum experiments, physicists themselves were led to raise philosophical questions, questions that had long been thought to be settled by a combination of Descartes' dualism (defined in terms of "extended" vs. "non-extended") and the subsequent empiricist methods for observing the "extended = objective = non-subjective" features of matter.[83]

Since the dawn of "scientific" thought, philosophers struggled with the relation between the so-called "subjective" and "objective" features of the investigation of "nature." The words in quotations marks here indicate that their concepts, as used today, are layered or sedimented with the meanings ushered in by the Modern period of philosophy. In fact, speculation about the "nature of things" extended (at least) as far back as the pre-Socratic philosophers. Using two examples to make this point, both Parmenides ("all is in stasis"), and Heraclitus ("all is in flux") recognized that a philosophic-scientific[84] understanding of being (all that is) is based in the psyche, not in the senses, which are misleading. The history of scientific thought has, in part, refined more and more the understanding of the relation between the "subjective" and the "objective" in scientific investigation, with the "objective" taking a more and more dominating role. Long before the nineteenth century, science had come to resist and reject "subjective" notions as "idols" or presuppositions likely to interfere with proper observation and interpretation of scientific experiments and their results.[85] After Descartes' clarification of the "extensional difference" between the subjective and the objective, results were more and more treated as properly "empirical" only insofar as they ignored any role that the ("subjective") researchers played in their experiments. Quantum physics brought this broad understanding

pp. 29-43. Originally published in *Pacific Philosophical Quarterly*, Vol. 62, no. 4, October 1981.

[82] Shimony, "The Reality of the Quantum World," p. 46.

[83] See, e.g., Cassidy, "Heisenberg, Uncertainty, and the Quantum Revolution," p. 110. One philosophical extreme of this view is Popper's "epistemology without a knowing subject." See *Objective Knowledge*, Ch. 3, pp. 106-152.

[84] It should be recalled here that the distinction between "philosophy" and "science" is only about two centuries old, and that the application of such terms to earlier periods must be at least in part anachronistic.

[85] Francis Bacon, *The New Organon*, aphorisms xxxix-lxv, pp. 34-45.

into question. At the quantum level, it seemed, the role of the observer could not be ignored in the observation and interpretation of experimental results. The subject's role had entered into the "objectivity" of empirical results.[86] As physicists themselves realized, this raised both epistemological and ontological questions about the nature of the quantum world. As Patrick Heelan noted,

> The Principle of Complementarity is not a physical principle like the Indeterminacy Principle, nor is it a heuristic principle in physics like the Correspondence Principle; but it is a philosophical (or epistemological) principle which attempts to explain how we know the atomic domain and how the inherent limitations of our knowing powers impede our conception and expression of the intrinsic nature of microphysical events.[87]

In quantum physics, Stephen Hawking espoused an idealist-sounding *anthropic principle*: "We see the universe the way it is because we exist."[88] John A. Wheeler stressed the centrality of human life in the holistic view of quantum mechanics:

> It is not only that man is adapted to the universe. The universe is adapted to man. Imagine a universe in which one or another of the fundamental dimensionless constants of physics is altered by a few percent one way or another? Man could never come into being in such a universe. That is the central point of the anthropic principle. According to this principle, a life-giving factor lies at the centre of the whole machinery and design of the world.[89]

John Gribbon puts this yet another way: "The story [of quantum mechanics] stresses the fundamental axiom of quantum theory, that no elementary phenomenon is a phenomenon until it is a recorded phenomenon."[90]

In phenomenology, Husserl's methodological clarification of the foundational epistemological role of ideas or *eidei* forced a similar questioning

---

[86] See Heisenberg, *Physics and Beyond*, p. 88, and cf. Patrick A. Heelan, *Quantum Mechanics and Objectivity*, p. xiii.

[87] Patrick A. Heelan, *Quantum Mechanics and Objectivity*, p. 45.

[88] Hawking, p. 124. Hawking's principle is not a clearly idealistic one, as he modifies it. Nonetheless, this shows that physicists have been led to such epistemological speculations even as Husserl had insisted is required for the proper founding of science.

[89] John D. Barrow and Frank J. Tippler, *The Anthropic Cosmological Principle*, (Oxford: Clarendon Press, 1986). Wheeler's comment is in the Introduction, p. vii.

[90] *In Search of Schrödinger's Cat*, pp. 209-210, my interpolation.

of the traditional restriction of "empirical" evidence to the purely non-subjective realm. Methodologically working out the philosophical and scientific implications of Brentano's focus upon intentionality, Husserl realized that the separation of the "subjective" from the "empirical" was in fact descriptively, and thus methodologically, false. No object is presented in science except to a scientist, and the subjectively experiencing scientist is continually bombarded with "objective" ideas resulting from "empirical" experiments. Realizing that science is a human enterprise,[91] Husserl discerned that the traditional prejudice against "the subjective" amounted to a scientific self-misunderstanding.[92] The "objects" of scientific investigation are only present-to-a-subject and never float in a world without "knowing subjects."[93]

A major stumbling block in philosophy's attempts to accomplish this foundation was the phenomenologically erroneous focus upon conscious acts as somehow "tinged" with a "truth-indicator,"

> Evidence is, in fact, not some sort of consciousness-index attached to a judgment (and usually one speaks of such evidence only in the case of judgment), calling to us like a mystic voice from a better world: Here is the truth; as though such a voice would have something to say to free spirits like us and would not have to show its title to legitimacy. We no longer need to argue with skepticism, nor take into consideration objections of the old type which cannot overcome the theory of evidence which resorts to indices and feeling: whether an evil genius (the Cartesian fiction) or a fateful change in the factual course of the world could make it happen that just any false judgment would be outfitted with this index, this feeling of intellectual necessity, of the transcendent oughtness; and the like.[94]

or discrete and unconnected in time:

> The continual obstacle that may have been sensed during this exposition is owing solely to the usual, fundamentally wrong, interpretation of evidence, an interpretation made possible by the utter lack of a serious phenomenological analysis of the effective performance common to all forms of evidence. Thus it happens that evidence is usually conceived as an ***absolute apodicticity,***

---

[91] Patrick A. Heelan, *Quantum Mechanics and Objectivity*, p. 9.

[92] This theme is discussed most clearly in *Crisis*, Part I, pp. 1-18; Hua. VI, pp. 1-17.

[93] The reference here is to Karl Popper, *Objective Knowledge*, Ch. 3, pp. 106-152.

[94] *Ideas*, p. 345: Hua. III/1, p. 334. Cobb-Stevens' discussion of eidetic reduction ("Husserl on Eidetic Intuition and Historical Interpretation") is very helpful here.

> an absolute security against deceptions - an apodicticity quite incomprehensibly ascribed to a single mental process torn from the concrete, essentially unitary, context of subjective mental living. The usual theorist sees in evidence an absolute criterion of truth; though, by such a criterion, not only external but also, in strictness, all internal evidence would necessarily be done away with. If, being unable to explicate evidence as a functioning intentionality, the theorist, by a kind of sensualistic substitution, falls back on so-called feelings of evidence, then their attainment of truth itself (an attainment he still ascribes to evidence) becomes a miracle, nay, at bottom a countersense. [95]

Thus, like phenomenology, contemporary physics has come to see the need to account for both the "knower of the known" and for the non-corpuscular nature of the grounding of knowledge of the known.

VIII. Ontological implications

Attempts to correlate quantum mechanics and the rest of science were made both methodologically and ontologically difficult by the radical difference between quantum probability and classical causality. Right from the start quantum theorists were troubled by this difference, leading to theoretical debates of the most fundamental kind. The scientists realized the possible ontological implications of their work, as they were "struggling with properties of nature that they believed to exist and to be embodied in their matrix mechanics."[96] One implication of the Heisenberg uncertainty principle was that, "For the first time since the Scientific Revolution, a leading physicist had proclaimed a limitation to scientific understanding [of being]."[97] Einstein stubbornly refused to accept the probability of quantum mechanics, with his famous claim that "God does not play with dice," in an ongoing debate with Niels Bohr.[98] Einstein could not accept the Copenhagen interpretation of quantum mechanics. Debates ensued between positivists, wanting to abstain from all ontological commitments, and non-positivists

---

[95] Husserl, *Formal and Transcendental Logic*, pp. 156-157; Hua. XVII, p. 165.

[96] Cassidy, "Heisenberg, Uncertainty, and the Quantum Revolution," p. 109.

[97] Cassidy, "Heisenberg, Uncertainty, and the Quantum Revolution," p. 106, my interpolation.

[98] Emilio Segrè, *From X-Rays to Quarks*, p. 100; Heisenberg, *Physics and Beyond*, pp. 79-80.

trying to salvage some (much modified) thread of naive realism.[99] Nevertheless, gone were the relatively unsophisticated attempts to capture our naive realism, in large part because causality had always been seen as a cornerstone of reality. According to the Copenhagen interpretation of quantum mechanics, however, "Objective reality does *not* have any place in our fundamental description of the universe, but action at a distance, or acausality, does have such a place."[100] Open discussions of ontological relativism appeared among quantum physicists, often with vehement objection.[101] Meanwhile, attempts to align the implications of quantum physics and relativity with astronomical, cosmological, and cosmogonical phenomena resulted in interpretation and confirmation of an understanding of very large-scale phenomena based upon the very small-scale, quantum-mechanical interpretation of nature. The so-called "macro-level" phenomena of human perception shifted gradually to become the exception, rather than the rule, for interpreting nature. With the suddenness of the "break" between the perceptual world and the quantum world, the new physics actually shared for a time analogous features with the pre-classical, Aristotelian "two spheres" view of causation. Just as causal rules operated in essentially different ways in the Aristotelian sublunary and superlunary spheres, causal rules seemed to act determinately in the "macro world" of perception and probabilistically in the quantum world. The Heisenberg uncertainty principle "leads to phenomena qualitatively different from those exhibited in classical mechanics."[102] Recent experiments demonstrating "macro-level" quantum effects have softened the line of demarcation between "micro-" and "macro-level" phenomena. Naive realism, based in the phenomena of human perception, became harder and harder to defend,[103] and debates raged over whether quantum mechanics and relativity theory constituted "evolutionary" or "revolutionary" science.[104]

---

[99]This debate was paralleled in philosophy by Popper's debates with the positivists. See Karl Popper, *The Logic of Scientific Discovery*, 2d. Harper ed., (N.Y.: Harper & Row, 1968). Originally published as *Logik der Forschung*, in Vienna in 1934, with the imprint '1935'.

[100]John Gribbon, *In Search of Schrödinger's Cat*, p. 183.

[101]David C. Cassidy's "Heisenberg, Uncertainty and the Quantum Revolution" captures some of the all too human tone of some of the debates swirling about early quantum physics.

[102]Halliwell, "Quantum Cosmology and the Creation of the Universe," p. 79.

[103]See, e.g., Heisenberg, *Physics and Beyond*, p. 76; and Popper's attempts via "verisimilitude," (p. 143) and an ontology of "three worlds" (Ch. 3, pp. 106-152) in *Objective Knowledge.*

[104]See, e.g., the debate between Popper and Kuhn. T.S. Kuhn, "Reflections on My Critics" in Imre Lakatos and Alan Musgrave, eds., *Criticism and the Growth of Knowledge*, (Cambridge: Cambridge University Press, 1970), pp. 231-278; Kuhn, "Logic of Discovery or Psychology of Research?" in Imre Lakatos and Alan Musgrave, eds., *Criticism and the Growth of Knowledge*, (Cambridge: Cambridge University Press, 1970), pp. 1-23, also published in T.S. Kuhn, *The*

Since Aristotle science had been seen as dealing exclusively with the causal properties of things, properties that seemed to cover Aristotle's efficient, material, and formal causes. Aristotle's final cause had dropped out of the scientific picture. However, some formulations of the anthropic principle seem to verge on pronouncements of a cosmic final principle.[105] Such thinking has long been thought to be unscientific because it implies some sort of conscious reason for things. If science is all based upon the bedrock assumption that all things happen because a non-conscious, mechanistic cause, where does quantum mechanics, with its acausality, leave us as scientists? If the real is not what was caused by something else that is real, this leaves us quite puzzled about the nature of the real, of being itself. The puzzles about causality and being are perhaps at their most troublesome in the cases of virtual particles and a famous thought experiment known as "Schrödinger's Cat."

There are two kinds of virtual particles, those that carry forces, and those that appear in seemingly empty space.[106] Our discussion will focus upon the latter. Because of Heisenberg's uncertainty principle, space cannot be empty, because then it would have both a precise value and a precise rate of change, which is impossible.[107] Because of this, "Spontaneous *random* fluctuations in the structure of matter, and even spacetime, inevitably occur," so that, "matter can appear out of nowhere."[108] In addition, the gravity of black holes can bring into existence pairs of photons, one of which falls into the black hole and the other of which is released into the universe.[109] These phenomena raise profound questions about existence and causality. Since ancient times it has been accepted as basic to science that "nothing comes from nothing." According to quantum mechanics, however, matter itself may be created by forces in the fields of spacetime. The randomness of this mechanism necessitates a profound re-thinking of the relationship

---

Essential Tension: Selected Studies in Scientific Tradition and Change, (Chicago: University of Chicago Press, 1977), Ch. 11, pp. 266-292; Popper, "Replies to My Critics," in Paul A. Schillp, ed., *The Philosophy of Karl Popper*, (Library of Living Philosophers, Vol. XIV, Book II), LaSalle, IL: Open Court, 1974), pp. 1144-1153; and Popper, "Normal Science and its Dangers," in Lakatos, Imre, and Musgrave, Alan, eds., *Criticism and the Growth of Knowledge*, (Proceedings of the International colloquium in the Philosophy of Science, London, 1965, Vol. 4), (Cambridge: Cambridge University Press, 1970), pp. 51-58. (This paper was delivered as a lecture at the International Colloquium in the Philosophy of Science, London, 1965.)

[105] See above, notes 88 and 89.

[106] Hawking, *A Brief History of Time*, pp. 69-73, 105-106.

[107] Hawking, *A Brief History of Time*, pp. 105-106; Halliwell, "Quantum Cosmology and the Creation of the Universe," p. 79.

[108] Paul Davies and John Gribbon, *The Matter Myth: Dramatic Discoveries That Challenge Our Understanding of Physical Reality*, (N.Y.: Simon & Schuster, 1992), p. 142.

[109] Kip Thorne, *Black Holes & Time Warps*, p. 440.

between reality and causation, a re-thinking that continues to this day.

A classic thought-experiment of quantum mechanics, one that captures the poignancy of these puzzles about reality and causality, is that of Schrödinger's cat.[110] In the thought experiment, inside a box is a bit of fissionable material, a detector that records any radioactive particles present, a sealed glass vial of poisonous gas, and a live cat. The detector is turned on long enough that there is a fifty-fifty chance that the detector will record a particle released by the radioactive material. The cat lives if no particle is detected, but if a particle is detected the detector breaks the glass vial, which in turn kills the cat. The ontological puzzle arising from this thought experiment concerns the existence of the cat. Once we open the box, we see whether the cat is dead or alive. So far, no problem. However, two features of quantum mechanics leave us unable to make a final pronouncement about the existence of the cat *before the box is opened.*[111] Our ordinary, naive-realist thinking assures us of the objective reality of the fact that the cat in the box must be either dead or alive. But quantum mechanics, with its placing of the subject into the objective system, and the principle of superposition,[112] lead to quite different ways of describing the situation. Let us look at three different interpretations proposed by physicists to see the ontological puzzle suggested by quantum mechanics. We will call these interpretations the "observer determines," the "superposition," and the "many universes" interpretations.

Since the quantum-mechanical interpretation of the state of the system is in part determined by our act of observing the system, it leads some scientists to say that the cat is *neither alive nor dead* until we make our observation; the observation "makes" the cat be dead or alive. This view stems from the mathematical "description" of the quantum state of things:

> Prior to actually measuring the disintegration [of the fissionable material], the state vector of the atom of radioactive substance must be expressed as a linear superposition of the measurement eigenstates, corresponding to the physical states of the intact atom and the disintegrated atom. However . . . treating the measuring instrument as a quantum object and using the equations

[110]See John Gribbon, *In Search of Schrödinger's Cat*, pp. 203-208; and Shimony, "The Reality of the Quantum World," p. 52, for clear explanations of the thought-experiment. The above way of talking is, of course, the "Copenhagen interpretation" of the issue. This interpretation is wide-spread, but not universal. See, e.g., Jonathan J. Halliwell, "Quantum Cosmology and the Creation of the Universe," pp. 76-85, especially p. 82.

[111]The meaning of this thought experiment is still the subject of debate. See John Gribbon, *In Search of Schrödinger's Cat*, p. 203.

[112]". . .an arbitrary, well behaved state vector can be expanded as a linear superposition of the complete set of eigenstates of any hermitian operator," Baggott, *The Meaning of Quantum Theory*, p. 50.

> of quantum mechanics leads us to . . . a superposition of the two possible outcomes of the measurement. . . . Prior to measurement, the physical state of the cat is therefore 'blurred'-it is neither alive nor dead but some peculiar combination of both states. We can perform a measurement on the cat by opening the chamber and ascertaining its physical state. Do we suppose that, at that point, the state vector of the system-plus-cat collapses and we record the observation that the cat is alive or dead as appropriate? [113]

Theorists interpret this scenario in various ways. On one interpretation the observation of the sciences brings about the existence of the cat as alive or dead, so that the cat was neither alive nor dead until *the observation made it so.* This is the "observer determines" interpretation. According to the "superposition" interpretation, the cat exists both as alive and as dead, as well as neither alive nor dead, until the observation is made:

> The whole experiment, cat and all, is governed by the rule that the superposition is "real" until we look at the experiment, and that only at the instant of observation does the wave function collapse into one of the two states. Until we look inside, there is a radioactive sample that has both decayed and not decayed, a glass vessel of poison that is neither broken nor unbroken, and a cat that is both dead and alive, neither alive nor dead.[114]

This interpretation is also suggested by the mathematics of quantum mechanics. Given the probabilistic nature of quantum mechanics and the principle of superposition, the fissionable material actually exists both in a state of having released the particle and the state of *not* having released the particle. This implies that the cat exists both in the living and the dead state *until we look into the box.* As if these two interpretations were not puzzling enough, according to the "many universes" interpretation, there exist two parallel universes, one in which the cat is alive even before we observe it, and another in which the cat is dead even before we observe it.[115]

As these examples show, quantum mechanics has led to a drastic reshaping of our notions of "what there is," with the concepts of matter, being, time, and causation moving far beyond our everyday picture of the world.

---

[113] Baggott, *The Meaning of Quantum Theory*, pp. 104-106, my interpolation.

[114] John Gribbon, *In Search of Schrödinger's Cat*, pp. 204-205. As Gribbon later notes, (p. 208), "It is impossible to reconcile with the strict Copenhagen interpretation without accepting the "reality" of the dead-alive cat . . ."

[115] Davies and Gribbon, *The Matter Myth*, p. 219.

As in physics' understanding of quanta, in phenomenology new methods of investigation required to ground the eidei, the universal features of things in general and acts of knowing in particular, required a radical rethinking of being. Husserl's critiques of metaphysics notwithstanding, he saw the need to account philosophically for all that there is, and to tie it to judgments based in self-evidence. To avoid methodological and ontological presuppositions of the sort that plagued Modern philosophy, phenomenology required a new openness to being in its various modes of appearing. Anything presented to consciousness "is," in some ontological sense. Rather than presupposing the subjective vs. objective distinction that had developed both in individual features and in the self-concealing nature of the categories "subjective" and "objective" that resulted from the scientific revolution and the Enlightenment, Husserl recognized that the foundation of a science of science required a *regional ontology*,[116] in which each *de facto* appearance is to be grounded as to its *de jure* modes of appearing, with the *act* of appearing serving as co-foundational with the eidetic, *de jure* properties of the appearances of that sort of object.[117]

Husserl's focus upon the *de facto* grounding of acts of knowing stemmed from his recognition that all evidence is at base self-evidence, that is, the givenness in experience of an object to an intentionally related consciousness. [118] It was the philosophic/scientific tradition's lack of attention to the *acts* of knowing that constituted the logical and philosophical naiveté of Western thought's culmination in empiricistic, sensual forms of evidence.[119] The sundering of the objects of knowledge from their acts of appearing was the philosophic self-misunderstanding leading to the crisis of Western humanity in the early twentieth century.[120]

The uniqueness of the appearance of eide as a result of epoche and eidetic reduction was discovered precisely because Husserl's overall project was to find an evidential founding for logic and mathematics. The failure of his attempting to find this foundation in psychological acts forced him to re-assess his presuppositions about psychological presentation, just as results in quantum mechanics forced physicists to re-think the categories guiding their experimental methods. The theories and equations of quantum mechanics had led scientists to become aware of the possibility, and

---

[116]Husserl, *CM*, §64, pp. 152-157; Hua. I, pp. 178-183.

[117]See José Huertas-Jourda, "On the Two Foundations of Knowledge According to Husserl," in Lester Embree ed., *Essays in Memory of Aron Gurwitsch*, (Current Continental Research, 007), (Washington, D.C.: Center for Advanced Research in Phenomenology and University Press of America, 1983), pp. 195-211. Husserl's insight is a refinement of Aristotle's view that we know the *tode ti* through apprehension of its universal features.

[118]*LI*, I, pp. 58-59; Hua. XVIII, pp. 25-26; FTL, pp. 11-17; Hua. XVII, pp. 16-21; EJ, pp. 18, 21; EU, pp. 9-10, 13-14.

[119]FTL, p. 2; Hua. XVII, p. 6.

[120]Husserl, *Crisis*, Part II.

then experimentally confirm the existence, of virtual particles. These theories and equations resulted from a loosening of old theories, concepts, and methods. The virtual particles "exist as needed" by laws of physics, and then cease to exist. Similarly, in order to demonstrate the grounding of the normative systems of logic and mathematics, and of scientific knowledge, Husserl had to focus both more carefully and more reflectively upon the life of an intentionally-living consciousness. Husserl was driven to break through to the transcendental level of reflection and description precisely because he recognized that the *de jure* nature of eidei, which can appear in the very specialized acts of eidetic, transcendental reflection, was required by the *de facto* appearance of many acts of knowing the same intentional object. His guiding empiricist theme, that all evidence is based in the self-evident confrontation of intentional subjects and intentional objects in intentional acts,[121] forced him to widen the concepts of intentionality, subjectivity, and objectivity into a coherent grounded validation of knowledge[122] in acts of knowing, acts that are repeatable both over time and among intersubjective tests by related researchers.[123] Thus the being of eidei must be in some sense assured.[124] We can be sure that eide exist insofar as they may appear (with greater or lesser clarity and distinctness, to be sure)[125] in acts of knowing. We know that they exist because we can find their existing traces as they "exist as needed" in intentional acts of fulfilled knowledge or meaning. The nominalistic prejudices of the classical empiricists resulted from their focus upon the external senses as the presumed sole source of knowledge. A more careful, reflective, and open-minded approach, phenomenology, finds that such a presumption is false, descriptively false, because it "hides" important "empirical phenomena" through the ideology of what has come to be known as sense-datum theory. Eidei do not exist in the same sense as (with the some modes of appearing as) sensory bodies, any more than quanta exist in the same sense as sensory, particle- or wavelike perceptual objects. They do, however, exist, and have been demonstrated to exist by many a follower of Husserl's transcendental method.

IX. Conclusion

It has been demonstrated that the paths of quantum mechanics and phenomenology have been in many ways parallel in their methodological problems and solutions. Their puzzles, objects, methodologies, shifts in

---

[121]Husserl, *Crisis*, p. 189; Hua. VI, pp. 192-193.

[122]Husserl, *LI*, I, pp. 60-62; Hua. XVIII, pp. 27-29.

[123]Husserl, *Crisis*, p. 163; Hua. VI, p. 166.

[124]Husserl, *LI*, I, pp. 351-353; Hua. XIX/1, pp. 128-131.

[125]Husserl, *LI*, II, *Investigation* VI, §§8-39; Hua. XIX/2, pp. 566-656.

language, re-conception of the norms of science, re-evaluation of the scientific investigator's effect upon the objects studied, and the ontological implications of their researches all shifted in similar ways, as required by newly-established empirical evidence, evidence that required a broadening of the category of "the empirical." This evidence supports Husserl's claim that phenomenology is – at one level, and a necessary one – an important part of our understanding of the nature of science and scientific evidence. Rather than challenging individual researches in physics, chemistry, biology, etc. (which Husserl makes it clear that he is *not* doing),[126] Husserl challenged our culture's over-all understanding of science, reintegrating it with our understanding of the everyday world. Husserl demonstrated that science is a human enterprise, and as such it cannot be reduced to a combination of logic, mathematics, and sensory perceptions – although these are, to be sure, *necessary conditions* of what makes science the sort of unique enterprise that it is – precisely because, as human beings, our understanding of scientific knowledge must somehow fit in with the rest of our knowledge, including that of the everyday *Lebenswelt*, which involves many hermeneutical, open-ended, and teleological features. To straddle the gaps between the micro-, macro-, and cosmological levels of understanding of the world, we need a breadth of grasp of the relationship between scientists and the world (including the rest of us) that is richer than the traditional rationalistic and empiricistic accounts. Both physicists and phenomenologists agree that newer categories of understanding are required by new evidence and new methodological insights. This supports Husserl's claim that phenomenology is (a philosophical part of) a strict science.

[126]Husserl, *LI*, I, *Prolegomena* §4, pp. 58-59;Hua. XVIII, pp. 25-26; *Crisis*, p. 189; Hua. VI, p. 193.

The Constitution of Qi in Traditional Chinese Medicine: A Phenomenological Hypothesis

Lester Embree

" Qi is dynamic, active, and invisible." [1]

I. Introduction

While it might be thought otherwise, phenomenologists can and do develop and use hypotheses in their investigations. The hypothesis ventured here and how it might be tested are described late in the second part of the following exposition. The first part consists of a sketch of traditional Chinese medicine ("TCM" hereafter) with an emphasis on Qi, which is pronounced "Chee" and sometimes also transliterated at "C'hi." From Korean it is transliterated as "Ki." There are various English translations.

It could be considered presumptuous that a Westerner discuss TCM. The author is certainly an outsider to East Asian thought, but the sources drawn on not only appear reputable but are clearly intended to make TCM intelligible to Westerners and the present admission of cultural outsiderhood may help reduce suspicion. That one is also a disciplinary outsider regarding medicine may be less obvious in philosophy of science and technology, but is also a problem the acknowledgment of which is at least the beginning of a solution.

II. A Selective Sketch of Traditional Chinese Medicine

The following sketch is mostly a collection of passages, the selection and arrangement of which is not the responsibility of the authors used. So that they be more easily read, some passages are not printed in reduced form. There are variations in translation and transliteration, but they should not mislead the reader.

Traditional Chinese medicine relates to Daoism and thus shares much with Daoist cosmology and also with the practice of Feng Shui and several types of martial art, but the concern here is with medicine. Its history goes back to the Shang Dynasty (ca. 1,000 BC) and no doubt stems from

[1]Shen Zinin and Chen Zelin, *The Basis of Traditional Chinese medicine* (Boston & London: Shambhala Publications, 1994), p. 39. Hereafter this source will be cited as "Basis."

Shamanism as well as the observation of animals, but, above all, from observation of the effects of massage and acupuncture. There was opposition to it within China as well as beyond in recent centuries, but the People's Republic of China began to support it strongly in 1954 and there is also currently much less resistance to it elsewhere as well.[2]

TCM is as much preventative as crisis medicine and thus also involves recommendations concerning diet and exercise. Presumably the same general approach can be taken to non-human animals, but only remarks about human medicine have been noticed in the sources consulted for this essay. In TCM the human is considered a whole within which everything is interdependent and mutually interacting, mind and body included:

> Under ordinary conditions, emotions are normal reactions to external stimuli. 'Being joyful, angry, sorry, and gay are natural emotions for human beings,' says traditional Chinese medicine. Without these emotions, disease would occur. However, if emotional excitement is extremely abrupt or intense, or if it is persistent and exceeds the normal endurance of the human body, emotions may produce functional disorders of the *zang-fu* organs, impeding the harmonious balance of *yin* and *yang*, *Qi*, and blood. The emotions then become pathogenic factors, producing disease and organic lesions. These are classified as 'endogenous injuries' since the diseases they cause originate in the interior of the body and directly affect the related internal organs.[3] Rage, for example, is said to injure the liver; excessive fear disrupts the kidney, and so on.[4]

There is much classification within TCM. Yin and Yang are considered basic pairs, like up and down or night and day. The former denotes "the dark side of the mountain" and connotes cold, still, passive, dark, inside, and potential, while the latter denotes "the bright side of the mountain"

---

[2]Tom Williams, *The Complete Illustrated Guide to Chinese Medicine* (Shaftsbury, Dorset: Element Books, 1996), pp. 14 f. Hereafter this source will be referred to as "Complete."

[3]"Emotions have a broader meaning in Chinese medicine than in Western science. In traditional Chinese medical thought, emotions are closely related to the functioning of the internal organs. Mental disorders may injure the internal organs, while functional disturbances of the internal organs may also find their reflection mentally. According to traditional Chinese medicine, there are seven basic emotions. These are: joy, anger, sadness, pensiveness, grief, fear, and fright. Each of these emotions corresponds to a particular *zang* organ." ["While there are seven emotions and five *zang* organs, two of the *zang* organs - the heart and lung - each have an additional emotion associated with them ... "]

[4]Liu Yanchi, *The Essential Book of Traditional Chinese Medicine*, trans. Fang Tingyu and Chen Laidi, New York: Columbia University Press, 1988, Vol. I, p. 156. Hereafter this source will be cited as "Essential."

and connotes warm, active, light, outside, and expression. Everything manifests both Yin and Yang, but emphases vary and there are many combinations. Fever is too much Yang and chills are too much Ying. Health is a balance to be preserved or restored.

Then again, there are five elements, the names for which also have connotations:

Water : wet, cool, descending, flowing, yielding

Fire : dry, hot, ascending, moving

Wood : growing, flexible, rooted

Metal : cutting, hard, conducting

Earth : productive, fertile, potential for growth

And these are associated with psychical as well as somatic components and physical elements:[5]

———	WOOD	FIRE	EARTH	METAL	WATER
Yin ORG.	Liver	Heart	Spleen	Lungs	Kidney
Yang ORG.	Gall Blad.	Sm.Intes.	Stomach	Lg.Intes.	Bladder
ORIFICE	Eyes	Tongue	Mouth	Nose	Ears
TISSUE	Tendons	Bld. Vesl.	Muscles	Skin	Bones
EMOTION	Anger	Joy	Pensiveness	Grief	Fear

What are the *zang-fu* organs? These include most of the internal organs of Western medicine, but include other structures of the body: *Zang-fu* is a general term which stands for the five solid organs and the six hollow viscera of the human body. The five *zang* organs refer to the heart, liver, spleen, lung, and kidney, while the six *fu* organs comprise the gall bladder stomach, small intestine, large intestine, bladder, and the *sanjiao* ...[6] It

[5] "Complete," pp. 21-27.

[6] "The *sanjiao* (*san* means three, but *jiao* has no exact English equivalent) is a functional unit consisting of three portions, the upper *jiao* of the chest (heart and lung), the middle *jiao* of the upper abdomen (spleen and stomach) as well as the lower *jiao* of the lower abdomen (kidney and bladder). The *sanjiao* are not actually organs, but are three zones of the body within which various channels connect to govern the flow of nutrients and *qi* to that zone. The *sanjiao* have dual functions. They distribute and circulate *qi* and *blood*; and dredge the water passages so that excessive body fluids flow to the bladder for excretion." ("Basis," 30)

must be noted that these *zang-fu* organs may not always coincide with the anatomical organs. According to TCM, the *zang* organs store the essence and *qi* of the body and are functionally more important than the six *fu* organs, which are responsible for absorption and assimilation. ("Basis," p.23)

Finally, there are five factors, (1) Qi, which is responsible for movement, activity, warming, transformation, protection, and containment (and to be returned to presently); (2) Jing, which is responsible for growth, reproduction, development, marrow, etc.; (3) Blood, which nourishes, moistens, and aids Shen; (4) body Fluids, which moisten and nourish; and (5) Shen, which keeps mind sharp and alert ("Complete," p. 45).

Qi is central. It can hardly be discussed without the consideration of meridians or channels through which it flows in the person. Traditional Chinese doctors know about meridians like Western doctors know about anatomy and physiology. Probably everyone has seen maps of the body with the meridians traced on the surface with lines connecting what are called "acupoints." For example, "*The Spleen Meridian of the Foot Taiyin* - Beginning from the medial tip of the big toe, this meridian runs upwards along the first metatarsal bone. It passes in front of the medial malleolus and ascends along the posterior side to the tibia and the anteromedial aspect of the thigh. Through the abdomen, it arrives at the chest where a tributary ascends to the root of the tongue. A branch of the meridian separates in the stomach region and finds its way both to the spleen as well as the heart after crossing the diaphragm. There are 21 points along the channel." ("The Basis," p. 174)

More generally, "*Qi* is the motive force promoting the physiological activities of all the *zang-fu* organs. There are two types of *qi* in the body. *Congenital qi* begins at birth and is inherited from one's parents. This energy originates from the kidneys and is stored in the '*dantian*,' a place three *cuns* (Chinese inches) below the navel. The other type of *qi* is acquired after birth. This is the *acquired qi* we get from food and water, which is assimilated by the spleen and stomach, and from the air inhaled by the lungs. The *acquired qi* is constantly replenished, and is a fundamental substance maintaining the life activities of the human body. It is said that 'human life is completely dependent upon this kind of *qi*.'

> Both types of *qi* work together, circulating in the body along the channels and nourishing the body. *Qi* is capable of producing and controlling blood, warming and nourishing the tissues, building up resistance against diseases as well as activating the physiological functions of the *zang-fu* organs. *Qi* is function-specific and carries different names according to the role it plays or the *zang-fu* organ it serves. ("Basis," p.39)

Furthermore,

> The *qi* that circulates throughout the body is the most vigorous form of *qi*. It has four basic patterns of movement: ascending, descending, exiting, and entering. The channels are the passageways along which these movements occur. - In addition to activating the body, *qi* performs several other functions, it changes character. For example, *yang qi* is the form of *qi* that warms the body. It regulates body temperature. A deficiency of *yang qi* results in symptoms such as chills and cold limbs. - Finally, *qi* is also the actual activity - the physiological functioning - of the organs, channels, and tissues. Thus, liver *qi*, for instance, is the action of the liver on the body. ("Essential," p. 69)

Then there is diagnosis:

> Thus diseases of the affected *zang-fu* organs often show physical signs along the related meridians. For example, low back pain may occur in kidney disease, and chest pain may be noticed in heart and lung diseases. This is because the meridians, passing information of what is happening inside the body, will affect other parts of the body and therefore provide valuable information for diagnosis. ("Basis," p. 158)

And finally, in therapy the acupoints are used in acupuncture or needling, cupping with bamboo, clay, or glass cups first heated inside with burning paper, and "moxibusion," which is scorching the skin with moxa leaves in cones or sticks by non-blistering and non-scarring techniques.

TCM is of course far more complex in its theories and especially in its skills than these few pages even begin to suggest. Since it is a form of medicine, a practical discipline, the first question is whether it works. By all indications seen by the present author thus far, it meets this test. In good hands, it is safe and effective.

III. A Phenomenological Hypothesis

Like in principle any other practice, TCM and, more specifically, its theoretical component can be reflected upon phenomenologically. Groups can be reflectively observed, but this is a matter of doctors practicing upon patients, both of whom are individuals in this medical relationship. Investigation of TCM from the patient's side is possible and might be helpful in some connections, but here the concern is with how the doctor relates to the patient.

This relating can be observed in two ways reflectively. If one was a traditional Chinese doctor, one could reflect on how one oneself treats patients. If one is not, there is still reflection on others. In that case one's theme is, as usual in phenomenology, dual. One reflects on how the doctor relates to patients and patients as related to by the doctor. This reflection on others does not usually have the high quality of evidencing available in self-observation, but can accomplish its cognitive objective where there is sufficient data and the practice is highly disciplined, as it is in TCM. Such reflecting on others via texts, interviews, participation, etc. is a matter of course in history-oriented philosophy of science and technology.

For analysis to begin with, the theoretical component of the medical practice can be distinguished. Medicine is of course a practical discipline with the objectives of the prevention and cure of illness or, positively speaking, the fostering of health. This implies that health has positive value and illness negative. Such values hold for the patient and the doctor as do the ends and means they justify. Interestingly, however, in the literature consulted for this essay, the account of how the doctor knows about the patient is treated separately in chapters on matters of the sort presented above in Section I. The phenomenologist need only follow along in this abstracting of the cognitive component from the whole concrete encounter of the patient by the doctor in order to focus on the theory in this science-based practice.

Secondly, what is fundamental to the medical knowledge in TCM is something best called "observation." This consists of awareness and thinking. The awareness could include the values and purposes of patients in its objects, in which case the observation would be best called "cultural," or since it is also a matter of theorizing, even "cultural-scientific observation."

In this case, however, the observation appears naturalistic. Nothing in the literature consulted is said about differences among patients according to class, gender, language, race, religion, or other cultural variations. (Even relatively little is said about differences in age and sex [cf. "Essential," pp.212 ff.], so that either adult males or an idealized person in general is the typical patient.) This naturalistic observation may be an artifact of presentation of TCM to Western readers for whom medicine is as a matter of course naturalistic, but it seems not and, until it is shown otherwise, it can be assumed that TCM has a naturalistic theory.

What then is observed? The whole, dynamic, and situated person as a natural object. This is not a physical object because, as seen above, psychical states are included. The observation is then in part a matter of other-awareness. Otherwise, however, it is an observation of the surface coloration and temperatures and, through touching, some of the interiors, e.g., pulses, as well as the movements of the patient's body. Perhaps enough for present purposes has been said about that above, but it needs to be added here that by all indications this medical observation needs to be subtle, highly skilled, and is thus the result of extensive training.

As for the other component of that which is best called "observation," namely thinking, two points are especially important. In the first place, there should be no doubt that one can learn to observe in this fashion. It is no more difficult to do so than it is to observe in the way of Aristotelian natural science, i.e., in terms of Air, Earth, Fire, and Water, the Formal,

Material, Efficient, and Final Causes, etc. (and there is also, of course, Aristotelian medicine with the doctrine of the four humors). In the second place, it is regularly admitted in the sources consulted that what one most deeply thinks about in TCM are strictly not observable. Thus, e.g.,

> The channel system is a system of pathways throughout the body. However, just as the *zang-fu* organs are not strictly analogous to the concrete organs that bear the same names in Western medicine, the channels of Chinese medicine are not analogous to any tangible channel in the human body, such as the veins and arteries. Rather, they are a way of describing the flow of blood, *qi* (or vital energy), and information that supports the life functions of the body. In this sense, they are more invisible than visible. (Essential 95)

Attempts have of course been made to find observable matters corresponding to the acupuncture maps.

> Three hundred and twenty-four frequently used acupuncture points have been dissected to discover their anatomical relationship to the nerves, blood vessels, and lymphatics. Nerve roots of varying sizes were detected nearby in 323 cases. Dissection along the paths of the meridians also revealed major blood vessels or nerves underneath. The course of meridians occasionally was found to be similar to the route of the lymphatic, suggesting that the meridians are related to, though not identical with, nerves and blood vessels. ("Basis," p. 160)

In thinking, then, it would seem that the traditional Chinese doctor conceives of and believes in unobservable structures and factors that account for what is observable. Besides the coloration, temperature, etc. mentioned above, there are also the observed effects of needling, cupping, moxibustion, etc. in particular places to identify the acupoints. There must have been billions of particular observations conducted during the three millennia of TCM, certainly the most massive induction ever performed for anything like scientific purposes. And in thinking there must have been an interrelating of separate results into elegant arrangements no different in kind (but different in referent) than what occurs in the Ptolemaic and Copernican cosmologies.

Nevertheless, the foregoing description or descriptive sketch of observation as practiced in TCM must be considered to involve hypotheses and this in two respects. In the first place, the thinking involved in the medical observation that is reflectively observed posits unobservables in order to account for observables. These are not unobserved matters that could become observed. Such positing of unobservables for explanatory purposes is hypothesizing in one signification of the word.

In another signification of "hypothesis" and related words, however, the description just outlined is at once phenomenological and hypothetical. In this second and phenomenological signification, reference is made via the hypothesis to observables, i.e., patterns of naturalistic awareness and biomedical thinking, that have yet to be at all adequately observed in reflection on others at least by the present writer, who is accordingly offering these remarks as extremely tentative.

How could this phenomenological hypothesis be tested? This requires obtaining better evidencing than indicated above. Three ways seem possible. In the first place, much more could be comprehended through reading about TCM, including ultimately the classics of TCM studied in Chinese. In the second place, one might obtain training in TCM and hopefully be also able to practice self-observation on one's own medical practice. And in the third place, one can observe Chinese doctors at work and thus rely on reflection on others. These are not mutually exclusive but rather mutually supporting approaches and, as mentioned, they are already relied on in history-oriented philosophy of science.

At least one problem remains. It is very likely that the traditional Chinese doctor does not consider Qi, the meridians, etc. to be essentially constructed and hypothetical in the observation that he or she has learned to perform. Rather, it is quite likely that these unobservable matters are considered within TCM to be what is ultimately most real. The same is no doubt the case for Psychoanalysts with respect to the unconscious id and super-ego and indeed the physical world for the physicist, which Western philosophers have sometimes called the outer world. This is of course the problem of realism vs. in strumentalism in the philosophy of science.

That the biomedical theorist, psychologist, or physicist unreflectively believes in as real that which can be recognized upon reflection to be constructed and hypothetical does not, however, require the phenomenological philosopher of science to agree with the believing in the conscious life reflected upon. If there were such agreement, it would not be sufficiently justified by the fact of that this belief was found in the life reflected upon and, in any case, it would very quickly lead to major contradictions, especially if this approach were extended to religions, but already where Asian and Western medical traditions are concerned. Furthermore, there needs to be motivation to explore such a possibility, a motivation has yet to arise in the present account, which, again, is offered as a phenomenological hypothesis to be tested in less amateurish inquiry than the present effort, which may, nevertheless, be considered a start.

Heideggers Deutung des „Unterwegs“

Jae-Chul Youm

Wenige Tage vor seinem Tod hat Heidegger den Leitspruch für seine Gesamtausgabe letzter Hand zusammen mit dem Titelblatt handschriftlich aufgesetzt: „Wege - nicht Werk“.[1] Zur Erläuterung des Leitspruches sagt Heidegger in den nachgelassenen Aufzeichnungen für das Vorwort zur derselben: „Die Gesamtausgabe soll auf verschiedene Weisen zeigen: ein Unterwegs im Wegfeld des sich wandelnden Fragens der mehrdeutigen Seinsfrage.“[2] Als eine Anleitung sowohl für deren Herausgeben als auch für deren Lesen weist dies darauf hin, daß das Denken Heideggers ein sich wandelndes, d.h. ein Unterwegs ist, sei es ein daseinsanalytisches(vgl. *Sein und Zeit*), sei es ein seinsgeschichtliches(vgl. *Beiträge zur Philosophie*), sei es ein seinssprachliches(vgl. *Unterwegs zur Sprache*).

Noch einmal: Heideggers Denken bewegt sich als ein Unterwegs - nicht einmal als ein abgeschlossenes - in einer langen Wanderung auf den verschiedenen ‚Holzwegen‘ und ‚Feldwegen‘, und zwar dies bis zu seinem letzten Schritt. In dieser Wanderung kann der vormalige Standort des Denkens jeweils „nur ein Aufenthalt in einem Unterwegs“[3] bleiben. Eben daraufhin heißt es schon in der Vorlesung *Was heißt Denken?*: „Das eigentliche Wesen des Denkens könnte sich uns zeigen, wenn wir unterwegs bleiben. Wir sind unterwegs. Was meint dies? Wir sind noch unter Wegen, inter vias, zwischen verschiedenen Wegen. Über den einen unumgänglichen und deshalb wohl einzigen Weg ist noch nicht entschieden. Also unterwegs - müssen wir mit einer besonderen Sorgfalt auf die Wegstelle achten, die unsere Schritte durchlaufen.“[4] Die vorliegende Arbeit nimmt solche Forderung Heideggers ernst, auf den sich wandelnden Denkweg zu achten, und versucht, ihn in seinen einigen bedeutendsten Wegstrecken sichtbar zu machen.

Allein Heideggers Denkweg bleibt, trotz seiner verschiedenen Aufenthaltsorte, von der Sache des Denkens her gesehen, derselbe: der Weg in das „was das Wort *sein* einst als zu Denkendes enthüllt hat, was es einst vielleicht als Gedachtes verhüllen wird.“[5] Das Sein ist nach Heidegger ‚das Älteste des Alten im abendländischen Denken‘ und so bleibt das zentrale Thema der Metaphysik, die sich in ihrer langen Geschichte im Grunde als Theorie des Seins des Seienden ausgelegt hat.

In diesem Hinblick bezieht sich das Seinsdenken Heideggers wiederholt auf die Frage ‚Was ist Metaphysik? ‘, dies aber auch mit den sich wandelnden Stellungen zu ihr: nämlich zuerst ihrer ‚Grundlegung‘, sodann

---

[1] Heidegger, *Frühe Schriften*, Gesamtausgabe Bd. 1. S. 437
[2] ebd.
[3] Heidegger, *Unterwegs zur Sprache*, GA. Bd. 12. S. 94
[4] Heidegger, *Was heißt Denken?*, Tübingen 1971^3, S. 61
[5] Heidegger, *Wegmarken*, GA. Bd. 9. Vorbemerkung

ihrer ‚Überwindung' und schließlich ihrer ‚Verwindung'. Heideggers Verwandlung der Stellung zur Metaphysik geschieht doch vor allem auf Grund des ihr vorangehenden Wandels der Erfahrung des Seins, welche wesentlich mit der Erfahrung der Wahrheit zusammengeht, in der erst das eigentliche Vermächtnis des Heideggerschen Gedankens in der Moderne zu finden ist.

Die genannte nachgelassene Aufzeichungen führen demnach fort: „Die in der Ausgabe versammelte Bemühung bleibt ihrerseits nur ein schwaches Echo des immer ferner sich entziehenden Anfangs: die ansichhaltende Verhaltenheit der *aletheia*. Sie ist in gewisser Weise offenkundig und stets erfahren; ihr Eigentümliches bleibt jedoch im Anfang notwendig ungedacht, welcher Sachverhalt allem nachkommenden Denken eine eigenartige Zurückhaltung auferlegt."[6]

Eben das schwache Echo der Wahrheit des Seins, das schon in die Sprache Heideggers und zwar in der Gestalt der Vorlesung und des Aufsatzes gesammelt ist, hörend und dem ent-sprechend, werden wir im Folgenden die drei Phasen des Heideggerschen Denkweges (I, II, III) in Kürze zusammenfassen. Dabei wird jede Phase in Hinsicht auf die Deutung der Seinsfrage (a), den Grundzug des Denkens (b), und seine Grenze (c), welche zum Umbruch des Denkens führen läßt, betrachtet werden.

I. (a) Heideggers Denkweg beginnt mit der Erfahrung der „ontologischen Differenz", welche den Standort der Seinsfrage im Umkreis von *Sein und Zeit* bildet. Sie will heißen: Das Sein ist vom Seienden gründlich unterschieden und ist das Apriori am Seienden, aus dem und in dem jedes Seiende als es selbst gezeigt wird. Das Sein ist aber für Heidegger weder abstrakte Allgemeinheit des Seienden noch höchstes Seiendes. Doch betrifft es als „das Sich-an-ihm-selbst-zeigende" jedes Seiende, derart, daß in ihm jedes Seiende als Seiendes entdeckt wird.

An der Erfahrung des Seins als des „Sich-an-ihm-selbst-zeigenden" und so der „Entdecktheit" (des Seienden) ist schon Heideggers Erfahrung der Wahrheit als „Unverborgenheit" (*aletheia*) angedeutet. Sie ist sein erstes Wahrheits-Verständnis, und dies zwar im Abstoß vom überkommenen, geläufigen Wahrheitsbegriff als „Übereinstimmung". Im *Streit um die Wahrheit* sagt Heidegger deutlich: „Zur Ausweisung steht nicht eine Übereinstimmung von Erkennen und Gegenstand oder gar von Psychischem und Physischem, aber auch nicht eine solche zwischen *Bewußtseinsinhalten* unter sich. Zur Ausweisung steht einzig das Entdeckt-sein des Seienden selbst, es im Wie seiner Entdeckheit."[7]

Das Sein ist also als die Entdecktheit (Unverborgenheit) des Seienden die allererst auszuweisende Wahrheit. Heidegger versucht nun, das so erfahrene Sein wiederum auf seinen Sinn, d.h. die Zeit hin auszuweisen: - eine ‚Sinnfrage', die er von seinem Lehrer E. Husserl übernommen hat. Heideggers

[6]Heidegger, *Frühe Schriften*, GA. Bd. 1. S. 438
[7]Heidegger, *Sein und Zeit*, GA. Bd. 2. S. 289

Sinnfrage vollzieht sich aber in der Gestalt einer Verwandlung, nämlich nicht mehr als die Frage nach dem Sinn vom ,wahrhaft Seienden', sondern als die Frage nach dem Sinn von seinem ,Sein'. Die Aufgabe der Seinsfrage in der ersten Phase des Heideggerschen Denkwegs liegt demnach darin, alle positiven Wissenschaften und sogar die Metaphysik durch das Ausweisen des Sinnes von Sein zu ,begründen', wie dies auch Husserl in seiner eigenen Weise wollte, wenn er die reine Phänomenologie als die ,erste Philosophie' angesehen hat.

Innerhalb dieser Aufgabe zeigt sich das ,,Dasein" als das primär zu Befragende, denn: In ihm ist das Sein und in eins damit sein Sinn jedenfalls insofern erschlossen, ,da', als es ihm in seinem Sein um dieses selbst geht. Die Erschlossenheit des Daseins ist nach Heidegger im Grunde das existenziale Verstehen, welches von jeder Art des bewußtseinsmäßigen Erkennens zu unterscheiden ist. Heideggers Ausweisen des Sinnes von Sein wendet sich somit an die existenziale Verständlichkeit des Seins des Daseins, nicht an das ,reine Bewußtsein' des phänomenologischen Ich. Sachlich gedacht, bedeutet diese Wendung deshalb nichts anderes als die Analytik des Seins des Daseins, weil das existenziale Verstehen selbst der Grundmodus des daseinsmäßigen Seins ist.

Heidegger formuliert die so gedachte Seinsfrage wie folgt: ,,Philosophie ist universale phänomenologische Ontologie, ausgehend von der Hermeneutik des Daseins, die als Analytik der Existenz das Ende des Leitfadens alles philosophischen Fragens dort festgemacht hat, woraus es entspringt und wohin es zurückschlägt."[8] Mit der Analytik der Existenz, die sich eigens für die Fundamentalontologie hält, will Heidegger seine Idee der Grundlegung der Metaphysik verwirklichen.

(b) Die Analytik der Existenz vollzieht sich, wie gesagt, durch das existenziale Verstehen. Darin steckt sich aber eine merkwürdige Tatsache, daß das Verstehen selber als ein Grundmodus der Existenz versucht, diese, d.h. sich selbst ins Wissen zu heben. Hier ist Heideggers treffende Bemerkung : ,, ... in der Frage nach dem Sinn von Sein liegt eine merkwürdige *Rück- oder Vorbezogenheit* des Gefragten (Sein) auf das Fragen als Seinsmodus eines Seienden. Die wesenhafte Betroffenheit des Fragens von seinem Gefragten gehört zum eigensten Sinn der Seinsfrage."[9] Das Verstehen ist, so gedacht, gleichsam ein produktives Wissen. Die hier gemeinte Produktivität ist aber nicht diejenige des ,reinen Bewußtseins von sich selbst', sondern diejenige des Existierens der Existenz, welche sich apriorisch als das In-der-Welt-Sein ansieht und deshalb von Anfang an so etwas wie ,Reduktion zum reinen Bewußtsein' unmöglich macht.

Das produktive Wissen des Verstehens geht demgemäß vor allem in die Explikation der apriorischen Seinsverfassung des Daseins als des In-

---

[8] a. a. O., S. 51
[9] a. a. O., S. 11

der-Welt-Seins ein, aus dem allein das daseinsmäßige Verstehen seine ursprüngliche ,Weltlichkeit' gewinnt. Die Weltlichkeit des Seinsdenkens bekundet an sich, daß zum Seinsverständnis des Daseins nicht nur das Verständnis des Seins des Daseins gehört, sondern auch das des Seins des nicht daseinsmäßigen Seienden: - das Verständnis von Sein überhaupt. Die weltliche Bestimmung des existenzialen Verstehens ist sozusagen die Wegbahnerin vom Dasein zum Sein überhaupt, welcher Weg den Grundcharakter des Seinsdenkens in der ersten Wegphase bildet und ihn als „Transzendentales" nennen läßt. Im unabläßlichen Zierkel des existenzialen, produktiven und weltlichen Verstehens bestimmt sich das Sein des Daseins als „Sorge", und in Hinsicht auf seine Ganzheit als das „Sein zum Tode". Eben aus diesem erschließt sich der Sinn des daseinsmäßigen Seins: - die Zeitlichkeit. Sie als „der mögliche Himmelt eines jeden Seinsverständnisses überhaupt "[10] wird für das Fragen nach dem Sein überhaupt richtungsweisend.

(c) Auf die existenziale Explikation der Zeit hin wollte Heidegger den Weg von der ,existenzialen' Zeit zum Sinn des Seins überhaupt - d.h. Weg von „Zeit und Sein" in *Sein und Zeit* - weiter gehen, wo vermutlich die eigentliche Bestimmung des Seins überhaupt erörtert werden sollte. Aber der Weg von „Zeit und Sein" mußte insofern ausbleiben, als sich die Seinsfrage im Umkreis von *Sein und Zeit* von Haus aus als der ,Weg vom Dasein zum Sein und seinen Sinn' verstanden hat. Zur Erinnerung: *Sein und Zeit* schließt in der Tat mit der existenzialen Explikation der Zeit ab. Dies bedeutet für die Seinsfrage in der ersten Wegphase, daß die existenziale Zeit als der mögliche Himmelt des Verstehens des Seins gerade den Sinn von Sein überhaupt bildet. Die Seinsfrage von *Sein und Zeit* bewegt sich durch und durch in einer zirkelhaften Struktur, in deren Mitte immer schon das Dasein bleibt.

Dies gilt ebenfalls für das Welt-Verständnis, an der allein wir die Spur von so etwas wie Sein überhaupt in der ersten Wegphase gewahren können. Die von Heidegger verstandene Welt ist im Unterschied zum vulgären Weltbegriff als ,Summe des Seienden' die „Bedeutsamkeit", nämlich die Ganzheit der Seins-Bezüge des „Um-zu", „Wozu", „Dazu", „Um-willen" usw. Sie als solche erweist sich als die Strukturganzheit des Seins des innerweltlich Seienden. Doch bleibt immer in der Mitte dieser Welt das Dasein, genauer, sein „Worum-willen" als „das primäre *Wozu* ". Der Entwurf des Daseins bleibt die Mitte der Welt. Nur in ihm und durch ihn geschieht das Welten der Welt. Die Welt im Umkreis von *Sein und Zeit* ist genau so wie die Zeit diejenige der Existenz. Und nur weil die Welt diejenige der Existenz blieb, konnte Heidegger die Weltlichkeit am „Zeug" erfragen, dem der daseinsmäßige Umgang - „Besorgen" - vornehmlich begegnet. Solange die Seinsfrage sich ganz und gar in der daseinsanalytisch-Transzendentalen Fragestellung bewegt, gibt es keinen Weg zum Sein als solchen mehr.

---

[10] *a. a. O., S. 1*

II. (a) In der zweiten Wegphase wird die Heideggersche Seinsfrage der Grenze der Transzendentalen Fragestellung inne und läßt sich von ihr ab. Diese Ablösung bedeutet für ihn zugleich diejenige vom philosophischen, d.h. metaphysischen Denken, insofern die Transzendentale Fragestellung hinsichtlich ihres eigenmächtigen Verfahrens - es gilt immer noch, wenn das entwerfende Verstehen gleich ein gestimmtes ist - wesentlich mit dem metaphysischen Denken verwandt ist. Allein das Innewerden der Grenze der daseinsanalytisch-Transzendentalen Fragestellung und so seine Ablösung vom metaphysischen Denken überhaupt geschieht mit der ursprünglichen Erfahrung der anfänglichen Wesung des Seins, zum deren Zeugnis Heidegger Heraklits Wort ablegt: „*physis kryptesthai philei* (Physis neigt dazu, sich zu verbergen)" (Frg. 123, Diels-Kranz).

Die anfängliche Wesung des Seins - dieses nun als *physis* im Sinne des „aufgehend-verweilenden Waltens" - liegt nicht so sehr im Entbergen wie „eine starre Bühne mit ständig aufgezogenem Vorhang, auf der sich das Spiel des Seienden abspielt",[11] vielmehr im Ververgen, welches als „die Seinsverlassenheit in der Offenbarkeit des Seienden"[12] für das Denken der ‚Verborgenheit' den Vorrang läßt und im solchen Sinne als die ursprüngliche Ortschaft der daseinsmäßigen Seinsvergessenheit west.

Das Sein als das ursprünglich Sichverbergende für die Lichtung ist selbst die Un-wahrheit (Verborgenheit), die unumgängliche Irre, in der der Menschentum, sein Irrtum sich abspielt, derart, daß der Mensch innerhalb der von Sein entdeckten Offenbarkeit des Seienden nur auf diesem verharrt, und zwar auf die subjektivistische Weise ‚vom Seienden aus, über das Seiende hinaus und mit der erfundenen Seiendheit des Seienden auf dieses zu.' Der Spielraum solchen menschlichen Irrtums ist nach Heidegger die Geschichte der Metaphysik. Damit erweist sich die Metaphysik nicht mehr als das zu Erneuernde, zu Begründende wie in der ersten Wegphase, sondern vielmehr als das Abzulösende und zu Überwindende, so wie bei Nietzsche. [13]

---

[11] Heidegger, *Holzwege*, GA. Bd. 5. S. 41

[12] Heidegger, *Beiträge zur Philosophie*, GA. Bd. 65. S. 111

[13] Nietzsches Gedanke bewegt sich bekanntlich in der Idee der ‚Umwertung aller Werte', vornehmlich der Werte der christlichen Moral, welche die ganze bisherige abendländische Zivilisation verderbend bestimmt hat. Daraufhin will Nietzsche uns zeigen, „daß es immer noch ein metaphysischer Glaube ist, auf dem unser Glaube an die Wissenschaft ruht, daß auch wir Erkennenden von heute, wir Gottlosen und Antimetaphysiker, auch unser Feuer noch von dem Brande nehmen, den ein jahrtausendealter Glaube entzündet hat, jener Christenglaube, der auch der Glaube Platos war, daß Gott die Wahrheit ist, daß die Wahrheit göttlich ist ..." (Nietzsche, Kritische Gesamtausgabe, V 2, S. 259). Genau auf diesem Boden steht nach Nietzsche die ganze abendländische Kultur, d.h. die Metaphysik, die Religion, die Moral, die Wissenschaft usw. und ist in eins als ein Irrtum zu überwinden. In seiner zweiten Wegphase begegnet Heidegger entscheidend dem nietzscheschen Überwindungswillen der Metaphysik und geht in die Dimension hinein, welche Nietzsche, sein Vorgänger eröffnet hat.

Der Standort der Seinsfrage in der zweiten Wegphase ist das Ververgen des Seins und so die ursprüngliche Verborgenheit (*lethein*) innerhalb der Wahrheit, welche die Griechen mit ihrem privativen Namen *a-letheia* erfahren, aber, so meint Heidegger, nicht einmal sie als solche gedacht haben. In diesem neuen Frageort innestehend, er-fragt Heidegger nun die Wahrheit des Seins, noch genauer, die Lichtung des sichverbergenden Seins: - eine ‚Wahrheitsfrage‘ im Unterschied zur ‚Sinnfrage‘ der ersten Wegphase. In *Beiträge zur Philosophie* formuliert er dies wie folgt: „Die Frage nach dem Sein wird jetzt zur Frage nach der Wahrheit des Seyns. Das Wesen der Wahrheit wird jetzt aus der Wesung des Seyns erfragt, als die Lichtung des Sichverbergenden begriffen und damit als zugehörig zum Wesen des Seyns selbst.“ [14] Mit dem Er-fragen der Wahrheit des Seins, das sich als der ‚andere Anfang‘ der Philosophie versteht, will Heidegger den ‚ersten Anfang‘ der Philosophie, nämlich den metaphysischen Anfang überwinden.

(b) Die zum Er-fragen der Wahrheit des Seins verwandelte Seinsfrage wendet sich ‚dem in sich kehrigen Ereignis‘ zu. Für Heidegger bedeutet solche Zuwendung, sachlich gesehen, den Einsprung in die Geschichte des Seins im Sinne des „Grundgeschehnisses der Verbergung und Lichtung.“ Das Fragen nach dem Sein denkt also jetzt nicht mehr von der Existenz und ihrer Welt her - so war es in der ersten Wegphase -, sondern ganz und gar durch die Seinsgeschichte und als ihr zugehöriges. Daraus gewinnt das Seinsdenken seine ursprüngliche ‚Geschichtlichkeit‘, in der es sich als die sich fügende Verfügung über die Seinsgeschichte und so sich als deren Mitgründendes - nicht mehr als ‚produktives‘ wie in der ersten Wegphase - bestimmt. Dem Zwiespalt der Seinsgeschichte m.a.W. dem Grundgeschehnis der Verbergung und der Lichtung gemäß vollzieht sich das seinsgeschichtliche Denken auch in der Zwiespältigkeit, nämlich: das Der-Verborgenheit-Entreißen und das Stiften der Wahrheit des Seins. Jenes Denken als das Bedenken der „Enteignungsgeschichte“ will in seinem Angriff auf die Verborgenheit in der Geschichte der Metaphysik zeigen, inwiefern sich der erste Anfang der Philosophie in der Irre bewegt, und inwiefern die metaphysische Enteignungsgeschichte der Irrtum des subjektivistischen Denkens und so das zu Überwindende ist. In eins damit will das Denken in der „Entfernung“, „Scheidung“, „Verneinung“ und „Übersprung des ganzen Verlaufes der Verunstaltung und des Verfalls“ [15] die darin verschüttete und so vergessene Wahrheit des Seins „erobern“ und „gründen“. Eben dieses Denken vollzieht sich für Heidegger insbesondere als das Stiften. Es als das Ins-Werk-setzen will die unzerstörte Wahrheit des Seins als solche in einem Offenen, nämlich im Kunstwerk verwahren, indem es den Streit von Welt und Erde, weil den Ur-streit der Wesung der Wahrheit, anstiftet. Die in dieser Anstiftung streitende Welt und Erde

---

[14] Heidegger, *Beiträge zur Philosophie*, GA. Bd. 65. S. 428
[15] Heidegger, *Einführung in die Metaphysik*, GA. Bd. 40. S. 16

erweisen sich als das zu bewahrhende Eigentum des Seins und so als die „Ereignisgeschichte."

(c) Aber die Absicht der Seinsfrage im Umkreis von *Holzwege*, durch die Ablösung von der Transzendentalen Fragestellung überhaupt die Wahrheit des Seins als solche zurückzugewinnen, ist nicht gründlich erfüllt. Dies deshalb, weil das Denken trotz seiner Verhaltenheit und Zugehörigkeit zur Seinsgeschichte immer noch ein „Wissen-wollen" bleibt, welches nichts anderes als das abzulösende Erbe der Eigenmächtigkeit des metaphysischen Denkens ist. Inwiefern das Denken wesentlich ein Wissen-wollen bleibt, zeigt sich schon im zwiespältigen Seinsdenken, d.h. im Stiften und im Der-Verborgenheit-Entreißen. Während dieses ein Überwinden-wollen der Verborgenheit ist, bewegt sich jenes in einem Verwahren-wollen der Unverborgenheit. Heideggers Er-fragen der Wahrheit des Seins beim ‚Kunstwerk', das weder dem ‚Zeug' noch ‚reinem Ding' gleicht, geht vor allem von dem Faktum aus, daß das Kunstwerk eben dasjenige ist, worin sich das Verwahren-wollen der Wahrheit des Seins ausgezeichneterweise findet. Um zu erinnern: Daß die Welt in einem - obwohl künstlerischen - Wissen-wollen der Sterblichen zu stiften und zu verwahren ist, macht einen klaren Unterschied zur „Welt des Gevierts" der dritten Wegphase, in der der Sterbliche nur als ein von Ereignis Ereignetes, ein von „Welt des Gevierts" Gewährtes west. Solange das Denken solchermaßen noch ein Wissen-wollen bleibt, ist es immer noch schwer, einen Wink von der Wahrheit des ‚bestimmenden' Seins zu empfangen. [16]

III. (a) In der dritten Phase des Heideggerschen Denkweges gibt das Denken die bis dahin noch verbliebene Gewalttätigkeit seines Entdeckens, jede Art von Wissen-wollen auf. Dies wird jetzt genötigt, und zwar aus der Erfahrung des Seins als „Verbindlichkeit, die jedes Denken bindet, gesetzt daß es sich dem Geheiß des zu Denkenden fügt" [17] : - will sagen: Das Sein ist das Bestimmende, das Heißende, das Verbindliche für das Denken. Das Sein ist nie durch das Denken zu er-bringen, sondern sie ist wesenhaft eine von sich her Kommende, Schickende. Die von sich her kommende Bestimmung des Seins bildet nun den dritten Standort der Seinsfrage und führt Heidegger zum vollkommenen „Umdenken", welches er in seiner zweiten Wegphase trotz der Entzugs-Erfahrung nicht erreichen konnte. In solcher Erfahrug des Seins als der bestimmenden Verbindlichkeit steckt sich auch Heideggers neue Erfahrung der Wahrheit, die die von sich her schickende Lichtung des ‚Bergens' im (das Seiende) entbergenden Ververgen ist. Heideggers Besinnung auf die Wahrheit, die sich in der Schrittfolge von der „Üereinstimmung (Richtigkeit)" über die „Unverborgenheit (Entdecktheit)" zur „Verborgenheit (Verbergung)" entwickelte, geht sich damit über die griechische Erfahrung der Wahrheit hinaus schließlich in die waltende „Lichtung des

[16] Heidegger, *Was heißt Denken?*, S. 91

[17] Heidegger, *Zur Sache des Denkens*, Tübingen, 1976^2. S. 25

Bergens" ein. Dies geschieht im radikalen Gewahren des Ververgens innerhalb des schrankenlosen Entbergens der modernen Technik, deren Wesen das „Ge-stell" ist. Heidegger erfährt hier, daß das Sichverbergen des Seins im Wesen der modernen Technik nicht nichts ist, sondern das Bergen des Eigentums, welches dem reinen Schicken angewiesen ist, daß die Lichtung des Geschickes des geborgenen Seins „die Entbergung der sich entziehenden Befugnis ist". [18] Als solche Lichtung waltet sie immer schon als die vorgängige „Bestimmung der Sache des Denken", die einzig und allein das Denken überhaupt bestimmt und es in den Anspruch nimmt.

Auf die maßgebende Erfahrung der „Bestimmung der Sache des Denken" hin gilt es dem Seinsdenken, jede Art der Eigenwilligkeit des Denkens zu tilgen und zum Verwinden des heißenden Seins zu werden. Solche Tilgung ist allerdings für das Seinsdenken die schwierigste Aufgabe, denn: da sollte das Denken die kleinste Kluft zum hartnäckigen Erben der Eigenmächtigkeit des Denkens auftun und sich davon ablösen, um dann die reinste Gelassenheit in die Bestimmung des Seins zurückzugewinnen. Insofern aber das Denken im Verhältnis zum Sein, mit Heidegger zu sprechen, von Haus aus „das die Subjektivität verlassende Denken" [19] ist, kann dies nur durch die radikale Tilgung jeder Art des Entdecken-wollens endgültig gelingen. Wenn es gelingt, wird das Verhältnis zwischen „Sein und Denken" nicht einmal mehr das Verhältnis des Denkens zum Sein, sondern das Verhältnis des Seins zum Denken sein.

In der Seinsfrage der dritten Wegphase sollten wir nicht wegsehen, daß die Erfahrung des Bestimmungscharakters des Seins schon mit der Erfahrung des Sprachcharakters des Seins zusammengeht. Für ihn ist die Sprache im Grunde nichts anderes als die Zeige, die jedes Seiende als solches zeigt: - die ursprüngliche Rücknahme der Sprache auf die Zeige, d.h. die Sage. Das Sein selbst ist ursprünglich die Sprache, insofern es als die Lichtung das Seiende im Ganzen in seinem Wesen zeigt. Die Erfahrung von der Sein-Sprache und in eins damit seiner Bestimmungscharakter ist eben dasjenige, was den Weg im Umkreis von *Feldweg* von dem Weg im Umkreis von *Holzwege* unterscheidet und ihn *unterwegs zur Sprache* bleiben läßt. Daraufhin gewinnt das Seinsdenken die ursprüngliche ‚Sprachlichkeit', in der das Denken als das Ent-sprechen bestimmt. ‚Das Ent-sprechen der heißenden Sein-Sprache' ist die vollkommene Gestalt der Seinsfrage in der dritten Phase des Heideggerschen Denkweges. Heidegger sammelt das soeben Gewiesene in den Monolog auf seinem *Feldweg* wie folgt: „Das Einfache ist noch einfacher geworden. Das immer Selbe befremdet und löst. Der Zuspruch des Feldweges ist jetzt ganz deutlich. Spricht die Seele? Spricht die Welt? Spricht Gott? Alles spricht den Verzicht in das Selbe. Der Verzicht nimmt nicht. Der Verzicht gibt. Er gibt die unerschöpfliche Kraft des Einfachen. Der

---

[18] Heidegger, *Aus der Erfahrung des Denkens*, GA. Bd. 13. S. 224
[19] Heidegger, *Wegmarken*, S. 327

Zuspruch macht heimisch in einer langen Herkunft." [20]

(b) Das zum Entsprechen der Sein-Sprache verwandelte Denken achtet vor allem auf die gewesene Geschichte der Metaphysik, in der das Sein von einst her als ‚Geschick des Entzugs' gekommen ist. Es west in den verschiedenen epochalen Seinsprägungen (z. B. idea, Gott, absoluter Geist usw.) der Metaphysik als der Anspruch der Differenz als solcher, und kommt inmitten dieses Anspruches als der Zuspruch des Vor- und Aufbehaltenen, wenn das Denken sich ihm fügt. Demgemäß bestimmt sich das dem Geschick des Entzugs entsprechende Denken als das ‚Andenken des Seinsanspruches' und zugleich als das ‚Vordenken des vor- und aufbehaltenen Zuspruches des Seins' : - das ist die Verwindung der Metaphysik im Umkreis von *Feldweg* im Unterschied zur Überwindung der Metaphysik im Umkreis von *Holzwege.*

Den vor- und aufbehaltenen Zuspruch des Seins, der im metaphysisch Gesprochenen viel Mühe vorzudenken ist, hört Heidegger weniger Mühe im dichterisch Gesprochenen, insbesondere in den Gedichten von Hölderlin, Trakl, George. Das Sein kommt dort zum ‚Geläut der Stille.' Das Sein spricht, d.h. läutet, indem es als die Sage die vier Weltgegenden (Erde und Himmel, die Göttlichen und die Sterblichen) lautlos rufend versammelt und in dieser stillen Versammlung jegliches es selbst bleiben läßt. Das dem Geläut der Stille entsprechende Denken bestimmt sich also als das ‚hörende Entsprechen' - nicht mehr als das verwahrende Stiften-Wollen im Umkreis von *Holzwege.*

Wenn das Sein im Bereich der Welt kommt, kommt es zur ‚Nähe der Ferne'. Zunächst als die Ferne west es in der modernen technischen Welt als der Anspruch des Ge-stells, welches nach Heidegger der Vollendungsort des Wesens der Metaphysik ist. Inmitten dieses Anspruches kommt das Sein als der Zuspruch der geborgenen Welt des Gevierts: - es ist die Nähe. Diese möglicherweise kommende Welt ist eben das in der „Gefahr" des Ge-stells wachsende Rettende. Hierfür gilt nur das Denken als das ‚Danken', nämlich dasjenige, das dankt, daß es danken darf.

c) Soweit die knappe Zeichnung des Heideggerschen langen Denkweges, welcher auf die Besinnung auf die Wahrheit des Seins hin gegangen ist. [21] Auf diesem Weg wandelt sich das Seinsdenken, wohl gemerkt, in den drei Grundzügen, nämlich: erstlich das Verstehen des Sinnes von Sein, sodann das Der-Verborgenheit-Entreißen und Stiften der Wahrheit des Seins, und letztlich das der heißenden Sein-Sprache Ent-sprechen. Als ganzes gedacht, ist Heideggers Denkweg ein Unterwegs zur verbindlichen „Bestimmung der Sache des Denkens". [22] Was das Denken anlangt, gilt er aber als der Weg

---

[20] Heidegger, *Aus der Erfahrung des Denkens*, S. 90

[21] Freilich läßt sich der lange Weg Heideggers in dieser Kürze nicht ausführlich entwickeln; ich darf deshalb auf meine Darstellung *Heideggers Verwandlung des Denkens* (Würzburg, 1995) verweisen.

[22] Heidegger, *Wegmarken*, GA. Bd. 9. Vorbemerkung

der Tilgung der Eigenmächtigkeit des Denkens. Im letzten Schritt des Unterwegs bleibt das Denken als das Danken, das dankt, daß es danken darf. Wann und wie es danken darf, weiß niemand. Dies deshalb, weil das Danken das Geschenk des von sich her kommenden „Es gibt“ ist. Insofern deutet das Denken letztlich in das ‚Warten‘, in dem wir in der Gelassenheit zum Offenen des „Es gibt“ dieses offen lassen. Dieses Warten ist doch keine Untätigkeit, sondern eine Vorbereitung der Sterblichen mit Wachsamkeit. Das ‚Warten mit Wachsamkeit‘: - das ist der eigentliche Sinn des Heideggerschen „Unterwegs“. Und so bleibt die Seinsfrage in der Vorläufigkeit, weil der sich entziehende Endlichkeit des bestimmenden „Es gibt“.

Contributors

Kah Kyung Cho received Ph.D. from Heidelberg in 1957. Professor of Philosophy at the State University of New York at Buffalo. Publications: *Philosophy of Existence* (Seoul 1961, 13th ed. 1995), *Philosophy and Science in Phenomenological Perspective* (ed.) (Martinus Nijhof 1984), *Bewußtsein und Natursein* (Freiburg 1987, Japanese Edition: Tokyo 1994). Member of the Editorial Board: *Husserl Studies* and *Phänomenologie, Texte und Kontexte.* General Editor: *Orbis Phaenomenologicus* (with Y. Nitta, H. R. Sepp).

Lester Embree received Ph.D. from New School for Social Research in 1972. William F. Dietrich Eminent Scholar and Professor of Philosophy at Florida Atlantic University and President of the Center for Advanced Research in Phenomenology. Authored, translated, and edited a number of books and articles chiefly in constitutive phenomenology. Editor of the *Encyclopedia of Phenomenology* (Kluwer 1997). Areas of interest: history and philosophy of science (cultural sciences, archeology in particular), technology, and environmentalism.

Klaus Held received Ph.D. in 1963 and submitted *Habilitation* in 1970 in Köln. Professor of Philosophy at the Bergische University of Wuppertal. President of the Deutsche Gesellschaft für phänomenologische Forschung 1987-1994. Publications: *Lebendige Gegenwart: Zur Zeitproblematik in der Spätphilosophie Husserls* (1966), *Heraklit, Parmenides und der Anfang von Philosophie und Wissenschaft. Eine phänomenologische Besinnung* (1980), *Stato, interessi e mondi vitali. Per una fenomenologia della politica* (1981), *Treffpunkt Platon. Philosophischer Reiseführer durch die Länder des Mittelmeers* (2. Aufl., 1991), *la fenomenologia del mondo e i Greci* (1995).

Hwa Yol Jung studied phenomenology and existential philosophy with John Wild at Northwestern and Yale. Professor of Political Science at Moravian College. Publications: *Existential Phenomenology and Political Theory: A Reader* (1972), *The Crisis of Political Understanding: A Phenomenological Perspective in the Conduct of Political Inquiry* (1979), *The Question of Rationality and the Basic Grammar of Intercultural Texts* (1989), *Rethinking Political Theory: Essays in Phenomenology and the Study of Politics* (1993). Currently engaged in multi-volume work on carnal hermeneutics/body politics.

Nam-In Lee received Ph.D. in 1991 in Wuppertal. Professor of Philosophy at Seoul National University. Publications: *Edmund Husserls Phänomenologie der Instinkte* (1993), *Problems of Reality in East and West* (co-author, Korean, 1994), "Wissenschaftliche Lebensphilosophie als Grundcharackter der Phänomenologie" (1995), "E. Husserl's Genetic Phenomenology and M. Heidegger's Hermeneutic Phenomenology" (Korean, 1997),

"Edmund Husserl's Phenomenology of Mood" (1998). Major research fields: phenomenology, hermeneutics, existential philosophy, philosophy of life, philosophy of nature.

Seung-Chong Lee received Ph.D. in philosophy at the State University of New York at Buffalo. Associate Professor of Philosophy at Yonsei University in Seoul. Field of specialization: philosophy of language with special reference to Wittgenstein. Co-authored with Newton Garver: *Derrida and Wittgenstein* (1994). Publications: "The Philosophy of Mathematics in Plato and Aristotle" (Korean, 1993), "Natural Language and Artificial Intelligence" (Korean, 1994), "Naturalism with a Human Face" (Korean, 1995), "Reading Wittgenstein Reading Gödel" (Korean, 1997).

Young-Ho Lee graduated from Seoul National University in 1961, received M.A. in 1967. Alexander von Humboldt Research Fellow 1972-1974. Professor of Philosophy at Sungkyunkwan University since 1977. Numerous books and articles on Nietzsche, Husserl, especially on Husserl's views of history. President of Korean Phenomenological Society 1993-1997, President of Korean Society for Philosophy 1997-1998.

Yoshihiro Nitta studied philosophy at Tohoku University. Professor of Philosophy at Toyo University. Editor of the volumes on Phenomenology, Hermeneutics and Contemporary Philosophy (including the volume *Japanische Beiträge zur Phänomenologie* (1984)). Co-editor of *Orbis Phaenomenologicus*. Publications: *What is Phenomenology?* (Japanese, 1968; 1992), *Phenomenology* (Japanese, 1978), *History of the Philosophical Question* (Japanese, 1989), *Phenomenology and Modern Philosophy* (Japanese, 1995), *Philosophy of the Contemporary Phenomenology and Hermeneutics* (Japan-ese, 1997).

Aiko Ogoshi studied religious philosophy at Kyoto University. Professor in Women's Studies at Kinki University. Founding member of the Association for Research on the Impact of War and Military Bases on Women's Human Rights. Publications: *Women in Western and Eastern Thought* (Japanese, 1985), *Sexist Buddhism* (Japanese, 1993), *A Deconstructive Analysis of Buddhism* (Japanese, 1994), *A Feminist Criticism of Japanese Culture* (Japanese, 1996), *A Guidebook of Feminist Theories* (Japanese, 1996), *Gender in Modern Japan* (Japanese, 1997), *Women and Religion* (Japanese, 1997), "Dualistische Sicht der Natur in Japan" (1996).

Ernst Wolfgang Orth studied philosophy, psychology, German literature and history in Freiburg and Mainz. Professor of Philosophy in Trier. President of Deutsche Gesellschaft für phänomenologisch Forschung 1983-1987. Publications: *Bedeutung, Sinn, Gegendstand. Studien zur Sprachphilosophie Edmund Husserls und Richard Hönigswalds* (1967), *Wilhelm Dilthey und die Philosophie der Gegenwart* (1985), *Von der Erkenntnistheorie zur Kulturphilosophie. Studien zu Ernst Cassirers Philosophie der symbolischen*

Formen (1996), *Kultur und Organismus. Studien zur Philosophie Richard Hönigswalds* (1997). Editor of *Phänomenologische Forschungen* (1975ff.). Co-editor of *Studien und Materialien zum Neukantianismus* (1992ff), *Texte und Kontexte'/Alber Phänomenologie* (1997ff).

Otto Pöggeler received Ph.D. in Bonn in 1955. Habilitation with Hans-Georg Gadamer in 1966. Professor of Philosophy at the Ruhr-University at Bochum and Director of the Hegel-Archives. Professor emeritus since 1994. Member of Nordrhein-Westfälische Akademie der Wissenschaften. Publications: *Der Denkweg Martin Heideggers* (1963, 1990), *Philosophie und Politik bei Heidegger* (1972, 1974), *Hegels Idee einer Phänomenologie des Geistes* (1973, 1993), *Heidegger und die hermeneutische Philosophie* (1983), *Die Frage nach der Kunst* (1984), *Spur des Wortes* (1986), *Preußische Kulturpolitik im Spiegel von Hegels Ästhetik* (1987), *Neue Wege mit Heidegger* (1992), *Schritte zu einer hermeneutischen Philosophie* (1994), "Über die moderne Kunst" (1995).

Harry P. Reeder studied philosophy at University of Illinois at Champaign-Urbana and The University of Waterloo, Ontario. Associate Professor of Philosophy at The University of Texas at Arlington. Publications: *The Work of Felix Kaufmann* (1991), *The Theory and Practice of Husserl's Phenomenology* (1986), *Language and Experience: Descriptions of Living Language in Husserl and Wittgenstein* (1984), "Felix Kaufmann" and "Ludwig Wittgenstein" in *The Encyclopedia of Phenomenology* (1997), "Husserl's Phenomenology and Contemporary Science" in Burt Hopkins (ed.), *Husserl in Contemporary Context: Prospects and Projects for Phenomenology* (1997), "Hermeneutics and Apodicticity in Phenomenological Method" in *Southwest Philosophy Review* (1990), "Wittgenstein Never Was a Phenomenologist" in *Journal of the British Society for Phenomenology* (1989), "A Phenomenological Account of the Linguistic Mediation of the Public and the Private" in *Husserl Studies* (1984).

Hans Rainer Sepp, studied at the University of Munich. Fellow of the Husserl-Archives of the University of Freiburg. Co-editor of the collected works of Edmund Husserl (*Husserliana*). General editor of *Orbis Phaenomenologicus* (together with Kah Kyung Cho and Yoshihiro Nitta). Co-editor of the series *Phänomenologie. Texte und Kontexte* with Karl-Heinz Lembeck and Ernst Wolfgang Orth. Publications: *Edmund Husserl und die phänomenologische Bewegung* (editor, 1988), *Husserl in Halle* (co-editor, 1994), *Praxis und Theoria* (1997). Major fields of research: phenomenology, phenomenological theories of ethics and art, philosophy of the 19th century, and intercultural philosophy.

Kiyoko Shimizu studied philosophy at Osaka University. Professor at Otemon Gakuin University in Osaka. Publications: *The Feminine Studies as a Way of Life* (co-author, 1989), *Ishiki-to Shizen* (transl. with Yamamoto et. al., Japanese edition of *Bewußtsein und Natursein* by Kah

Kyung Cho, 1994). Publications: continuous series on "Hannah Arendt's Political Philosophy" in the *Faculty of Letters Review*, Otemon Gakuin University. Many article length contributions to topics of general philosophy, Kant, philosophical lexicon, feminism. Founding member of the Association for Research on the Impact of War and Military Bases on Women's Human Rights.

Toru Tani studied at Keio University. Professor of Philosophy at Josai International University. Publications: *Shiki no Shizen* (1998), *Genshogaku to Kaishakugaku* (co-author, 1988), *Genshogaku no Genzai* (1989), *Genshogaku - Ekkyo no Genzai* (1992), *Genshogaku Undo* (1993), *Seiyo Tetsugaku-shi* (1994), "Life and the Life-World" (1986), "Heimat und das Fremde" (1993), "The Physics of Consciousness and Metaphysics" (1998).

Helmuth Vetter studied philosophy, German literature, and classical philology at the University of Vienna. Professor of the Institute of Philosophy at University of Vienna. President of the Austrian Society for Phenomenology. Publications: *Stadien der Existenz. Eine Untersuchung zum Existenzbegriff Sören Kierkegaards* (1979), *Der Schmerz und die Würde der Person* (1980). Numerous papers on phenomenology (especially Heidegger, Kierkegaard and analysis of Dasein). Editor of *Wiener Reihe. Themen der Philosophie* (9 volumes now). Founder and editor of the *Reihe der Öst. Ges f. Phänomenologie*; Vol. 1: *Krise der Wissenschaften - Wissenschaften der Krisis? Im Gedenken an Husserls „Krisis“ -Abhandlung* (1988); Vol. 2:*Heidegger und das Mittelalter* (1998); Vol. 3: *Siebzig Jahre „Sein und Zeit“* (1999).

Bernhard Waldenfels studied philosophy, psychology, classical philology and history in Bonn, Innsbruck, Munich and Paris. Professor of Philosophy at the University of Bochum. Publications: *Spielraum des Verhaltens* (1980), *Phänomenologie in Frankreich* (1983), *In den Netzen der Lebenswelt* (1985), *Ordnung im Zwielicht* (1987), *Einführung in die Phänomenologie* (1992), *Antwortregister* (1994), *Deutsch-Französische Gedankengänge* (1995), *Topographie des Fremden* (1997), *Grenzen der Normalisterung* (1998), *Sinnesschwellen* (1999), *Vielstimmigkeit der Rede* (1999). Editor of the anthologies on Schütz/Gurwi-tsch, Merleau-Ponty, Foucault and Derrida.

Jae-Chul Youm received Ph.D in 1993 with Heribert Boeder in Osnabrück. Habilitation work with Heribert Boeder, 1993-1995. Lecturer at Seoul National University. Publications: *Heideggers Verwandlung des Denkens* (1995), "Die Stellung der Kunst beim heideggerschen Denken" (Korean, 1996), "Heideggers Erfahrung der Sein-Sprache" (Korean, 1997), "Wozu Kunst? Nietzsche und Heidegger" (Korean, 1998), "Heidegger und die Geschichte der Philosophie" (Korean, 1998). Major research fields: ontology, aesthetics, existential philosophy, phenomenology, hermeneutics.

Personenregister/*Name Index*

Sachregister/*Subject Index*